Fond Best Wishes
in 2009,
Annie Bones

# CELESTIAL FORECASTER ®
# 2009

## *EVERYONE'S*
## DAILY ASTROLOGY GUIDE

## FEATURING:

- Daily forecasts based on planetary alignments
- Monthly overview of significant aspects
- Lunar aspects guide
- Time zone adjustments chart
- Daily table of aspect influences
- Full year calendar, and
- Built-in ephemeris

Loon Feather Publications
Box 47031 Victoria, B.C.
V9B 5T2  Canada
www.metaphysical.ca/forecaster
email: loonfeather@metaphysical.ca

## Acknowledgements:

Thanks to all of you for continuing to make the Celestial Forecaster
a success. Your enthusiasm is what keeps the Forecaster going.
Thanks to Soror SSH for the great work editing,
and to Frater 72 for production.
Special thanks and "Aloha" to Wray Arrenz and Steve Smeltzer
for their hospitality in Maui,
and for their extra enthusiasm and support for this year's book.

Printing and Binding:     Data Reproductions Corporation
Production & cover:       Frater 72
Editing:                  Soror SSH
Inside Graphics:          Merx Toledo International
ISBN:                     978-0-9731518-6-2

# TABLE OF CONTENTS

# TIME ZONE ADJUSTMENTS

In the *Celestial Forecaster* we show Pacific Time and Eastern Time. Most poeple in North America are familiar with adjusting to one of those two zones. If you use **Central Time**, add two hours to Pacific Time. For **Rocky Mountain Time**, add one hour to Pacific Time. To get **Greenwich Mean Time**, add 8 hours to Pacific Time (PST) or seven hours to Pacific Daylight Time (PDT). If you live outside North America, you can refer to the Time Zone Map below.

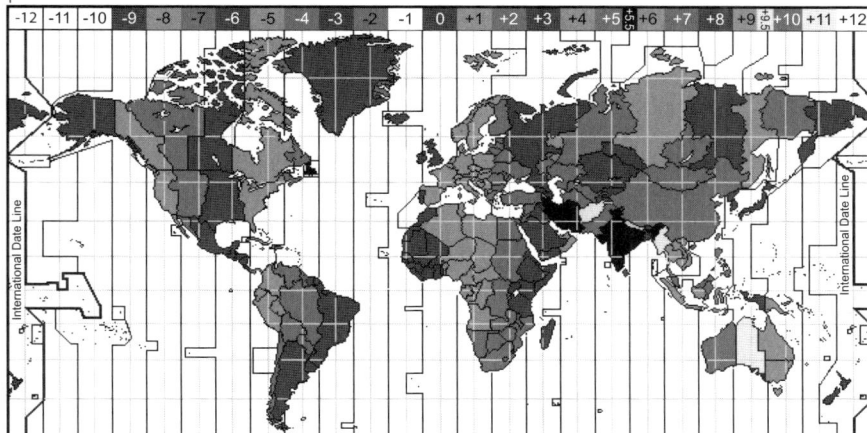

# Definitions of Terms

**Aspect:** Planets are said to be "in aspect" with each other when their location in the sky forms particular angles with the earth which are deemed significant. The main aspects and angles used in this book are as follows:

✳ **Sextile (60°):** The sextile aspect is considered to be favorable, and opens up possibilities and opportunities to work energies out between the two planetary influences.

☐ **Square (90°):** The square aspect indicates a struggle or stress between two planetary influences. This aspect often brings obstacles, or difficulties in our ability to learn and understand. A positive way to address this aspect is to see it as a time when we need to work through our challenges. In these blocks or obstacles a great deal of energy is concentrated. If one acts with caution and care, the energy released by dealing with our challenges can be harnessed, and overcoming the obstacle becomes a personal triumph that leads to growth and the strengthening of character.

△ **Trine (120°):** The most advantageous and harmonious aspect. It is considered to bring the most positive effects. A trine aspect brings gifts, and talents are often realized and acted upon.

☍ **Opposition (180°):** The opposition is the furthest apart the two planets are able to be in their orbits. This aspect brings an acute awareness of the energies that two planetary influences have upon us. It can also bring an overwhelming effect, and handling the polarity often requires awareness and caution.

☌ **Conjunction (0°):** Conjunction is the act of joining, or the state of being joined. When two planets have reached the same degree in the sky this is called a conjunction. It represents the direct confrontation of these energies which will be positive or negative depending on the nature of the planets which are in conjunction.

**The Orb:** The orb is the area of influence before and after an exact aspect, measured in degrees. The smaller the orb, the closer we are to an exact aspect, and the more strongly we feel the planetary influences. Orbs are divided into two parts: applying and separating. **Applying** — the part of the orb when the planetary aspect is approaching the exact time of reaching its peak. **Separating** — the part of the orb when the planetary aspect is moving away from the peak point of the aspect. Orbs in this book have been calculated using an orb of 6° applying, and 3° separating for all aspects except the sextile, for which 4° applying and 2° separating have been used.

V/C **Void-of-course Moon:** As it travels through a zodiacal sign, the Moon is in aspect with a number of planets. The final major aspect it reaches in a sign marks the time when the Moon goes void-of-course (v/c), meaning it will undergo no further aspects while in that zodiac sign. The Moon will remain void-of-course until it enters the next zodiac sign. While the Moon is void-of-course is a time of less direction and more confusion, particularly on the emotional or mood level.

R **Retrograde:** This occurs when the orbit of a planet causes it to appear to move backward through the sky. It represents a time of moving back over old ground, and inverting influences. The section on Mercury retrograde (page 8) gives examples of how retrogrades work. The Sun and Moon, not being planets, do not go retrograde.

D **Direct:** After a period of retrograde motion, the planet ceases its backward motion and moves forward again through the zodiacal signs. It represents a time of release and forward movement, though the old ground that was just covered in retrograde fashion must be gone over again before any new progress can be made.

# Glossary of Astrological Symbols

| | | | | |
|---|---|---|---|---|
| Aries | ♈ | Sun | ☉ | |
| Taurus | ♉ | Moon | ☽ | |
| Gemini | ♊ | Mercury | ☿ | |
| Cancer | ♋ | Venus | ♀ | |
| Leo | ♌ | Mars | ♂ | |
| Virgo | ♍ | Jupiter | ♃ | |
| Libra | ♎ | Saturn | ♄ | |
| Scorpio | ♏ | Neptune | ♆ | |
| Sagittarius | ♐ | Uranus | ♅ | |
| Capricorn | ♑ | Pluto | ♇ | |
| Aquarius | ♒ | | | |
| Pisces | ♓ | | | |

# How to Use this Book

**To adjust for time zones** other than Pacific or Eastern USA, use the *Time Zone Adjustments* table on page 5.

**For planetary aspectarian and for the phases of the Moon:** use the *Overview of Significant Aspects in 2009* found on pages 9 – 19.

**For major daily influences at a glance:** look at the *Table of Aspect Influences* on pages 20 - 23.

**For exact zodiacal position of a planet:** use the *Ephemeri*s on pages 266-272.

**For daily commentary and analysis:** see the main section pages 39-265, including:

<u>Sun Signs:</u> The glyph for the current sun sign is shown in the upper right margin on each page of the daily commentary.

<u>Headers:</u> The date headers at the top of each day show the date, the day of the week, and a selection of notable holidays.

<u>Moon signs and void-of-course periods:</u> Below the date header is the Moon's sign. The Moon's void-of-course period and entry to the next sign is shown chronologically with the day's planetary aspects. The numerous lunar aspects are included this year, and are interpreted in the new *Lunar aspects guide* on pages 25 - 37.

<u>Aspects:</u> Below the Moon's sign in the header is a list of the day's exact planetary and lunar aspects, together with their time of occurrence. Also listed are aspects whose orb of influence is just beginning, and the aspect's date of exact occurrence. Occasionally the aspect information is followed by quotes from famous people.

<u>Mood Watch:</u> Each day features a *Mood Watch* section. This commentary examines key lunar aspects of the day, and explains their likely influence on our moods. Like our moods, these lunar aspects are generally short-lived.

<u>Aspect Analysis:</u> Below the *Mood Watch* section are shown the day's main planetary aspects, the dates their orb of influence occurs, and an in-depth aspect analysis.

# Mercury retrograde periods: 2009

| BEGINS (Mercury goes retrograde) | | ENDS (Mercury goes direct) | |
|---|---|---|---|
| Jan. 11 | in Aquarius | Jan. 31 PDT / Feb. 1 EDT | in Capricorn |
| May 6 PDT / 7 EDT | in Gemini | May 30 | in Taurus |
| Sept. 6 PDT / 7 EDT | in Libra | Sept. 29 | in Virgo |
| Dec. 26 | in Capricorn | *(Jan. 14, 2010 in Capricorn)* | |

### Mercury Retrograde through the Air and Earth Signs

Mercury represents how we process information and communicate. Mercury retrograde is a term that describes an orbital shift as it moves backwards through a sign. Technically it only appears to move backwards through the degrees of the zodiac from our geocentric view. Astrologically, this is a time of communication related setbacks, reiterations, or inconsistencies; particularly the first few days going into and out of the retrograde period. Mercury retrograde periods take place for an average of three weeks at a time, and will occur on the average of three times a year. This year ends with a fourth period just beginning.

Mercury retrograde is a time of going back over various topics, and repeating or correcting, a lot of information. General misinformation and absentmindedness are the most common symptoms.

This year Mercury will go retrograde in the three air signs of the zodiac; Aquarius, Gemini, and Libra. In the final half of each phase, it will also be retrograde in the three earth signs; Capricorn, Taurus, and Virgo.

As Mercury goes retrograde through the air signs, communications of an intellectual nature are likely to be easily misinterpreted. It is best not to underestimate (or overestimate) the intellect of others when attempting to communicate. Mercury retrograde through the earth signs will bring a tendency towards misplacing physical items, and there may be a lot of miscommunication over necessities, money, practical matters, and the physical wellbeing of things.

While Mercury is retrograde in the air sign, Aquarius, communication mistakes will be apparent in topics such as technology, science, and politics. Mercury retrograde in Capricorn brings miscommunications over large scale contracts, issues of control and, time restraints. While Mercury is retrograde in the Mercury-ruled air sign, Gemini, be careful not to get caught up in gossip, disputes, and confusion over minor but important details. Also, be on the look out for frequent bouts of dyslexia, and other communication mistakes in activities such as writing, speaking, and journalism. Mercury retrograde in Taurus may bring disputes over possessions, or over the necessity for practicality and economic viability. Mercury retrograde in Libra often brings miscommunications between friends and loved ones. Also, there may be several delays, and re-scheduling, occurring in various levels of the justice system. Mercury retrograde in the Mercury-ruled earth sign, Virgo, may bring miscommunications with regard to matters of health and in situations involving the maintenance of resources and re-sale goods.

# Overview of Significant Aspects in 2009

## Particular aspects of note in 2009

- Jupiter enters Aquarius - See January 5th

- Saturn opposite Uranus - See February 5th

- Jupiter conjunct Neptune - See May 27

- Uranus square Pluto (non exact) - See June 7th

- Saturn enters Libra - See October 29th

- Saturn square Pluto - See November 15th

## Monthly overviews

| January | | PST | EST | |
|---|---|---|---|---|
| 1 | Mercury enters Aquarius | 1:52 AM | 4:52 AM | |
| 3 | Venus enters Pisces | 4:35 AM | 7:35 AM | |
| 4 | **First QTR Moon in Aries** | 3:55 AM | 6:55 AM | |
| | Venus sextile Pluto | 11:32 AM | 2:32 PM | |
| 5 | Jupiter enters Aquarius | 7:41 AM | 10:41 AM | |
| 9 | Sun sextile Uranus | 7:27 AM | 10:27 AM | |
| 10 | **Full Moon in Cancer** | 7:27 PM | 10:27 PM | |
| 11 | Mercury goes retrograde | 8:44 AM | 11:44 AM | |
| | Sun trine Saturn | 10:01 AM | 1:01 PM | |
| 18 | Mercury conjunct Jupiter | 11:04 AM | 2:04 PM | |
| 17 | **Last QTR Moon in Libra** | 6:46 PM | 9:46 PM | |
| 19 | Sun enters Aquarius | 2:40 PM | 5:40 PM | |
| 20 | Sun conjunct Mercury | 7:59 AM | 10:59 AM | |
| | Mercury enters Capricorn | 9:36 PM | 12:36 AM | (Jan. 21) |
| 22 | Mars sextile Uranus | 8:59 AM | 11:59 AM | |
| | Venus conjunct Uranus | 5:01 PM | 8:01 PM | |
| 23 | Sun conjunct Jupiter | 9:44 PM | 12:44 AM | (Jan. 24) |

# January (Cont'd)

| | | PST | EST | |
|---|---|---|---|---|
| 24 | Mars trine Saturn | 12:04 AM | 3:04 AM | |
| | Venus opposite Saturn | 12:15 AM | 3:15 AM | |
| | Venus sextile Mars | 1:07 AM | 4:07 AM | |
| 25 | **New Moon in Aquarius** | 11:54 PM | 2:54 AM | (Jan. 26) |
| 26 | Mercury sextile Venus | 3:32 PM | 6:32 PM | |
| | Mercury conjunct Mars | 10:15 PM | 1:15 AM | (Jan. 27) |
| 31 | Mercury goes direct | 11:11 PM | 2:11 AM | (Feb. 1) |

# February

| | | | | |
|---|---|---|---|---|
| 2 | **Candlemas** | | | |
| | **First QTR Moon in Taurus** | 3:12 PM | 6:12 PM | |
| | Venus enters Aries | 7:41 PM | 10:41 PM | |
| 4 | Mars enters Aquarius | 7:55 AM | 10:55 AM | |
| 5 | Saturn opposite Uranus | 2:55 AM | 4:55 AM | |
| | Venus square Pluto | 8:25 PM | 11:25 PM | |
| 9 | **Full Moon in Leo** | 6:49 AM | 9:49 AM | |
| 12 | Sun conjunct Neptune | 4:40 AM | 7:40 AM | |
| 14 | Mercury enters Aquarius | 7:37 AM | 10:37 AM | |
| 16 | **Last QTR Moon in Scorpio** | 1:37 PM | 4:37 PM | |
| | Venus sextile Jupiter | 8:49 PM | 11:49 PM | |
| 17 | Mars conjunct Jupiter | 8:27 AM | 11:27 AM | |
| 18 | Venus sextile Mars | 1:27 AM | 4:27 AM | |
| | Sun enters Pisces | 4:46 AM | 7:46 AM | |
| 21 | Sun sextile Pluto | 12:03 AM | 3:03 AM | |
| 23 | Mercury conjunct Jupiter | 10:51 PM | 1:51 AM | (Feb. 24) |
| 24 | **New Moon in Pisces** | 5:34 PM | 8:34 PM | |
| 25 | Mercury sextile Venus | 4:59 PM | 7:59 PM | |

# March

| | | | | |
|---|---|---|---|---|
| 1 | Mercury conjunct Mars | 7:04 PM | 10:04 PM | |
| 3 | **First QTR Moon in Gemini** | 11:45 PM | 2:45 AM | |
| 5 | Mercury conjunct Neptune | 1:39 AM | 4:39 AM | |
| 6 | Venus goes retrograde | 9:18 AM | 12:18 PM | |

# March (Cont'd)

| | | PDT | EDT | |
|---|---|---|---|---|
| 8 | Mars conjunct Neptune | 5:50 AM | 8:50 AM | |
| 20 | Mercury enters Pisces | 11:55 AM | 2:55 PM | |
| | Sun opposite Saturn | 12:53 PM | 3:53 PM | |
| 10 | Mercury sextile Pluto | 10:37 AM | 1:37 PM | |
| | **Full Moon in Virgo** | 7:38 PM | 10:38 PM | |
| 11 | Venus sextile Jupiter | 5:34 AM | 8:34 AM | |
| 12 | Sun conjunct Uranus | 6:27 PM | 9:27 PM | |
| 14 | Mars enters Pisces | 8:19 PM | 11:19 PM | |
| 18 | **Last QTR Moon in Sagittarius** | 10:47 AM | 1:47 PM | |
| | Mercury opposite Saturn | 8:59 PM | 11:59 PM | |
| | Mars sextile Pluto | 11:14 PM | 2:14 AM | (March 19) |
| 20 | **Vernal Equinox** | | | |
| | Sun enters Aries | 4:43 AM | 7:43 AM | |
| 21 | Sun square Pluto | 11:35 AM | 2:35 PM | |
| | Mercury conjunct Uranus | 10:01 PM | 1:01 AM | (March 22) |
| 25 | Mercury enters Aries | 12:54 PM | 3:54 PM | |
| 26 | **New Moon in Aries** | 9:05 AM | 12:05 PM | |
| 27 | Mercury square Pluto | 5:15 AM | 8:15 AM | |
| | Sun conjunct Venus | 12:23 PM | 3:23 PM | |
| 28 | Mercury conjunct Venus | 7:31 PM | 10:31 PM | |
| 30 | Sun conjunct Mercury | 8:28 PM | 11:28 PM | |

# April

| | | | | |
|---|---|---|---|---|
| 2 | **First QTR Moon in Cancer** | 7:33 AM | 10:33 AM | |
| 3 | Venus square Pluto | 3:24 AM | 6:24 AM | |
| 4 | Mercury sextile Jupiter | 7:58 AM | 10:58 AM | |
| | Pluto goes retrograde | 10:36 AM | 1:36 PM | |
| | Mars opposite Saturn | 5:54 PM | 8:54 PM | |
| 7 | Mercury sextile Neptune | 5:37 AM | 8:37 AM | |
| 9 | Mercury enters Taurus | 7:21 AM | 10:21 AM | |
| | **Full Moon in Libra** | 7:56 AM | 10:56 AM | |
| 10 | Sun sextile Jupiter | 6:42 AM | 9:42 AM | |
| | Mercury trine Pluto | 10:52 PM | 1:52 AM | (April 11) |

11

# April (cont'd)

|     |                              | PDT      | EDT      |            |
| --- | ---------------------------- | -------- | -------- | ---------- |
| 11  | Venus enters Pisces          | 5:47 AM  | 8:47 AM  |            |
| 15  | Mars conjunct Uranus         | 3:00 AM  | 6:00 AM  |            |
|     | Sun sextile Neptune          | 12:54 PM | 3:54 PM  |            |
| 17  | **Last QTR Moon in Capricorn** | 6:36 AM  | 9:36 AM  |            |
|     | Venus goes direct            | 12:25 PM | 3:25 PM  |            |
|     | Mercury trine Saturn         | 5:51 PM  | 8:51 PM  |            |
| 19  | Sun enters Taurus            | 3:44 PM  | 6:44 PM  |            |
| 21  | Venus conjunct Mars          | 4:20 PM  | 7:20 PM  |            |
| 22  | Mars enters Aries            | 6:44 AM  | 9:44 AM  |            |
|     | Mercury square Jupiter       | 5:52 PM  | 8:52 PM  |            |
|     | Sun trine Pluto              | 10:44 PM | 1:44 AM  | (April 23) |
| 24  | Venus enters Aries           | 12:12 AM | 3:12 AM  |            |
|     | Mercury sextile Uranus       | 12:41 PM | 3:41 PM  |            |
|     | **New Moon in Taurus**       | 8:21 PM  | 11:21 PM |            |
| 25  | Mercury square Neptune       | 5:54 PM  | 8:54 PM  |            |
| 26  | Mars square Pluto            | 9:14 AM  | 12:14 PM |            |
| 30  | Mercury enters Gemini        | 3:33 PM  | 6:33 PM  |            |

# May

|     |                              | PDT      | EDT      |          |
| --- | ---------------------------- | -------- | -------- | -------- |
| 1   | **Beltane / May Day**        |          |          |          |
|     | **First QTR Moon in Leo**    | 1:44 PM  | 4:44 PM  |          |
| 2   | Venus square Pluto           | 10:08 AM | 1:08 PM  |          |
| 5   | Sun trine Saturn             | 2:34 AM  | 5:34 AM  |          |
| 6   | Mercury goes retrograde      | 10:01 PM | 1:01 AM  | (May 7)  |
| 8   | **Full Moon in Scorpio**     | 9:02 PM  | 12:02 AM |          |
| 13  | Mercury enters Taurus        | 4:51 PM  | 7:51 PM  |          |
| 16  | Sun square Jupiter           | 1:45 AM  | 4:45 AM  |          |
|     | Sun sextile Uranus           | 6:08 AM  | 9:08 AM  |          |
|     | Saturn goes direct           | 7:07 PM  | 10:07 PM |          |
|     | Sun square Neptune           | 10:05 PM | 1:05 AM  | (May 17) |
| 17  | **Last QTR Moon in Aquarius** | 12:25 AM | 3:25 AM  |          |
| 18  | Sun conjunct Mercury         | 3:01 AM  | 6:01 AM  |          |

# May (Cont'd)

| | | PDT | EDT | |
|---|---|---|---|---|
| 20 | Mercury square Neptune | 2:22 AM | 5:22 AM | |
| | Sun enters Gemini | 2:51 PM | 5:51 PM | |
| | Mercury square Jupiter | 8:45 PM | 11:45 PM | |
| | Mercury sextile Uranus | 11:47 PM | 2:47 AM | (May 21) |
| 24 | **New Moon in Gemini** | 5:10 AM | 8:10 AM | |
| 26 | Mars sextile Jupiter | 8:19 PM | 11:19 PM | |
| | Mars sextile Neptune | 9:36 PM | 12:36 AM | |
| 27 | Jupiter conjunct Neptune | 1:07 PM | 4:07 PM | |
| 28 | Neptune goes retrograde | 9:30 PM | 12:30 AM | |
| 30 | Mercury goes direct | 6:22 PM | 9:22 PM | |
| | **First QTR Moon in Virgo** | 8:22 PM | 11:22 PM | |
| 31 | Mars enters Taurus | 2:18 PM | 5:18 PM | |

# June

| | | | | |
|---|---|---|---|---|
| 2 | Venus sextile Neptune | 8:53 AM | 11:53 AM | |
| | Venus sextile Jupiter | 4:39 PM | 7:39 PM | |
| 3 | Mars trine Pluto | 9:36 PM | 12:36 AM | |
| 5 | Sun square Saturn | 12:10 PM | 3:10 PM | |
| 6 | Venus entersTaurus | 2:06 AM | 5:06 AM | |
| 7 | **Full Moon in Sagittarius** | 11:12 AM | 2:12 PM | |
| 8 | Venus trine Pluto | 12:22 PM | 3:22 PM | |
| 9 | Mercury sextile Uranus | 2:42 PM | 5:42 PM | |
| | Mercury square Neptune | 2:50 PM | 5:50 PM | |
| 10 | Mercury square Jupiter | 8:30 AM | 11:30 AM | |
| 13 | Mercury enters Gemini | 7:45 PM | 10:45 PM | |
| 15 | Jupiter goes retrograde | 12:50 AM | 3:50 AM | |
| | **Last QTR Moon in Pisces** | 3:13 PM | 6:13 PM | |
| 17 | Sun trine Neptune | 3:45 AM | 6:45 AM | |
| | Sun square Uranus | 7:56 AM | 10:56 AM | |
| | Sun trine Jupiter | 7:28 PM | 10:28 PM | |
| 20 | **Summer Solstice** | | | |
| | Sun enters Cancer | 10:45 PM | 1:45 AM | (June 21) |

## June (Cont'd)

| | | PDT | EDT | |
|---|---|---|---|---|
| 21 | Venus conjunct Mars | 6:09 AM | 9:09 AM | |
| | Venus trine Saturn | 11:30 PM | 2:30 AM | (June 22) |
| 22 | Mars trine Saturn | 7:44 AM | 10:44 AM | |
| | **New Moon in Cancer** | 12:34 PM | 3:34 PM | |
| 23 | Sun opposite Pluto | 12:41 AM | 3:41 AM | |
| 26 | Mercury square Saturn | 1:30 AM | 4:30 AM | |
| 29 | **First QTR Moon in Libra** | 4:29 AM | 7:29 AM | |

## July

| | | | | |
|---|---|---|---|---|
| 1 | Uranus goes retrograde | 12:38 AM | 3:38 AM | |
| | Venus square Neptune | 1:00 PM | 4:00 PM | |
| | Mercury trine Neptune | 1:47 PM | 4:47 PM | |
| | Mercury trine Jupiter | 6:34 PM | 9:34 PM | |
| | Mercury square Uranus | 7:12 PM | 10:12 PM | |
| | Venus square Jupiter | 9:24 PM | 12:24 AM | (July 3) |
| | Venus sextile Uranus | 10:41 PM | 1:41 AM | (July 3) |
| 3 | Mercury enters Cancer | 12:18 PM | 3:18 PM | |
| 4 | Mercury opposite Pluto | 8:28 AM | 11:28 AM | |
| 5 | Venus enters Gemini | 1:22 AM | 4:22 AM | |
| 6 | Mars square Neptune | 7:42 AM | 10:42 AM | |
| | Mars square Jupiter | 1:47 PM | 4:47 PM | |
| 7 | Mars sextile Uranus | 12:48 AM | 3:48 AM | |
| | **Full Moon in Capricorn** | 2:21 AM | 5:21 AM | |
| 9 | Sun sextile Saturn | 12:09 AM | 3:09 AM | |
| 10 | Jupiter conjunct Neptune | 2:11 AM | 5:11 AM | |
| 11 | Mercury sextile Saturn | 6:55 PM | 9:55 PM | |
| | Mars enters Gemini | 7:55 PM | 10:55 PM | |
| 13 | Sun conjunct Mercury | 7:15 PM | 10:15 PM | |
| 15 | **Last QTR Moon in Taurus** | 2:52 AM | 5:52 AM | |
| 16 | Mercury trine Uranus | 12:33 AM | 3:33 AM | |
| 17 | Mercury enters Leo | 4:07 PM | 7:07 PM | |
| 18 | Sun trine Uranus | 5:35 PM | 8:35 PM | |

14

# July (Cont'd)

| | | PDT | EDT | |
|---|---|---|---|---|
| 20 | Mercury sextile Mars | 4:32 PM | 7:32 PM | |
| 21 | Venus square Saturn | 1:05 PM | 4:05 PM | |
| | **New Moon in Cancer** | 7:34 PM | 10:34 PM | |
| 22 | Sun enters Leo | 9:35 AM | 12:35 PM | |
| 26 | Venus trine Jupiter | 9:07 PM | 12:07 AM | |
| 27 | Venus trine Neptune | 10:51 PM | 1:51 AM | (July 28) |
| 28 | Venus square Uranus | 1:38 PM | 4:38 PM | |
| | **First QTR Moon in Scorpio** | 3:00 PM | 6:00 PM | |
| 30 | Mercury opposite Jupiter | 3:38 AM | 6:38 AM | |
| 31 | Mercury opposite Neptune | 12:47 AM | 3:47 AM | |
| | Venus enters Cancer | 6:27 PM | 9:27 PM | |

# August

| | | PDT | EDT |
|---|---|---|---|
| 1 | **Lammas / Lughnassad** | | |
| | Venus opposite Pluto | 4:35 PM | 7:35 PM |
| 2 | Mercury enters Virgo | 4:07 PM | 7:07 PM |
| 5 | **Full Moon in Aquarius** | 5:54 PM | 8:54 PM |
| 3 | Mercury trine Pluto | 7:11 AM | 10:11 AM |
| 7 | Mercury sextile Venus | 8:55 PM | 11:55 PM |
| 10 | Mars square Saturn | 5:16 PM | 8:16 PM |
| 13 | Mars trine Jupiter | 9:29 AM | 12:29 PM |
| | **Last QTR Moon in Taurus** | 11:53 AM | 2:53 PM |
| 14 | Sun opposite Jupiter | 10:52 AM | 1:52 PM |
| 17 | Mercury conjunct Saturn | 8:14 AM | 11:14 AM |
| | Sun sextile Mars | 3:57 AM | 6:57 AM |
| | Sun opposite Neptune | 1:54 PM | 4:54 PM |
| | Mars trine Neptune | 6:28 PM | 9:28 PM |
| 18 | Mars square Uranus | 7:24 PM | 10:24 PM |
| 19 | Venus sextile Saturn | 3:10 AM | 6:10 AM |
| 20 | **New Moon in Leo** | 3:01 AM | 6:01 AM |
| 21 | Mercury opposite Uranus | 4:47 AM | 7:47 AM |
| 22 | Venus trine Uranus | 4:31 PM | 7:31 PM |
| | Sun enters Virgo | 4:38 PM | 7:38 PM |

# August (Cont'd)

| | | PDT | EDT | |
|---|---|---|---|---|
| 23 | Sun trine Pluto | 11:19 AM | 2:19 PM | |
| 25 | Mars enters Cancer | 10:15 AM | 1:15 PM | |
| | Mercury enters Libra | 1:20 PM | 4:20 PM | |
| | Mercury square Mars | 9:03 PM | 12:03 AM | |
| 26 | Mars opposite Pluto | 1:34 PM | 4:34 PM | |
| | Mercury square Pluto | 9:11 AM | 12:11 PM | |
| | Venus enters Leo | 9:11 AM | 12:11 PM | |
| 27 | **First QTR Moon in Sagittarius** | 4:42 AM | 7:42 AM | |
| 28 | Mercury sextile Venus | 6:24 AM | 9:24 AM | |

# September

| | | PDT | EDT | |
|---|---|---|---|---|
| 3 | Mercury square Mars | 9:09 AM | 12:09 PM | |
| 4 | **Full Moon in Pisces** | 9:02 AM | 12:02 AM | |
| 6 | Mercury goes retrograde | 9:45 PM | 12:45 AM | (Sept. 7) |
| 11 | Venus opposite Jupiter | 12:54 AM | 3:54 AM | |
| | Pluto goes direct | 9:58 AM | 12:58 PM | |
| | **Last QTR Moon in Gemini** | 7:15 PM | 10:15 PM | |
| 15 | Saturn opposite Uranus | 5:51 AM | 8:51 AM | |
| | Venus opposite Neptune | 2:36 PM | 5:36 PM | |
| 17 | Sun opposite Uranus | 2:41 AM | 5:41 AM | |
| | Mercury square Pluto | 4:44 AM | 7:44 AM | |
| | Sun conjunct Saturn | 11:22 AM | 2:22 PM | |
| | Mercury enters Virgo | 8:25 PM | 11:25 PM | |
| 18 | **New Moon in Virgo** | 11:45 AM | 2:45 PM | |
| 20 | Sun conjunct Mercury | 3:04 AM | 6:04 AM | |
| | Venus enters Virgo | 6:32 AM | 9:32 AM | |
| | Venus trine Pluto | 7:57 PM | 10:57 PM | |
| 22 | **Autumnal Equinox** | | | |
| | Mercury conjunct Saturn | 2:09 AM | 5:09 AM | |
| | Sun enters Libra | 2:18 PM | 5:18 PM | |
| 23 | Sun square Pluto | 7:22 AM | 10:22 AM | |
| | Mercury opposite Uranus | 8:39 AM | 11:39 AM | |
| 25 | **First QTR Moon in Capricorn** | 9:50 PM | 12:50 AM | |

## September (Cont'd)

|    |                        | PDT       | EDT       |          |
|----|------------------------|-----------|-----------|----------|
| 29 | Mercury goes direct    | 6:14 AM   | 9:14 AM   |          |
| 30 | Mercury sextile Mars   | 11:28 PM  | 2:28 AM   | (Oct. 1) |

## October

| 3  | **Full Moon in Aries**            | 11:09 PM  | 2:09 AM   | (Oct. 4)  |
|----|-----------------------------------|-----------|-----------|-----------|
| 4  | Mercury sextile Mars              | 4:25 AM   | 7:25 AM   |           |
|    | Mercury opposite Uranus           | 1:59 PM   | 4:59 PM   |           |
|    | Mars trine Uranus                 | 6:36 PM   | 9:36 PM   |           |
| 7  | Mercury conjunct Saturn           | 11:30 PM  | 2:30 AM   | (Oct. 8)  |
| 9  | Venus opposite Uranus             | 3:00 PM   | 6:00 PM   |           |
|    | Mercury enters Libra              | 8:43 PM   | 11:43 PM  |           |
| 10 | Mercury square Pluto              | 11:42 AM  | 2:42 PM   |           |
|    | Sun trine Jupiter                 | 1:38 AM   | 4:38 AM   |           |
| 11 | **Last QTR Moon in Cancer**       | 1:55 AM   | 4:55 AM   |           |
| 12 | Mars sextile Saturn               | 1:51 PM   | 4:51 PM   |           |
|    | Jupiter goes direct               | 9:35 PM   | 12:35 AM  | (Oct. 13) |
| 13 | Venus conjunct Saturn             | 3:51 AM   | 6:51 AM   |           |
|    | Venus sextile Mars                | 11:30 AM  | 2:30 PM   |           |
| 14 | Venus enters Libra                | 3:46 PM   | 6:46 PM   |           |
| 15 | Venus square Pluto                | 10:21 AM  | 1:21 PM   |           |
| 16 | Mars enters Leo                   | 8:32 AM   | 11:32 AM  |           |
|    | Sun trine Neptune                 | 5:46 PM   | 8:46 PM   |           |
| 17 | **New Moon in Libra**             | 10:34 PM  | 1:34 AM   | (Oct. 18) |
| 20 | Mercury trine Jupiter             | 2:49 PM   | 5:49 PM   |           |
| 22 | Sun enters Scorpio                | 11:43 PM  | 2:43 AM   | (Oct. 23) |
| 24 | Sun sextile Pluto                 | 2:57 AM   | 5:57 AM   |           |
|    | Mercury trine Neptune             | 9:55 AM   | 12:55 PM  |           |
| 25 | **First QTR Moon in Aquarius**    | 5:42 PM   | 8:42 PM   |           |
| 28 | Mercury enters Scorpio            | 3:08 AM   | 6:08 AM   |           |
|    | Venus trine Jupiter               | 7:01 PM   | 10:01 PM  |           |
|    | Mercury sextile Pluto             | 8:53 PM   | 11:53 PM  |           |

17

# October (Cont'd)

| | | PDT | EDT |
|---|---|---|---|
| 29 | Saturn enters Libra | 10:09 AM | 1:09 PM |
| | Sun square Mars | 12:55 AM | 3:55 AM |
| 31 | **All Hallows / (Halloween) / Samhain / Witches' New Year** | | |

# November

| | | PST | EST |
|---|---|---|---|
| 1 | Mercury square Mars | 4:50 PM | 7:50 PM |
| 2 | **Full Moon in Taurus** | 11:12 AM | 2:12 PM |
| | Venus trine Neptune | 3:21 PM | 6:21 PM |
| 4 | Neptune goes direct | 10:10 AM | 1:10 PM |
| 5 | Sun conjunct Mercury | 12:02 AM | 3:02 AM |
| 7 | Venus enters Scorpio | 4:23 PM | 7:23 PM |
| 8 | Mercury square Jupiter | 6:42 AM | 9:42 AM |
| | Venus sextile Pluto | 9:34 PM | 12:34 AM (Nov. 9) |
| 9 | **Last QTR Moon in Leo** | 7:56 AM | 10:56 AM |
| 10 | Sun square Jupiter | 10:41 AM | 1:41 PM |
| 11 | Mercury trine Uranus | 3:37 AM | 6:37 AM |
| | Mercury square Neptune | 4:11 PM | 7:11 PM |
| 14 | Sun trine Uranus | 5:40 PM | 8:40 PM |
| 15 | Saturn square Pluto | 7:20 AM | 10:20 AM |
| | Sun square Neptune | 3:10 PM | 6:10 PM |
| | Mercury enters Sagittarius | 4:28 PM | 7:28 PM |
| 16 | **New Moon in Scorpio** | 11:14 PM | 2:14 PM |
| | Mercury sextile Saturn | 9:00 PM | 12:00 AM (Nov. 17) |
| 19 | Venus square Mars | 12:22 AM | 3:22 AM |
| 21 | Sun enters Sagittarius | 8:22 PM | 11:22 PM |
| 23 | Venus square Jupiter | 2:02 PM | 5:02 PM |
| 24 | Sun sextile Saturn | 7:34 AM | 10:34 AM |
| | **First QTR Moon in Pisces** | 1:38 PM | 4:38 PM |
| 25 | Venus trine Uranus | 7:00 PM | 10:00 PM |
| 26 | Mercury trine Mars | 6:53 AM | 9:53 AM |
| | Venus square Neptune | 4:15 PM | 7:15 PM |
| 29 | Mercury sextile Jupiter | 3:53 AM | 6:53 AM |
| 30 | Mercury square Uranus | 11:52 AM | 2:52 PM |

18

# December

| | | PST | EST | |
|---|---|---|---|---|
| 1 | Mercury sextile Neptune | 6:52 AM | 9:52 AM | |
| | Uranus goes direct | 12:28 PM | 3:28 PM | |
| | Venus enters Sagittarius | 2:03 PM | 5:03 PM | |
| | **Full Moon in Gemini** | 11:29 PM | 2:29 AM | (DEC. 2) |
| 4 | Venus sextile Saturn | 3:44 AM | 6:44 AM | |
| 5 | Mercury enters Capricorn | 9:24 AM | 12:24 PM | |
| 7 | Mercury conjunct Pluto | 1:12 AM | 4:12 AM | |
| | Mercury square Saturn | 6:35 PM | 9:35 PM | |
| 8 | **Last QTR Moon in Virgo** | 4:13 PM | 7:13 PM | |
| 10 | Sun trine Mars | 5:18 PM | 8:18 PM | |
| 14 | Sun square Uranus | 7:26 AM | 10:26 AM | |
| | Sun sextile Jupiter | 4:16 PM | 7:16 PM | |
| 15 | Sun sextile Neptune | 4:16 PM | 7:16 PM | |
| 16 | **New Moon in Sagittarius** | 4:02 AM | 7:02 AM | |
| 17 | Venus trine Mars | 4:39 AM | 7:39 AM | |
| 19 | Venus square Uranus | 5:52 PM | 8:52 PM | |
| 20 | Mars goes retrograde | 5:27 AM | 8:27 AM | |
| | Venus sextile Jupiter | 8:52 PM | 11:52 PM | |
| | Venus sextile Neptune | 9:23 PM | 12:23 AM | (Dec. 21) |
| 21 | **Winter Solstice** | | | |
| | Jupiter conjunct Neptune | 12:50 AM | 3:50 AM | |
| | Sun enters Capricorn | 9:46 AM | 12:46 PM | |
| 24 | Sun conjunct Pluto | 9:31 AM | 12:31 PM | |
| | **First QTR Moon in Aries** | 9:34 AM | 12:34 PM | |
| 25 | Venus enters Capricorn | 10:17 AM | 1:17 PM | |
| | Sun square Saturn | 3:57 PM | 6:57 PM | |
| 26 | Mercury goes retrograde | 6:39 AM | 9:39 AM | |
| 27 | Venus conjunct Pluto | 10:49 PM | 1:49 AM | (Dec. 28) |
| 28 | Venus square Saturn | 10:54 PM | 1:54 AM | (Dec. 29) |
| 31 | **Full Moon in Cancer** | 11:12 AM | 2:12 PM | |

# TABLE OF ASPECT INFLUENCES

## JANUARY 2009

| 1 | 2 | 3 | 4 | 5 | 6 | 7 | 8 | 9 | 10 | 11 | 12 | 13 | 14 | 15 | 16 | 17 | 18 | 19 | 20 | 21 | 22 | 23 | 24 | 25 | 26 | 27 | 28 | 29 | 30 | 31 |
|---|---|---|---|---|---|---|---|---|----|----|----|----|----|----|----|----|----|----|----|----|----|----|----|----|----|----|----|----|----|----|

Aspects: ♄☍♅  ♂△♄  ♂✶♅  ♀✶♂  ♀☍♄  ♀☌♅  ♀☌♃  ♀✶♀  ♂□♀  ♀☌♂  ☿✶♅  ☿✶♀  ☉△♄  ☉✶♅  ☉☌♀  ☿△♄  ☉☌♃

## FEBRUARY 2009

| 1 | 2 | 3 | 4 | 5 | 6 | 7 | 8 | 9 | 10 | 11 | 12 | 13 | 14 | 15 | 16 | 17 | 18 | 19 | 20 | 21 | 22 | 23 | 24 | 25 | 26 | 27 | 28 |
|---|---|---|---|---|---|---|---|---|----|----|----|----|----|----|----|----|----|----|----|----|----|----|----|----|----|----|----|

Aspects: ♄☍♅  ♂☌♃  ♀✶♃  ♀✶♂  ♀□♀  ♀☌♃  ☿✶♅  ☉☌♆  ☿☌♂  ☿△♄  ☿✶♀  ☉✶♀

## MARCH 2009

| 1 | 2 | 3 | 4 | 5 | 6 | 7 | 8 | 9 | 10 | 11 | 12 | 13 | 14 | 15 | 16 | 17 | 18 | 19 | 20 | 21 | 22 | 23 | 24 | 25 | 26 | 27 | 28 | 29 | 30 | 31 |
|---|---|---|---|---|---|---|---|---|----|----|----|----|----|----|----|----|----|----|----|----|----|----|----|----|----|----|----|----|----|----|----|

Aspects: ♂✶♀  ♂☍♄  ♂☌♆  ♀□♀  ♀✶♃  ♀☌♀  ☿☌♆  ☿☍♄  ♀□♀  ☿☌♂  ☿✶♀  ☉☌♀  ☉☌♅  ☉☍♄  ☉□♀

20

# TABLE OF ASPECT INFLUENCES

## APRIL 2009

| 1 | 2 | 3 | 4 | 5 | 6 | 7 | 8 | 9 | 10 | 11 | 12 | 13 | 14 | 15 | 16 | 17 | 18 | 19 | 20 | 21 | 22 | 23 | 24 | 25 | 26 | 27 | 28 | 29 | 30 |
|---|---|---|---|---|---|---|---|---|----|----|----|----|----|----|----|----|----|----|----|----|----|----|----|----|----|----|----|----|----|

Aspects:
- ♃☍♆
- ♂☍♄
- ♂□♀
- ♂☌♅
- ♀☌♂
- ♀☌♅
- ♀□♀
- ♀□♀
- ♀✳♆
- ♀□♃
- ♀✳♃
- ♀△♀
- ♀□♆
- ☉✳♃
- ♀△♄
- ♀✳♅
- ☉✳♆
- ♀✳♀
- ☉△♀

## MAY 2009

| 1 | 2 | 3 | 4 | 5 | 6 | 7 | 8 | 9 | 10 | 11 | 12 | 13 | 14 | 15 | 16 | 17 | 18 | 19 | 20 | 21 | 22 | 23 | 24 | 25 | 26 | 27 | 28 | 29 | 30 | 31 |
|---|---|---|---|---|---|---|---|---|----|----|----|----|----|----|----|----|----|----|----|----|----|----|----|----|----|----|----|----|----|----|----|

Aspects:
- ♃☌♆
- ♂△♀
- ♀□♀
- ♂✳♆
- ♂✳♃
- ☉✳♅
- ♀✳♃
- ☉□♆
- ♀☌♂
- ☉△♄
- ☉☌♀
- ♀✳♆
- ♀□♃
- ♀□♆
- ☉□♃
- ☉□♄
- ♀✳♅

## JUNE 2009

| 1 | 2 | 3 | 4 | 5 | 6 | 7 | 8 | 9 | 10 | 11 | 12 | 13 | 14 | 15 | 16 | 17 | 18 | 19 | 20 | 21 | 22 | 23 | 24 | 25 | 26 | 27 | 28 | 29 | 30 |
|---|---|---|---|---|---|---|---|---|----|----|----|----|----|----|----|----|----|----|----|----|----|----|----|----|----|----|----|----|----|----|

Aspects:
- ♅□♀
- ♃☌♆
- ♂△♀
- ♂△♄
- ♂□♆
- ♀△♀
- ♀✳♃
- ♀△♄
- ♂□♃
- ♀✳♆
- ♀□♃
- ♀☌♂
- ♀□♆
- ♀□♆
- ♀✳♅
- ♀✳♅
- ☉△♆
- ♀□♄
- ♀□♃
- ☉☍♀
- ♀□♅
- ☉□♄
- ☉□♅
- ♀△♃
- ☉△♃
- ♀△♆

21

# TABLE OF ASPECT INFLUENCES

## JULY 2009

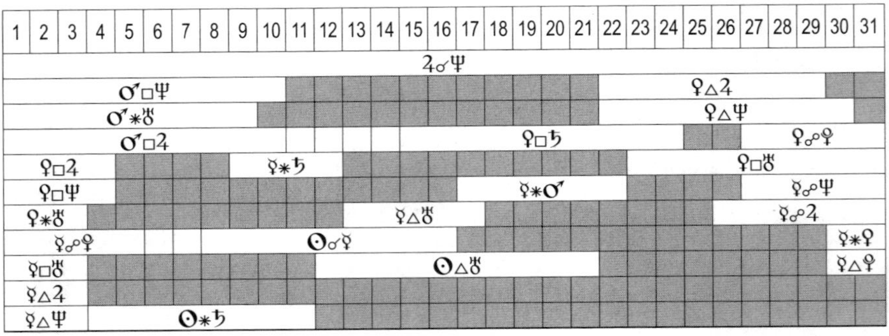
1 2 3 4 5 6 7 8 9 10 11 12 13 14 15 16 17 18 19 20 21 22 23 24 25 26 27 28 29 30 31
♃☌♆
♂□♆
♀△♃
♂✶♅
♀△♆
♂□♃
♀□♄
♀☍♇
♀□♃
☿✶♄
♀□♅
♀□♆
☿✶♂
☿☍♆
♀✶♅
☿△♅
☿☍♃
☿☍♇
☉☌☿
☿✶♀
☿□♅
☉△♅
☿△♀
☿△♃
☿△♆
☉✶♄

## AUGUST 2009

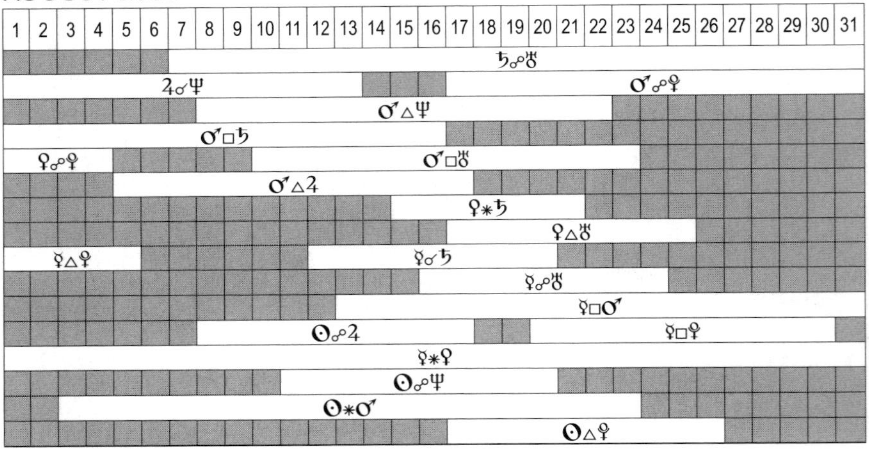
1 2 3 4 5 6 7 8 9 10 11 12 13 14 15 16 17 18 19 20 21 22 23 24 25 26 27 28 29 30 31
♄☍♅
♃☌♆
♂☍♇
♂△♆
♂□♄
♀☍♇
♂□♅
♂△♃
♀✶♄
♀△♅
☿△♇
☿☌♄
☿☍♅
☿□♂
☉☍♃
☿□♀
☿✶♀
☉☍♆
☉✶♂
☉△♇

## SEPTEMBER 2009

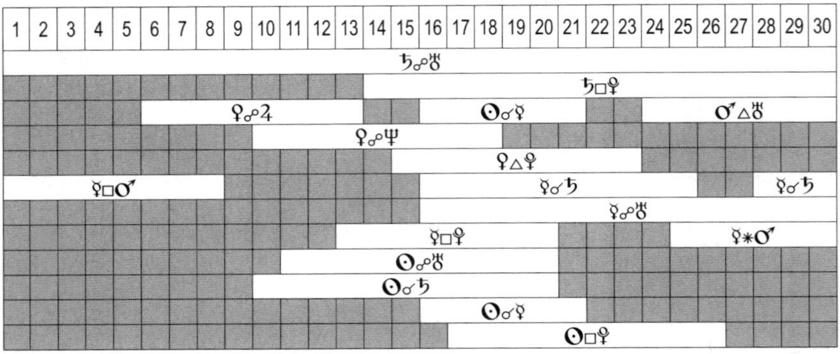
1 2 3 4 5 6 7 8 9 10 11 12 13 14 15 16 17 18 19 20 21 22 23 24 25 26 27 28 29 30
♄☍♅
♄□♇
♀☍♃
☉☌☿
♂△♅
♀☍♆
♀△♇
☿□♂
☿☌♄
☿☌♄
☿☍♅
☿□♇
☿✶♂
☉☍♅
☉☌♄
☉☌☿
☉□♇

# TABLE OF ASPECT INFLUENCES

## OCTOBER 2009

| 1 | 2 | 3 | 4 | 5 | 6 | 7 | 8 | 9 | 10 | 11 | 12 | 13 | 14 | 15 | 16 | 17 | 18 | 19 | 20 | 21 | 22 | 23 | 24 | 25 | 26 | 27 | 28 | 29 | 30 | 31 |
|---|---|---|---|---|---|---|---|---|---|---|---|---|---|---|---|---|---|---|---|---|---|---|---|---|---|---|---|---|---|---|
| | | | | | | | | | | | | | | | ♄□♇ | | | | | | | | | | | | | | | |
| | ♄☍♅ | | | | | | | | | | | ♀□♇ | | | | | | | | | | | | | | ♀△♃ | | | | |
| | | | | | | | | | ♂✶♄ | | | | | | | | | | | | | | | | | | | | ♀△♆ | |
| | | | | ♂△♅ | | | | | | | | | | | | | | | | | | | | | | | | | | |
| | | | | | | | | | | ♀✶♂ | | | | | | | | | | | | | | | | | | | | |
| | | | ☿☍♅ | | | | | | | | | | | | | | | | | | | | | | | | | | | |
| | | | | | | | | | | ♀☌♄ | | | | | | | | | | | | | | | | | | | | |
| | | | | | | | ♀☍♅ | | | | | | | | | | | | | | | ☿△♆ | | | | | | | | |
| | | | | | ☿☌♄ | | | | | | | | | | | | | ☿△♃ | | | | | | | | | | ☿□♂ | | |
| | | | | ☿✶♂ | | | | | | | | | | ☉△♆ | | | | | | | | | | | | | | ☿✶♇ | | |
| | | | | | | | ☿□♇ | | | | | | | | | | | | | | | | | | | | | ☉☌☿ | | |
| | | | | | | | ☉△♃ | | | | | | | | | | | | | | | | ☉□♂ | | | | | | | |
| | | | | | | | | | | | | | | | | | | | | | | ☉✶♇ | | | | | | | | |

## NOVEMBER 2009

| 1 | 2 | 3 | 4 | 5 | 6 | 7 | 8 | 9 | 10 | 11 | 12 | 13 | 14 | 15 | 16 | 17 | 18 | 19 | 20 | 21 | 22 | 23 | 24 | 25 | 26 | 27 | 28 | 29 | 30 |
|---|---|---|---|---|---|---|---|---|---|---|---|---|---|---|---|---|---|---|---|---|---|---|---|---|---|---|---|---|---|
| | | | | | | | | | | | | | | ♄□♇ | | | | | | | | | | | | | | | |
| | | | | | | | | | | | | | | ♃☌♆ | | | | | | | | | | | | | | | |
| | | ♀△♆ | | | | | | | | | | | | | | | | | | | ♂☍♃ | | | | | | | | |
| | | | | | | ♀✶♇ | | | | | | | | | | | | | | | ♀□♃ | | | | | | | | |
| | | | | | | | | | | | | | | | | ♀□♂ | | | | | | | | | | | | | |
| | | | | | | ☿□♃ | | | | | | | | | | | | | | | | | | ♀□♆ | | | | | |
| | ☿□♂ | | | | | | | | ☿□♆ | | | | | | | | | | | | | | ♀△♅ | | | | | | |
| | | | | | | | | | | | | | | | ☿✶♄ | | | | | | | | | | | | ☿□♅ | | |
| | ☉□♂ | | | | | | | | ☿△♅ | | | | | | | | | | | | | | | | | | | ☿✶♆ | |
| | | | | ☉☌☿ | | | | | | | | | | | | | | | | | | | | | | | ☿✶♃ | | |
| | | | | | | | ☉□♃ | | | | | | | | | | | | | | | | ☿△♂ | | | | | | |
| | | | | | | | | | | | | | ☉□♆ | | | | | | | | | ☉✶♄ | | | | | | | |
| | | | | | | | | | | | ☉△♅ | | | | | | | | | | | | | | | | | | |

## DECEMBER 2009

| 1 | 2 | 3 | 4 | 5 | 6 | 7 | 8 | 9 | 10 | 11 | 12 | 13 | 14 | 15 | 16 | 17 | 18 | 19 | 20 | 21 | 22 | 23 | 24 | 25 | 26 | 27 | 28 | 29 | 30 | 31 |
|---|---|---|---|---|---|---|---|---|---|---|---|---|---|---|---|---|---|---|---|---|---|---|---|---|---|---|---|---|---|---|
| | | | | | | | | | | | | | | | ♄□♇ | | | | | | | | | | | | | | | |
| | | | | | | | | | | | | | | ♂☍♆ | | | | | | | | | | | | | | | | |
| | | | | | ♂☍♃ | | | | | | | | | | | | | ♀✶♃ | | | | | | | | ♀□♄ | | | | |
| | | ♀✶♄ | | | | | | | | | | | | ♀△♂ | | | | | | | | | | | ♀☌♇ | | | | | |
| | | | | ☿☌♇ | | | | | | | | | | | | | | ♀✶♆ | | | | | | | | | | | | |
| | | | | | ☿□♄ | | | | | | | | | | | | ♀□♅ | | | | | | | | | | | | | |
| ☿□♅ | | | | | | | | | | | ☉□♅ | | | | | | | | | | | | | ☿✶♅ | | | | | | |
| ☿✶♆ | | | | | | | | | | | | | | | | | | | | | ☉☌♇ | | | | | | | | | |
| | | | | | | | ☉△♂ | | | | | | | | | | | | | | | | ☉☌♀ | | | | | | | |
| | | | | | | | | | | | | | ☉✶♆ | | | | | | | | | | | | | | | | | |
| | | | | | | | | | | | | ☉✶♃ | | | | | | | | | | ☉□♄ | | | | | | | | |

# Phases of the Moon

Times in Pacific Time (for Eastern add 3 hours)

| | ☽ 1st Qtr | ◯ Full | ☾ 3rd Qtr | ● New | |
|---|---|---|---|---|---|
| **January** | 4th 3:55AM Aries | 10th 7:26PM Cancer | 17th 6:46PM Libra | 25th 11:54PM Aquarius | |
| **Febuary** | ☽ 2nd 3:12PM Taurus | ◯ 9th 6:49AM Leo | ☾ 16th 1:37PM Scorpio | ● 24th 5:34PM Pisces | |
| **March** | ☽ 3rd 11:45PM Gemini | ◯ 10th 7:38PM Virgo | ☾ 18th 10:47AM Sagittarius | ● 26th 9:05AM Aries | |
| **April** | ☽ 2nd 7:33AM Cancer | ◯ 9th 7:56AM Libra | ☾ 17th 6:36AM Capricorn | ● 24th 8:21PM Taurus | |
| **May** | ☽ 1st 1:44PM Leo | ◯ 8th 9:02PM Scorpio | ☾ 17th 12:25AM Aquarius | ● 24th 5:10AM Gemini | ☽ 30th 8:22PM Virgo |
| **June** | ◯ 7th 11:12AM Sagittarius | ☾ 15th 3:13PM Pisces | ● 22nd 12:34PM Cancer | ☽ 29th 4:29AM Libra | |
| **July** | ◯ 7th 2:21AM Capricorn | ☾ 15th 2:52AM Aries | ● 21st 7:34AM Cancer | ☽ 28th 3:00PM Scorpio | |
| **August** | ◯ 5th 5:54PM Aquarius | ☾ 13th 11.53AM Taurus | ● 20th 3:01AM Leo | ☽ 27th 4:42AM Sagittarius | |
| **September** | ◯ 4th 9:02AM Pisces | ☾ 11th 7:15PM Gemini | ● 18th 11:45AM Virgo | ☽ 25th 9:50PM Capricorn | |
| **October** | ◯ 3rd 11:09PM Aries | ☾ 11th 1:55AM Cancer | ● 17th 10:34PM Libra | ☽ 25th 5:42PM Aquarius | |
| **November** | ◯ 2nd 11:12AM Taurus | ☾ 9th 7:56AM Leo | ● 16th 11:14AM Scorpio | ☽ 24th 1:38PM Pisces | |
| **December** | ◯ 1st 11:29PM Gemini | ☾ 8th 4:13PM Virgo | ● 16th 4:02AM Sagittarius | ☽ 24th 9:34AM Aries | ◯ 31st 11:12AM Cancer |

# LUNAR ASPECTS GUIDE

## MOON TO SUN ASPECTS

In general, the Moon aspects to the Sun bring us a greater awareness of our feelings with regard to the season through which we are passing.

### Moon sextile Sun

Moon sextile Sun brings optimism, or a brighter spirit, towards whatever seasonal activities are occurring and our moods are more likely to be encouraged by the endearing qualities of the season. This aspect helps our moods to accept and be at peace with the relevant seasonal factors, getting in tune with the seasonal pace. It assists us in making the shift from the early stage of emotional experience to the next stage of emotional development. In general, Moon sextile Sun brings positive vibrations, and acts as a catalyst in the ebb and flow of the emotions. It brings the promising potential for acceptance and reassurance and, where such moods are absent, there is the driving hope to reach a happy medium. Moon sextile Sun brings inspiration to our dreams and gives us a sense of where we are going next.

### Moon square Sun (First and Last Quarter Moons)

Moon square Sun represents the First and Last Quarter stages of the Moon. It is the middle road, the half-way mark between the waxing and waning process of the Moon. It is the pinnacle of the in-between stage, and it represents the crux of what we hope to establish in our emotional process as it is affected by the Moon. The square aspect represents struggle or challenge; this tends to be the point where we exercise our emotions with diligent effort. The square of the Moon to the Sun is a time when we tend to make extra adjustments with our emotional process, and we take extra steps towards the place we have determined that our emotions are headed. This is characterized by the sign the Moon is in, and how we respond, individually, with the qualities of that sign. Moon square Sun summons some very lively and busy emotional responses in the course of our dreams.

**First Quarter Moon** (Waxing Quarter Moon) Halfway in between the New and Full Moon, the First Quarter Moon has built up some momentum in our emotional process. This is a positive, upbeat, anticipatory time. The sign that the Moon is in will denote the types of focuses and themes that will preoccupy us, and these are the things we will be building up and strengthening in our emotional core. As the waxing Moon reaches this First Quarter mark, this is a good time for maintaining and nurturing positive emotional vibrations.

**Last Quarter Moon** (Waning Quarter Moon) Halfway in between the Full and New Moon, the Last Quarter Moon breaks down the emotional momentum that was built up during the Full Moon period of the previous week. This is a time of letting go, of finishing or completing certain aspects of the emotional process. The waning Moon allows us to process and let go of emotionally taxing sensations, and from there we begin to be less weighted down by our feelings. When we struggle with letting go, it is highlighted through this stage of lunar development. As the waning Moon reaches this Last Quarter mark, this is a good time for weeding out and cleaning up emotional negativity, and for letting go of unnecessary emotional baggage.

## Moon trine Sun

Overall, Moon trine Sun brings good vibes; it allows us to create or to access congenial, hopeful, and positive moods. Moon trine Sun always reminds us of the aspects of the current season that are inspiring and uplifting. Whenever the trine aspect occurs, the Moon and Sun will both (usually) be in the same element together: a fire, water, air, or earth sign. This brings synchronization and focuses the energy of our moods on positive and cohesive emotional responses. Moon trine Sun brings beautiful harmony to the mood of the day. In general, this aspect brings sunny, cheerful moods, and a positive outlook on life. Moon trine Sun influences dreams with positive vibrations, and it brings sparkling delights and gifts of happiness.

## Moon opposite Sun (Full Moon)

The Full Moon represents the fruition of our emotional process. Moon opposite Sun magnifies the emotional or spiritual qualities of the season. This is a time when we access and harness a great deal of emotional energy. It's a great time to establish positive affirmations, and to celebrate the bountiful fullness of the season. Often, the Full Moon time brings a whirlwind of activity, and this represents the crescendo or climax of our emotional process as it is affected by the Moon. This climax of the Moon's luminous reflections of the Sun brings the greatest amount of light to our emotional experience, and this is a very good time to count your blessings and enjoy the wonders of your life. Moon opposite Sun brings astonishing images and rich, fulfilling, experiences to the dream world.

## Moon conjunct Sun (New Moon)

The New Moon represents the beginning; a starting point, where our feelings begin their development, and where our pre-established feelings are renewed, confirmed, or re-established. This is a dark time of night, as the Moon joins forces with the daytime Sun. Through this time, our emotional process is often internalized, where it is replenished with a sense of newness. Here, newer feelings may emerge with a certain affirmation or assurance. It is here that we muster new hope, new faith, and there is a subtle – but certain – expression of re-birth in our emotional understanding. This is the time to tap into the wiser parts of the soul, to allow our older feelings to be recycled and renewed, and to open up to, and give room for, new feelings as they begin to emerge. It is also important to remember to rest, to let emotions just be, without adding complexity to them. Moon conjunct Sun brings insightful, regenerative, and profound images to the dream world.

# MOON TO MERCURY ASPECTS

## Moon sextile Mercury

Moon sextile Mercury brings the potential for inspiring news and communications. This lunar aspect brings clear and succinct communications which will assist us to keep business running along smoothly. It's a good time to reiterate plans, schedules, and messages and to handle communications very thoroughly. Moon sextile Mercury inspires our moods with informative talk and information but, when Mercury is retrograde, it would be wise to follow up any new information with careful research. This time brings the potential for inspiration through thoughts and ideas, and all this is possible despite the travails of Mercury retrograde periods. Moon sextile Mercury brings the potential for some intelligent brainstorming between people, and this will be a very good time to run your ideas by others. It brings intellectually stimulating dreams and reveals a lot about your thoughts and ideas.

## Moon square Mercury

Moon square Mercury often brings a challenging time for communications. This may be a time when it is difficult to reassure others, and moods may be challenged by intellectual debates and discussions. It may be difficult to get the message across in the way it was intended. It may also bring uncommunicative moods, or we may find that it is difficult to describe our moods. This lunar aspect is the least ideal aspect for communications under the influence of Mercury retrograde. Moon square Mercury tends to bring moods or emotional responses which are thwarted by complex communications and difficult subjects, and defensive moods may become argumentative. This is a good time to use caution with our words and to consider the impact that harsh statements may have on others. Moon square Mercury adds mental nervousness to the course of our dreams, and may contribute to nightmarish feelings and thoughts about our dreams.

## Moon trine Mercury

Moon trine Mercury brings moods in harmony with communications. This is an excellent time to talk, relay thoughts, and communicate with greater ease. Moon trine Mercury brings the gift of thoughtfulness, making communications very harmonious. This aspect brings pleasantly talkative and mindful moods, leading to discussions that may clarify misinterpreted facts. It will assist us to communicate more clearly during Mercury retrograde periods. Moon trine Mercury brings a superb time for us to communicate amicably and effectively. As a general rule, this is the time to promote positive thoughts. As the day closes, Moon trine Mercury brings a helpful time to rest the mind, but for those who are awake, this may seem like an excellent time to think matters through more easily. Moon trine Mercury brings positive thoughts to our dreams.

## Moon opposite Mercury

Moon opposite Mercury brings a deeper sense of awareness – or curiosity – while we are communicating. This lunar aspect inspires a surge of thoughts and discus-

27

sion, and it may be necessary to comprehend a lot of things at once. This is a time when we tend to be overwhelmed or overloaded by communications or the communication process. Our feelings are more readily challenged by our thoughts. Sometimes this lunar aspect gives us the feeling that there is a great deal more to be communicated. Beware of exhausting arguments. Moon opposite Mercury brings an intense need to communicate, to reiterate on complex messages, and to set the record straight when Mercury retrograde periods have brought havoc to our communications. Moon opposite Mercury brings complex nervous responses and complex thoughts with regard to what we are feeling or sensing. As for dreams, this aspect brings very nervous or restless kinds of dreams which may seem overwhelming and possibly loaded with too much information.

## Moon conjunct Mercury

Moon conjunct Mercury brings mental clarity and acuity, inspiring thoughtful and communicative moods – this is a great time to catch up on journals, research, and correspondence. Moon conjunct Mercury brings a pensive time, and our moods will be as clearly succinct as our thinking. It engages us in mindful and resourceful planning. Moon conjunct Mercury invites us to take some time to explain various matters very carefully, especially when Mercury is retrograde. This aspect reminds us of our need to pay attention to what is being communicated, and to stay on top of communications. It allows us to drop nervous tension in our sleep, and lets those who can't sleep think clearly and relevantly through their mental processes. Moon conjunct Mercury affects our dreams and moods with the desire to connect to brilliance and intelligent ideas.

## MOON TO VENUS ASPECTS

## Moon sextile Venus

Moon sextile Venus brings moods inspired by beauty and there are opportunities for our moods to tune into the power of love and affection. This aspect brings moods inspired by kind and attractive feminine influences, finding us easily captivated by the law of attraction. Moon sextile Venus brings the potential for very pleasurable, affectionate, and beautiful feelings to occur. It holds the potential to bring moods that will be responsive to love, affection and gentle kindness. It also brings the potential for positive vibes between loved ones, but a definite effort to create those positive vibes will have to be made. Moon sextile Venus brings pleasant dreams touched by infinite beauty.

## Moon square Venus

Moon square Venus brings moods challenged by matters of love and attraction. It's also bound to bring some challenging weather between loved ones, and this may be a good time to avoid making idealistic promises that could possibly go unfulfilled. Our moods are likely to be strained by the effort to maintain beauty and comfort. Moon square Venus tests our affections and our ability to feel and express love, and may cause unpleasant moods due to a lack of kindness or love wherever it is needed. This lunar aspect may be a difficult time for us to find the kind of affections we need, but it's best to patiently persevere through love related challenges. Moon square Venus brings dreams that may seem particularly unpleasant, and dreams that may leave us feeling abandoned, torn asunder, or separate from the things to which we are attached.

## Moon trine Venus

Moon trine Venus is the most receptive and advantageous time to spread loving energy. This lunar aspect generally brings moods which will be pleasant and easily prone to affection. Moon trine Venus brings gentle, beautiful, and harmonious moods and vibrations. It often blesses our moods with kindness, and increases our fondness and appreciation for beauty. Moon trine Venus brings the strong urge for love, and loving energy won't be too hard to find. This lunar aspect helps to smooth over chaotic energies with loving and kind moods. Moon trine Venus puts us in the mood for love and for all those things that bring us comfort, inspiring especially beautiful, alluring, and relaxing dreams.

## Moon opposite Venus

Moon opposite Venus brings moods that will make us acutely aware of our affections – both the giving of, and the desire for, all kinds of affection. This aspect will draw relationships and love related situations into focus, and it may be especially difficult to try to please everyone, especially our loved ones. Moon opposite Venus may bring overwhelming or obsessive desires for beauty and pleasure. This aspect implies that our moods may be dominated by feminine expression or demands. Lady Justice is blind, but that doesn't mean that her logic is not sound. Sometimes, Moon opposite Venus brings obsessive or agitating moods with regard to love. Here, we often find that our affections have been spread too thin. We may feel overwhelmed by compelling attractions. This lunar aspect brings dramatic moods and dreams about our needs for affection and beauty.

## Moon conjunct Venus

Moon conjunct Venus brings gentleness, kindness, and love to our moods. It puts us directly in touch with those things we are attracted to. This lunar aspect can bring deeply affectionate and sometimes very intense loving moods. Different levels and expressions of affection occur, depending on the sign in which the Moon and Venus are conjunct. Moon conjunct Venus brings moods that will be instantly drawn to beauty and love wherever it exists. This is a good time to seek pleasure and to appreciate beauty to the fullest. Moon conjunct Venus brings dazzling beauty and pleasure to the scope of our dreams.

## MOON TO MARS ASPECTS

## Moon sextile Mars

Moon sextile Mars tends to bring energetic moods which are motivated by force and activity, and inspired by high energy levels. Incisive action and the affirmation of will infuse our moods. Moon sextile Mars brings moods that may point to the need to take action, but this inclination is not always acted upon. Generally, Moon sextile Mars brings positive energy, strength and courage to our moods. It brings strong impulses and urges, and our dreams will seem triumphant, although somewhat martial and headstrong in attitude.

## Moon square Mars

Moon square Mars suggests our moods will be challenged by invasive forcefulness, our patience levels will be tested, and it may be difficult to get amicably motivated. This aspect brings offensive and maddening challenges to our moods where abrupt energies and unbalanced temperaments will seem like bullying martial forces. Moon square Mars – this is a recipe for accidents, fights, headaches – and many people will find that they are being especially defensive as well as impatient. This lunar aspect may lead to difficulty or conflict when one is attempting to take initiative to do things, and it often tests our temper, strength, and willpower. Moon square Mars usually brings challenging moods with regard to masculine energies. While we sleep, cruelty or mad aggression may be evident in our dreams.

## Moon trine Mars

Moon trine Mars brings moods that will be gifted with lots of vibrant, positive energy and our moods are often in harmony with masculine energies and courageous activities. This aspect invites optimism that inspires action. For some, this aspect brings vibrant emotional and physical energy, positive strength and might. It's an advantageous time to build on our strength, get motivated, and to get things rolling. Moon trine Mars harmoniously energizes our dreams, often making us stronger than we ever imagined.

## Moon opposite Mars

Moon opposite Mars brings moods which are opposed to offensive kinds of pressures. Some may find that they are opposed to, or overwhelmed by, masculine force. In general, it brings moods at odds with some disharmonizing force. Forcefulness and brazen activity are highlighted, and Moon opposite Mars brings exceedingly energetic and feisty moods which are sometimes offensive. A surge of emotional heat may lead to anger for some. This lunar aspect is known for its extreme force, and may stimulate alarming kinds of offensive and defensive behavior. Some folks may be overwhelmed or affronted by the activities and actions occurring around them. Without a doubt, Moon opposite Mars motivates us, and brings a sharp awareness of martial forces and masculine energies. Some folks may appear to be obsessed by or preoccupied with aggressive forces. This may also be an accident prone time. Moon opposite Mars may bring pushy, impatient, or overly defensive moods, and it can bring bloody battles to the forefront of our dream world.

## Moon conjunct Mars

The sign where the Moon and Mars are conjunct will have a strong bearing on the type of energy conjured by this lunar conjunction. Moon conjunct Mars activates our moods with a feeling of get-up-and-go, stirring our moods with energy and adrenaline that may seem refreshingly positive for some and overly aggressive for others. While Moon conjunct Mars occurs, our moods are active, hot, and eager to take action. Energized moods may lead to incredulous force. Moon conjunct Mars may bring moods activated by complex and reactionary kinds of aggression. Sometimes, this conjunction puts us in touch with our anger issues. Moon conjunct Mars impresses our moods with the need to take action on some level, and to get in touch with our true will. It's bound to stir up raw energy and action in our dreams.

## MOON TO JUPITER ASPECTS

### Moon sextile Jupiter

Moon sextile Jupiter brings the potential for our moods to be inspired by a sense of joviality, prosperity, travel, and adventure. It also brings moods inspired by opportunity, generosity, and extravagance. This lunar aspect invites moods which are generally hopeful and optimistic, inspired by promising prospects and propositions. It brings the potential for a warm and generous spirit, and sets the tone of the day with the potential for positive, upbeat feelings, and a sense of wellbeing and prosperity. Moon sextile Jupiter brings adventurous dreams.

### Moon square Jupiter

Moon square Jupiter may cause our moods to be less generous than usual. We may find we are less willing to extend ourselves beyond our limits. Moon square Jupiter often brings moods challenged by matters of expenses and wealth. This lunar aspect may bring some apprehension with regard to the need to prosper, and this often leads to prudent or unreceptive moods. Jupiter's influence represents joy, and some folks may be prone to depression as they struggle with their ability to find joy or to express it. Many people may be irritated by rising costs or hidden expenses. We may find difficulty in handling large productions. Sometimes, our moods are challenged by travel related expenses, inconveniences, and delays. Our dreams may appear like a gambler's losing streak. Moon square Jupiter brings moods that are challenged by overextension — or perhaps, overexertion — especially in the dream world. The events in our dreams are often reflected by the fear of loss.

### Moon trine Jupiter

Moon trine Jupiter brings moods that will be very generous, joyous, and gregarious, and it tops our experience with optimistic and prosperous moods. This aspect is an excellent time to appreciate good fortune, and to enjoy parties, fund raisers, and social affairs. Good luck, happiness, and positive vibes, often ensure a sense of wellbeing, bringing a healthy desire to prosper. Moon trine Jupiter harmonizes our moods with an outgoing spirit and an enthusiastic sense of adventure. Generally speaking, this aspect brings especially pleasant moods, and our dreams are bound to lead us into a pot of gold.

## Moon opposite Jupiter

Moon opposite Jupiter brings moods that may be overwhelmed by abundance and rapid growth. People may be put off by, or suspicious of, extreme generosity. Moon opposite Jupiter brings deeply involved moods, especially with regard to our livelihoods, our fortunes, and our sense of wellbeing. This aspect brings an acute awareness of the need to excel and to prosper, and there may be something very tempting calling out to us at this time. Our moods could seem overwhelmed by overextension, either on a financial or a psychological level. Moon opposite Jupiter brings a bit of a roller coaster ride on the collective wheel of fortune, which in turn brings a lot of excitement with regard to our expenditures and our sense of wellbeing. Beware of a tendency towards compulsive gambling. In some cases, this lunar aspect puts us in touch with the feeling of greed, as Jupiter brings the compulsory need to gain, profit, and get ahead of all the financial commotion. Moon opposite Jupiter brings a tendency to overindulge, and there may be a lot of defensiveness over expenditures. In the dream world, we may get lost, or find that we have gone too far out on a limb, leaving us with the feeling of overextension.

## Moon conjunct Jupiter

For those who are willing to tap into it, this lunar aspect impresses our moods with rich and prosperous feelings. Moon conjunct Jupiter brings abundant enthusiasm. Moods are especially extravagant and optimistic, connecting us with a sense of joy, wealth, joviality, prosperity, and wellbeing. This is a good time to count your blessings. Moon conjunct Jupiter puts us in touch with our visions and our hopes. It's a great time to enjoy feasts and epicurean delights. This is also an excellent time to exercise, travel, and to explore new territory. With this lunar conjunction, our dreams are often gratifyingly joyous and prosperous in nature.

## MOON TO SATURN ASPECTS

## Moon sextile Saturn

Moon sextile Saturn opens up our moods to employment opportunities. This is a great time to instill discipline and a sense of duty, to teach, and to work. Moon sextile Saturn inspires discipline and focus, but this usually only starts to occur when some effort towards work is made. In other words, just do the work, and the inspiration to carry on will follow. Our moods tend to be expressed a little more seriously, or with greater expectation towards seeing results. Here, seeing others apply discipline can often inspire us to do the same, making this a great time to set an example, and to focus on getting things done rather than putting them off. The Moon sets the tone of the mood, the sextile aspect brings raw potential and opportunity, and the influence of Saturn gets things done. Moon sextile Saturn brings serious dreams that inspire a sense of duty and discipline.

## Moon square Saturn

Moon square Saturn brings moods which are tested by deadlines, responsibilities, and limitations. It often causes challenges with our ability to concentrate, stay focused and handle pending deadlines. Sometimes, Moon square Saturn infringes on the comfort zones of our moods which may seem overshadowed by a foreboding kind of seriousness. Moon square Saturn brings another dimension to our moods, as many folks will be troubled by the burdensome responsibility of difficult work, adding a feeling of being restricted. Moon square Saturn sometimes brings moods challenged by authority. Sometimes, time is warped, or we may find ourselves wishing that time would go by a little faster. While we sleep, Moon square Saturn slips into the night and into our dreams, bringing moods often irritated by the need for discipline; with any luck, this is a time to rest and not to worry. Moon square Saturn may bring troublesome dreams about our struggles over having control, or not having it. Sleeplessness is usually filled by obsessions over career challenges, troublesome work, or burdensome responsibilities. Hang in there – stay on course with your efforts.

## Moon trine Saturn

Moon trine Saturn often inspires an amicable work mood. It is a superb time to practice disciplines and to work on things that require perfect timing, allowing for a greater sense of control, precision, and focus. Moon trine Saturn brings harmonious moods with regard to our approach to discipline, or to work in general, and this usually results in more effective teamwork. It also brings moods that are likely to be in harmony with our responsibilities and, as a result, basic duties and tasks may be carried out much more smoothly than expected. This favorable aspect assures us that time is the healer. Moon trine Saturn brings dreams that allow us to feel in control, and to go beyond our limitations, possibly accomplishing the impossible.

## Moon opposite Saturn

Moon opposite Saturn is a very challenging time for our moods to stay the course of our work, and it may seem tedious to fulfill our responsibilities. These are times when we may feel overworked. Moon opposite Saturn brings moods which may appear opposed to — or overwhelmed by — restrictions and limitations. This will be a good time to keep work schedules light and to anticipate serious or reluctant moods with regard to work tasks. This is usually not an easy time to hold people's attention for very long, or to get them to perform tasks beyond their usual pace. Difficult jobs will seem that much harder and may take longer than usual to do. Moon opposite Saturn brings a serious tone to our dreams and we may tend to over-extend ourselves, even in the dream world. In general, this aspect puts us in touch with our limitations and reminds us of the mortal side of ourselves.

## Moon conjunct Saturn

Moon conjunct Saturn brings serious moods in general, and there is often a strong sense of determination present. We also tend to be guarded, cautious, and work oriented. This conjunction occurs once a month, and it is therefore a good time to reiterate on personal goals and achievements. Moon conjunct Saturn brings moods that will be inclined towards discipline and responsibility, and will appeal to our protective instincts as well. It brings moods that awaken us to the awareness of our limitations. The act of completion is an important part of the Moon/Saturn conjunction, and this is a good time to recognize what level of completion has been achieved in the various stages of our lives. It's also a good time to count blessings as well as setting goals.

## MOON TO NEPTUNE ASPECTS

### Moon sextile Neptune

Moon sextile Neptune brings peaceful moods, responsive to spiritual expression. It can bring a calmness that allows us to pace ourselves comfortably, and our moods will be pleasant for the most part. This aspect brings moods inspired by spiritual perspectives. This time holds the potential for us to experience more accepting and flexible kinds of moods. Here, forgiveness is possible. Whenever it's convenient, this is a good lunar aspect to seek the comfort of a sanctuary and to enjoy some tranquility. Moon sextile Neptune brings moods that are influenced strongly by our beliefs. It inclines our moods towards simplicity or the path of least resistance. People tend to respond more intuitively to many situations. Moon sextile Neptune brings spiritual hope and reassuring beliefs. It assists us by bringing peaceful rest and calming dreams.

### Moon square Neptune

Moon square Neptune brings struggles with regard to our beliefs and in spiritual matters. Our moods may be challenged by passivity, resignation, or perhaps even laziness, and they are often nebulous or vague. Moon square Neptune brings difficult spiritual forces into the picture, challenged by inactivity and passiveness. Moon square Neptune brings moods which may seem troubled by a lack of spiritual harmony, or possibly by addictions, temptations, and a lack of resistance. This aspect brings less tolerance of the beliefs of others and quite a bit of spiritual doubt. People may be questioning the burdening imposition or inconvenience of some beliefs. This is a time when people may be more susceptible to illusion. In general, Moon square Neptune brings disquieting moods, and many folks may have an insatiable urge to find a peaceful sanctuary away from the complexities of emotional clamor. This lunar aspect brings spiritually disturbing moods and dreams, and it may haunt our dreams with deceptive misconceptions.

### Moon trine Neptune

Moon trine Neptune blesses our moods with spiritually uplifting vibrations. It settles our moods with a calm, cool acceptance of the way things are and brings the blessing of peacefulness. Moon trine Neptune brings our moods into perfect harmony with the spiritual energies around us, bringing tranquil and passive energy that is positive in nature. People will be inclined to kick back, relax and to accept their beliefs as they stand. This aspect adds calmness to the astrological atmosphere, and helps to smooth over the sting of any conflicting aspects that are simultaneously occurring. It also brings positive inspiration to our moods and is a superb time to apply, or enjoy, artistic expression. This is a great lunar aspect to share in spiritual ceremonies and customs with others. Moon trine Neptune brings relaxing and enchanting dreams filled with blessed tranquility and divine pleasures.

## Moon opposite Neptune

Moon opposite Neptune brings moods that will be strongly stimulated by spiritual encounters and experiences, often challenging, and overwhelmed by doubt. This lunar aspect invites weakness with regard to our addictive tendencies. Moon opposite Neptune brings an especially strong awareness of our spiritual needs, but our feelings tend to be at odds with our beliefs. This lunar aspect brings moods that may be opposed to, or overwhelmed by, spiritualism. Moon opposite Neptune brings a strong and compelling awareness of the art, poetry, music, and spiritual beliefs that shape and form who and what we are in spirit and at heart. This lunar aspect awakens our spiritual nature and impresses upon us the need to apply our faith. It could be challenging for some folks to feel comfortable or spiritually in tune with others. Moon opposite Neptune may bring escapist tendencies and the potential for overindulgent moods, and we may be more easily susceptible to life's little deceptions. This aspect brings remarkable and impressionable subliminal images to our dreams.

## Moon conjunct Neptune

Moon conjunct Neptune connects our moods with our beliefs and our spirituality. It brings a stronger spiritual awareness of life and there is the general feeling of connectedness among people. Moon conjunct Neptune brings moods that will be responsive to the need for tranquility and peacefulness, and our moods are able to merge easily with spiritual awareness. It brings us closer to a sense of spiritual oneness with the universe, and the common bonds that connect us are felt beyond the physical realms. This lunar conjunction brings peaceful and comforting dreams.

## MOON TO URANUS ASPECTS

## Moon sextile Uranus

Moon sextile Uranus brings lively and outgoing expressions of mood as well as the potential for wild and disorderly moods. As a general rule, it inspires us to let loose and feel free. When Moon sextile Uranus rolls around, our moods are more prone towards, or sympathetic to, reckless activity or behavior. It helps us to embrace the unusual and to find freedom from the mundane. Moon sextile Uranus brings freedom-loving rebelliousness and our dreams are likely to be explosive and colorful, reflecting a feeling of liberation.

## Moon square Uranus

Moon square Uranus is often very challenging, as unexpected outbursts and radical surprises create chaotic moods complicated by explosive conflict. This aspect often brings disruptive disorder; moods may be intensified by undisciplined forces and by radical attitudes. During this time, many people tend to be less forgiving, particularly around unusual behavior and unconventional tones of expression. Moon square Uranus brings chaos – the kind of chaos which requires extra clean up work. It also brings confused and difficult dreams. To some folks, these dreams may seem more like explosive nightmares.

## Moon trine Uranus

Moon trine Uranus brings crazy, fun-loving, and unusual kinds of moods and focuses. There's a feeling of wild and reckless abandon, and all is in harmony with the forces of chaos. Moon trine Uranus brings a sense of freedom and our moods will be carefree, or blithely reckless, but not with malicious intent. This lunar aspect can also inspire brilliance and spontaneous inventiveness. Moon trine Uranus brings very exciting and liberating dreams often in harmony with chaos and disorder.

## Moon opposite Uranus

Moon opposite Uranus brings discordant sounds, disruptive energies, and explosive distractions. This lunar aspect ignites a strong urge for freedom from oppression, and makes us acutely aware of – and sensitive to – disruption of any kind. Our moods are agitated with an overwhelming feeling of chaos and disorder. Explosively contradictory moods shaken up by extreme or disruptive actions and expressions of thought are common. Moon opposite Uranus brings alarming dreams and unsettled feelings.

## Moon conjunct Uranus

Moon conjunct Uranus brings moods that may seem out of the ordinary. It aligns us with the need for freedom, and we may find ourselves being somewhat counter-productive. Beware of the tendency towards irrational or unusual behavior; rules may be broken. Moon conjunct Uranus may bring a feeling of acceptance for disorder, or it may inspire us to tackle disorder with unabashed determination. Either way, chaotic fortitude will be the energy of our mood. This lunar aspect animates our moods and our dreams with turbulent emotions.

## MOON TO PLUTO ASPECTS

## Moon sextile Pluto

Moon sextile Pluto brings moods inspired by vigilant efforts in the face of intensity and strife often affected by life's unchangeable circumstances. Our moods may be preoccupied with the need for trouble-shooting and problem solving. Moon sextile Pluto brings moods inspired by the opportunities that are shaped by fate and intensified by powerful and variable situations. This aspect allows us to be receptive to the inevitable factors of life, and many folks will feel as though they can tolerate just about anything. Moon sextile Pluto brings moods that are influenced by the deeds of superpowers, and gives us the incentive to look for solutions to the troubles they generate. It also brings positive moods geared towards the necessity to find ways to change our apparent destiny. Moon sextile Pluto brings dreams that are open to helping us work out our individual struggles.

36

## Moon square Pluto

Moon square Pluto brings moods challenged by the unforeseeable factors of life, by matters of fate and by perplexing transformations. This may be a difficult time to collaborate with people of another generation or those of a different cultural background. Our moods may be challenged by our hidden fears, particularly with regard to those irreversible processes of life. We may find that our moods are oppressed by dramatic losses, hopelessness, and troublesome realities. Moon square Pluto brings dramatic complexity to our moods, which very often ends up affecting everyone. It can bring troublesome and sometimes fearful moods and dreams.

## Moon trine Pluto

Moon trine Pluto brings moods that will be inspired by transformation and permanent change. It gives us the strong incentive to tackle problems and find solutions and brings harmonious and therapeutic strength to our moods, especially with regard to matters of fate and the unchangeable factors of life. It also brings moods that will be attuned to the influences of superpowers. This lunar aspect promotes accordance among generations, and those with difficult realities will feel more in tune with the sympathies of others. Moon trine Pluto brings moods enriched with the acceptance of hardships and allows us to confront hardship with a lot less difficulty. This lunar aspect helps the process of healing wounds, and it brings moods that will lean amicably towards therapeutic methods of easing pain. Moon trine Pluto inspires a profound sense of renewed hope and brings a cathartic, as well as therapeutic, breakthrough in our dreams.

## Moon opposite Pluto

Moon opposite Pluto makes us conscious of the troubles and the transformations occurring in our lives, especially those likely to be opposed by the influences of superpowers. This aspect causes moods which will be strongly affected by the generation gaps or the cultural gaps that exist between different folks. It also may be the cause of relentless kinds of obsessions, bringing moods that will inspire awareness of life's more intense qualities and hardships. There's a potential for dramatic, rocky moods. Moon opposite Pluto may be the cause of some sleepless energy for various folks, and there may be some overwhelming intensity to the scope of our dreams.

## Moon conjunct Pluto

Moon conjunct Pluto brings intensity and extraordinary perspectives to our moods. It leads to an awareness of the influence of superpowers and how these forces affect everyone. Moon conjunct Pluto also brings moods which will be at one with a sense of acceptance of those things which we cannot change. It puts us in touch with world events, and our moods may be surprised by the peculiar ways in which destiny evolves. Moon conjunct Pluto puts our moods and dreams in tune with the relevance and importance of world events, which are busily shaping our individual lives and our lifestyles forever.

## Table of Planetary Dignities

| Planet | Sign of Rulership | Sign of Detriment | Sign of Exaltation | Sign of Fall |
|---|---|---|---|---|
| Sun | Leo | Aquarius | Aries | Libra |
| Moon | Cancer | Capricorn | Taurus | Scorpio |
| Mercury | Gemini, Virgo | Sagittarius, Pisces | Aquarius, Virgo | Leo, Pisces |
| Venus | Taurus, Libra | Scorpio, Aries | Pisces | Virgo |
| Mars | Aries | Taurus, Libra | Capricorn | Cancer |
| Jupiter | Sagittarius | Gemini | Cancer | Capricorn |
| Saturn | Capricorn | Cancer | Libra | Aries |
| Uranus | Aquarius | Leo | Scorpio, Aquarius | Taurus, Leo |
| Neptune | Pisces | Virgo | Cancer | Capricorn |
| Pluto | Scorpio | Taurus | Pisces | Virgo |
| Moon's North Node | | | Gemini | Sagittarius |
| Moon's South Node | | | Sagittarius | Gemini |

## Table of Planetary Associations

| Planet | Day | Incense | Metal | Body Part |
|---|---|---|---|---|
| Sun | Sunday | Frankincense | Gold | Heart |
| Moon | Monday | Jasmine | Silver | Eyes |
| Mercury | Wednesday | Storax | Mercury | Nerves |
| Venus | Friday | Rose, Benzoin | Copper | Skin |
| Mars | Tuesday | Tobacco | Iron | Muscles |
| Jupiter | Thursday | Cedar | Tin | Diaphram |
| Saturn | Saturday | Myrrh | Lead | Bones |
| Uranus | | | | |
| Neptune | | | | |
| Pluto | | | | |

# CAPRICORN

Key Phrase: "I USE"
Cardinal Earth Sign
Symbol: The Goat
Ruling Planet: Saturn
December 21st, 2008
through January 19th, 2009

## January 1st Thursday

**New Year's Day**

**Moon in Pisces**

|  | PST | EST |
|---|---|---|
| Moon sextile Mars | 11:47 PM (Dec. 31) | 2:47 AM |
| Mercury enters Aquarius | 1:52 AM | 5:52 AM |
| Moon sextile Sun | 3:08 PM | 6:08 PM |

*Mood Watch*: A New Year begins at the stroke of midnight and within the first hour, the first lunar aspect of the year, Moon sextile Mars, brings a strong feeling of ambition – there is likely to be a positive, emotionally active start to the New Year. Today's Moon is waxing in Pisces, and places an emphasis on our need for spiritual fortification. Many will seek to find some form of validation for their beliefs or their sense of intuition. Waxing Moon in Pisces is a great time to kick off the New Year with musical and artistic expressions of celebration.

**Mercury enters Aquarius** (Mercury in Aquarius: January 1 – 20) Today, Mercury enters Aquarius, the fixed air sign of the zodiac which represents humanity's knowledge. As the force of communication (Mercury) travels through the constellation of fixed thought and meditation (Aquarius), there are great opportunities for us to share and to empower each other through our knowledge. This is a splendid time to communicate ideas and investigate the latest in technology, science, and the world of invention. That said, Mercury will go retrograde January 11 – February 1, causing communications to be challenged by technological glitches, as well as human related inaccuracies and misunderstandings. Mercury in Aquarius is also a special time to speak out on humanitarian issues and the rights of freedom. Eccentric talk and unusual subjects will fill the airwaves while Mercury is in Aquarius. For more information on Mercury retrograde in Aquarius, see the section in the introduction about Mercury retrograde periods.

Still in effect: **Venus sextile Pluto** (occurring Dec. 31, 2008 – Jan. 6, 2009) – *see January 4.*

**Mercury conjunct Jupiter** (occurring Dec. 28, 2008 – Jan. 3, 2009) This conjunction is still occurring, having reached its peak on December 31, 2008. Mercury and Jupiter are conjunct in Capricorn. News and discussions (Mercury) revolve around our joys, our prosperity, and our wealth (Jupiter) – particularly with regard to fulfilling our desires and abiding by our deep passions in life. This aspect creates expansive talk which spreads quickly with news about the state of economic affairs. Thoughts and information (Mercury) with regard to a prosperous and visionary breakthrough (Jupiter) will be highlighted. It's a great time to boost the morale of others by complimenting them on their skills. This could be a prosperous conjunction for communicating the need for a job or financial loan. Early born Capricorns having birthdays at this time are about to be showered with a wealth of information and opportunities which are worthy of their time and effort.

# January 2nd Friday

| Moon in Pisces | PST | EST |
|---|---|---|
| Moon conjunct Uranus | 5:40 AM | 8:40 AM |
| Moon opposite Saturn | 10:22 AM | 1:22 PM |

*Mood Watch*: It is often true that the imagination likes to roam on a Pisces Moon day. Pisces Moon puts us in touch with our belief systems and the personal trials we must endure concerning our individual beliefs. For some, there is a creative process unfolding; for others, there is a battle going on with addictive behavior or the need to escape. For most, the dreamlike quality of this time drifts in a timeless fashion connecting us with our past as well as showing us the future as we open ourselves up in the now.

# January 3rd Saturday

| Moon in Pisces / Aries | PST | EST |
|---|---|---|
| Moon sextile Jupiter goes v/c | 12:49 AM | 3:49 AM |
| Moon enters Aries | 1:48 AM | 4:48 AM |
| Moon square Pluto | 4:19 AM | 7:19 AM |
| Venus enters Pisces | 4:35 AM | 7:35 AM |
| Moon sextile Mercury | 6:41 AM | 9:41 AM |
| Moon square Mars | 12:16 PM | 3:16 PM |

*Mood Watch*: Long before the break of dawn, the waxing Moon in Pisces goes void-of-course for an hour and then enters Aries. Our moods begin a phase of confidence. Aries Moon generates energy and gives many of us the impetus to tend to personal needs and projects requiring attention. Waxing Aries Moon is a great time to start new projects, particularly new routines that fall under the category of New Year's resolutions. This is an advantageous time to take to the art of motivation. Waxing Moon in Aries invites us to initiate projects, to motivate ourselves and others, and to tackle dormant energies with an inspired new outlook.

**Venus enters Pisces** (Venus in Pisces: January 3 – February 2) Venus, the planet of magnetism and love, will be focusing our attraction on Pisces related subjects. From today through February 2, music, poetry, the arts, psychic phenomena, and spiritual and religious practices will all be endearing and lively pursuits. Over the next few weeks, as Venus crosses over their natal Sun sign, it will touch the personal realms of our Pisces friends with an awareness of the need for love and beauty in their lives. Venus is the feminine planet of love, and Pisces is an extremely feminine, dreamy, and spiritual placement for the love force of Venus. Matters of the heart will emphasize passivity, tenderness, sensitivity and the need for a gentle approach towards love's expression. Venus will travel through Pisces for an extended period this year, since it will go retrograde March 6 – April 17, causing it to reenter Pisces on April 11, and it will remain in Pisces until April 24.

# January 4ᵗʰ Sunday
## FIRST QUARTER MOON in ARIES

|  | PST | EST |
|---|---|---|
| Moon square Sun | 3:55 AM | 6:55 AM |
| Venus sextile Pluto | 11:32 PM | 2:32 PM |
| Moon sextile Neptune goes v/c | 6:43 PM | 9:43 PM |

*Mood Watch*: **First Quarter Moon in Aries** (Moon square Sun) This Moon energizes our moods, and inspires an upbeat, outgoing, and forward manner. This is the time to get in tune with your own personal levels of energy, strength and vitality. There is a self-starter energy in the air and the active ones among us are on the prowl. Aries Moon brings on an expression of courageous vigor, as well as a sense of bold adventure. As a general rule, moods are marked by confidence and the drive to make a lasting impression. Moon in Aries squaring to the Sun in Capricorn is a good time to apply diligence and inspired ability to your work. Later, while the Moon is void-of-course, people may seem easily distracted, and they may also have a tendency to start things that they aren't very likely to finish. Take it easy later tonight; beware of the potential for arguments and avoid head butting with others.

**Venus sextile Pluto** (occurring Dec. 31, 2008 – Jan. 6, 2009) Venus is in Pisces where the law of attraction is irresistible, easy going, and artistically uplifting. Pluto in Capricorn brings dutiful allegiance to matters of fate. Venus sextile Pluto implies that even in the midst of hardship, opportunities are arising with regard to the things we treasure and are attracted to, and also in matters of love and affection (Venus). These opportunities often are born out of fate or destiny (Pluto), or sometimes are a result of an unpredictable factor. For some, this aspect may be teaching them the lessons of acceptance, of learning to let go of attachments, as well as finding liberation through the transformative process of acceptance, particularly in matters of love. This aspect will reoccur, November 5 – 10, and will reach its peak on November 8 with Venus in Scorpio.

# January 5ᵗʰ Monday

| Moon in Aries / Taurus | PST | EST |
|---|---|---|
| Jupiter enters Aquarius | 7:41 AM | 10:41 AM |
| Moon enters Taurus | 7:44 AM | 10:44 AM |
| Moon square Jupiter | 7:44 AM | 10:44 AM |
| Moon trine Pluto | 10:12 AM | 1:12 PM |
| Moon sextile Venus | 12:03 PM | 3:03 PM |
| Moon square Mercury | 4:27 PM | 7:27 PM |
| Moon trine Mars | 8:32 PM | 11:32 PM |
| Sun sextile Uranus begins (see January 9) | | |
| Sun trine Saturn begins (see January 11) | | |

41

*Mood Watch*: The day begins with the Moon void-of-course in Aries. At first, the day may seem to start off with some disappointments, or with struggles to get things started right. Swiftly though, the Moon enters Taurus, and many folks will gravitate towards simple luxuries and comforting pleasures. Waxing Moon in Taurus brings an emphasis on financial security, or desires to get ahead in business, and on the attainment of simple and practical necessities. This is a good time to put the physical world in order and to tackle doing holiday clean-up and gift returns.

**Jupiter enters Aquarius** (Jupiter in Aquarius: January 5, 2009 – January 18, 2010) A technological era of economic advancement begins today with the planet of luck and fortune, Jupiter, newly entering the constellation Aquarius. Jupiter in Aquarius brings innovative solutions to economic problems. It also allows us to realize our economic strength as whole communities, bringing people together to work towards building financial strength and salvation.

**A review of the past: JUPITER IN CAPRICORN** (December 18, 2007 – January 5, 2009)

Since December 18, 2007, Jupiter was traveling through Capricorn, focusing the magic of great wealth and expense on such Capricorn-like things as construction, building, banking, corporate growth, architectural feats, estate management, and administrative expertise.

Jupiter in Capricorn brought numerous types of business endeavors with regard to corporate takeovers, big shifts in property management and, as we've seen in last year's American housing crunch, foreclosures in the banking industry. Capricorn's key phrase is "I use," and there has been no mistaking the fact that many people's misfortune or mismanagement of financial affairs has been to the prosperous advantage of wealthy real estate tycoons and other such shifty manipulators of the economic slump which openly reared its ugly head in early 2008. It was also evident that big economic change was headed our way when, on December 11, 2007, Jupiter reached an exact conjunction with the power-monger, Pluto – on the Sagittarius/Capricorn cusp – bringing some seriously disruptive changes to our economic powers and to our overall perception of what it means to maintain and experience wealth.

The past year of Jupiter in Capricorn has been a time of loss and financial misman-agement for many folks in North America, yet we must remember that Jupiter's domain focuses on gain, and those areas of life where fortunes continue to rise, not fall. Just as it is in any era of marked recession, where many have fallen, some do excel at unprecedented rates. As a general rule, Jupiter's influence brings enthu-siasm, stimulates economy and focuses on prosperity. Even in difficult economic times, Jupiter puts us in touch with the necessity to find, to develop, or to create new skills and new means to generate prosperity. Jupiter is often the catalyst in raising the overall morale. Out of the drive to create competent caregivers, and practical management strategies, comes the hope of maintaining and rebuilding a stable economic future. While Jupiter was in Capricorn, the key to successful gains came with the proper management of goods and services.

Capricorn is conservative by nature, and requires the flow of prosperity to be useful, attainable, applicable, substantive, and controllable. The old Capricorn adage,

"I use," implies that favors have been hard won, wages have been compromised, and bargains haven't come cheap. The demands and expectations of Capricorns ♑ are often high, and their stealth and thrifty propensity to achieve material growth through unrelenting persistence gives this sign its not-so-jovial reputation of being cold, calculating, profiteering and exclusive. Despite the downside of this corporate attitude, efficient and well organized frontiers of economic growth continue to thrive in many parts of the world. While Jupiter was in Capricorn, economic shifts have indeed had some weight to them, and this past year has been an especially useful time to take note of exactly who prospered – and why.

**JUPITER IN AQUARIUS** (January 5, 2009 – January 18, 2010) Jupiter now travels through the humanitarian domain of Aquarius, bringing the focus of knowledge and science to economic systems. Jupiter in Aquarius implies a time of experiment and taking chances. It is here that the term "thinking outside the box" is accentuated, with Aquarius representing eccentric and unconventional means of thought, while Jupiter represents unyielding increase and rapid growth. No such "box" has a chance to contain the type of expansion and unusual avenues of economic strategy that we (humanity) are about to encounter. Jupiter in Aquarius may lead to unusual, but very humane and conscientious encounters with richness and prosperity. Aquarius is ruled by Uranus, bringing the radical and unpredictable qualities of chaos into the human equation. Jupiter expansively provides, while the radical energy of Uranus blatantly destroys all superfluous or unnecessary matter. Jupiter gloats over wealth, skill, and abundance; Uranus depletes, destroys, and strips away dysfunctional realities. Jupiter's social appeal represents prosperous growth, valuable talents, fascination, joy, joviality, and the spreading of happiness. When Jupiter traverses through the Uranus ruled domain of Aquarius, the act of prospering occurs with a consciousness raising purpose, with innovative knowledge, and with a certain degree of chance taking and experiment. Jupiter in Aquarius brings economic changes which will affect the quality of our institutions and our public funding programs, which in turn affects each one of us individually. If there is a lack of expansion and growth for everyone, and too much economic suffering is occurring around us, the quality of life will eventually affect us on a personal level.

Aquarius focuses on how the overall good of humanity may operate and evolve. It seeks to undo and re-create outmoded or dysfunctional systems. This time of Jupiter in Aquarius will bring large sums of revenue that will be spent in the effort to create workable systems through the chaos of volatile markets. Jupiter in Aquarius takes us to a place where people can expand in unusual occupations and expertise. This may well be the time to invest in future markets that hold the most practical and feasible potentials for creating alternative resources and sources of power. Over the course of the next year, we will find ourselves adapting very quickly to some especially innovative uses of technology. Joy may be found in the power of invention. Through applied systems of knowledge and highly prized creative skills, as well as through unpredictable risks and the discovery of unbridled talents, Jupiter in Aquarius is likely to bring a very revealing picture of where our prosperous growth can be found.

Aquarius people will be able to enjoy some abundant opportunities and joyous personal experiences while Jupiter crosses over their natal Sun throughout the year to come. They will also have a strong influence on the wave of the economic future. The other air signs of the zodiac, Gemini and Libra, will enjoy the fruits of Jupiter being trine to their natal Sun signs in the next year. This will bring the potential for travel or financial boons of some kind for Gemini and Libra people. Leo folks would be wise to use their sensibilities and take precautions with their expenditures while Jupiter opposes their natal Sun over the next year. They may also find that the effort to handle massive volumes of business, or a large inheritance, may be overwhelming at times in the next year. Taurus and Scorpio people may discover that it will be especially difficult to keep up with expenses and opportunities in their lives while Jupiter squares to their natal Sun signs. They would be wise to proceed cautiously in business. Sagittarius and Aries people's natal Sun signs will be in the sextile position to Jupiter this year, bringing the potential for business or career opportunities in those areas of life where these people have already been working hard, or where they have made some genuine effort to succeed over time.

This is a time of great change, as the slow moving planet Neptune, also in Aquarius, will be conjunct with Jupiter on December 21, bringing expansive spiritual growth to those seeking to broaden their awareness for social and economic growth. Jupiter conjunct Neptune will bring oil and gas resources into a revealing light as Neptune represents the realm of the oceanic underworld, the sea, and oil is one of the big commodities found in this realm. The time of Jupiter conjunct Neptune in Aquarius will also give strong clues about the spiritual evolution of our ideas of prosperity, and it will be one of the eye opening trendsetters of our economic outlook for the next decade or so. For more information on Jupiter conjunct Neptune, *see May 27.*

Jupiter in Aquarius is bound to assist us towards an effort to uplift whole communities and to expand our awareness of the needs of others. Many social programs will be designed to improve people's outlook, hope, and enthusiasm. We can also expect to see some very profitable breakthroughs for specific technological systems and in certain fields of science.

# January 6th Tuesday

| Moon in Taurus | PST | EST |
|---|---|---|
| Moon trine Sun | 12:07 PM | 3:07 PM |
| Moon sextile Uranus | 4:45 PM | 7:45 PM |
| Moon trine Saturn | 8:34 PM | 11:34 PM |
| Moon square Neptune goes v/c | 10:03 PM | 1:03 AM (January 7) |

*Mood Watch*: The steadily waxing Moon in Taurus will bring practical desires to the forefront of today's focuses. Many folks will emphasize the need to make life more functional and comfortable. The majority of today's lunar aspects are positive in nature, making this a good time to focus on enjoying life. However, for those who have been putting off necessary material tasks and duties, it won't be long before they will find they can no longer ignore the bull in the china shop. It's time to clean up the mess, lazy folks; you'll feel *sooo* much better once you do. Sun in Capricorn and Moon in Taurus is an excellent time to plan financial strategies to achieve material goals. Much later tonight, the Moon goes void-of-course just as it squares to Neptune – this would be the best time to quit torturing yourself and get some rest.

♑

# January 7th Wednesday

| Moon in Taurus / Gemini | PST | EST | |
|---|---|---|---|
| Moon enters Gemini | 10:10 AM | 1:10 PM | |
| Moon trine Jupiter | 10:59 AM | 1:59 PM | |
| Moon square Venus | 6:09 PM | 9:09 PM | |
| Moon trine Mercury | 9:00 PM | 12:00 AM | (January 8) |
| Venus sextile Mars begins  (see January 24) | | | |

*Mood Watch*: The day begins with a distinct air of laziness, stubbornness, and the tendency for some folks to misplace things while the waxing Moon in Taurus is void-of-course. Finally, as the Moon enters Gemini, thoughtful moods swiftly bring ideas. Communication will play an integral role in today's activities. This is a good time to exchange thoughts with others and to take the time to consider various possibilities. That said, this evening it would be wise to be cautious and patient when attempting to communicate with loved ones while the Moon is square to Venus.

# January 8th Thursday

| Moon in Gemini | PST | EST | |
|---|---|---|---|
| Moon square Uranus | 6:34 PM | 8:34 PM | |
| Moon square Saturn | 9:04 PM | 12:04 AM | (January 9) |
| Moon trine Neptune goes v/c | 10:39 PM | 1:39 AM | (January 9) |

*Mood Watch*: The Moon in Gemini tends to bring a nervous air to our moods, or perhaps a naïve sort of impatience occurs. Talkative moods bring bustling chatter. The more our thoughts stir the pot of the general mood, the thicker this gumbo stew of busy thoughts becomes. The mutable air sign of Gemini engages us in the urge to communicate. There is a strong need to satiate our curiosities, and to indulge in our need to bounce our ideas off someone else. That's what the twin does, isn't it? One twin complements the other. Later tonight, the Gemini Moon goes void-of-course; this is a most important time to rest the mind, and to silence those restless thoughts.

# January 9th Friday

Moon in Gemini / Cancer          PST          EST
*Full Moon Eve*

| | PST | EST | |
|---|---|---|---|
| Sun  sextile Uranus | 7:27 AM | 10:27 AM | |
| Moon enters Cancer | 10:13 AM | 1:13 PM | |
| Moon opposite Pluto | 12:42 PM | 3:42 PM | |
| Moon trine Venus | 9:31 PM | 12:31 AM | (January 10) |

*Mood Watch*: The day begins with the Moon void-of-course in Gemini, a time when our thoughts may appear particularly scattered. While the Moon is waxing so heavily, morning moods will be fickle as we tend to be quite easily distracted.  It isn't long before the nearly Full Moon, set to reach its fullness tomorrow evening, will enter its home base, Cancer. Our moods will be highlighted with emotional concerns, which are often worked out at home or in domestic settings where the

nurturing spirit of Mother Moon brings responsive and sympathetic conscientious-
ness.

**Sun sextile Uranus** (occurring Jan. 5 – 11) This occurrence of Sun sextile Uranus
particularly affects those Capricorn folks celebrating birthdays January 5 – 11.
These birthday people are being given an opportunity to blow off some chaotic
steam and to reach for qualities of freedom that may have been absent in their recent
past. This will be your time to make radical breakthroughs, birthday Capricorn;
your natal Sun is currently sextile Uranus for a good reason – to find a liberating
balance in the midst of the chaos and to use the chaos in your life to your advantage.
Once you've done this, you'll be ready to take the next step. Right now, there is no
holding back, so go for it; discover your freedom. The victory of creative change
will bring a more optimistic outlook on life. This aspect will repeat on May 16,
affecting the lives of Taurus people whose birthdays fall between May 11 – 18.

# January 10ᵗʰ Saturday

| FULL MOON in CANCER | PST | EST |
| --- | --- | --- |
| Moon opposite Mars | 3:04 AM | 6:04 AM |
| Moon trine Uranus | 5:06 PM | 8:06 PM |
| Moon opposite Sun | 7:27 PM | 10:27 PM |
| Moon sextile Saturn goes v/c | 8:26 PM | 11:26 PM |

*Mood Watch*: The **Full Moon in Cancer** (Moon opposite Sun) emphasizes Mom
and maternal energy, and people may be moody or especially preoccupied with their
feelings. Nurturing activities and emotional support are the best ways to approach
the Full Cancer Moon. Be careful not to overeat, but be sure to enjoy heartwarming,
delicious, and nourishing foods. Later this evening, as the Full Cancer Moon goes
void-of-course, beware of the tendency strong for emotional responses to dominate
the course of events. This is an especially vulnerable time for communications to
be misinterpreted, as Mercury is currently stationary and about to go retrograde;
*see tomorrow*.

# January 11ᵗʰ Sunday

| Moon in Cancer / Leo | PST | EST | |
| --- | --- | --- | --- |
| Mercury goes retrograde | 8:44 AM | 11:44 AM | |
| Moon enters Leo | 9:41 AM | 12:41 PM | |
| Sun trine Saturn | 10:01 AM | 1:01 PM | |
| Moon opposite Jupiter | 11:59 AM | 2:59 PM | |
| Moon opposite Mercury | 10:03 PM | 1:03 AM | (January 12) |

*Mood Watch*: An emotional hangover is the likely response to last night's Full
Cancer Moon gone void-of-course. Also, it does not help matters much that
Mercury is going retrograde this morning. Fortunately, the emotional impact of
this weekend's Full Moon will begin to seem less disorienting as the Moon enters
Leo. The Leo Moon gives us a sense of humor, warms our senses, and awakens our
creative side. Leo Moon is a splendid time to enjoy family activities and to focus on
personal hobbies and projects.

46

**Mercury goes retrograde** (Mercury retrograde: Jan. 11 – Feb. 1) Mercury goes retrograde today in the sign of Aquarius; it will travel back to the later degrees of Capricorn before going direct at the 21 degree mark of Capricorn on February 1. Mercury retrograde in Aquarius is likely to disrupt communications with misinformation, particularly for topics that cover science, education, human rights issues and philanthropic endeavors. Despite rational and fair minded attempts to spontaneously articulate ingenuous and profound subjects, Mercury retrograde in Aquarius will often leave us dissatisfied and tongue tied. On January 21, Mercury enters the tail end of Capricorn, the final half of Mercury retrograde. Mercury retrograde in the cardinal earth sign, Capricorn, is likely to bring a number of communication mishaps over building contracts, corporate mergers, and in matters with regard to authority and control. A real test of everyone's patience occurs; this leaves us susceptible to arguments and confusion over who's in control, and over the means, methods, and issues of control. Eventually, as Mercury retrograde completes its cycle, there will be less doubt as to how these issues of control will be played out. Meanwhile, establishing a clear understanding will be the most important part of engaging in various kinds of agreements. Expect to repeat yourself more than once or twice, and to be persistent as well as patient during this time. Whatever you agree on, if it's very important, *get it in writing*! Mercury will go retrograde in Capricorn again this year on December 26, ending our year with Mercury in a retrograde cycle. For more information on Mercury retrograde, see the section in the introduction about *Mercury retrograde periods*.

**Sun trine Saturn** (occurring Jan. 5 – 14) This aspect particularly affects Capricorn people celebrating birthdays January 5 – 14. This is a positive time for these Capricorn folks to get a handle on their lives, and it may be easier for them to take on the responsibilities of life with fewer complications and less difficulty in the year to come. These birthday folks may notice more acceptable forms of control, responsibility and work occurring in their lives. Now is your time (birthday people) to successfully work on putting some structure into your life; the kind of structure you've needed and wanted awaits you in the coming year. It is possible that time (Saturn) is on your side to make that move you've wanted to make. This aspect will reoccur April 29 – May 8, reaching its peak on May 5, affecting the birthday Taurus people of that time.

# January 12ᵗʰ Monday

**Moon in Leo**

| | PST | EST |
|---|---|---|
| Moon opposite Neptune goes v/c | 10:39 PM | 1:39 AM (January 13) |

*Mood Watch*: This could be a day to enjoy some lazy lolling about! The waning Leo Moon of winter is a good time to slow down the pace and to enjoy introspective reflections. Personal needs will stand out and this is the time to tend to them. It is also a time to enjoy friends, and our interests will be focused on the theater, entertainment, and similar activities that make for some good fun. Lucky, lazy, lions love to lounge in the library.

# January 13ᵗʰ Tuesday

| Moon in Leo / Virgo | PST | EST |
|---|---|---|
| Moon enters Virgo | 10:34 AM | 1:34 PM |
| Moon trine Pluto | 1:26 PM | 4:26 PM |

*Mood Watch*: Throughout the morning, a lazy attitude emerges and it is magnified by the void-of-course Leo Moon. This morning may be a troublesome time to attempt to get some harmonious teamwork in order, as people may seem to be self-absorbed. Communications are at a standstill in this shifting time of Mercury, newly retrograde since Sunday. The day will begin to improve as the waning Moon enters Virgo, and our moods will be more inclined towards taking care of practical matters. Moon in Virgo energies emphasize cleanliness, order, and precision.

# January 14ᵗʰ Wednesday

| Moon in Virgo | PST | EST |
|---|---|---|
| Moon opposite Venus | 6:20 AM | 9:20 AM |
| Moon trine Mars | 10:15 AM | 1:15 PM |
| Moon opposite Uranus | 8:16 PM | 11:16 PM |

*Mood Watch*: This morning may seem somewhat busy with the Moon in strong aspects to Venus and Mars. Prudent resourcefulness comes in handy during waning Virgo Moon. Sun in Capricorn with Moon in Virgo is a good time to get organized and to purge the world around us of all its physical clutter; do this early in the day. Later tonight, Moon opposite Uranus makes us especially aware of the extreme levels that chaos is capable of reaching. Tomorrow will bring a long void-of-course phase of the Moon in Virgo, and this may be the time to give into the mayhem and to prepare to accept the state of matters as they currently stand.

# January 15ᵗʰ Thursday

| Moon in Virgo / Libra | PST | EST |
|---|---|---|
| Moon conjunct Saturn | 11:33 AM | 2:33 AM |
| Moon trine Sun goes v/c | 6:37 AM | 9:37 AM |
| Moon enters Libra | 2:30 PM | 5:30 PM |
| Moon square Pluto | 5:43 PM | 8:43 PM |
| Moon trine Jupiter | 6:55 PM | 9:55 PM |

*Mood Watch*: This morning the waning Virgo Moon goes void-of-course and remains that way for eight lengthy hours. Mercury is retrograde and the void-of-course Moon in the Mercury-ruled sign, Virgo, is likely to throw some frustration our way, particularly with regard to communications. When communications aren't going well, Virgo Moon energy can be nerve wracking, Accounting, secretarial duties, analytical science, writing, research, therapy, and matters of physical hygiene are just some of the areas where communications may appear rather challenging. Health issues or depression may also be affecting some folks today. Not all of the day is lost; by the time the Moon enters Libra, our moods will settle down into a much more amenable effort to create peace and harmony. Libra Moon brings a better sense of unity.

# January 16<sup>th</sup> Friday

| Moon in Libra | PST | EST |
|---|---|---|
| Moon  trine Mercury | 12:43 AM | 3:43 AM |
| Moon  square Mars | 7:21 PM | 10:21 PM |
| Mercury conjunct Jupiter begins (see January 18) | | |
| Mars sextile Uranus begins  (see January 22) | | |
| Venus conjunct Uranus begins  (see January 22) | | |
| Sun conjunct Jupiter begins  (see January 23) | | |
| Mars trine Saturn begins  (see January 24) | | |

*Mood Watch*: Moon in Libra brings an emphasis on the need for balance and harmony, particularly in law and family related matters. The Libra Moon keeps our senses in a careful pacing pattern. As the search for harmony continues, making balanced decisions regarding loved ones remains the focus of many. Waning Libra Moon often brings the need to release emotional misgivings in order to function peacefully in an imperfect world of complex relationships. There will always be a need for adjustments. Libra also focuses our attention on accessing information, although we must be careful with that now that Mercury is retrograde (Jan. 11 – Feb. 1). Beware of dicey tempers while the Moon is square to Mars tonight. Libra Moon times also focus on creating a pleasing and artistic atmosphere. Don't forget the epicurean delights!

# January 17<sup>th</sup> Saturday
## LAST QUARTER MOON in LIBRA

| Moon in Libra / Scorpio | PST | EST | |
|---|---|---|---|
| Moon  trine Neptune | 8:56 AM | 11:56 PM | |
| Moon  square Sun goes v/c | 6:46 PM | 9:46 PM | |
| Moon  enters Scorpio | 10:21 PM | 1:21 AM | (January 18) |
| Sun conjunct Mercury begins  (see January 20) | | | |

*Mood Watch*: **Last Quarter Moon in Libra** (Moon square Sun) reminds us of the need to continue working on the imbalances in our relationships, much of which is probably caused by Mercury retrograde (Jan. 11 – Feb. 1). Libra's adage is simple: "I balance." This is the time to let the emotional pressure be released, and to handle matters with friends and loved ones carefully and congenially. The Last Quarter Moon aspect confirms the need to make amends with others and unite peacefully. If some aspect of your connection to a friend or loved one disrupts your sense of peace, reach within for the answers. A balanced response will soon follow, but don't expect instant answers – the Moon will be void-of-course for sometime during the evening, causing rampant indecisiveness.

# January 18<sup>th</sup> Sunday

| Moon in Scorpio | PST | EST |
|---|---|---|
| Moon  sextile Pluto | 1:57 AM | 4:57 AM |
| Moon  square Jupiter | 4:09 AM | 7:09 AM |
| Moon  square Mercury | 4:53 AM | 7:53 AM |
| Mercury  conjunct Jupiter | 11:04 AM | 2:04 PM |
| Venus opposite Saturn begins  (see January 24) | | |

49

*Mood Watch*: Today's waning Scorpio Moon will focus our energies on secretive, deep rooted and introspective moods and emotions. Early morning moods may seem stifling at times while the Moon takes on some somewhat challenging planetary aspects. This is a good time to be especially careful not to rock the boat of unsettled emotions. Taking the time to enjoy special interest hobbies and to practice valuable skills brings a certain degree of satisfaction.

**Mercury conjunct Jupiter** (occurring Jan. 16 – 20) The retrograde Mercury and Jupiter are now repeating the December 31, 2008 conjunction. The essential difference here – besides the fact that Mercury is retrograde (since January 11) – is that Jupiter recently entered Aquarius *(see January 5,)* and these two planets are currently conjunct in Aquarius. Retrograde Mercury and Jupiter conjunct in Aquarius may bring rumors of prosperity and promises of hope to the disadvantaged participants of society. People handling civil rights issues and humanitarian efforts may be going through a tailspin at this time, particularly over an attempt at raising funds. Not all civil servants will triumph, but for the time being, they are being given a lot of lip service from politicians and the media. News and discussions (Mercury) revolve around our joys, our prosperity, and our wealth (Jupiter) – particularly with regard to fulfilling our desires and abiding by our deep passions in life. This conjunction creates expansive talk which spreads quickly with news about the economic state of affairs. Thoughts and information (Mercury) with regard to a prosperous and visionary breakthrough (Jupiter) will be highlighted. It's a great time to boost the moral of others by complimenting them on their skills. This could be a prosperous time for communicating the need for a job or financial loan, but beware of false promises while Mercury is retrograde. Idle promises made at this time will be challenged again once Mercury has gone direct (February 1,) and this favorable conjunction returns, from February 17 – 26, to set the economic records straight on February 23.

# AQUARIUS
Key Phrase: "I KNOW"

Fixed Air Sign

Ruling Planet: Uranus

Symbol : The Water Bearer

January 19th through February 18th

# January 19th Monday
**Dr. Martin Luther King Junior Day**

| Moon in Scorpio | PST | EST |
|---|---|---|
| Moon  trine Venus | 6:59 AM | 9:59 AM |
| Moon  sextile Mars | 8:59 AM | 11:59 AM |
| Moon  trine Uranus | 1:18 PM | 4:18 PM |

50

| Sun enters Aquarius | 2:40 PM | 5:40 PM |
| Moon sextile Saturn | 4:21 PM | 7:21 PM |
| Moon square Neptune goes v/c | 7:37 PM | 10:37 PM |

♒

*" I believe that unarmed truth and unconditional love will have the final word in reality. That is why right, temporarily defeated, is stronger than evil triumphant. "* - Martin Luther King Jr. (1929 – 1968), Accepting Nobel Peace Prize, Dec. 10, 1964

***Mood Watch***: Today's moods express a deep underlying perception, an intense awareness that laces the events of the day with strong doses of emotion. A waning Moon in Scorpio calls to us to let go of strong destructive tendencies, and challenges us to cease hurting ourselves and others, and to transform our lower impulses into higher aspirations. Beware of the tendency for blithely inaccurate facts to be misconstrued as harmful lies or deception, particularly after the Moon goes void-of-course this evening. Under favorable circumstances, this is a good time to let go of the pain you've been concealing.

**Sun enters Aquarius** (Sun in Aquarius Jan. 19 – Feb. 18) Aquarius is ruled by the enigmatic planetary force of Uranus, the often strange villain who forges new clarity and hope through the storms of chaos and disruption. Freedom fighters will remind us always that we must find a solution to every great atrocity that dampens the human spirit. We must always take measures to prevent tomorrow's health crisis and to insure the perpetuity of our species. Aquarius is the "fixed air" sign which represents the sum of human knowledge. It is an old world oppression that we must address in this Aquarian time – through knowledge we will succeed. This is a time for opening up new ideas and possibilities. Aquarians are usually very clever people who love a good challenge. Next Month, Mars will trot through Aquarius like a brazen warrior horse, bringing a great deal of energy, fiery force, and action into the lives of Aquarians *(see Mars enters Aquarius, February 4)*. Over the course of this year, Aquarians have the worthy advantage of Jupiter crossing through their natal sun sign *(see Jupiter enters Aquarius, January 5)*. Early born Aquarians having birthdays at this time are currently being showered with a wealth of information and opportunities which are worthy of their time and effort. As the year progresses, Jupiter will sweep through the constellation Aquarius bringing inspired visions and a deepening sense of joy to our Aquarius friends. This is your time, Aquarians, to show us what you know through the opportunities you are bound to come across.

# January 20th Tuesday

| Moon in Scorpio / Sagittarius | PST | EST | |
| --- | --- | --- | --- |
| Sun conjunct Mercury | 7:59 AM | 10:59 AM | |
| Moon enters Sagittarius | 9:30 AM | 12:30 PM | |
| Moon sextile Mercury | 10:41 AM | 1:41 PM | |
| Moon sextile Sun | 11:15 AM | 2:15 PM | |
| Moon sextile Jupiter | 4:46 PM | 7:46 PM | |
| Mercury enters Capricorn | 9:36 PM | 12:36 AM | (January 21) |

***Mood Watch***: The start of the day can have emotionally disruptive ramifications with the waning Moon void-of-course in Scorpio. As the Moon enters Sagittarius, philosophical views are revealed to give us a better perspective on matters. All of today's lunar aspects just happen to be sextile; this brings an upbeat effort to focus on the positive side of life, and to look for opportunities as we settle more thoroughly into a new mind-set with the Sun newly in Aquarius.

**Sun conjunct Mercury** (occurring Jan. 17 – 21) This conjunction will occur half a dozen times this year – it is a common occurrence due to the closeness of Mercury to the Sun. It will create a much more thoughtful, communicative, and expressive year ahead for those Capricorn and Aquarius people celebrating birthdays from January 17 – 21. This is your time (birthday folks) to record ideas, relay important messages, and pay close attention to your imaginative thoughts as they are touched by Mercury, creating the urge to speak and be heard. Birthday Capricorns and Aquarians, your thoughts will reveal a great deal about who you are, now and in the year to come.

**Mercury enters Capricorn** (Mercury in Capricorn: Jan. 20 – Feb. 14) Today the retrograde Mercury (Jan. 11 – Feb. 1) enters the tail end of Capricorn. While Mercury travels through Capricorn, communications tend to be more serious and to the point, although not necessarily less complex, especially due to Mercury's confusing retrograde effects. In the heart of perplexing negotiations, there is an emphasis on enterprise and the need to take the upper hand in matters. While this versatile planet goes through Capricorn, our realms of communications have a determined and persistent quality of expression, like a demanding voice waiting to be heard and received with hospitality. Communication is one of the tools of survival, and this is an important time to use those skills wisely and sensibly while Mercury remains retrograde, here in the throes of winter. Mercury in Capricorn focuses talk on such issues as commercial and corporate progress, market control, and the attainment of goods and resources. It will also emphasize the necessity for discipline in a demanding time of change.

# January 21st Wednesday
## Moon in Sagittarius – *No Exact Aspects*

*Mood Watch*: There are no significant aspects of any kind occurring today, just the simple philosophical hopefulness of a waning Sagittarius Moon. The waning Sagittarius Moon brings an explorative process of internal reflection. It allows us to perceive emotional patterns a little more objectively, as well as optimistically. The waning Sagittarius Moon of winter is the time to prepare for the days ahead, to focus on our visions, to shed old pretenses, and to gather our courage. This is the time to broaden our awareness through exploration, and to do so with enthusiasm and wit.

# January 22nd Thursday

| Moon in Sagittarius / Capricorn | PST | EST |
|---|---|---|
| Moon square Venus | 12:43 AM | 3:43 AM |
| Moon square Uranus | 1:59 AM | 4:59 AM |
| Moon square Saturn | 4:41 AM | 7:41 AM |
| Moon sextile Neptune goes v/c | 8:23 AM | 11:23 AM |

| Mars sextile Uranus | 8:59 AM | 11:59 AM | |
| Venus conjunct Uranus | 5:01 PM | 8:01 PM | |
| Moon enters Capricorn | 10:18 PM | 1:18 AM | (January 23) |

*Mood Watch*: This morning's waning Sagittarius Moon brings insightfulness and contemplative moods. By dawn, our perceptions may feel somewhat out on a limb with so many pre-dawn lunar squares putting a damper on the overall mood; this is accentuated by the Sagittarius Moon going void-of-course this morning, and remaining so for the remainder of the day. This is a good time to stick to familiar territory, as the Sagittarian void-of-course Moon is an easy time to get lost or to go off track. Spacey philosophical moods will be the theme of the day. It may be best to keep plans simple while all of this is going on during Mercury retrograde (Jan. 11 – Feb. 1).

**Mars sextile Uranus** (occurring Jan. 16 – 25) Mars in Capricorn is sextile to Uranus in Pisces. Serious forces of combat are ignited in unanticipated ways. Mars governs all activities and forces of action. The sextile aspect puts this exalted Capricornian Mars energy into a position of opportunity and hope with regard to the explosive, unpredictable and chaotic energies of Uranus in Pisces. Both of these planets are charged with forceful energy and vitality as well as being violent and unsettled at times. Masculine forces are forging ahead abruptly and loudly right now, especially since the warrior spirit, Mars, was conjunct with the planet of permanent change, Pluto, last month (Dec. 28, 2008). The overall qualities of Mars sextile Uranus are very fiery, although not necessarily completely destructive. It is important to look for the opportunity and potential in all sources of raw masculine energy. This aspect will reoccur July 1 – 9, reaching its exact peak on July 7 with Mars in Taurus.

**Venus conjunct Uranus** (occurring Jan. 16 – 26) It's no wonder that love matters seem wild or chaotic – this conjunction brings an element of shock value to the expression of love. Venus conjunct Uranus in Pisces creates the potential for lively encounters with spiritual love and affection, wherein there is sometimes an exceedingly wise, though often unusual, counsel of love. A radical or explosive attraction or fascination may occur with this conjunction, opening our senses to a more artistic understanding of chaos. For those who are strongly affected, mischievous, brilliant, outgoing and challenging modes of love and affection now occur. Hang in there. Chaos is often considered a true test of love. Be positive and open to the challenge of love with chaos. Venus will *almost* be conjunct with Uranus in April (see Venus-conjunct-Uranus-non-exact April 10,) but this will not be an exact conjunction since Venus will be retrograde when the orbital conjunction begins, and it will go direct before the conjunction has a chance to reach an exact position.

# January 23rd Friday
## Moon in Capricorn

| | PST | EST | |
| --- | --- | --- | --- |
| Moon conjunct Pluto | 2:25 AM | 5:25 AM | |
| Sun conjunct Jupiter | 9:44 PM | 12:44 AM | (January 24) |
| Mercury-trine-Saturn-non-exact (occurring Jan. 23 to Feb. 6 – see below) | | | |
| Mercury conjunct Mars begins (see January 26) | | | |

*Mood Watch*: Overnight, the long-winded void-of-course Sagittarius Moon entered Capricorn. Our moods are likely to be dominated by a serious phase of expression throughout the day. Capricorn Moon keeps our moods focused on important matters and relentlessly reminds us to get a handle on our unfinished business. For some, the important "task" may be the job of resting, but if that's not the case for you, don't use this as an excuse! Whatever you do, enjoy the work while the atmosphere invites success.

**Sun conjunct Jupiter** (occurring Jan. 16 – 27) This conjunction brings those Aquarians celebrating birthdays at this time into an especially favorable position of their natal sun to Jupiter. This represents a time of gifts and expansion for these Aquarius folks, and there are good times in the works for these people. Financial or career advancement as well as skill building, exploration, travel, inheritance, and perhaps just plain happiness, becomes a bonus for these folks, now and in the year to come. Be sure to count your blessings birthday people; you may find that there are a great deal more blessings opening up for you this year than you might have expected! As Jupiter continues to travel through the later degrees of Aquarius, it will cross over the solar degrees of later born Aquarius people. Although it won't exactly occur at the time of their birthdays, they too will reap the benefits of promising opportunities in the year to come.

**Mercury-trine-Saturn-non-exact** (occurring Jan. 23 – Feb. 6) The retrograde Mercury (Jan. 11 – Feb. 1,) is beginning to trine with Saturn. Due to the fact that Mercury is retrograde, this aspect will never actually reach an *exact* trine. Despite this, the energy of Mercury trine Saturn is still assuredly there, creating an ideal time to edit. Normally this would also be a good time to practice memorization skills, but with Mercury retrograde, one must take precautions not to memorize the wrong information. Mercury retrograde in Capricorn creates the need for some serious perfectionism and there is often a very demanding tone to our communications. However, as a general rule this aspect is positive in nature, and timely information often represents a gift or blessing. For more information on Mercury trine Saturn, see April 17, when it actually reaches an exact trine, with Mercury in Taurus and Saturn in Virgo.

# January 24ᵗʰ Saturday

**Moon in Capricorn**

| | PST | EST |
|---|---|---|
| Mars  trine Saturn | 12:04 AM | 3:04 AM |
| Venus  opposite Saturn | 12:15 AM | 3:15 AM |
| Venus  sextile Mars | 1:07 AM | 4:07 AM |
| Moon  sextile Uranus | 3:04 PM | 6:04 PM |
| Moon  trine Saturn | 5:19 PM | 8:19 PM |
| Moon  conjunct Mars | 6:35 PM | 9:35 PM |
| Moon  sextile Venus | 6:51 PM | 9:51 PM |
| Mercury sextile Venus  (see January 26) | | |

*Mood Watch*: The commitment to carrying on time honored traditions, and discharging the workload with a sense of accomplishment, brings favorable moods today. Long winded planetary aspects keep this day busy and eventful as the waning Capricorn Moon emphasizes the necessity to pay attention, avoid distractions, and to steer clear of sticky or complex emotional responses.

**Mars trine Saturn** (occurring Jan. 16 – 27) Exalted Mars in Capricorn is trine the retrograde Saturn in Virgo. Large scale projects can expect to move ahead,

54

although it may not necessarily occur on time. Our actions bring gifts with this aspect, provided there is an application of discipline and timing. At best, Mars trine Saturn provides a sense of good timing, but while Saturn is retrograde, the good timing tends to occur most effectively during the completion of projects, rather than during the initiation of projects. Activities will be very physical while these two planets are in earth signs. This may be a good time to apply diligent practice with one's favorite sport, especially those physical activities which demand precision and perfect timing. The timely gift of willpower and discipline brings rewards and positive results. To fully benefit from this aspect, one must use the energy (Mars) responsibly (Saturn). This is usually a time of harmonious transitions, when endings and new beginnings are easily merged. This aspect will reoccur June 13 – 26, reaching its exact peak on June 22, when Mars will be in Taurus.

**Venus opposite Saturn** (occurring Jan. 18 – 27) Venus in Pisces is opposite Saturn in Virgo. Artistic and spiritually oriented expressions of love, beauty, and magnetism are at odds with the scrutiny of restrictive kinds of discipline. While there is a very strong need to attain a sense of beauty, to stop and smell the roses, there is a constantly compelling and obsessive compulsion to press on with work and vital responsibilities. This may be a difficult time for some to feel in tune with loved ones, and career related disciplines may be impeding on recreational needs and desires. This may be particularly so because Saturn is currently retrograde (Dec. 31, 2008 – May 16, 2009). Love matters – and the things we are attracted to – are subjected to unavoidable trials and restrictions. There will be folks among us thrust into the challenges of facing jealousy, guilt, offensive outbreaks, anguish, oppression, defeat or despair. There are always lessons where our sheltered passions lie. We must be careful how our passions are stirred or handled. Hold steadfast to all principles of wisdom. Be careful not to bite off more than you can chew, especially with regard to irresistible attractions and restrictive love matters. This is the only time Venus will oppose Saturn this year.

**Venus sextile Mars** (occurring Jan. 7 – Feb. 24) Mischievous, talkative, and outgoing kinds of affection are evident while Venus is sextile to Mars. Venus in Pisces sextile Mars in Capricorn brings intuitively astute attractions and ambitious displays of worthiness. It is here that feminine (Venus) and masculine (Mars) forces have an opportunity (the sextile aspect) to support each other. The Mars influence emphasizes the awareness and application of action, movement, involvement, and also harnesses strength and energy. Venus reminds us to draw towards ourselves the pleasures we desire. Here we have the incentive to apply action with love. This aspect will reach another peak on February 18, with Venus in Aries and Mars in Aquarius. It will also occur October 7 – 16, reaching its exact peak on October 13 with Venus in Virgo and Mars in Cancer.

# January 25th Sunday
## NEW MOON in AQUARIUS – Annular Solar Eclipse

| Moon in Capricorn / Aquarius | PST | EST | |
|---|---|---|---|
| Moon conjunct Mercury goes v/c | 1:08 AM | 4:08 AM | |
| Moon enters Aquarius | 10:55 AM | 1:55 PM | |
| Moon conjunct Jupiter | 8:35 PM | 11:35 PM | |
| Moon conjunct Sun | 11:54 PM | 2:54 AM | (January 26) |

*Mood Watch*: The **New Moon in Aquarius** (Moon conjunct Sun) is a good time to begin new social and philanthropic endeavors, and to gain fresh knowledge by learning something new about ourselves or our ever changing world. Moods created by this New Moon may be bold or daring, with a flair for experimenting with life. This is the time to open up to new feelings and greater comprehension of science and technology and of these changing times, adding to our power. Today is also the day to work on getting a good head start on the coming work week, especially since tomorrow's Moon in Aquarius will be void-of-course for most of the day.

An **Annular Solar Eclipse in the sign of Aquarius** brings an emphasis on the needs of humanity and the systems by which it operates. This may be a time of technological glitches or accidental breakthroughs. There may also be some form of inspiration or liberating change as a result of longer and harder looks at the way systems operate. For some, the act of thinking comprehensively may be overshadowed by the solar eclipse energy, particularly now that Mercury is retrograde. This is a good time to pace ourselves through the motions of this shadowy time.

# January 26th Monday
## Chinese New Year: OX (Year 4707) *Earth Ox*

| Moon in Aquarius | PST | EST | |
|---|---|---|---|
| Mercury sextile Venus | 3:32 PM | 6:32 PM | |
| Mercury conjunct Mars | 10:15 PM | 1:15 AM | (January 27) |
| Mercury-sextile-Uranus-non-exact | (occurring Jan. 26 to Feb. 4 – see below) | | |

*Mood Watch*:  As the darkly waning Moon enters Aquarius, a thoughtful approach to the day makes matters run a little more smoothly. Today will be a good day for research and experimentation.

**Mercury sextile Venus** (occurring Jan. 24 – 27) Retrograde Mercury in Capricorn sextile Venus in Pisces teaches us of the necessity to speak up responsibly about our love needs, and it focuses talk and discussion on the things in life we are most attracted to. While Mercury is retrograde (Jan. 11 – Feb. 1,) we may find this aspect is tricky when negotiating in love related matters. However, the sextile aspect of Mercury to Venus brings hope and good possibilities for our love needs. This is a good time to speak up clearly yet cautiously with regard to the things and people we treasure. This aspect will reoccur February 21 – 27, reaching its peak on February 25 with Mercury in Aquarius and Venus in Aries. Mercury sextile Venus will be non-exact in April, as it *almost* occurs, beginning on April 26 and ending before its fruition on May 1. It will finally occur July 30 – August 31, reaching its exact peak on two separate occasions; first on August 7 with Mercury in Virgo and Venus in Cancer, and secondly on August 28 with Mercury in Libra and Venus in Leo.

56

**Mercury conjunct Mars** (occurring Jan. 23 – 29) This conjunction brings the forces of communication (Mercury) together with the forces of action (Mars). This is currently occurring just as Mercury begins to complete its final phase of retrograde motion (Jan. 11 – Feb. 1). This is not a very good time to bluff! This aspect brings words and deeds together, and in this case, the greatest action occurs with communication and is empowered in the expression of the message. This is an excellent time to get others motivated through speech, but it is likely that this speech will have to be modified, and eventually, repeated, as Mercury tends to throw curve balls during communications while it is retrograde. This may be a time of angry words being spoken. Also, with the Mercury retrograde factor, it is likely that properties will be rigorously disputed while Mercury and Mars are conjunct in the physically conscientious – and methodically goal oriented – sign of Capricorn. Some might say, the best way to win an argument is to begin by being right; taking this approach during this time is likely to win you favors but not friendship. Take caution with your words; if they are intended to incite a battle, this would be a marvelous time to put that message out there! Note: due to Mercury retrograde, this conjunction will reoccur on March 1, with both planets conjunct in Aquarius.

**Mercury-sextile-Uranus-non-exact** (occurring Jan. 26 – Feb. 4) Mercury is in Capricorn placing a determined emphasis on our efforts to communicate. Uranus is in Pisces, stirring up chaos in the arts and religion. Mercury sextile Uranus gives us the opportunity to freely speak our minds and to address the turmoil that exists in our lives. Even though this aspect does not actually reach a peak, due to Mercury retrograde (Jan. 11 – Feb. 1), the affects of the struggle to be heard over the calamity of confusion is still affecting us, in subtle – but definite – ways. This aspect will reach an actual peak on three separate occasions; April 24, May 20, and June 9. Mercury sextile Uranus will begin to occur again on December 20, but due to Mercury retrograde on December 26, it will not reach an exact peak until February 5, 2010.

**Happy Chinese New Year! – Year of the Ox** (occurring: Jan. 26, 2009 *Earth OX* – Feb. 13, 2010 – next year's animal will be *Metal TIGER*). In the Chinese calendar, we have reached the year 4707, and this time marks the *Year of the Earth* Ox. Every twelve years, the Year of the Ox rolls around, and every sixty years, we come to the specific oxen sign known as the Earth Ox. People born under the Year of the Ox are very earthy in character, so you can imagine that those who are born in the Year of the Earth Ox are especially grounded in their ways. The personality of the Ox may be likened to the qualities of the zodiac signs, Capricorn and Taurus. If you combined those two zodiac signs, you'd have the perfect description of the Ox personality. Of course, Taurus represents the bull, which is similar to the Ox. Capricorn's symbol is the mountain goat. The bull and the mountain goat are stubborn, persistent, and methodical, and so are the people born in the Year of the Ox. The Ox personality does not change easily, which makes them dependable, but also very predictable.

The ox is a highly respected and revered animal in China, and often represents the livelihood and proud symbol of the farmer. Many Chinese families still rely on the oxen to assist them in harvesting foods and moving heavy equipment. As for those born in the Year of the Ox, these folks are diligent, reliable, sincere, strong, and generally have very sound judgment. However, they are rarely looked to for entertainment, stylish dress codes, or a refreshing sense of humor. These people are hard working, stable, security conscious, tolerant, and revered for their strong, respectable character. These are not the sort of people who seek get-rich-quick schemes, but they are often wealthy by virtue of their scrupulous ability to save money and build up a lifelong accumulation of savings. If you know someone born in the Year of the Ox who does not fit these descriptions, please remember that systems such as Western and Chinese Astrology are multifaceted parts to an intricate and complex human makeup. Sometimes the vast combination of celestial traits in humans can bring surprising results, and sometimes, through sheer persistence of will – as well as environmental and cultural influences – people change completely from their inherent nature into something phenomenal. This is why it is not wise to blithely accept every probability predicted in this book. You have the power to change what's around you! Meanwhile, don't expect to change a person who easily fits the description of the Year of the Ox personality. It's up to them to change, not you. Anything is possible, but it's generally easier to go with the flow of nature.

# January 27th Tuesday

**Moon in Aquarius / Pisces**

| | PST | EST |
|---|---|---|
| Moon conjunct Neptune goes v/c | 9:11 AM | 12:11 PM |
| Moon enters Pisces | 10:11 PM | 1:11 AM (January 28) |

*Mood Watch*: For most of the day and all of the evening, the newly waxing Aquarius Moon will be void-of-course. This is classically a time of technological glitches, and some issues may arise with regard to human rights or systems that don't work. This is magnified by the fact that Mercury is retrograde (Jan. 11 – Feb. 1,) causing further complications with the relaying of messages. Today is a good day to stick with what you know best and to avoid trying to explain matters that are too complex for overtaxed minds.

# January 28th Wednesday

**Moon in Pisces**

| | PST | EST |
|---|---|---|
| Moon sextile Pluto | 2:26 AM | 5:26 AM |

*Mood Watch*: Something intrinsically special and often incommunicable touches the heart in the newly waxing inspiration of Pisces Moon. This is the time to recognize an inherent gift that exists within, and to visualize the ways in which that gift can manifest. Spiritual moods put us in touch with our ability to withstand adversity and to accept how we feel.

# January 29th Thursday

**Moon in Pisces**

| | PST | EST |
|---|---|---|
| Moon conjunct Uranus | 1:14 PM | 4:14 PM |
| Moon opposite Saturn | 2:30 PM | 5:30 PM |
| Moon sextile Mercury | 4:33 PM | 7:33 PM |
| Moon sextile Mars | 11:40 PM | 2:40 AM (January 29) |
| Venus square Pluto begins (see February 5) | | |

58

*Mood Watch*: Pisces Moon entices our attraction to art and music as well as escapism and dreamy distractions. Pisces Moon, now waxing, creates the need for many to access an internal part of their understanding. Our intuition begins to surface. This is a time of reverie and reflection. Our moods will tend to take the path of least resistance, particularly while Uranus shakes things up in Pisces, and in the spiritually adept environment that Pisces Moon creates. Even when we are under pressure, strong and instinctual inclinations are enhanced on a waxing Pisces Moon.

# January 30ᵗʰ Friday

**Moon in Pisces / Aries**

| | | PST | EST |
|---|---|---|---|
| Moon | conjunct Venus goes v/c | 1:22 AM | 4:22 AM |
| Moon | enters Aries | 7:24 AM | 10:24 AM |
| Moon | square Pluto | 11:37 AM | 2:37 PM |
| Moon | sextile Jupiter | 6:33 PM | 9:33 PM |

*Mood Watch*: Before dawn, the Pisces Moon goes void-of-course, creating some rather spacey moods early this morning. As the Moon enters Aries, the morning moods swiftly sober up into a creative and determined drive to get down to business. From our various slow starts, to those who got off to a running start, the race of the tortoise and hare is on, as we continue our mad dash through the trials of winter.

# January 31ˢᵗ Saturday

**Moon in Aries**

| | PST | EST | |
|---|---|---|---|
| Moon sextile Sun | 5:15 AM | 8:15 AM | |
| Mercury goes direct | 11:11 PM | 2:11 AM | (February 1) |
| Moon square Mercury | 11:20 PM | 2:20 AM | (February 1) |

*Mood Watch*: Today's only outstanding planetary aspect, Moon sextile Sun, brings moods which are inspired by the seasonal factors of this time. Waxing Moon represents a time of increasing the awareness of our feelings. Winter restlessness stirs our hearts. The desire to start up new projects is also a symptom of the youthfully waxing Aries Moon. Overall, we can expect to get a lot of things accomplished on this Aries Moon Saturday. Aries Moon generates energy and gives many of us the impetus to tend to personal needs and projects requiring attention. Aries Moon on the last day of the month accentuates the strong anticipation affecting those people who are in a state of rapid change, thus making today's mover tomorrow's new occupant.

**Mercury goes direct** (Mercury direct: Feb. 1 – May 6/7) Since January 11, Mercury has been retrograde in the signs Aquarius and Capricorn, commonly causing communication mix-ups. In Aquarius, the retrograde Mercury often causes communication glitches with regard to social engagements, charity efforts, and technological events. Since January 20 the retrograde Mercury in Capricorn has been causing communication mix-ups that revolve around issues of control, stability, and inaccurate timing. Now we can breathe a greatly needed sigh of relief as Mercury, the planet governing the realms of communication, becomes stationary and will soon begin to move forward in the late degrees of Capricorn. Take note that our faculties and manner of communicating will definitely improve within the next few days. Although perhaps not today – when the stationary Mercury often freezes communication efforts – but very soon our communications will run more smoothly; this will be a good time to begin clearing up various misunderstandings that have occurred over the past few weeks. For more information on this recently completed phase of Mercury retrograde, see January 11. For more on Mercury retrograde patterns throughout this year, see the introduction on *Mercury retrograde periods*.

# February 1ˢᵗ Sunday

**National Freedom Day, USA**

| Moon in Aries / Taurus | PST | EST |
|---|---|---|
| Moon sextile Neptune | 2:31 AM | 5:31 AM |
| Moon square Mars goes v/c | 10:07 AM | 1:07 PM |
| Moon enters Taurus | 2:07 PM | 5:07 PM |
| Moon trine Pluto | 6:16 PM | 9:16 PM |

*" If a nation values anything more than freedom, it will lose its freedom,*

*and the irony of it is that if it is comfort or money that it values more, it will lose that too. "* - W. Somerset Maugham (1874 – 1965)

*Mood Watch*: The first day of the month begins with the Moon in the first sign of the zodiac, Aries, and kicks off the morning with ambitious vigor. Then, as the Moon squares with Mars, it goes void-of-course for exactly four hours during midday. The potential for angry, confused, or frustrated moods is strong. This may be the time to temper impatience – or high expectations – with guarded tolerance. To complicate matters, Mercury is now stationary and has just gone direct. This is the most problematical part of the Mercury retrograde cycle, when communications seem suspended by insufficient delivery of information. Later in the day, as our midday bewilderment blows off, the Moon enters Taurus and our moods begin to ground out and settle. The Taurus Moon waxes and our enthusiastic stubbornness to get the job done, despite faulty communications, will make the difference. Moon in Taurus brings positive moods, and the evening nightcap of Moon trine Pluto allows us to look for the silver lining in the hardships of life.

# February 2ⁿᵈ Monday

**Candlemas / Groundhog Day**
**FIRST QUARTER MOON in TAURUS**

| | PST | EST |
|---|---|---|
| Moon square Jupiter | 1:42 AM | 4:42 AM |
| Moon square Sun | 3:12 PM | 6:12 PM |
| Venus enters Aries | 7:41 PM | 10:41 PM |

*Mood Watch*: **First Quarter Moon in Taurus** (Moon square Sun) brings the pressure to take care of essential needs. Taurus is the *fixed earth* sign, and the nature of Taurus Moon leads many folks to watch their pocketbook and make sure they're getting the most value possible out of all expenditures. There is also a need to let the beauty of our surroundings be accented and appreciated. Somewhere in between the processes of earning and reaping rewards, a happy medium is struck.

The Moon is *exalted* in the place of Taurus, and positive harmony brings satisfaction.

**Today is Candlemas**, a celebration of the return of the light. Out of the darkness and into the light – this represents a time of blossoming knowledge and a time to acknowledge one's own growth. We are now one half of the way through winter season. This holiday is also known as **Imbolc**, the breakthrough of winter's darkness. The days to come bring prismatic sparkling color through crystals suspended from windows. The light awakens and stirs the seeds of hope, and touches us from within. The legendary Irish Saint, Bridget, dons a crown of candles. Light candles and celebrate the return of the light! Today is also Groundhog Day, when the absence or presence of the groundhog's shadow predicts the course of the final half of winter season.

**Venus enters Aries** (Venus in Aries: Feb. 2 – April 11) Venus will be in Aries (off and on) for an extended time this year, as Venus will go retrograde (March 6 – April 17), then it will enter Pisces for a short time (April 11 – 24). It will then reenter Aries (April 24), keeping this planet busy in Aries throughout most of the spring season (April 24 – June 6). As Venus enters Aries, the expression of beauty, love and attraction assumes a fascination for the warrior spirit. Venus represents magnetic draw and attraction, and now the planet of love and beauty focuses our attention on the force and fire of Aries related interests. This brings sheer love of and appreciation for such activities as competition, rights (or rites) of selfhood, and initiation into new endeavors. Aries is considered to be the detrimental place for Venus, since Venus rules the opposite of Aries, which is the peace loving realm of Libra. In Aries, Venus brings out the warrior spirit or quality in people, and a new sense of life and vitality will be evident. Venus in Aries emphasizes ardent, open and forthright expressions and proposals of love, especially from our Aries friends who may be blinded by the lust for beauty. New hobbies, crafts and talents will spring forth. Remember, Aries rules the head; there are numerous ways you can use your head before plunging head first into love matters. Try not to be too militant in the display of personal defenses and in the expression of true feelings of affection. New love is inspired with Venus in Aries, although without stronger influences at work, a new love may be somewhat impulsive or fleeting when initiated in this sign.

# February 3rd Tuesday

| Moon in Taurus / Gemini | PST | EST |
|---|---|---|
| Moon sextile Uranus | 2:06 AM | 5:06 AM |
| Moon trine Saturn | 2:28 AM | 5:28 AM |
| Moon trine Mercury | 4:40 AM | 7:40 AM |
| Moon square Neptune | 7:19 AM | 10:19 AM |
| Moon trine Mars goes v/c | 5:26 PM | 8:26 PM |
| Moon enters Gemini | 6:14 PM | 9:14 PM |
| Moon sextile Venus | 7:37 PM | 10:37 PM |

*Mood Watch*: The waxing Taurus Moon focuses our moods on practical needs and comforts. The momentum of our efforts begins to pick up today as we work our way through physical tasks, and beautify and warm up our surroundings with a

61

renewed outlook on the second half of winter season. This evening, Taurus Moon goes void-of-course for a short time, then enters Gemini. The cloud of Mercury retrograde (Jan. 11 – Feb. 1) has lifted; tonight's Gemini Moon has us talking again.

# February 4ᵗʰ Wednesday

| Moon in Gemini | PST | EST | |
|---|---|---|---|
| Moon trine Jupiter | 6:07 AM | 9:07 AM | |
| Mars enters Aquarius | 7:55 AM | 10:55 AM | |
| Moon trine Sun | 9:59 PM | 12:59 AM | (February 5) |

*Mood Watch*: Gemini Moon playfully waxes and loves to play tricks on the mind. Don't overdo the caffeine and take it easy on the nervous system. When in doubt, apply humor. Jovial and positive lunar aspects bring optimistic moods. At last, we can begin to straighten out the facts as the Moon in the Mercury-ruled sign, Gemini, brings communicative moods that will assist us to find supportive and encouraging words to face the (already penetrating) hard and heavy aspects of tomorrow.

**Mars enters Aquarius** (Mars in Aquarius: Feb. 4 – March 14) As Mars, the red warrior planet, moves through Aquarius, a surge of energy and vitality takes place in the lives of Aquarius people. Now the fixed signs of the zodiac go into an activity mode, for as Mars goes through Aquarius, Scorpio and Taurus people will experience Mars squaring with their natal Sun signs, causing their lives to be more prone towards accidents, fights, fevers, and unyielding activities of great challenge. Mars in Aquarius will be opposing the fixed sign Leo, making our Leo friends realize that the activities in their lives are a challenge to keep up with; occasional bouts of exhaustion will be common. Mars in the air sign of Aquarius shows that activities will emphasize science, technology and computer data banks, as well as humanitarian endeavors. Watch out for the tendency of electrical equipment to overheat and fry during this time of Mars in Aquarius.

# February 5ᵗʰ Thursday

| Moon in Cancer | PST | EST |
|---|---|---|
| Saturn opposite Uranus | 2:55 AM | 5:55 AM |
| Moon square Saturn | 4:45 AM | 7:45 AM |
| Moon square Uranus | 4:45 AM | 7:45 AM |
| Moon trine Neptune goes v/c | 9:43 AM | 12:43 PM |
| Moon enters Cancer | 7:04 PM | 10:04 PM |
| Venus square Pluto | 8:25 PM | 11:25 PM |

*Mood Watch*: As Saturn reaches an exact opposition to Uranus (see below,) the Moon ties us into this big event by squaring with Saturn at the same time it squares with Uranus. The Gemini Moon energy keeps our moods busy by jumping the hurdles of great change with urgent discussions. This Gemini Moon has us talking, and gives us the blow-by-blow details of how to interpret the trials we now face. We may also encounter a lot of confusion with the Moon void-of-course the whole day. In the midst of it all, Moon trine Neptune reminds us to keep the faith, and hold a positive outlook on the spiritual ramifications of this exciting and explosive time of the new millennium. Tonight, as the Moon enters Cancer, our moods are emotionally touched by the strength of our difficulties with life. Take heart; every

62

difficult phase of life must have the emotional flushing that Cancer Moon moods often bring. Let the spirit of Cancer Moon cleanse your cup with grace.

**Saturn opposite Uranus** (occurring Oct. 12, 2008 – March 23, 2009) This is a big one. Saturn has been in the Mercury-ruled planet, Virgo, since September 2, 2007, and Uranus has been in the Neptune-ruled sign, Pisces, since March 10, 2003. This aspect reached an exact opposition for the first time (this century) during the USA's last presidential election on November 4, 2008. Out of the maintenance of the structurally unsound elements of the past (Saturn in Virgo,) comes the belief altering disruption and explosive chaos of the future (Uranus in Pisces). The stark reality of this aspect suggests Saturn, which represents order and structure, is indeed the very opposite kind of energy in the very opposite position to its opponent, Uranus, which represents chaos and disorder. What are the results of this significant polarization? Which of the two masters' energy will outweigh the other? Saturn being control, and Uranus being disruption, one might surmise the very best to hope for would be an elaborate exercise in learning to control the uncontrollable. From storms, earthquakes, shifts of ocean currents, and volcanic activity come all kinds of earth shifts. Saturn is in an earth sign, the *mutable earth* sign, Virgo. This represents the mutability and the adaptability of the physical world, and the shifting of the physical realm will be unpredictable and chaotic while Uranus's opposing influence continues to bring immense and irreparable change.

Saturn, whose orbital phase through a single astrological sign takes a couple of years or more to complete, has finally caught up to the late degrees of Virgo, and is now traversing through a lengthy opposition phase to the power packed outer planet, Uranus. Both of these slower moving planets have a strong impact on societies as a whole, and this aspect has been dramatically affecting the world at large for the past six months. This aspect implies that there has been an acute awareness of explosive endings occurring on the planet. Saturn represents our guard or defense, which is being placed in a challenged state of awareness (the opposition), over the radically revolutionary surge of consciousness and chaotic urgency that Uranus' energy creates.

The Saturn-Uranus opposition occurred back in the mid-1960s, bringing with it a wave of authority-questioning skepticism, revolution, rebellion, civil unrest, and massive protests. The essential difference of that time verses now lies in the fact that Saturn was in Pisces and Uranus was in Virgo, while now, the opposite holds true. The polarity of Pisces and Virgo emphasizes the struggle between belief (Pisces,) and doubt (Virgo). This polarity examines the compelling power of intuition (Pisces) verses the temptation (or propensity) to question or analyze with skepticism (Virgo). It represents an unconditional acceptance (Pisces) opposed to a conditional lack of acceptance (Virgo). The Neptune-ruled sign, Pisces, does not usually seek to explain that which can only be categorized as nebulous or uncertain, whereas the Mercury-ruled sign, Virgo, requires explanation, and needs evidence to support every argument – in short, Virgo needs certainty before abandoning all doubt. What binds the traits of this polarity is summed up in one word: susceptibility. We are made susceptible to all kinds of unpredictable trouble the moment we begin to believe or to doubt anything. Uranus in Virgo during the 60s brought a revolution of doubt and resistance; whereas Uranus in Pisces, this time around,

63

brings a revolution of belief, intuition, and spiritual rebellion.

What's bound to happen is the severe collapse of infrastructures and systems of rules and regulations. Saturn contains structure, while Uranus breaks structure that is no longer feasible for containment. This aspect, at worst, implies the potential for nuclear destruction, as Uranus' volatile influence is associated with extreme explosiveness, while Saturn's timely influence represents the structural beginning and ending of all things. Revolution will be evident, and catastrophic natural disasters may also be evident. Since Saturn is currently in a retrograde phase (Dec. 31, 2008 – May 16, 2009,) this aspect will begin reoccurring later this year (August 7 – October 3) and it will reach an exact opposite position on September 15.

**Venus square Pluto** (occurring Jan. 29 – Feb. 10) Venus in Aries is square to Pluto in Capricorn. The energetic, swift and intrepid qualities of our affections are likely to take a pretty good beating. Our concepts of beauty may be challenged as the corruption of superpowers prompts action which threatens or alters the beauty and pleasure in our lives. There may be environmental destruction that intrudes on our sense of natural aesthetics. Venus square Pluto often involves such difficulties as loss or death of a loved one, the obstacles of rejection, and general oppression for those aspects of life to which we are undeniably attached and which we hold dear. If something of this nature is occurring for you, it is best to recognize that love will triumph in every dimension, despite the pain of separation, or the disease and strife of the beloved. While Pluto is in Capricorn, the square of Venus in Aries may create the sense that loving efforts are unreciprocated. Some people may feel used, unappreciated, or disadvantaged. Be both strong and gentle in matters of love. Let the obstacles of love's pain become the building blocks of a better outlook, and a stronger love will supersede these current trials of the heart. This time may seem difficult, but bear it in mind that Venus will go retrograde on March 6 and this aspect will repeat again March 24 – April 10, reaching its peak on April 3. When Venus is retrograde, the turmoil surrounding issues of affection at that time may be harder to openly share with others than it is now. Venus square Pluto also occurs April 29 – May 7, reaching its peak on May 2. Finally, this aspect will occur for the fourth and last time – October 10 – 17, reaching its exact aspect on October 15, with Venus in Libra and Pluto in Capricorn.

# February 6ᵗʰ Friday

| Moon in Cancer | PST | EST |
|---|---|---|
| Moon opposite Pluto | 12:05 AM | 3:05 AM |
| Moon square Venus | 12:17 AM | 3:17 AM |
| Sun conjunct Neptune begins (see February 12) | | |
| Mars conjunct Jupiter begins (see February 17) | | |

*Mood Watch*: Today the Moon is in Cancer, where our moods are geared towards nurturing and appeasing the emotions. Some do this with an emphasis on food, cooking, and dining. Others may choose to pamper themselves with luxury baths, while others just need to spill the emotional core and let off some steam in the hope that someone will listen sympathetically. Since Mercury went direct (Feb. 1) communications have been steadily improving, and today we may find that our feelings will seem more easily reconcilable. This may be a time to reflect on life's recent

64

episodes with a calm and encouraging demeanor. Cancer Moon clearly assists us in feeling our way through situations. There are loads of ways to nurture and give emotional support. Sometimes it's as simple as applying the listening ear.

# February 7<sup>th</sup> Saturday

| Moon in Cancer / Leo | PST | EST |
|---|---|---|
| Moon sextile Saturn | 5:25 AM | 8:25 AM |
| Moon trine Uranus | 5:47 AM | 8:47 AM |
| Moon opposite Mercury goes v/c | 11:07 AM | 2:07 PM |
| Moon enters Leo | 8:43 PM | 11:43 PM |
| Venus sextile Jupiter begins  (see February 16) | | |

*Mood Watch*: After a seemingly endless week, the weekend has arrived, and the morning's heavily waxing Cancer Moon keeps our emotionally highlighted internal process turning. Saturn is opposite Uranus (Feb. 5) and the Moon, along with our moods, finally takes the positive approach to Mr. Saturn and Mr. Uranus. Since they reached the peak of dancing the big opposition dance on our lives this week, this morning's positive lunar aspects will assist us to patch up certain disruptive responses that have been too much to bear. However, all too soon, Moon opposite Mercury brings a void-of-course phase that makes it very difficult to talk about things. Sheer moodiness is the most common symptom of this time. Hang in there, and try not to fall victim to overreaction.

# February 8<sup>th</sup> Sunday

| Moon in Leo – *Full Moon Eve* | PST | EST |
|---|---|---|
| Moon opposite Mars | 1:23 AM | 4:23 AM |
| Moon trine Venus | 3:31 AM | 6:31 AM |
| Moon opposite Jupiter | 9:42 AM | 12:42 PM |

*Mood Watch*: Last night the Moon entered Leo, and it's a welcome change, as the long void-of-course Cancer Moon of yesterday may have worn some folks' patience down to a frazzle. Restlessness strikes the heart. It is no wonder that we awaken to wild and beastly moods. Such moods as these will get the chance to break out of their cage, as we gear ourselves up for a Full Moon eve. There may be an opportunity here to enhance and harmonize friendships and family situations in a fulfilling and enriching manner. This is a good time to stretch out your paws, seek warmth and light, enjoy affectionate hearts, and to reaffirm the strength of willpower. However, it would be wise to pace yourself today, as tomorrow brings yet another long and arduous void-of-course Moon phase.

# February 9<sup>th</sup> Monday

**FULL MOON in LEO – Penumbral Lunar Eclipse**

| Moon in Leo / Virgo | PST | EST | |
|---|---|---|---|
| Moon opposite Sun | 6:49 AM | 9:49 AM | |
| Moon opposite Neptune goes v/c | 11:29 AM | 2:29 PM | |
| Moon  enters Virgo | 9:39 PM | 12:39 AM | (February 10) |

*Mood Watch*: **FULL MOON in LEO – Penumbral Lunar Eclipse.** Life improves as the **Full Moon in Leo** (Moon opposite Sun) captivates our moods with a wild and instinctual push. The Full Moon in Leo reaches its peak this morning, leading to playful, imaginative, and creative expressions of mood. Most of us are easily drawn towards the need to find warmth and affection, or just plain attention. Pretty soon though, the energy shifts as the morning fades; this afternoon brings Moon opposite Neptune and another long void-of-course lunar phase begins. This sets the tone for nebulous, self-absorbed, spacey, tired, lazy, and un-engaging kinds of moods. This is a good time to give yourself and others some space.

**Penumbral Lunar Eclipse:** What we are likely to observe, with this eclipse in Leo, is the sense that things may not appear to be going our way, and at times, annoying, mean or negative people may have some affect on the shadowy emotional subtleties of this Leo Lunar Eclipse atmosphere. Trifling details, particularly of other people's lives, may be part of today's annoyances. Coarse or sly behavior, coupled with subtle bouts of cruelty and oppression may also be prevalent. Failing, giving up, and also being nagged, mocked, or ignored may send some folks into a reckless frenzy. The death of prominent people may be notable. This lunar extravaganza influences actors, directors, dramatists, entertainers, dancers, musicians, teachers, and hypnotists. The quality of our instincts may seem compromised by extravagance, arrogance, egotism, pride, or by confrontation. The fixed fire sign of Leo in the ecliptic state also influences earthquakes, hurricanes, floods, storms, drought, thunder and lighting. This is the time to reassure the self with confidence, to calm the heart, and to ease the steady beat of the heart with diligent care. A lunar eclipse occurs when the Earth moves between the moon and the sun, blocking the light that reflects off the moon's surface back to Earth. Every year there are at least two lunar eclipses, this year there are four. Today brings the first of the four lunar eclipses. The other penumbral lunar eclipses occur on July 7 and August 5. The final eclipse – a partial lunar eclipse – occurs on December 31. The darkness of a "penumbra" varies gradually from total darkness at one edge to full brightness at the other. Darkness is the key, as there tends to be the common belief that the casting of a shadow upon the Moon brings darker than average moods. Some view this as mere superstition while others may base this belief on their personal experiences.

# February 10th Tuesday

| Moon in Virgo | PST | EST |
|---|---|---|
| Moon trine Pluto | 1:53 AM | 4:53 AM |

*Mood Watch*: Last night the Moon entered Virgo. Practical matters now come to the surface. Despite business as usual, the waning Virgo Moon keeps us cautious, suspicious, and carefully poised. This is a good time to concentrate on the cleansing process of the soul. Virgo Moon emphasizes the need to focus on such things as accounting, dieting, research and analysis. Sun in Aquarius and Moon in Virgo brings out the need to get the technical world of communications in order.

# February 11ᵗʰ Wednesday

**Moon in Virgo**

| | PST | EST | |
|---|---|---|---|
| Moon conjunct Saturn | 7:43 AM | 10:43 AM | |
| Moon opposite Uranus | 8:56 AM | 11:56 PM | |
| Moon trine Mercury goes v/c | 8:18 PM | 1:18 AM | (February 12) |

*Mood Watch*: The Virgo Moon is an excellent time to focus on organization and communication. Moon conjunct Saturn brings serious morning moods that allow for greater concentration. A little later, Moon opposite Uranus focuses our attention on the chaotic energies that have been disrupting our lives. Virgo Moon allows our moods to take the pure and simple approach to our needs. This is a good time to tend to health matters and to clean up the environment.

# February 12ᵗʰ Thursday

**Moon in Libra**

| | PST | EST |
|---|---|---|
| Moon enters Libra | 12:33 AM | 3:33 AM |
| Sun conjunct Neptune | 4:40 AM | 7:40 AM |
| Moon square Pluto | 5:08 AM | 9:08 AM |
| Moon trine Mars | 11:41 AM | 2:41 PM |
| Moon opposite Venus | 1:28 PM | 4:28 PM |
| Moon trine Jupiter | 4:29 PM | 7:29 PM |

*Mood Watch*: Today's Libra Moon reminds us of the importance of applying logic to the structure of our lifestyle and our choices in life. Moon square Pluto may start off the morning with a bit of a struggle. By afternoon, Moon trine Mars will assist us to get things moving favorably. This is followed by Moon opposite Venus, which implies that our moods may be dominated by feminine types of expression or demands. Lady Justice is blind, but that doesn't mean her logic is not sound. This evening, Moon trine Jupiter brings moods which will be inspired by notions of travel, or by expansion of some nature. Positive evening moods bring joy and peace.

**Sun conjunct Neptune** (occurring Feb. 6 – 15) This occurrence of Sun conjunct Neptune particularly affects Aquarius people celebrating birthdays February 6 – 15 with intuitive inclinations and spiritual desires. Your visions (Aquarius birthday folks) will inspire great feats, and the higher, more spiritually refined parts of the soul are going to be speaking to you throughout the upcoming year. Listen! This may be a time to let go of personal attachments and outmoded desires that appear to be going nowhere. Your highly complex Aquarian idealism will work up your spiritual beliefs into a kind of peak performance level, even if you don't believe you have such a thing as spiritual beliefs. Birthday Aquarians, you will continue to encounter a kind of spiritual catharsis and, by the time you've come through this, you'll know what that means. This is all magnified by your ruling planet, Uranus, which has been traveling through the Neptune-ruled sign of Pisces since March 2003. Integrate a listening pattern concerning the Great Spirit in your life; focus on the spiritual part of the self (or higher self) that rules over personal destiny and guides the true desires of the soul. Can you handle that, birthday folks?

# February 13th Friday

**Friday the 13TH**

| Moon in Libra | PST | EST |
|---|---|---|
| Moon trine Neptune | 7:41 PM | 10:41 PM |
| Moon trine Sun | 10:52 PM | 1:52 AM (February 14) |

*Mood Watch*: Libra says: "I balance," and today's Libra Moon holds the promise of doing just that. Lunar aspects are positive in nature, and this is the time to infuse the world with a positive attitude towards teamwork and relationships. Sun in Aquarius and Moon in Libra is an excellent time to work on finding solutions that will work for everyone.

Why is **Friday the 13TH** considered such a bad omen? Friday the 13TH in October of the year 1307 was a really bad day in the life of Jacques DeMolay, fearless leader of the (notorious) Knights Templar. By sundown on that fateful day nearly all the Knights Templar throughout France were seized and thrown into dungeons. Thousands of men who were at one time considered nobles had their properties seized, and many suffered torture and inhumane conditions. The French King and the Pope conspired against the Templars to plunder their wealth; the Templars were then discarded as heretics and banned from the power they had held for so long. Seven years after the Friday the 13TH incident, DeMolay was executed. The fall of the Templars left such a bitter mark on the soul of Europe that Friday the 13TH has held a notorious reputation. Friday the 13TH is often still considered unlucky, however, there are some people who think of thirteen as an auspicious number, and to them this day is considered to be a lucky time. These people naturally tend to have a better experience of this day, by virtue of their more optimistic outlook. On a positive note, the Knights Templar still remain a fascination and a fraternally honored memory to this day. Perhaps their fortunes will yet revive.

# February 14th Saturday

**Saint Valentine's Day**

| Moon in Libra / Scorpio | PST | EST |
|---|---|---|
| Moon square Mercury goes v/c | 6:47 AM | 9:47 AM |
| Moon enters Scorpio | 6:51 AM | 9:51 AM |
| Mercury enters Aquarius | 7:37 AM | 10:37 AM |
| Moon sextile Pluto | 11:53 AM | 2:53 PM |
| Moon square Mars | 10:25 PM | 1:25 AM (February 15) |

*Mood Watch*: This morning the Moon in Libra goes void-of-course just as it squares to Mercury. Fortunately, this void-Moon factor only disrupts our decision making process for all of four minutes, but the square of the Moon to Mercury reminds us to choose our words wisely – it would be a good idea to avoid barking orders during this hypersensitive time of communications. Moon sextile Pluto focuses our attention on big issues that have been shaping the views between the generations. As the Moon enters Scorpio, our passion begins to surface on this Valentine's Day. Scorpio Moon is an intense and ardent place for displays of affection. Passionate moods will lead to a memorable Saturday evening experience, but beware of Moon square Mars much later this evening; this lunar aspect often results in defensive or offensive moods, and sometimes forces people into a place where they are just not comfortable.

**Mercury enters Aquarius** (Mercury in Aquarius: February 14 – March 8) Mercury in Aquarius is a time when we explore the power of knowledge through our communications. Due to Mercury's last retrograde process, January 11 – February 1, Mercury is currently entering Aquarius for the second time this year. This is a splendid time to communicate ideas and investigate the latest in technology, science, and the world of invention, particularly due to the fact that this period of Mercury in Aquarius won't be retrograde, promising more accurate communications. Mercury in Aquarius is also a special time to speak out on humanitarian issues and the rights of freedom. Eccentric talk and unusual subjects will fill the airwaves while Mercury is in Aquarius. For more information on Mercury retrograde in Aquarius, see the section in the introduction about Mercury retrograde periods.

# February 15th Sunday

| Moon in Scorpio | PST | EST | |
|---|---|---|---|
| Moon  square Jupiter | 1:00 AM | 4:00 AM | |
| Moon  sextile Saturn | 9:06 PM | 12:06 AM | (February 16) |
| Moon  trine Uranus | 11:34 PM | 2:34 AM | (February 16) |

*Mood Watch*: Waning Scorpio Moon emphasizes the need for release of tension and emotional buildups. This is a good time to work on allowing emotional expression to flow, however harsh it may appear on some levels, and trust that the release will bring a greater sense of healing. This month's emotional stresses, which have built up to this point, can no longer hide. Under secure circumstances, this may be the best time to let go of the pain you've been concealing.

# February 16th Monday

**Presidents' Day, Washington's Birthday, USA**
**LAST QUARTER MOON in SCORPIO**

| Moon in Scorpio / Sagittarius | PST | EST | |
|---|---|---|---|
| Moon  square Neptune | 5:11 AM | 8:11 AM | |
| Moon  square Sun goes v/c | 1:37 PM | 4:37 PM | |
| Moon  enters Sagittarius | 4:53 PM | 7:53 PM | |
| Venus  sextile Jupiter | 8:49 PM | 11:49 PM | |
| Moon  sextile Mercury | 10:37 PM | 1:37 AM | (February 17) |

Sun sextile Pluto begins  (see February 21)
George Washington's actual birthday is February 22, 1732
*" Be courteous to all, but intimate with few, and let those few be well tried before you give them your confidence. True friendship is a plant of slow growth, and must undergo and withstand the shocks of adversity before it is entitled to the appellation "* – George Washington (1732 – 1799)

*Mood Watch*: The **Last Quarter Moon in Scorpio** (Moon square Sun) occurs later this evening, and it focuses our attention on issues of passion and compassion. It is likely the dark secrets of our life will be touched on somehow. This Moon urges us to release stored up tension, and to find release for our emotions without imposing them on others. Late in the day, unobtrusive emotional release may not be all that simple, as the Moon will be void-of-course for over three hours. Physical workouts are excellent for this, provided safety consciousness is maintained. Safety consciousness of any kind is particularly important during Scorpio Moon. Don't forget to keep an eye out for suspicious activity – beware of thieves, smooth talkers, and the potential for violent outbreaks. Tonight's waning Moon in Sagittarius allows us explore our feelings more easily, and our outlook on life will be more philosophical.

**Venus sextile Jupiter** (occurring Feb. 7 – March 15) Venus is in Aries, the place of ardent and forceful love play. Jupiter is in Aquarius, bringing a humane outreach for fulfillment and a joyful effort towards getting in touch with the things we love. Creative – as well as impulsive – attractions and pleasures (Venus in Aries) lead us to prosperous opportunities in humanitarian related focuses, science, research, technology, civil service, and politics (Jupiter in Aquarius). This is an excellent time to shower loved ones with gifts and compliments. A lovers' getaway may be just the ticket to recapture some romance. This is the time to allow expansion to occur in love matters, and to take the next step towards enlivening and enhancing the beauty of life. A greater opportunity for increasing skills or augmenting your livelihood is available, especially if your focus remains on doing what you love most. Due to Venus retrograde (March 6 – April 18), this aspect goes on for an extended period and will reoccur on March 11. This aspect returns on May 29 – June 4, reaching its peak on June 2. It will also occur December 17 – 22, reaching its exact aspect on December 20, when Venus will be in Sagittarius.

# February 17ᵗʰ Tuesday

| Moon in Sagittarius | PST | EST |
|---|---|---|
| Mars conjunct Jupiter | 8:27 AM | 11:27 AM |
| Moon sextile Jupiter | 1:12 PM | 4:12 PM |
| Moon sextile Mars | 1:26 PM | 4:26 PM |
| Moon trine Venus | 1:41 PM | 4:41 PM |
| Mercury conjunct Jupiter begins (see February 23) | | |

*Mood Watch*: It's the last full day of Sun in Aquarius and the Moon wanes in Sagittarius, bringing an outgoing and free flowing expression of creativity and innovative thought. Moods are inclined towards optimism and energetic enthusiasm with Moon sextile both Jupiter and Mars. Moon trine Venus encourages our feelings to seek beauty and comfort. Overall, we can expect to make the most of the day and to enjoy the optimism brought to us by the Sagittarius Moon.

**Mars conjunct Jupiter** (occurring Feb. 6 – 22) Mars is conjunct with Jupiter in Aquarius. Strong actions will occur, possibly even warlike or defensive actions with regard to the distribution and management of large sums of wealth and revenue. While Mars and Jupiter are conjunct in Aquarius, these active shifts of revenue will occur around such Aquarius related things as broadcasting, television, computer sciences, civil services, social galas and events, political ventures, and economic or humane recovery programs. Mars represents action as it occurs, while Jupiter symbolizes expansion and matters of skill building, investing, joviality, vision quests, and achievement. This could be a time of exceedingly active break-

70

throughs with great wins or losses in economic endeavors. This is an especially
active time for fund raising and humanitarian efforts. Market mergers will bring
great fortune where great losses may have otherwise occurred. Opportunities to
enhance or perfect talents or skills make this a good time to activate a business or
career, especially in such Aquarius related endeavors as science and technology.
This is the only time this planetary conjunction will occur in 2009. It's an excellent
time to attempt to prosper, and to act on personal and community needs.

# PISCES

Key Phrase: "I Believe"

Mutable Water Sign

Ruling Planet: Neptune

Symbol : The Fishes

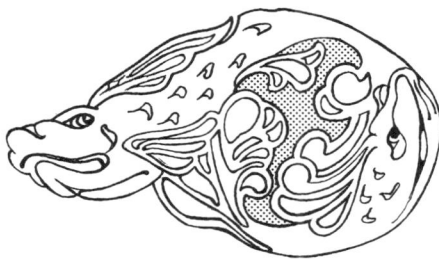

## February 18ᵗʰ Wednesday
**Moon in Sagittarius**

| | PST | EST |
|---|---|---|
| Venus sextile Mars | 1:27 AM | 4:27 AM |
| Sun enters Pisces | 4:46 AM | 7:46 AM |
| Moon square Saturn | 8:40 AM | 11:40 AM |
| Moon square Uranus | 11:51 AM | 2:51 PM |
| Moon sextile Neptune goes v/c | 5:36 PM | 8:36 PM |
| Mercury conjunct Mars begins (see March 1) | | |

*Mood Watch*: The waning Sagittarius Moon allows our moods to explore and roam
freely as the current shift of energy moves from the Sun in Aquarius to Sun in
Pisces – the mutable phase of winter. Both Sagittarius and Pisces are mutable signs,
focusing our energies on completion, adaptability, and change. Sagittarius Moon
brings the energy and vitality that make room for change to occur in our hearts. As
the Moon squares with both Saturn and Uranus, we may be challenged by deadlines
or limitations, as well as by chaos and erratic energies. Tonight will be a good time
to take it easy, as spacey moods will seem evident after the Moon sextile Neptune
aspect brings a long phase of Moon void-of-course. A calm sanctuary – and some
rest – might be the best course of action tonight.

**Venus sextile Mars** (occurring Jan. 7 – Feb. 24) During this occurrence period,
this aspect last reached its peak on January 24, only at that time, Venus was in
Pisces and Mars was in Capricorn. Now the two planets of yin and yang are in
the opportunistic sextile position again – Venus in Aries and Mars in Aquarius
will bring swift and intrepid attractions, and humane displays of heroism and
worthiness. It is here that feminine (Venus) and masculine (Mars) forces have an
opportunity (the sextile aspect) to support each other. At this time, many vital love
matters are being stirred, bringing numerous opportunities. This aspect will also

71

occur October 7 – 16, reaching its exact peak on October 13 with Venus in Virgo and Mars in Cancer.

**Sun enters Pisces** (Sun in Pisces: Feb. 18 – March 20) Out of Aquarius we take the extraordinary knowledge and experience of humanity, and in Pisces we purify that experience and seek further insight by getting in touch with divinity. Pisces is the last sign of the zodiac, representing the completion of a cycle. This mutable water sign is adaptive and Pisceans can absorb all kinds of influence. However, if bogged down by oppressive influences, the Piscean becomes burnt out, oversensitive, and depressed; it's important to find ways to vent heavy feelings of oppression. Pisces people are very psychic as a general rule, and they are also quite artistic and imaginative. The Pisces time of year is a good time to get in touch with personal beliefs and divinity.

## February 19ᵗʰ Thursday

| Moon in Sagittarius / Capricorn | PST | EST |
|---|---|---|
| Moon enters Capricorn | 5:25 AM | 8:25 AM |
| Moon sextile Sun | 7:43 AM | 10:43 AM |
| Moon conjunct Pluto | 11:06 PM | 2:06 PM |

*Mood Watch*: The earliest morning hours may seem quite spacey with the waning Sagittarius Moon still void-of-course. As the Moon enters Capricorn, a much more determined and down-to-earth set of moods begin to surface. Capricorn Moon brings out a serious effort to tackle big jobs. We are likely to feel a slight blow of intensity with the Moon conjunct Pluto. Waning Capricorn Moon is the time when we tend to set strong feelings aside, to subdue emotional tides with sober intent. Many folks may seem to be intolerant of emotional weakness. This is a time when we commonly deal with our problems through stalwart labor and persistent effort.

## February 20ᵗʰ Friday

| Moon in Capricorn | PST | EST | |
|---|---|---|---|
| Moon square Venus | 5:20 AM | 8:20 AM | |
| Moon trine Saturn | 9:11 PM | 12:11 AM | (February 21) |

*Mood Watch*: Moon in Capricorn commonly decrees that our moods become distinctly more serious and more work conscious. Throughout the day our moods exhibit a sense of diligent, persistent, and disciplined focus. There is a need today to get things done, to face up to unfinished business and to handle whatever comes along with strict effort.

## February 21ˢᵗ Saturday

| Moon in Capricorn / Aquarius | PST | EST |
|---|---|---|
| Sun sextile Pluto | 12:03 AM | 3:03 AM |
| Moon sextile Uranus goes v/c | 1:00 AM | 4:00 AM |
| Moon enters Aquarius | 6:06 PM | 9:06 PM |
| Mercury sextile Venus begins (see February 25) | | |

*Mood Watch*: Our day begins with somewhat placid moods, but as we attempt to get things moving, we soon discover the futility of our efforts. The void-of-

72

course Moon in Capricorn is upon us, and for the entire day into the evening, our moods may drive us to perform, but with no incentive to work and no inclination to concentrate. Needless to say, not much is likely to get done. As the Moon enters Aquarius, innovative perspectives open our minds. Our moods will enter into a humanitarian kind of acceptance of all things past and present.

**Sun sextile Pluto** (occurring Feb. 16 – 23) The Sun in Pisces is sextile Pluto in Capricorn, bringing opportunities that appear both vast and demanding to Pisces/ Aquarius cusp born people celebrating birthdays between February 16 – 23. These birthday people are experiencing the sextile aspect of their natal sun to Pluto, giving them opportunities to take charge, to step into positions of power, and to accept and embrace permanent change in their lives. These are powerful transformations which provide opportunities to embody what has been learned from the personal trials of the past. Go thee forth and conquer, master Pisceans and Aquarians! Persist with diligence to resolve the conflicts of your life with self-respect and assurance. Your time to triumph is always available when your will to achieve is balanced by knowledge and hard work. This holds true for all signs of the zodiac. This aspect will reoccur October 20 – 26, reaching its exact aspect on October 24 with the Sun in Scorpio.

# February 22nd Sunday

| Moon in Aquarius | PST | EST | |
|---|---|---|---|
| Moon conjunct Mercury | 1:32 PM | 4:32 PM | |
| Moon conjunct Jupiter | 4:37 PM | 7:37 PM | |
| Moon sextile Venus | 7:47 PM | 10:47 PM | |
| Moon conjunct Mars | 10:47 PM | 1:47 AM | (February 23) |

*Mood Watch*: Today brings excellent opportunities to undo the spell of yesterday's long void-of-course Moon. The waning Aquarius Moon brings innovative and inspired moods. Today's lunar aspects are all positive in nature and they will assist our moods to communicate amicably, tap into beneficial resources, to find affection, and to muster up some energy. For the most part, people are likely to be helpful, cheerful, and pleasant.

# February 23rd Monday

| Moon in Aquarius | PST | EST | |
|---|---|---|---|
| Moon conjunct Neptune goes v/c | 6:07 PM | 9:07 PM | |
| Mercury conjunct Jupiter | 10:51 PM | 1:51 AM | (February 24) |

*Mood Watch*: As the Moon wanes darkly in Aquarius, our moods are sensing the ways in which large groups of people are being affected by the build up of celestial energies. The waning Aquarius Moon draws our attention to the need for logic, knowledge, and scientific wisdom. The Pisces Sun carries us through the final days of winter with the trepidation of storms, both internal and external. Sun in Pisces with the Moon in Aquarius is a time when people tend to deeply contemplate humanitarian needs, starting with their own. Tonight's void-of-course Moon in Aquarius will probably highlight those things in life which make us feel small, like, simple human foibles, thoughtless mistakes, and technical glitches. These are only symptoms of another lunar cycle. Whatever you do, remember, it's only temporary, so don't let the feeling of helplessness get you down!

**Mercury conjunct Jupiter** (occurring Feb. 17 – 26) Last month's Mercury retrograde period (Jan. 11 – Feb. 1,) is the reason this conjunction is repeating for a second time this season. This is a time to set the record straight with regard to ownership, achievement, and attainment of all natures. Jupiter recently entered Aquarius *(see January 5,)* and these two planets are currently conjunct in Aquarius. News and discussions (Mercury) revolve around our joys, our prosperity, and our wealth (Jupiter) – particularly with regard to fulfilling our desires and abiding by our deep passions in life. Especially now that Mercury is no longer retrograde, this is a great time to boost the morale of others by complimenting them on their skills. This could be a prosperous conjunction for communicating the need for a job or financial loan. This conjunction last occurred from January 16 – 20, and reached its peak on January 18.

# February 24th Tuesday
## NEW MOON in PISCES

|  | PST | EST |
|---|---|---|
| Moon enters Pisces | 4:59 AM | 7:59 AM |
| Moon sextile Pluto | 10:32 AM | 1:32 PM |
| Moon conjunct Sun | 5:34 PM | 8:34 PM |

*Mood Watch*: **New Moon in Pisces** (Moon conjunct Sun) focuses our attention on the need to get in touch with our own beliefs and to inspire those beliefs with devotion and renewed faith. Tendencies towards escapism may be strong today, particularly for those who are unwilling to let go of the past. The New Moon in Pisces inspires a new outlook on our moods. This is a time of both emotional as well as spiritual purging. The spirit of what is now emerging and showing through our moods is a sense of renewed faith, in something divine and omnipotent. The world of magic exists in the melding mutable water of the Piscean expression.

# February 25th Wednesday
**Moon in Pisces**

|  | PST | EST |  |
|---|---|---|---|
| Mercury sextile Venus | 4:59 PM | 7:59 PM | |
| Moon opposite Saturn | 5:25 PM | 8:25 PM | |
| Moon conjunct Uranus goes v/c | 10:08 PM | 1:08 AM | (February 26) |

*Mood Watch*: Ever so new is the light of the waxing Pisces Moon. Crisp new psychic and intuitive inclinations lead to a spark of inspiration that carries us through the dwindling days of winter towards the renewed light of Spring Equinox, set to occur next month. Let the intuitive and creative process begin! Let the spirit of renewed faith cleanse our beliefs. This is the time to allow for new inspiration to come through in such Piscean kinds of things as art, music, poetic thought and prose, as well as spiritual reverie and meditation.

**Mercury sextile Venus** (occurring Feb. 21 – 27) Mercury in Aquarius sextile Venus in Aries teaches us of the necessity to speak up for all those we love and care about, particularly those who activate our most ardent love needs. It also focuses talk and discussion on the things in life we are most attracted to. While Mercury was retrograde (Jan. 11 – Feb. 1,) this aspect occurred on January 26, while Mercury was retrograde in Capricorn and sextile to Venus in Pisces. During that time we may have found it was tricky negotiating with regard to love related matters. However, the sextile aspect of Mercury to Venus brings hope and good possibilities for our love needs. Now that Mercury is no longer retrograde, this is an especially good time to speak up for the things and the people of our lives – those things and people we treasure. This aspect last occurred January 24 – 27, reaching an exact peak on January 26, when Mercury was retrograde in Capricorn and Venus was in Pisces. Mercury sextile Venus will begin to occur in April but it will not reach its peak; despite this, it will be an active aspect, beginning on April 26 and ending before its fruition on May 1. This aspect will finally occur July 30 – August 31, reaching its exact peak on two separate occasions: first on August 7 with Mercury in Virgo and Venus in Cancer, and secondly on August 28 with Mercury in Libra and Venus in Leo.

## February 26ᵗʰ Thursday

**Moon in Pisces / Aries**

| | PST | EST |
|---|---|---|
| Moon enters Aries | 1:23 PM | 4:23 PM |
| Moon square Pluto | 6:47 PM | 9:47 PM |

*Mood Watch*: Overnight, the newly waxing Pisces Moon went void-of-course, finally entering Aries this afternoon. Until then, our moods will seem spacey, distant, out of sorts, and somewhat isolated at times throughout the day. As the Moon enters Aries, our moods will seem more abruptly motivated to establish some clarity and focused intent.

## February 27ᵗʰ Friday

**Moon in Aries**

| | PST | EST | |
|---|---|---|---|
| Moon sextile Jupiter | 12:02 PM | 3:02 PM | |
| Moon conjunct Venus | 3:56 PM | 6:56 PM | |
| Moon sextile Mercury | 8:19 PM | 11:19 PM | |
| Moon sextile Mars | 10:47 PM | 1:47 AM | (February 28) |

*Mood Watch*: The basic mood-setting for today focuses on the need to stand out and be in control of events. There is eagerness and a quality of anticipation in our moods with the waxing Moon in Aries. Today's lunar aspects are all positive in nature and our moods will be filled with determination and inspiration. Sometimes the Aries Moon causes too much inspiration, and the search for a good fight or release of raw aggression must come out. This may be a difficult time to ignore pushy aggressors; nonetheless, being aware of this behavior and attempting to avoid it by watching for the signs — before the oppressor gets out of hand — may well be in your favor today.

# February 28th Saturday

**Moon in Aries / Taurus**

| | PST | EST |
|---|---|---|
| Moon sextile Neptune goes v/c | 9:50 AM | 12:50 PM |
| Moon enters Taurus | 7:32 PM | 10:32 PM |
| Mercury conjunct Neptune begins (see March 5) | | |
| Mars conjunct Neptune begins (see March 8) | | |

*Mood Watch*: The day begins with energetic moods, but by the time the waning Aries Moon goes void-of-course, there will be a definite tendency towards false starts, restless moods, and impatience. Irritable moods will probably lead to a lot of complaints. It's a good time to keep an eye out for drivers who aren't paying attention. Later this evening, the Moon enters Taurus and this will shift our moods into a much more relaxed and down-to-earth state of being. Taurus Moon brings a comforting close to a long day of minor annoyances.

# March 1st Sunday

**Moon in Taurus**

| | PST | EST |
|---|---|---|
| Moon trine Pluto | 12:50 AM | 3:50 AM |
| Moon sextile Sun | 3:53 PM | 6:53 PM |
| Moon square Jupiter | 6:18 PM | 9:18 PM |
| Mercury conjunct Mars | 7:04 PM | 10:04 PM |

*Mood Watch*: The waxing Moon in Taurus starts up this new month with pleasure seeking moods. Many folks will be focused on their finances and on practicalities. Our moods enter into the need for beauty and – just as important – the need for comfort, too. This is a good time to tackle physical projects and to begin spring cleaning.

**Mercury conjunct Mars** (occurring Feb. 18 – March 5) This conjunction brings the forces of communication (Mercury) together with the forces of action (Mars). It brings words and deeds together, and in this case, the greatest action occurs with communication and is empowered in the expression of the message. This is an excellent conjunction to get others motivated through speech and to actively clarify your intentions through communication. This may be a time of angry words being spoken, some of which may be about things that were poorly communicated while Mercury was retrograde during the last occurrence of this conjunction on January 26, when Mercury and Mars were conjunct in Capricorn. This phase of Mercury conjunct Mars is currently taking place in the dynamic sign of Aquarius, and it is likely to bring very interesting debates and discussions with regard to human rights, science, and social programs. Take caution with your words; if they are intended to incite a battle, this would be a marvelous time to put that message out there! This conjunction last occurred January 23 – 29, reaching its peak on January 26.

# March 2ⁿᵈ Monday

♓

| Moon in Taurus | PST | EST | |
|---|---|---|---|
| Moon trine Saturn | 4:43 AM | 7:43 AM | |
| Moon square Mars | 7:01 AM | 10:01 AM | |
| Moon square Mercury | 7:41 AM | 10:41 AM | |
| Moon sextile Uranus | 10:10 AM | 1:10 PM | |
| Moon square Neptune goes v/c | 2:41 PM | 5:41 PM | |
| Moon enters Gemini | 11:58 PM | 2:58 AM | (March 3) |
| Sun opposite Saturn begins (see March 8) | | | |

*Mood Watch*: While many desire comfort and practicality with the Taurus Moon, practical needs require effort. There is a determined, almost stubborn, effort on the part of many folks to get to the place of comfort and to feel a sense of security. Meanwhile, our finances demand attention, and so does our physical environment. Count on Taurus Moon to get us in the mood to address the physical issues in our life. Today is as good a time as any to beautify and simplify the value of our surroundings. Tonight's void-of-course Moon brings the potential for a great deal of laziness and there may be a tendency for things to be misplaced. After the hard drive to achieve results, tonight would be a good time to kick back and relax.

# March 3ʳᵈ Tuesday

## FIRST QUARTER MOON in GEMINI

| Moon in Gemini | PST | EST | |
|---|---|---|---|
| Moon trine Jupiter | 10:57 PM | 1:57 AM | (March 4) |
| Moon square Sun | 11:45 PM | 2:45 AM | (March 4) |

*Mood Watch*: The Gemini Moon focuses our moods on the power of thought. This is the time to open up conversations with others and to communicate the things that have been on our minds. Sun in Pisces and Moon in Gemini brings a curious, imaginative, and creative outlook on the situations of life. People will tend to be a whole lot more flexible and, under harsh or difficult circumstances, negotiations may tend to go a lot more smoothly than expected. It doesn't hurt that the only planetary aspect occurring today, Moon trine Jupiter, will tend to put people into a more generous and adventurous mood.

# March 4ᵗʰ Wednesday

| Moon in Gemini | PST | EST |
|---|---|---|
| Moon sextile Venus | 2:16 AM | 5:16 AM |
| Moon square Saturn | 7:59 AM | 10:59 AM |
| Moon trine Mars | 1:33 PM | 4:33 PM |
| Moon square Uranus | 1:49 PM | 4:49 PM |
| Moon trine Mercury | 5:17 PM | 8:17 PM |
| Moon trine Neptune goes v/c | 6:10 PM | 9:10 PM |

*Mood Watch*: Overnight, the **First Quarter Moon in Gemini** (Moon square Sun) brings the necessity for our moods to be changeable and adaptable. Our moods are easily affected by the busy buzz of intellectual focuses and pursuits. The emphasis of covering many details at once becomes the primary objective, but not necessarily the answer to our insatiable curiosity. The act of processing information becomes essential. Do not let gossip and idle chatter be the cause of disruption in your day – thoughtlessness is also a symptom of the Gemini Moon atmosphere. The Gemini Moon puts us in touch with how we feel about our thoughts. If you don't like how you feel about your thoughts, endeavor to alter your way of thinking. Omit thoughts which attempt to defeat your sense of purpose; encourage thoughts that uplift and inspire your spirit. Be careful not to overdo the caffeine. This evening, the Moon goes void-of-course and our thoughts may seem jumbled by too much chatter. It's a good time to work on quieting the mind and avoiding disruptive subjects and discussions.

# March 5ᵗʰ Thursday

| Moon in Gemini / Cancer | PST | EST |
|---|---|---|
| Mercury conjunct Neptune | 1:39 AM | 4:39 AM |
| Moon enters Cancer | 3:06 AM | 6:06 AM |
| Moon opposite Pluto | 8:16 AM | 11:16 AM |

*Mood Watch*: The waxing Cancer Moon is generally a time when we find ourselves reviewing and expounding on the heartbeat of our emotional patterns. The Sun and Moon are in water signs and there is no escaping from emotionalism of some nature. This is a time when our feelings tend to come to the surface and require the nurturing and reassuring touch. To gain the sympathy of others, a listening ear has great merit. To persuade others, we must begin by sympathizing with their needs. It won't take long to figure out who really cares. To find oneself in an environment where nobody cares, especially in work related situations, Cancer Moon activity requires that we take some extra measures to ensure that our emotional protection mechanisms are all in place.

**Mercury conjunct Neptune** (occurring Feb. 28 – March 7) This year's only conjunction of Mercury and Neptune inspires communications on the hypersensitive issues of people's belief systems. Aquarius represents humanity, and Neptune in the sign of Aquarius focuses on the essential need for belief in humankind; that is, we must believe in ourselves and our own capabilities in order to survive spiritually. Mercury in Aquarius focuses news, talk, and discussion on human rights issues. Many people, especially Aquarians, are deeply moved to speak about their convictions. This conjunction also presents a good time to learn from the news and talk concerning humanitarian issues and to pray, meditate on, and connect with that higher spirit that dwells within.

# March 6ᵗʰ Friday

| Moon in Cancer | PST | EST |
|---|---|---|
| Moon square Venus | 5:05 AM | 8:05 AM |
| Moon trine Sun | 6:14 AM | 9:14 AM |
| Venus goes retrograde | 9:18 AM | 12:18 PM |
| Moon sextile Saturn | 10:15 AM | 1:15 PM |
| Moon trine Uranus goes v/c | 4:28 PM | 7:28 PM |
| Sun conjunct Uranus begins (see March 12) | | |

**Mood Watch**: Throughout the day, the waxing Moon in Cancer brings out our maternal instincts, and focuses our moods and feelings on the desire to nurture emotional needs. As night falls, the void-of-course Cancer Moon brings a tendency for some folks to feel disoriented, and perhaps they are emotionally out of sorts. Even those people who are good at hiding their emotions may feel challenged by the fears or uncertainties they are currently facing. Let those feelings flow; there is no point in keeping them in, as they will only continue to build up and resurface later, sometimes when least expected.

**Venus goes retrograde** (Venus retrograde: March 6 – April 17) Today the planet of love and magnetism, Venus, begins the retrograde process at the fifteen degree mark of Aries. While Venus is retrograde in Aries, the expression of love and beauty is internalized with impetuous and often impatient fervor. Love related activities tend to be forcibly or outwardly pursued, or they can be obsessively internalized. Aries is a detrimental position for Venus to begin with, and while Venus is retrograde in Aries, the internal processes of our love related focuses may undergo episodes of jealousy or competition. Those who struggle with their own sense of self-love may have a difficult time with this retrograde period. Venus brings a yearning for affection, pleasure, beauty, and for the things we love. If we cannot identify with who we are and love ourselves unconditionally, then we are likely to attract people and things to ourselves that cause conflict and confrontation. It is important to maintain and respect the source from which love flows, to recognize true love for what it is, as well as maintaining a love and respect for yourself and your personal needs. The retrograde Venus will reenter the tail end of Pisces on April 11, bringing an emphasis on the need to internalize spiritual love. Hang in there, lovers, Venus retrograde in Aries and Pisces will be teaching us about the importance of not trying to control our love pursuits and pleasures, but simply to learn to enjoy what comes our way by attracting it to us naturally and without a struggle. True control comes from within, and the retrograde Venus helps us to internalize our understanding of love relationships altogether.

# March 7th Saturday
## Moon in Cancer / Leo

| | PST | EST |
|---|---|---|
| Moon enters Leo | 5:24 AM | 8:24 AM |
| Mercury sextile Pluto begins (see March 10) | | |

**Mood Watch**: A disoriented feeling lingers in the earliest part of the day as the residual qualities of the void-of-course Cancer Moon tend to bring defensive moods. It doesn't last long though, as the Leo Moon vaults our moods into an upbeat outlook on life. Family activities and personal hobbies allow us to blow off the work week with an open and optimistic heart. A certain degree of self confidence and playfulness comes with the spirit of the waxing Leo Moon. Sun in Pisces and Moon in Leo bring lightheartedness, a strong desire for entertainment, and many folks will find themselves thoroughly ready to escape from routine. Don't forget – Daylight Saving Time begins tomorrow. We will lose an hour this weekend, so use your time wisely.

# March 8ᵗʰ Sunday

## DAYLIGHT SAVING TIME BEGINS
*Turn clocks ahead one hour at 2:00 a.m.*

| Moon in Leo | PDT | EDT | |
|---|---|---|---|
| Mars conjunct Neptune | 5:50 AM | 8:50 AM | |
| Moon opposite Jupiter | 6:20 AM | 9:20 AM | |
| Moon trine Venus | 8:04 AM | 11:04 AM | |
| Mercury enters Pisces | 11:55 AM | 2:55 PM | |
| Sun opposite Saturn | 12:53 PM | 3:53 PM | |
| Moon opposite Neptune | 11:56 PM | 2:56 AM | (March 9) |

*Daylight Saving Time:* For the third year in a row: instead of the time changes occurring on the usual first Sunday in April and last Sunday in October, Daylight Saving Time will begin much earlier and end a bit later this year. Due to the United States' Energy Policy Act of 2005, Daylight Saving Time begins today and ends on Sunday, November 1.

*Mood Watch*: Today will have some minor, but certain, ups and downs. Nevertheless, Leo Moon activities can bring memorable pleasures. The watchword for this playful tune of a Moon is "will." If one or more facets of your personal will are purposefully executed and gratefully achieved, you will have experienced a successful Leo Moon time. Appease the despotic Leo beast's nature with loving admiration and all will be well.

**Mars conjunct Neptune** (occurring Feb. 28 – March 12) Mars, the planet of activity and action, is conjunct Neptune, the planet of mysticism and spiritual bounty. This planetary conjunction generally brings action to a fondness for the arts, and magnifies generosity, spiritual activity, and enthusiasm. There is mysticism, romance, and adventure in the air with this conjunction, which will also add a special and very spiritual quality to the activities of late winter. Mars comes on very strong, directing the forces of our actions, while Neptune evokes a deeper, more dramatic spiritual awareness. This is a time to be especially careful not to overindulge in strong beverages, rich fatty foods, drugs, chemicals, anesthetics, etc. It's an important time to ensure one has the proper nutrients. Mars conjunct Neptune can also create busy activity in temples, churches or any kind of spiritual retreat. On the downside, there may be a militant flare of energy brewing in the sanctuaries of holy places. However, on a more positive note, it is an active time for folks on spiritual quests as well as artists, musicians, choreographers and designers. Mars conjunct Neptune in Aquarius activates an openness to rise above mundane concerns with heightened awareness and newly inspired spiritual strength.

**Mercury enters Pisces** (Mercury in Pisces: March 8 – 25) Today Mercury enters Pisces and this brings the emphasis of news, media, and communications on our beliefs, spiritual growth, cultural expression, and our tendencies towards escapism and drug use. Today through March 25, Mercury in Pisces brings out the mystic in all of us and adds quite a bit of color and flair to the imagination in relayed messages. This is also a good time to immerse oneself in creative writing and music or to open up the channels to the spirit world, allowing for messages from the other side to penetrate our psyches. Listen and learn from the priests, holy teachers, loved ones, and spirit guides of your choosing. Sometimes the voice of sense and reason needs to surrender to the simplicity of just listening in silence.

**Sun opposite Saturn** (occurring March 2 – 11) This occurrence of Sun opposite ♓ Saturn particularly affects those Pisces people celebrating birthdays from March 2 – 11. These birthday folks are undergoing personal challenges with regard to patience, leaving them strongly aware of who and what is in control. These people are mindful of the crucial factors of time, limitations, and timing. Work demands may be overwhelming, and these Pisces folks will have to apply discipline and determination in order to achieve success. Work that requires self motivation may be the most challenging part of applying discipline while Saturn is in Virgo. Pisces birthday folks, this is a most important time in your life to persist! Endure! Keep up the Great Work! Take heart, as this may well be your year, Birthday Pisces, to accomplish something astounding.

# March 9ᵗʰ Monday
*Full Moon Eve*

| Moon in Leo / Virgo | PDT | EDT |
|---|---|---|
| Moon opposite Mars goes v/c | 12:56 AM | 3:56 AM |
| Moon enters Virgo | 8:34 AM | 11:34 AM |
| Moon opposite Mercury | 11:11 AM | 2:11 PM |
| Moon trine Pluto | 1:49 PM | 4:49 PM |

*Mood Watch*: Early morning moods may be affected by bouts of forgetfulness, laziness, and reluctance to face the work week. As the Moon enters Virgo, its fullness can be felt. The scrutinizing qualities of the Virgo Moon atmosphere will direct us toward a more compelling need to organize, purify, and apply some cleanliness to our existence. Efficiency, thoroughness, and the need for communication – especially while the Moon opposes Mercury – is the key to this lunar energy. Be aware of the tendency towards doubtfulness and skepticism.

# March 10ᵗʰ Tuesday
**FULL MOON in VIRGO**

| Moon in Virgo | PDT | EDT | |
|---|---|---|---|
| Mercury sextile Pluto | 10:37 AM | 1:37 PM | |
| Moon conjunct Saturn | 3:26 PM | 6:26 PM | |
| Moon opposite Sun | 7:38 PM | 10:38 PM | |
| Moon opposite Uranus goes v/c | 10:48 PM | 1:48 AM | (March 11) |

*Mood Watch*: The **Full Moon in Virgo** (Moon opposite Sun) which reaches its peak this evening reminds us of the need to organize, analyze, and constructively criticize our health and cleanliness practices. Virgo also puts the focus on organization, filing, accounting, preparing taxes, and handling all of life's mundane necessities. Virgo Moon energy purges and purifies our surroundings with sound resourcefulness and simple logic. Virgo rules the intestines of the body and represents the process of elimination. Now is an excellent time to focus on eliminating toxins and purifying the body. This is also a good time to purge the useless, destructive, or outmoded habits of our life. Celebrate your existing health and do something good for your body on this Full Virgo Moon.

**Mercury sextile Pluto** (occurring March 7 – 11) Communications and discussions are facilitated, with an opportunity to get your message across in negotiations with those in positions of power. Mercury is now in Pisces, ensuring the strong belief behind our topics of communication, while Pluto in Capricorn is forcing us to acknowledge our resources and to use them wisely. Vital information regarding treatments for illness or disease may frequent the news, and news in general may well have some critical impact. This is a good time to reach out to those of another generation and make an attempt to communicate something essential. This aspect will reoccur October 26 – 30, reaching its exact aspect on October 28 with Mercury in Scorpio.

# March 11ᵗʰ Wednesday

| Moon in Virgo / Libra | PDT | EDT |
|---|---|---|
| Venus sextile Jupiter | 5:34 AM | 8:34 AM |
| Moon enters Libra | 11:46 AM | 2:46 PM |
| Moon square Pluto | 5:15 PM | 8:15 PM |

*Mood Watch*: The effects of a post-full Virgo Moon still ring with a buzz of information-sharing and questioning. Doubtfulness and scrutiny are symptoms of the fact that the Virgo Moon is void-of-course. As we prioritize our personal needs and achieve success by cherry picking our way through numerous tasks, often physical in nature, we also pull in our reins and act with a great deal more subtlety and poise. As the Moon enters Libra, we balance our doubting insecurities with the need to apply teamwork and a much more caring attitude. Logic prevails with a much more cooperative spirit.

**Venus sextile Jupiter** (occurring Feb. 7 – March 15) Venus sextile Jupiter brings a greater opportunity for increasing skills or augmenting your livelihood, especially if your focus remains on doing what you love most. Due to the retrograde cycle of Venus (March 6 – April 18), this aspect is currently reaching an exact peak for the second time. For more information on Venus in Aries sextile Jupiter in Aquarius, *see February 16*, when it first occurred. This aspect will return for a third time on June 2 and, later this year, it will occur for a fourth and final time on December 20, when Venus will be in Sagittarius.

# March 12ᵗʰ Thursday

| Moon in Libra | PDT | EDT |
|---|---|---|
| Moon opposite Venus | 1:37 PM | 4:37 PM |
| Moon trine Jupiter | 2:41 PM | 5:41 PM |
| Sun conjunct Uranus | 6:27 PM | 9:27 PM |

*Mood Watch*: Today's Libra Moon brings the stability of balance into our moods. We naturally focus on those areas of life that require the most attention, as well as the most diplomacy and tact. This is the time to share experiences with friends and working partners, to develop a sense of teamwork and togetherness. As our moods enter into the need for balance, Moon opposite Venus highlights and accentuates important love related desires and the need for companionship. It may also emphasize the demands of love and its pitfalls. Moon trine Jupiter brings harmony

82

towards our sense of joy and the need to feel prosperous. Today will be a good day to exert some energy and accomplish some goals.

**Sun conjunct Uranus** (occurring March 6 – 15) This occurrence of Sun conjunct Uranus especially affects people celebrating birthdays March 6 – 15. There may well be a healthy dollop of disruption and chaos in the lives of these folks. Radical breakthroughs that create a sense of freedom will be apparent. Sun conjunct Uranus causes strong rebellious tendencies. There is a stronger than usual Piscean desire to roll with change and take life at a different pace, to fight oppression and injustice, possibly even with an entirely off-the-wall approach to deal with calamity. Where there is knowledge to back this radical new approach, there's a way to achieve a sense of freedom with a good chance to make an impression in the year to come. This will be your year (birthday folks) to express yourselves and your innovative desires and ideas.

# March 13th Friday
**Moon in Libra / Scorpio**

| | PDT | EDT | |
|---|---|---|---|
| Moon  trine Neptune | 8:14 AM | 11:14 AM | |
| Moon  trine Mars goes v/c | 3:40 PM | 6:40 PM | |
| Moon  enters Scorpio | 5:22 PM | 8:22 PM | |
| Moon  sextile Pluto | 11:15 PM | 2:15 AM | (March 14) |
| Mars sextile Pluto begins  (see March 18) | | | |

*Mood Watch*: With internal equilibrium, there is the potential for us to balance energies interactively. Libra Moon emphasizes relationships, and a good part of today's focuses will be based on our ability to enhance our lives through the act of finding the happy medium with those whom we love and admire. Later today, as the Moon goes void-of-course, indecision or uncertainty may be the common denominators that impede on our attempts to find harmony. By evening however, the Scorpio Moon brings clear and unabashed decisiveness to the spirit of the mood. Fortunately, this *Friday the 13th* has positive lunar aspects to get us through the day amicably.

# March 14th Saturday
**Moon in Scorpio**

| | PDT | EDT | |
|---|---|---|---|
| Moon  trine Mercury | 11:46 AM | 2:46 PM | |
| Mars  enters Pisces | 8:19 PM | 11:19 PM | |
| Moon  square Jupiter | 10:53 PM | 1:53 AM | (March 15) |

*Mood Watch*: The Sun and Moon are both in water signs and some folks may find this particular time a little emotionally taxing. Sun in Pisces and Moon in Scorpio often bring some tendencies towards escapism or melodramatic behavior. This is the time to face addictions and addictive behavior with brave fortitude. Hypersensitivity and emotional intensity may be some of the signs of today's mood setting. Gentleness and kindness may be difficult to come into contact with, but there is no better way to find it than to apply it yourself.

**Mars enters Pisces** (Mars in Pisces: March 14 – April 22) Mars represents the heated energy in our lives. Force, vitality, energy, and action are influenced by

Mars. While Mars traverses Pisces, much activity is taking place with regard to music and the arts, not to mention some heated action concerning the politics of our spiritual and religious beliefs. As Mars crosses over their natal Sun during this time, Pisceans will feel lots of hot and busy energy entering their realm. The nature of Pisces is fluid, passive, and dreamy – this is the spiritual realm of the zodiac. Mars in Pisces opens the gates to active visions and dreams. Intuitive strength is realized. This is a time to activate our creativity, and to work out hot feelings, such as anger, in an artful and healthy manner. Mars is also the famed god of war, reminding us to be especially cautious given the fact that hatred, violence, aggression and strife are often touching on the pulse of our belief structures (Pisces).

# March 15th Sunday

| Moon in Scorpio | PDT | EDT |
|---|---|---|
| Moon sextile Saturn | 2:53 AM | 5:53 AM |
| Moon trine Uranus | 12:18 PM | 3:18 PM |
| Moon square Neptune | 4:47 PM | 7:47 PM |
| Moon trine Sun | 5:43 PM | 8:43 PM |
| Mercury opposite Saturn begins (see March 18) | | |

*Mood Watch*: The Sun and Moon are both in water signs and this represents a very fluid and insightful time of adaptability and transformation. Embrace safe and therapeutic outlets for emotional build-ups. Waning Scorpio Moon is a good time to release emotional energy and face certain truths that may have been overlooked or avoided during the last Full Moon. Beware of addictive or violent tendencies. There is also the potential here for breathtaking art and creativity. Scorpio Moon is an excellent time to seek out and exercise talents and skills.

# March 16th Monday

| Moon in Scorpio / Sagittarius | PDT | EDT |
|---|---|---|
| Moon enters Sagittarius | 2:22 AM | 5:22 AM |
| Moon square Mars | 4:24 AM | 7:24 AM |

*Mood Watch*: A waning Sagittarius Moon day is upon us and despite the only aspect, Moon square Mars, bringing somewhat agitated moods or dreams at the pre-dawn hours, we have an opportunity to overcome our Monday morning blues with the optimism that this Moon often brings. Waning Moon opens the pathways towards emotional release, and the Sagittarius Moon inspires us to look beyond our difficult moments with a sense of hope and enthusiasm. A creative and enchanting quality of mood gives us the impetus to see life differently, and this is always a mood altering factor we can depend on. As the final days of winter dwindle, a new spirit of hope and happiness is waiting to be claimed and the mutable Sagittarius Moon prepares us for change.

# March 17th Tuesday

**Saint Patrick's Day**

| Moon in Sagittarius | PDT | EDT |
|---|---|---|
| Moon trine Venus | 4:12 AM | 7:12 AM |

| Moon | square Mercury | 7:39 AM | 10:39 AM | |
|------|----------------|---------|----------|---|
| Moon | sextile Jupiter | 10:38 AM | 1:38 PM | |
| Moon | square Saturn | 1:25 PM | 4:25 PM | |
| Moon | square Uranus | 11:57 PM | 2:57 AM | (March 18) |

Sun square Pluto begins  (see March 23)

♓

*"I showed my appreciation of my native land in the usual Irish way by getting out of it as soon as I possibly could. "* - George Bernard Shaw (1856 – 1950)

**Mood Watch**: You don't need an Irishman to tap into some lucky feelings today; no, Sir – they're already there. The Sagittarius Moon energy brings free spirited enthusiasm. That said, there are a couple of lunar square aspects to look out for. Square aspects aren't always bad, but they do require some ingenuity to work through puzzling or sometimes difficult feelings. Quite often when we are feeling enthusiastic there is a certain degree of anticipation or expectation. With a little bit of optimism, some extra effort towards communication, and with some extra patience or tolerance thrown in for good measure, this will be a good day to enjoy. Don't forget to apply humor, it's always a safeguard for keeping up the ole morale of everyone involved.

# March 18th Wednesday
## LAST QUARTER MOON in SAGITTARIUS

| Moon in Sagittarius / Capricorn | PDT | EDT | |
|---------------------------------|-----|-----|---|
| Moon sextile Neptune | 4:32 AM | 7:32 AM | |
| Moon square Sun goes v/c | 10:47 AM | 1:47 PM | |
| Moon enters Capricorn | 2:18 PM | 5:18 PM | |
| Moon sextile Mars | 8:41 PM | 11:41 PM | |
| Moon conjunct Pluto | 8:51 PM | 11:51 PM | |
| Mercury opposite Saturn | 8:59 PM | 11:59 PM | |
| Mars sextile Pluto | 11:14 PM | 2:14 AM | (March 19) |

Mercury conjunct Uranus begins  (see March 21)

**Mood Watch**: The **Last Quarter Moon in Sagittarius** (Moon square Sun) is a good time to internalize your new wishes and thoughts about the upcoming season. At the same time, focus on healing disruptive feelings and make a sporting effort to let go of unsatisfactory habits. Sagittarius Moon focuses our attention on such things as fitness, philosophy and travel. This is the time to broaden the mind and allow yourself to go further than anticipated in realizing your vision for the future. As soon as the Last Quarter Moon commences, it also goes void-of-course for a few hours, and this leads to a temporary lull in our ability to focus. Some folks may seem to be somewhat flippant, indiscreet, or perhaps just lost or uncertain. As the Moon enters Capricorn, the determination to get things moving and to be in control empowers us to face our responsibilities and focus our efforts towards getting some work done. Once we've tackled the minor setbacks, the game plan to deal with the big stuff in life will seem a little less daunting.

**Mercury opposite Saturn** (occurring March 15 – 20) This aspect brings a very strong awareness of the need to speak out on serious and important subjects. News, talk, discussions and media tend to revolve around matters of closure, deaths, endings, and the establishment of control. There may be an overwhelming tone of command or restriction in some of the more serious subjects being communicated. While Mercury opposes Saturn, be careful where you choose to draw the lines and what you agree to when negotiating. Mercury is in Pisces, where articulate precision is usually complex or abstract in nature. Saturn is in Virgo, where it emphasizes the perimeters and security of our health and other such Virgo-like issues as the need to strive for perfection and to have a clean and practical environment. At this time we may be especially aware of the delicate subject of how rules and laws are affecting our health and our wellbeing.

**Mars sextile Pluto** (occurring March 13 – 21) Mars, the planet of action is in a favorable position to Pluto, the planet of the generations. Mars is in the early degrees of Pisces sextile to Pluto in the early degrees of Capricorn. This is a superb time to take up activities with people of a different culture, or with someone who is of a different level of maturity or experience. This is also potentially a good time to reconcile differences. Those who are not in accordance with others at this time are likely to stand out – quite obviously. This may be a beneficial aspect for successfully recuperating from an illness. Mars represents the masculine push of our personal lives, the area where we activate our will, strength, and vitality; this brings opportunity, optimism, and the added boost to face otherwise tense situations and predicaments. The activities of Mars sextile Pluto will teach us about hardships and what we can learn from other generations. Some will make breakthroughs during this time. Some may choose to be more forgiving of the destructive behaviors of previous generations. All around, tender care is advised in your efforts to create peace.

# March 19th Thursday

| Moon in Capricorn | PDT | EDT |
|---|---|---|
| Moon square Venus | 2:31 PM | 5:31 PM |

*Mood Watch*: Yesterday's busy course of lunar events kept our moods diligently working through various emotional responses. Today's waning Capricorn Moon urges us to face our sense of duty with a lot less distraction. There is a great deal to comprehend and process as the Moon wanes in Capricorn, but the restrictive tendencies of emotional interruptions are often subdued for the sake of clarity and function. A time comes when we must set our emotions aside and deal with important matters and this is often the Moon to do the job. This is the last day of winter and as the nighttime hours give way to the dawning seasons of the Sun, our moods are steadied by the unwavering qualities of determination the Capricorn Moon brings.

# ARIES

Key Phrase: "I AM"
Cardinal Fire Sign
Ruling Planet: Mars
Symbol: The Ram
March 20th through April 19th

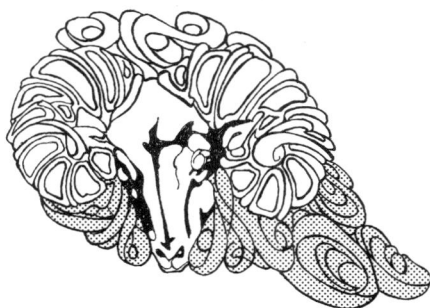

## March 20th Friday

Vernal Equinox

| Moon in Capricorn | PDT | EDT |
|---|---|---|
| Moon trine Saturn | 1:47 AM | 4:47 AM |
| Sun enters Aries | 4:43 AM | 7:43 AM |
| Moon sextile Mercury | 7:13 AM | 10:13 AM |
| Moon sextile Uranus goes v/c | 1:05 PM | 4:05 PM |

*Mood Watch*: The drive to get things done continues to influence our Capricorn Moon moods. As the new season commences, this is the time to develop and empower our goals and aims in life. Serious and determined moods empower us to give those goals the proper charge to achieve what we hope to accomplish. As the Moon goes void-of-course this afternoon, that drive to perform may be stunted by minor contingencies and unexpected setbacks. This evening would be a good time to lighten up on your expectations and apply some patience.

**Sun enters Aries** (Sun in Aries: March 20 – April 19) Today, the event classically called **Vernal Equinox**, also known as Spring Equinox, marks the start of a new season and the beginning of the zodiac. This is the time when the daylight hours are equal in length to the hours of the night. Spring arrives when the earth is tilted so the Sun is directly over the equator. In the northern parts of the world, the first day of spring is on or about March 20. In the northern hemisphere we are on the side of the Equinox that returns toward the light, as opposed to Autumnal Equinox when the Sun enters Libra, the opposite of Aries. With Daylight Savings Time already underway since March 8, we now celebrate the continued lengthening of the days.

The Sun in Aries inspires courageous and bold new beginnings, as well as instilling confidence and forcefulness. Many Aries folks have an inherent desire to not only survive, but to exceed, and to make a lasting impression. Aries is the cardinal fire sign that doesn't give up easily. Arians are known for beginning projects with a pioneering zeal. However, they are also infamous for suddenly leaping into a new venture, leaving someone else to complete their original endeavor. Some Aries folks love to start up businesses, but continue into other ventures once the business has been established and requires the dull monotony of upkeep and maintenance. The Aries character typically expresses quality of leadership in the fiery realm of the cardinal signs, and is ruled by the active and vital planet, Mars. Aries boasts of being the first, and works earnestly to defy all who would mock, criticize, or misunderstand their drive to reach a certain self-appointed plateau of excellence. There is a strong sense of devotion to the self and the need to excel in the Arian's chosen field. The Mars ruled Aries person is loaded with fervor and a relentless fortitude that often, at best, motivates and inspires – or, at worst, repels and puts off others around them. Sun in Aries serves as a good time to initiate new projects and apply diligence with inspired ability. The youthful vigor that is characteristic of Arians is reflected in the season, and this springlike sprouting and growth is inspiration for us all.

# March 21st Saturday
## Moon in Capricorn / Aquarius

| | PDT | EDT | |
|---|---|---|---|
| Moon enters Aquarius | 3:06 AM | 6:06 AM | |
| Moon sextile Sun | 5:08 AM | 8:08 AM | |
| Mercury conjunct Uranus | 10:01 PM | 1:01 AM | (March 22) |

*Mood Watch*: Yesterday was a partly winter and partly spring day. The day of spring equinox, which encompasses both Pisces and Aries, could be called a "win-spri" day. Today, however, the sun is in Aries for the entire day and that makes this the official first *full* day of spring. How much of it will be acting like spring remains to be seen as the travails of unexpected weather patterns continue to baffle us in these years of global warming. The Aquarius Moon urges us to consider all those people around us who both effect, and are affected by, the course of nature's actions. Aquarius Moon brings out our urges to tackle humankind's biggest puzzles. This is a time when awareness is easily absorbed; it's a good time to raise consciousness and increase knowledge.

**Mercury conjunct Uranus** (occurring March 18 – 23) Mercury and Uranus are conjunct in Pisces, giving birth to radical, bright, inspired and intuitive ideas. This may raise some very interesting and unusual questions about what we choose to believe in. Consciousness raising talk is prevalent. Mercury conjunct Uranus magnifies the volume of shocking or question-raising news, and stirs the minds and mouths of rebels and non-conformists who are inspired to speak out. Everyone is crying for some kind of freedom!

# March 22nd Sunday
## Moon in Aquarius

| | PDT | EDT |
|---|---|---|
| Moon sextile Venus | 12:17 AM | 3:17 AM |
| Moon conjunct Jupiter | 1:31 PM | 4:31 PM |

*Mood Watch*: Quite often, the waning Aquarius Moon opens up our sense of scientific foresight. Aquarius Moon gives us the incentive to tackle puzzling problems, and the waning Aquarius Moon often leaves us contemplative over the types of problems that could only be described as "man made." If there's some form of logic that got us into a mess, there is indeed another kind of logic that will get us out of it. The Aquarius Moon gives our moods the extra push to seek out the knowledge that is necessary to succeed.

# March 23rd Monday

| Moon in Aquarius / Pisces | PDT | EDT |
|---|---|---|
| Moon conjunct Neptune goes v/c | 5:08 AM | 8:08 AM |
| Sun square Pluto | 11:35 AM | 2:35 PM |
| Moon enters Pisces | 2:07 PM | 5:07 PM |
| Moon sextile Pluto | 8:21 PM | 11:21 PM |
| Sun conjunct Venus begins (see March 27) | | |

♈

*Mood Watch*: It just may be one of those Monday morning days, a day when the void-of-course Aquarius Moon has us frustrated by technical glitches, misinformation, and general attitudes brought on by laziness and ignorance. Later today, as the waning Moon enters Pisces, there may be tendencies towards escapism as well as the need for musical and artistic output. This is a good time to take things in stride and don't forget to laugh.

**Sun square Pluto** (occurring March 17 – 26) This aspect particularly affects late-born Pisces and early-born Aries people celebrating birthdays this month from March 17 – 26. For them, Pluto squaring their natal Sun brings disruptive changes and many challenges to overcome, such as the pain of loss and the severity of transformation. As well, Virgo and Libra people who are born at the exact opposite of this early Aries time of year must also change in order to progress through these necessary Pluto-inspired tests of transformation. These tests often involve dealing with illness and loss, irreparable damage, and dramatic life changes. Late-born Sagittarians and early-born Capricorns (Pluto conjunct natal Sun), as well as late-born Geminis and early-born Cancer people (Pluto opposite natal Sun) also know what these tests of Pluto are about, as Pluto continues to trace a slow moving path through the late degrees of Sagittarius and into the earliest degrees of Capricorn. Trying to hold onto the regrets and the pain of the past will only bring greater destruction later. This is the time to persevere through the obstacles of hardship. Yet, the hardships that are taking place now will resurface in time, so do take note of the struggles going on in the lives of Pisces/Aries, Virgo/Libra, Gemini/Cancer, and Sagittarius/Capricorn (cusp born) people affected by Pluto's tests. Realize this trend will be repeated, and so necessitates finding methods of release and attitude changes in order to survive the anxiety and stress. Take it one day at a time and do not let fear and worry rule this condition. Know that you are not alone in facing these challenges. Move steadily through the required transformation, as stagnation and fear will only bring extended suffering. This aspect returns during the same date range in September (Sept. 17 – 26), reaching its exact peak on September 23, when the Sun will be in Virgo at the cusp of Libra, affecting the Virgo/Libra birthday people of that time.

# March 24th Tuesday

| Moon in Pisces | PDT | EDT | |
|---|---|---|---|
| Moon conjunct Mars | 4:01 AM | 7:01 AM | |
| Moon opposite Saturn | 10:23 PM | 1:23 AM | (March 25) |
| Mercury square Pluto begins (see March 27) | | | |
| Sun conjunct Mercury begins (see March 30) | | | |
| Venus square Pluto begins (see April 3) | | | |

89

*Mood Watch*: The waning Pisces Moon brings reflective, intuitive, and energetic flow to the course of our moods. This is also a time when we may be especially hypersensitive to drugs and alcohol. Other symptoms of the waning Pisces Moon may bring susceptibility to foot problems and stress-related illnesses. This is a good time to seek beneficial health programs and therapeutic practices. Stressful times require a little bit of pampering.

# March 25th Wednesday
**Moon in Pisces / Aries**

| | PDT | EDT | |
|---|---|---|---|
| Moon conjunct Uranus goes v/c | 9:51 AM | 12:51 PM | |
| Mercury enters Aries | 12:54 PM | 3:54 PM | |
| Moon enters Aries | 10:01 PM | 1:01 AM | (March 26) |
| Moon conjunct Mercury | 11:35 PM | 2:35 AM | (March 26) |

*Mood Watch*: The darkly waning Pisces Moon goes void-of-course early today and, unfortunately, it will remain void-of-course for the entire day and evening. The prevalent mood of the day is likely to be spacey and inattentive. This is good if there's room to be creative, but wherever it is necessary to make progress during the midcourse of the week, we may find a lack of attentiveness – or cooperation with the universe – to complete tasks and chores on time. Much later tonight, the Aries Moon brings self-assurance and confidence to our moods.

**Mercury enters Aries** (Mercury in Aries: March 25 – April 9) Mercury now enters Aries, bringing a focus of communications on selfhood, initiation, new projects, and new ways of seeing and experiencing life. We are all perpetually in the process of being initiated into some aspect of selfhood, particularly given that we are constantly learning, acquiring new skills, growing and aging. Mercury in Aries brings some lively heat to our communications and discussions. Mercury is the messenger, activating information, and Aries is the warrior and the force of nature that takes on life with fearless vigor and aggression. Communications possess a quality of command and a pioneering spirit. Now through April 9, while Mercury is in Aries, talk, news and discussions will be actively focused on the challenging and demanding enterprises and battles that await us.

# March 26th Thursday
**NEW MOON in ARIES**
**Moon in Aries**

| | PDT | EDT |
|---|---|---|
| Moon square Pluto | 3:57 AM | 6:57 AM |
| Moon conjunct Sun | 9:05 AM | 12:05 PM |
| Moon conjunct Venus | 12:13 PM | 3:13 PM |
| Mercury conjunct Venus begins (see March 28) | | |

*Mood Watch*: The **New Moon in Aries** (Moon conjunct Sun) invokes the powers of initiation; it is the essential part of regenerative force to take the initiative and to start anew. This is the time when the new parts of the self begin to emerge, and our moods are encouraged by confidence, motivation, courageousness, and fiery intent. Now is the time to generate and promote inspiration and happiness. In general, the spirit of our moods brings a strong sense of newness and a great deal of activity.

# March 27ᵗʰ Friday

**Moon in Aries**

| | PDT | EDT |
|---|---|---|
| Mercury square Pluto | 5:15 AM | 8:15 AM |
| Moon sextile Jupiter | 6:37 AM | 9:37 AM |
| Sun conjunct Venus | 12:23 PM | 3:23 PM |
| Moon sextile Neptune goes v/c | 7:16 PM | 10:16 PM |

*Mood Watch*: Aries Moon brings ambitious, energetic, and sometimes competitive moods. This is a good time to build on self-confidence and courage. This youthful, newly emerging, and newly waxing Moon goes void-of-course this evening and, for some, false starts may occur as a result of impetuous and hasty behavior.

**Mercury square Pluto** (occurring March 24 – 28) Mercury in Aries is square to Pluto in Capricorn. Scrutiny and doubt make it difficult to communicate with those of another generation. This is a particularly difficult time to deal with burdensome issues and discuss them in a manner that relieves tension. Mercury square Pluto often brings harsh and sometimes fatal news. Talk revolves around the corruption of superpowers and the setbacks caused by this corruption. This may be an especially difficult time to discuss matters involving permanent change. Due to the retrograde cycle of Mercury this summer and autumn (Sept. 6/7 – 29,) this aspect will reoccur on three more occasions; August 26, September 17, and October 10, each time with Mercury at the zero degree mark of Libra.

**Sun conjunct Venus** (occurring March 23 – 29) The Sun and Venus are conjunct in Aries. This conjunction particularly affects the love lives of those Aries people celebrating birthdays from March 23 – 29. These birthday folks are being filled with the need to have or to express love as best as they can and this is the year for them to address the love matters in their lives. There is an attraction which draws us to beauty, romance, and love when Venus connects with the natal solar degrees. The issue of love is unavoidable, and these birthday folks's love needs become evident whether they wish to acknowledge them or not. It is through the attraction magnet of Venus that the personality (Sun sign) is assured of that with which they choose to identify, be affected by, and attracted to. Sometimes sheer magnetism is unavoidable and an event or relationship cannot be chosen – it just happens. This can encompass not only love matters, but also other areas such as the arts, aesthetics or appreciation of beauty. This will be a year of love, birthday Aries people. This is the only time this conjunction will reach an exact peak in 2009. However, Sun conjunct Venus will begin occurring again in the sign of Sagittarius on December 17, reaching the peak conjunction in Capricorn on January 10, 2010. At that time, the Sun and Venus conjunction will have a similar (love related) affect on Sagittarians and Capricorns celebrating birthdays from December 17, 2009 – January 21, 2010.

# March 28th Saturday

**Moon in Aries / Taurus**

| | PDT | EDT | |
|---|---|---|---|
| Moon enters Taurus | 3:08 AM | 6:08 AM | |
| Moon trine Pluto | 8:50 AM | 11:50 AM | |
| Mercury conjunct Venus | 7:31 PM | 10:31 PM | |
| Moon sextile Mars | 10:10 PM | 1:10 AM | (March 29) |
| Mars opposite Saturn begins (see April 4) | | | |

*Mood Watch*: The Moon is exalted in the constellation Taurus. The physical world is in a state of reflection with our sensibilities. This is where we turn to environmental awareness, practical sense, business savvy, and the necessities of the body. This is a good time to actively secure those aspects of life that are in need of improvement on the physical level. Taurus governs the neck, throat – including that muscular wonder, the tongue – as well as the taste buds and tonsils, voice box and windpipe, down to the thyroid and parathyroid glands. It's a good time to nurture and care for these parts of the body.

**Mercury conjunct Venus** (occurring March 26 – 29) Today's conjunction of Mercury and Venus takes place in the swift and intrepid sign, Aries, bringing ardent and heartfelt fervor to our communications. These two planets conjunct in Aries brings a very strong personal connection to the communication of love, particularly for those Aries folks celebrating a birthday during the time of this conjunction. Any words of love or adoration uttered now may come across more easily – and with better reception – as long as this expression of love is actually very sincere and genuine. Mercury conjunct Venus in Aries sometimes brings a demanding tone to discussions among loved ones, and it may create an urgent quality in negotiations over such prized items as art and valuables. At this time, communications are received best when they are delivered with considerable care. Be sure to let those whom you love know it; sometimes it's what isn't said that disquiets the heart. Hold no expectations in the expression of love, and take no offense if your attempts to express love are poorly interpreted. Know that there is a need to communicate love occurring now, and that the most simple and direct way to express love might be best.

# March 29th Sunday

**Moon in Taurus**

| | PDT | EDT | |
|---|---|---|---|
| Moon trine Saturn | 8:03 AM | 11:03 AM | |
| Moon square Jupiter | 11:17 AM | 2:17 PM | |
| Moon sextile Uranus | 7:38 PM | 10:38 PM | |
| Moon square Neptune goes v/c | 11:00 PM | 2:00 AM | (March 30) |

*Mood Watch*: Taurus Moon days are always there to remind us to revamp our financial situations and to tend to our physical needs, especially as month's end approaches. This morning starts out productively with the favorable Moon trine Saturn, which allows us to focus on our strengths and limitations, and to make headway with our duties. Later in the morning/afternoon Moon square Jupiter tends to slow down desires to reach into the pocketbook and people may be feeling a little less generous at this time. Later on in the evening, Moon sextile

Uranus shakes things up with our attitudes towards life and by this time there may be a little more flamboyance added to the affairs of the day. Much later, Moon square Neptune brings a void-of-course Moon, a good time to get some shut-eye and to avoid touchy spiritual or emotional subjects.

# March 30th Monday
**Moon in Taurus / Gemini**

| | PDT | EDT |
|---|---|---|
| Moon enters Gemini | 6:35 AM | 9:35 AM |
| Moon sextile Venus | 3:37 PM | 6:37 PM |
| Sun conjunct Mercury | 8:28 PM | 11:28 PM |

*Mood Watch*: Early this morning begins rather lazily with the Moon void-of-course in Taurus. Soon enough though, the Moon enters Gemini and the tendency of the day is to focus on and deal with details – lots and lots of them. This is a superb time to focus on organization and communication. Today's only lunar aspect, Moon sextile Venus, brings the potential for affectionate moods.

**Sun conjunct Mercury** (occurring March 24 – April 2) This aspect will create a much more thoughtful, communicative and expressive year ahead for those Aries folks celebrating birthdays March 24 – April 2. This is your time (birthday Aries) to record ideas, relay important messages, and pay close attention to your imaginative thoughts as they are touched by Mercury, creating the urge to speak and be heard. Birthday Aries, your thoughts will reveal a great deal about who you are, now and in the year to come.

# March 31st Tuesday
**Moon in Gemini**

| | PDT | EDT | |
|---|---|---|---|
| Moon sextile Sun | 12:49 AM | 3:49 AM | |
| Moon sextile Mercury | 1:12 AM | 4:12 AM | |
| Moon square Mars | 4:18 AM | 7:18 AM | |
| Moon square Saturn | 10:50 AM | 1:50 PM | |
| Moon trine Jupiter | 2:59 PM | 5:59 PM | |
| Moon square Uranus | 10:48 PM | 1:48 AM | (April 1) |

*Mood Watch*: The last day of the month comes with a waxing Gemini Moon and a number of early morning lunar aspects which keeps our predawn dreams hoppin'. Some folks may feel a little tired or somewhat lacking in motivation as the Moon squares with Saturn. Later today, Moon trine Jupiter picks up our attitudes with a nice jolt of joy, and the feeling of prosperity or advancement of some kind will enhance conversations. Much later on, Moon square Uranus tends to bring reckless or destructive feelings. Perhaps it was something someone said? Don't let the idle chatter of a waxing Gemini Moon depress your attitude; positive affirmations first thing in the morning, and last thing at night are important ways to empower personal freedom. Gemini Moon is a good time to weed out negative thoughts and to contemplate life's finer potential.

# April 1st Wednesday

**April Fool's Day**

| Moon in Gemini / Cancer | PDT | EDT |
|---|---|---|
| Moon trine Neptune goes v/c | 2:02 AM | 5:02 AM |
| Moon enters Cancer | 9:30 AM | 12:30 PM |
| Moon opposite Pluto | 3:06 PM | 6:06 PM |
| Moon square Venus | 4:28 PM | 7:28 PM |

*Mood Watch*: Early this morning the Gemini Moon goes void-of-course, which may put a damper on our morning endeavors with confusion over details. This may be a frustrating time to try to communicate effectively, or to get anyone to agree on the facts as you know them. No matter, by morning/early afternoon the Moon enters Cancer, and by then the focus of our mood may be virtually unpredictable. The waxing Cancer Moon tunes us into the true nature of our feelings, which for some people comes as a surprise, while to others, emotional responsiveness is a matter of course.

Happy **April Fool's Day**, also known as *All Fools' Day*. This is a holiday of uncertain origin, but just about everybody knows it as the day for practical joking. Before the adoption of the Gregorian calendar in 1564, April 1st was observed as New Year's Day by many cultures from the Roman to the Hindu. This holiday is considered to be related to the festival of the Vernal Equinox, when the Sun enters Aries, on or about March 20th. The English gave April Fool's Day its first widespread celebration during the 18th century, where it quickly spread to the American colonies. Remember the classic North American school prank of anonymously taping a sign on the back of a fellow classmate? The sign customarily reads something degrading such as: "Kick Me," or "April Fool." The French call April 1st *Poisson d'Avril,* (April Fish). French children tape a picture of a fish on the back of their schoolmates, crying "Poisson D'Avril," when the prank is discovered. Our Full Libra Moon moods allow us to take simple pranks in stride. If something fishy is occurring around you, remember to keep the jokes in perspective, and to watch the backs of those you care about. Cancer Moon can have a alarming affect on our ability to be the brunt of someone's victimizing sense of humor.

# April 2nd Thursday

**FIRST QUARTER MOON in CANCER**

| Moon in Cancer | PDT | EDT |
|---|---|---|
| Moon square Sun | 7:33 AM | 10:33 AM |
| Moon trine Mars | 10:12 AM | 1:12 PM |
| Moon square Mercury | 12:46 PM | 3:46 PM |
| Moon sextile Saturn | 1:31 PM | 4:31 PM |
| Mercury sextile Jupiter begins  (see April 4) | | |

*Mood Watch*: The **First Quarter Moon in Cancer** (Moon square Sun) urges us to share our feelings and take care of emotional needs, particularly in our home. Home focused activities bring warm expressions of contentment. With First Quarter Cancer Moon the emotional current tends to be magnified. Nutritional foods and trustworthy company are important components of today's activities. Treating ourselves and others in a nurturing way becomes the key to enhancing or cleansing our emotional perspective. Be careful not to push the buttons of sensitive people and use words wisely while considering the feelings of yourself and others.

# April 3rd Friday

| Moon in Cancer / Leo | PDT | EDT |
|---|---|---|
| Moon trine Uranus goes v/c | 1:58 AM | 4:58 AM |
| Venus square Pluto | 3:24 AM | 6:24 AM |
| Moon enters Leo | 12:32 PM | 3:32 PM |
| Moon trine Venus | 5:38 PM | 8:38 PM |
| Jupiter conjunct Neptune begins (see May 27) – NOTABLE CONJUNCTION | | |

*Mood Watch*: Today's void-of-course Cancer Moon may have a defensive, or offensive, quality of mood. This is not the time to push people's emotional buttons – that is, if one is not willing to bear the brunt of the consequences. Kindness and patience will go a long way, and a listening ear will also have its merits. If you need to avoid conflict, don't buy the guilt. There is no point in rubbing your nose in trouble if you are not emotionally prepared. As for the rest of the day, the welcoming moods of the Leo Moon allow for smoother family encounters, particularly with Moon trine Venus. Enjoy the creative energy of the Leo Moon atmosphere!

**Venus square Pluto** (occurring March 24 – April 10) Since March 6, Venus in Aries has been retrograde (March 6 – April 17) and it is currently working its way back through the earliest degrees of Aries. This brings a repeat of Venus square Pluto, currently reaching its second peak of the year since February 5. Bear in mind that as Venus is now retrograde, the loving qualities of dealing with hardship may appear somewhat withdrawn and people may tend to privately internalize their perceptions of beauty and love rather than openly share their tenderness and affections. This aspect will reoccur April 29 – May 7, reaching its exact aspect on May 2. This aspect will also reoccur October 10 – 17, reaching its peak on October 15, with Venus in Libra and Pluto in Capricorn. For a recap on the story of Venus in Aries square Pluto in Capricorn, *see February 5*, when it first occurred this year.

# April 4th Saturday

| Moon in Leo | PDT | EDT | |
|---|---|---|---|
| Mercury sextile Jupiter | 7:58 AM | 10:58 AM | |
| Pluto goes retrograde | 10:36 AM | 1:36 PM | |
| Moon trine Sun | 2:38 PM | 5:38 PM | |
| Mars opposite Saturn | 5:54 PM | 8:54 PM | |
| Moon opposite Jupiter | 10:35 PM | 1:35 AM | (April 5) |

*Mood Watch*: A Leo Moon Saturday invites us to enjoy personal hobbies, self-made adventure, and family endeavors. Sun in Aries and Moon in Leo brings a fiery and creative time, as well as strong urges.

**Mercury sextile Jupiter** (occurring April 2 – 5) This aspect offers the potential for good news of growth and prosperity, especially for those who are open to broadening their awareness. Mercury brings news and talk, while Jupiter brings wealth and prosperous advancement. The money flows where our attention goes. It may be an advantageous time to ask for a job or a loan. Communicating our aspirations (Mercury in Aries) brings opportunities and the potential for success (the sextile aspect) in typical Aquarian endeavors. These include the growth of invention, the expansion of technology, victories for human rights, and advancements in psychology, anthropology, charity work, and the unconventional sciences (Jupiter in Aquarius). Opportunity exists for both the employer and the employee. Mercury sextile Jupiter brings joyful and mind expanding conversations. This aspect will reoccur November 26 – 30, and reaches an exact peak on November 29 with Mercury in Sagittarius.

**Pluto goes retrograde** (Pluto retrograde: April 4 – Sept. 11) Processes governed by Pluto take the longest time to go through since, from our perspective, Pluto appears to move the slowest of all the planets because it's the furthest away from us. Pluto goes retrograde today and when it resumes a forward moving course late this summer, it will have traveled only a few degrees in the sky, which is average for a Pluto retrograde period. This means the types of hardships that have been created and brought to our attention in the past five months must be addressed all over again, and that we must acknowledge the evolution of humankind's current condition in order to survive the changes that are occurring on Earth.

Pluto deals with the changes that occur in attitude according to the overall group consciousness of each of the generations. Each generation has its own insight as to what hardship represents. This is a time to make life better by consciously transforming fear into determination and despair into belief in oneself, no matter what condition of fate surrounds you. The destructive habits, prejudices, sufferings and haunts of previous generations must be acknowledged and addressed – and of course – altered to enable us to tackle the world of the future. We will all face greater challenges and tests of epic proportions, and outdated concerns must be dealt with so that we may find solutions to the new problems in front of us.

With Pluto's changes we must face tragedies, diseases, losses, shattered dreams, and altered or unexpected doses of reality. Pluto retrograde forces us to look within; this is a good time to confirm our greatest strengths by directing abusive patterns into constructive and useful disciplines which will reshape and bring hope to the emerging outlook on life.

Pluto represents the forces of power and control, which are always in a state of flux due to our mortal tango with fate. Our old concepts and memories of how life once was, or is supposed to be, are dying with the times. Pluto will go retrograde back to the zero degree mark (the Cusp) of Capricorn, and although it doesn't actually return to the Sagittarius constellation, it is still making the transition from Sagittarius related changes. Reality and normality are illusions that Pluto sweeps away as its final salute to Sagittarius opens up the last visionary glimpses of our transformational understanding of global awareness, and as it increases our foresight of worldwide struggles. There are aspects of life that are not meant to be controlled, but how we react to the shifts of this time is something we do control. Pluto retrograde is a time of readdressing universal human problems that take decades to fix.

Pluto, newly in the sign of Capricorn (since Jan. 25, 2008), will now influence Capricorn such related focuses as corporate growth, architectural feats, monumental achievements, industrial capitalization, environmental control, and many unprecedented forms of success and goal attainment. It is through the retrograde process that Pluto in Capricorn will shape and re-examine our views and perspectives on the large scale changes occurring on our planet. ♈

**Mars opposite Saturn** (occurring March 28 – April 8) Mars opposite Saturn always makes us aware of the timeliness of our actions and the importance of acting in a timely manner, for example, doing something about a problem before it's too late. Medical emergencies often crop up with this particular aspect. There will also be an awareness of the dynamic polarity between offensive and defensive forces. For opposing forces in battle, this aspect often brings fiery and sometimes tragic endings. Mars in Pisces is opposing the retrograde Saturn in Virgo, which accentuates sneak attacks on the structure of our established rules and protocol. Saturn has been retrograde since December 31, 2008, and will go direct on May 16, 2009. Saturn is the restrictive discipline behind every effort to contain, guard, and hold onto what matters to us. Mars in Pisces brings unexpected action to all modes of attack. Saturn in the place of Virgo emphasizes the need to face our responsibilities, particularly with regard to communicating important information in a timely manner. Pay attention to those aspects of life that hold active potential for accidents. The popular old adage of "look before you leap" is a good meditation to apply during this crucial time of Mars opposite Saturn.

# April 5ᵗʰ Sunday

**Palm Sunday**

| Moon in Leo / Virgo | PDT | EDT | |
|---|---|---|---|
| Moon  trine Mercury | 12:55 AM | 3:55 AM | |
| Moon opposite Neptune goes v/c | 8:38 AM | 11:38 AM | |
| Moon  enters Virgo | 4:01 PM | 7:01 PM | |
| Moon  trine Pluto | 9:43 PM | 12:43 AM | (April 6) |
| Mercury sextile Neptune begins  (see April 7) | | | |
| Sun sextile Jupiter begins  (see April 10) | | | |

*Mood Watch*: Willpower is one of the keys to the Leo Moon, but since today's Leo Moon will be void-of-course for most of the day, our sense of willpower may be distracted, deterred by delays, or brought to an end by other people's infringements. Wishy-washy qualities of mood are at work. This is no time to get caught up in selfishness, be it yours, or others' self-delusions. As the Moon enters Virgo, a more analytical quality of mood allows us to speak out a little more clearly on our thoughts. This evening will be a good time to wash the day's events out of your hair.

# April 6ᵗʰ Monday

| Moon in Virgo | PDT | EDT | |
|---|---|---|---|
| Moon  conjunct Saturn | 8:11 PM | 11:11 PM | |
| Moon  opposite Mars | 11:27 PM | 2:27 AM | (April 7) |
| Mars conjunct Uranus begins  (see April 15) | | | |

*Mood Watch*: Virgo Moon moods bring ingenuity and the desire for cleanliness and keenness of spirit. Since Virgo is ruled by Mercury, we must not forget that there is a certain degree of willingness to debate, deliberate, and argue for the sake of our ideals or principles. In the midst of all this scrutiny, there is a shyness, or prudence in our demeanor that allows for some dignity and discernment. Not everything in the universe is worth debating. We must not forget our ignorance, as it is still quite impossible to know it all. The Virgo Moon keeps us curious and this is why we question so much. Keep a cool head and your day will be rewarding. It is easier to admit what you don't know than it is to argue what you do.

# April 7th Tuesday

**Moon in Virgo / Libra**

| | PDT | EDT | |
|---|---|---|---|
| Mercury sextile Neptune | 5:37 AM | 8:37 AM | |
| Moon opposite Uranus goes v/c | 9:52 AM | 12:52 PM | |
| Moon enters Libra | 8:22 PM | 11:22 PM | |
| Moon opposite Venus | 10:15 PM | 1:15 AM | (April 8) |
| Mercury trine Pluto begins (see April 10) | | | |

*Mood Watch*: Most of yesterday's Virgo Moon meditations are applicable today, especially since this Virgo Moon will be void-of-course for most of the day and well into evening. This is a good time to *avoid* arguments, or to expect to bear the wrath of some excruciating criticisms. Everyone is a critic, but the best critics are the ones who have walked in your shoes. Our questioning moods are likely to bring contingencies, delays, and missed appointments. If you want to be on time, you'll have to be blunt and frank, but this doesn't mean you have to be rude. Tonight's Libra Moon offers peace of mind, and perhaps, some balance to your thoughts.

**Mercury sextile Neptune** (occurring April 5 – 8) Mercury in Aries sextile Neptune in Aquarius brings bold, independent messages that inform us of opportunities for spiritual growth in humanity. This is an opportunistic time to cautiously attempt communication with regard to beliefs and spiritual matters. Mercury is in Aries adding a fiery urgency to the question of how to face such Neptune related subjects as spiritual strength, guidance, and inspiration. Address addiction problems with helpful instruction. Prayers, channeling, and spells are all very effective with Mercury sextile Neptune. This is the time to get the word out to Great Spirit, and to reinforce a sense of faith or an acceptance of the way life is going. Mercury sextile Neptune allows us to verbalize and share beliefs in a way that encourages people. This aspect will reoccur November 28 – December 2, reaching its exact aspect on December 1.

# April 8th Wednesday

**Holy Day of Thelema (Nuit) /** *Full Moon Eve*

**Moon in Libra**

| | PDT | EDT |
|---|---|---|
| Moon square Pluto | 2:12 AM | 5:12 AM |

" *Every man and every woman is a star.* " *- LIBER AL vel LEGIS,* 1904

*Mood Watch*: The Moon waxes brightly in Libra and it is currently on the brink of fullness. This is the time to ask, seek, and knock. It's a time to create equilibrium in your life, to address the excesses of your lifestyle and to balance those excesses with assertive diplomacy. Many of the lifestyle changes that we choose to make affect the people around us. It is wise to consider the nature of all things and the people who directly affect us before choosing to make personal adjustments. Full Libra Moon keeps us busy thinking about the consequences of our actions. Positive actions often have an infectiously optimistic affect on others. Spread the goodness!

# April 9th Thursday
**Holy Day of Thelema (Hadit)**
**FULL MOON in LIBRA**

| Moon in Libra | PDT | EDT |
|---|---|---|
| Mercury enters Taurus | 7:21 AM | 10:21 AM |
| Moon opposite Sun | 7:56 AM | 10:56 AM |
| Moon trine Jupiter | 9:21 AM | 12:21 PM |
| Moon trine Neptune goes v/c | 6:45 PM | 9:45 PM |

*" Let the rituals be rightly performed with joy & beauty ! "* - LIBER AL vel LEGIS, 1904

*Mood Watch*: **Full Moon in Libra** (Moon opposite Sun) brings events that revolve around such things as law, the justice system, friends, and marital partners. Relationships are a balancing act. Friends will share their strengths as well as their weaknesses. Troubled times can strengthen even the weakest links in friendship. Refuse to contribute to the weakness of a friend; nurture friendship with patience, understanding, and encouragement. Use this Full Libra Moon energy to empower your relationships. Diplomacy, peace and goodwill can be achieved among loved ones, but a definite effort is required. Tonight the post-full Libra Moon goes void-of-course and this is a good time to take it easy.

**Mercury enters Taurus** (Mercury in Taurus: April 9 – 30) Mercury moves into the sign of Taurus, and communications will focus on manifesting sales and generating economic growth. It is a good time to clarify matters involving valuables, and to focus on documents, contracts, speeches, and business procedures. Mercury in Taurus brings on a new wave of discussion about the natural beauties and luxuries that surround us, and there is also an equal concern for practicality. Mercury is the messenger, the speaker and the director of the subject matter at hand. Mercury is also classically known as "The Merchant," "The Trickster," and "The Thief." In the fixed earth sign of Taurus, Mercury inspires the inclination to buy, sell, trade, and barter. Issues of ownership and, undoubtedly, a "steal of a deal" will appear in the arena of barter. Resourceful thinking and information processing can lead to the extra buck. This is a time to accurately record practical matters and events, and to communicate about finances. Mercury will be in Taurus for an extended period this year since it will go retrograde (May 6/7 -30), and it will return to the late degrees of Taurus on May 13. Mercury retrograde in Taurus (May 13 – June 13) may bring disputes over possessions, or over the necessity for practicality and economic viability. For more information on Mercury retrograde, see the section in the introduction about *Mercury retrograde periods*.

# April 10ᵗʰ Friday

## Good Friday / Holy Day of Thelema (Ra-Hoor-Khuit)

| Moon in Scorpio | PDT | EDT | |
|---|---|---|---|
| Moon enters Scorpio | 2:23 AM | 5:23 AM | |
| Moon opposite Mercury | 5:51 AM | 8:51 AM | |
| Sun sextile Jupiter | 6:42 AM | 9:42 AM | |
| Moon sextile Pluto | 8:27 AM | 11:27 AM | |
| Mercury trine Pluto | 10:52 PM | 1:52 AM | (April 11) |

Venus-conjunct-Uranus-non-exact (occurring April 10 to 24 – see below)

*" There is success ! "*    - LIBER AL vel LEGIS, 1904

***Mood Watch***: Scorpio Moon puts us in touch with our passion. There is success in passion. Why let the great transformations of our lives go uncelebrated? Yes, for some, today may seem intense, tiring, and melodramatic in the face of a full, but waning, Scorpio Moon. Some of us may feel victimized or hard done by. There is no easy way to experience change, yet it happens all the time. Scorpio Moon is here to remind us of that fact.

**Sun sextile Jupiter** (occurring April 5 – 12) This aspect brings those Aries people celebrating birthdays from April 5 – 12 into a favorable natal Sun position to Jupiter. It's a time of opportunity and expansion for these birthday folks if they act on their desires and work towards their goals. Skills learned throughout this year will support their overall plans for career advancement and fortune building. This aspect will occur again December 10 – 17, reaching its peak on December 14, bringing a similar affect to the birthday Sagittarians of that time.

**Mercury trine Pluto** (occurring April 7 – 12) Mercury in Taurus is trine to Pluto in Capricorn. Resourceful thoughts and communications will bring powerful results. This aspect brings hope like a gift, and the myth of Pandora's Box shows us that hope regenerates our senses and fills us with the potential for triumph over difficulties. Mercury in Taurus gives a very practical and logical quality to our methods of communicating. This would be a good time to share tales of triumph, spreading those miraculous stories that remind us of the great potential of winning against all odds. This positive aspect aids communication about struggles with fate, trouble, loss, and fatal illnesses. This is a good time to express encouraging words and reinforce the troubled people of our world with a sense of hope. This aspect will reoccur July 30 – August 5, reaching its peak on August 3 with Mercury in Virgo.

**Venus-conjunct-Uranus-non-exact** (occurring April 10 – 24) The retrograde Venus at the zero degree mark of Aries is beginning a conjunction with Neptune at the 24 degree mark of Aquarius. The six degree orb is as close as it comes to reaching an exact conjunction this week. Venus is about to go direct next week (see April 17) so it will never actually reach an *exact* conjunction with Uranus this time – it will only hover in a stationary fashion until it moves forward and away from Uranus. Despite this, the energy of Venus conjunct Uranus is still assuredly there, creating love energies that may seem especially brilliant but, perhaps, chaotic. This serves as a good time to initiate creative and imaginative spiritual practices and ceremonies and to empower the personal outlook and spiritual wellbeing. For more information on Venus conjunct Uranus, see January 22, when it actually performed at the peak level of conjunction, with Venus and Uranus conjunct in Pisces.

100

# April 11th Saturday

♈

**Moon in Scorpio**

| | PDT | EDT |
|---|---|---|
| Venus enters Pisces | 5:47 AM | 8:47 AM |
| Moon sextile Saturn | 8:08 AM | 11:08 AM |
| Moon square Jupiter | 5:50 PM | 8:50 PM |
| Moon trine Mars | 7:21 PM | 10:21 PM |
| Sun sextile Neptune begins (see April 15) | | |

*Mood Watch*: By now the hubbub of the Full Moon has subsided and what remains is a Scorpio Moon in the early stages of waning. This would be a good time to relax, or to work out those stresses with safe physical activities. Scorpio Moon is sometimes a time of deception. People may lie to protect others, or they may lie for selfish reasons. The waning Scorpio Moon may bring jealousy, a lack or trust, or hypersensitivity to our moods. Some people may just seem desperate. This may be the time to treat matters seriously, to protect the pocketbook from theft, and to carry out promises with the delivery of action. Scorpio energy does not lie: it senses all things.

**Venus enters Pisces** (Venus in Pisces: April 11 - 24) Venus, the planet of magnetism and love, has been retrograde since March 6, and it is currently exiting Aries and reentering Pisces at the tail end of the Piscean constellation. While Venus is retrograde in Pisces, our sense of attraction and magnetism will be deeply internalized, and ultra-passive in nature, as we intuitively process the value of the higher and more refined qualities of love and beauty. On April 17, Venus will go direct at the 29 degree mark of Pisces and it will reenter Aries on April 24. For a recap on the story of Venus in Pisces, see January 3, when Venus first entered the Piscean realm (Jan. 3 – Feb. 2).

# April 12th Sunday

**Easter**

**Moon in Scorpio / Sagittarius**

| | PDT | EDT |
|---|---|---|
| Moon trine Uranus | 12:00 AM | 3:00 AM |
| Moon square Neptune | 3:05 AM | 6:05 AM |
| Moon trine Venus goes v/c | 10:29 AM | 1:29 PM |
| Moon enters Sagittarius | 11:01 AM | 2:01 PM |

*Mood Watch*: For a short time this morning, the waning Scorpio Moon goes void-of-course. The morning may have its intensities, and in other ways it may seem very profound or insightful. Eventually, the Moon enters Sagittarius and our moods will become a great deal more adventurous and explorative. Sagittarius Moon invites us to engage with others in creative and outgoing ways. Sun in Aries and Moon in Sagittarius opens minds and gives us something to go on. Although the Moon wanes, the spirit is willing to look beyond in positive ways.

# April 13th Monday

**Moon in Sagittarius**

| | PDT | EDT |
|---|---|---|
| Moon square Saturn | 6:03 PM | 9:03 PM |

*Mood Watch*: The Sun and Moon are both in fire signs and this brings a very

101

active and creative time. From Greek mythology, the centaur is the symbol of Sagittarius. Centaurs are a race of creatures that are half human and half horse. They are famous in children's books for being star-gazers, foretellers of the future, and they are also considered to be benevolent and wise, loyal to the very end. Throughout the course of the day, our moods are touched by the need to look ahead and to apply the wisdom and moral self-discipline to overcome the troublesome limitations of a treacherous and uncertain new century. Even when life's continuing difficulties seem insurmountable, the wisdom of the centaur reminds us to hold an optimistic outlook, no matter what.

# April 14th Tuesday

| Moon in Sagittarius / Capricorn | PDT | EDT | |
|---|---|---|---|
| Moon sextile Jupiter | 5:20 AM | 8:20 AM | |
| Moon square Mars | 10:11 AM | 1:11 PM | |
| Moon square Uranus | 11:12 AM | 2:12 PM | |
| Moon trine Sun | 12:20 PM | 3:20 PM | |
| Moon sextile Neptune | 2:18 PM | 5:18 PM | |
| Moon square Venus goes v/c | 9:07 PM | 12:07 AM | (April 15) |
| Moon enters Capricorn | 10:27 PM | 1:27 AM | (April 15) |
| Mercury trine Saturn begins (see April 17) | | | |
| Venus conjunct Mars begins (see April 21) | | | |

*Mood Watch*: Moon in Sagittarius is a time when our moods tend to be optimistic and adventurous. There are a lot of lunar aspects at work today, particularly a number of squares. This usually means that we will have to spend some extra time working through complexity. Some love a challenge, some do not. It is senseless to force others to change, or to be optimistic, when they are not. Inner growth is the key to a waning Sagittarius Moon. It is important to keep a philosophical outlook on matters, particularly in an introspective way. Later tonight, the Capricorn Moon demands practicality, which probably means rest after a long philosophically challenging day.

# April 15th Wednesday

| Moon in Capricorn | PDT | EDT |
|---|---|---|
| Mars conjunct Uranus | 3:00 AM | 6:00 AM |
| Moon conjunct Pluto | 5:03 AM | 8:03 AM |
| Sun sextile Neptune | 12:54 PM | 3:54 PM |

*Mood Watch*: The feeling of importance is hatching – springtime is here! The Capricorn Moon gives some folks the feeling they could create or crush a whole universe, while the courageous days of Aries lead us fearlessly onward. Capricorn Moon keeps us on the straight and narrow. A determined world of doers sets a busy, but steady, pace. This midweek Capricorn Moon brings the sense that there is some advancement occurring, and it gets the week rolling along progressively.

**Mars conjunct Uranus** (occurring April 6 – 19) Every couple of years the Mars/Uranus conjunction occurs. Since 2003, Mars and Uranus have been conjunct in the sign of Pisces. Activity and force of action (Mars) is in direct alignment with the explosive and chaotic energy of the rebel (Uranus). Both of these planets are charged with force, energy, and vitality, and are known for creating disruptive and unsettled energy. Masculine forces are erupting abruptly and loudly. The outlook is very fiery, although not necessarily completely destructive, as these masculine forces are tempered by the feminine element of the mutable water sign, Pisces. This may be a time of violence, accidents and upheaval in the world of religion. Activities are likely to be explosive over issues touching on the arts, drugs, our dreams, and those hypersensitive spiritual issues. Anger and frustration can be stifling at times, causing the fierce desire for freedom and the need for a definite revolution or revolt. Take caution with your own actions, and be aware of the potential for accidents and outbreaks of chaotic energy from others. This conjunction of Mars and Uranus is most advantageous for success in demolition projects and wherever strong force is needed to make a total breakthrough.

**Sun sextile Neptune** (occurring April 11 – 17) This occurrence of Sun sextile Neptune creates an opportunistic time for those Aries people celebrating birthdays from April 11 – 17. These Aries folks are experiencing an opportunity to awaken in the realm of spirituality and creativity. There is an awareness of the self that goes deep here, and these birthday people are likely to appear distracted and difficult to reach while this phenomenon of great depth is occurring. This will be your year, birthday folks, to explore personal opportunities of spiritual growth. It may be a time to get away from it all, and find a sanctuary in which to meditate and open up to some valuable answers to old questions. These folks are in a place that gives them an opportunity to better understand the work of their path, but this is probably only true if they act on their own intuitive sensibilities, without the influences of others. That shouldn't be too hard for the enterprising and self-motivated Aries natures among us. This will be your year (Aries birthday people) to enhance and strengthen your intuition and primal instincts by tapping into them while they are easily available. This aspect will reoccur December 11 – 17, reaching its exact aspect on December 15 with the Sun in Sagittarius.

# April 16ᵗʰ Thursday

| Moon in Capricorn | PDT | EDT |
|---|---|---|
| Moon trine Mercury | 12:12 AM | 3:12 AM |
| Moon trine Saturn | 6:16 AM | 9:16 AM |
| Sun trine Pluto begins (see April 22) | | |

*Mood Watch*: The advantage of Saturn in Virgo guarantees that whenever the Moon is in Capricorn, it will be trine to Saturn, the ruler of Capricorn. Moon trine Saturn this morning allows for a clear, controllable – or at least cut and dry – start on today's activities. Capricorn Moon puts us in the mood to tend to the call of duty. This is the time to review goals, apply some assertiveness, and to take care of business. Serious attitudes often accompany the Capricorn Moon, but it's healthy to take life seriously once in a while – perhaps just not *all the time*.

# April 17th Friday
## LAST QUARTER MOON in CAPRICORN

| Moon in Capricorn / Aquarius | PDT | EDT |
|---|---|---|
| Moon sextile Uranus | 12:14 AM | 3:14 AM |
| Moon sextile Mars | 3:13 AM | 6:13 AM |
| Moon square Sun | 6:36 AM | 9:36 AM |
| Moon sextile Venus goes v/c | 9:41 AM | 12:41 PM |
| Moon enters Aquarius | 11:18 AM | 2:18 PM |
| Venus goes direct | 12:25 PM | 3:25 PM |
| Mercury trine Saturn | 5:51 PM | 8:51 PM |

*Mood Watch*: **Last Quarter Moon in Capricorn** (Moon square Sun) is here. This Moon emphasizes issues of control – whether that means taking control or letting go of it where needed. The waning Capricorn Moon reminds us not to give up, to persist as the mountain goat does, and to find a way to overcome the steep and rocky roads. Capricorn Moon gives moods a serious undertone of needing and wanting to take hold of our goals and create results. Saturn ruled Capricorn emphasizes time and the timeliness of important events. This may be a time to address impending deadlines. Life is so serious with Capricorn Moon in its last quarter state; it reminds us that in order to be in control we must let go of that which we can't control. Attached to success? Persistence wins overall where there is a stubborn drive to excel. How important is success to you? For most of today, the Moon will actually be in Aquarius. The waning Aquarius Moon is a good time to experiment, think matters through, and to consider alternative methods of going about life.

**Venus goes direct** (Venus direct: April 17, 2009 – Oct. 7, 2010) Since March 6, Venus has been retrograde through the signs of Aries and Pisces. This has probably been creating many difficulties and challenges in the love lives of those born at the cusps of Gemini/Cancer, and also Sagittarius/Capricorn, who have been experiencing the square aspect of the retrograde Venus to their natal sun signs. Virgo/Libra cusp born people have been experiencing a particularly strong awareness of their love lives, or lack thereof, as Venus has opposed their natal sun signs during this retrograde period. It is not only our love lives or our affections and attractions that are affected by Venus; beauty, art, and aesthetics are impacted as well. Today Venus in the late degrees of Pisces goes direct, bringing a forward moving sense of faith and harmony in our relationships. Now that Venus is direct, expressions of affection and love matters can be begin to move forward with much more clarity and certainty.

**Mercury trine Saturn** (occurring April 14 – 19) Mercury is in Taurus where the emphasis of information is placed on the need for practicality in business. Mercury in Taurus trine Saturn in Virgo brings favorable communication which tells us how, and where, to draw the lines for ourselves. This is a good time to make an impression, to teach, and to communicate to others those important matters that must be clarified. This is a great time to study or practice memorization skills. Timely information and news represents a gift or blessing. News concerning the end of a long and arduous task brings relief. Due to this year's first Mercury retrograde cycle (Jan. 11 – Feb. 1,) this aspect *almost* occurred in its entirety back in January; see Mercury-trine-Saturn-non-exact – January 23.

# April 18ᵗʰ Saturday

**Moon in Aquarius**

| | PDT | EDT |
|---|---|---|
| Moon square Mercury | 10:23 PM | 1:23 AM (April 19) |
| Mercury square Jupiter begins (see April 22) | | |
| Mars square Pluto begins (see April 26) | | |

♉

*Mood Watch*: The Aquarius Moon often brings out the scientific, knowledgeable, and sometimes unusual qualities of our moods. This is the Moon that puts us in touch with our sense of humanity, or lack of humanity. Moral and ethical issues are often at the forefront of our intellectual pursuits, and this gives the overall mood a quality of irony or incongruity. How can we think freely if we are bound to ethical principles? The answer is simple: people change. Morals and ethics change, and this especially occurs through the ways we choose to think. Nonetheless, the rules of society must be applied and the laws must be obeyed, yet even these laws will change. Aquarius Moon gives us the impetus to keep an open mind and this is how we eventually evolve. Sun in Aries and Moon in Aquarius makes us bold, engaging, and sometimes insensitive. Technology can also make us irritable and ferocious. As the day closes and the Moon squares with Mercury, try not to let your thoughts and conversations get the best of you. We would all do well to uphold some positive thoughts for humanity.

# TAURUS

Key Phrase: "I HAVE"

Fixed Earth Sign

Ruling Planet: Venus

Symbol: The Bull

April 19ᵗʰ through May 20ᵗʰ

# April 19ᵗʰ Sunday

**Moon in Aquarius / Pisces**

| | PDT | EDT |
|---|---|---|
| Moon conjunct Jupiter | 7:52 AM | 10:52 AM |
| Moon conjunct Neptune goes v/c | 3:14 PM | 6:14 PM |
| Sun enters Taurus | 3:44 PM | 6:44 PM |
| Moon enters Pisces | 10:53 PM | 1:53 AM (April 20) |
| Moon sextile Sun | 11:30 PM | 2:30 AM (April 20) |

*Mood Watch*: Jovial moods kick off the morning with the Aquarius Moon conjunct Jupiter. Aquarius Moon brings thoughtful and interested moods. Later on, minor afternoon and evening foibles tend to be the way of things as the void-of-course Moon in Aquarius defies all remnants of common sense. Spacey moods bring basic kinds of stupidity. Our patience may be tested when it comes to machines. The late night entry of the Pisces Moon is a good time to concentrate on finding some peace and getting some rest.

**Sun enters Taurus** (Sun in Taurus: April 19 – May 20) Taurus is a Venus ruled sign whose attraction to beauty is second nature. As a general rule, Taurus energy promotes a strong desire to keep physically fit, and to keep possessions and personal effects shining and looking good. Taurus has a very matter-of-fact way of looking at life, and likes to keep the surroundings neat and functional as well as aesthetically pleasing and socially acceptable. This is not to say that Taurus folks are orderly according to the rest of the world! They have a very sensitive and often sentimental side, and find it difficult to change and adapt swiftly when their lives seem to be in perfect order. Taurus loves stability and security. Taurus folks have a knack for smelling money and for finding the value in all things. Taurus says "I have," and Taurus folks are interested in preserving and enhancing what they have attained and acquired in the course of their lives.

# April 20th Monday
**Moon in Pisces**

| | PDT | EDT |
|---|---|---|
| Moon sextile Pluto | 5:09 AM | 8:09 AM |
| Mercury square Neptune begins (see April 25) | | |

*Mood Watch*: The Moon wanes in Pisces. It's an intuitive and introspective time. Monday morning moods may seem dreamy, idealistic and, at times, unrealistic. Our moods may also be fairly accommodating, charming, and imaginative. This is a good time to tap into artistic methods of releasing pent up energies. It is also a time to be aware of addictive behavior patterns and weakness in abstinence. The Sun is newly in Taurus, focusing our energies on the growth and materialization of nature, as well as springtime activities. Pisces Moon gives us a chance to plan our springtime activities with artistic flare.

# April 21st Tuesday
**Moon in Pisces**

| | PDT | EDT | |
|---|---|---|---|
| Moon opposite Saturn | 4:22 AM | 7:22 AM | |
| Moon sextile Mercury | 3:23 PM | 6:23 PM | |
| Venus conjunct Mars | 4:20 PM | 7:20 PM | |
| Moon conjunct Uranus | 9:37 PM | 12:37 AM | (April 22) |
| Mercury sextile Uranus begins (see April 24) | | | |

*Mood Watch*: A youthful fervor greets our moods. Let music, art, and beauty abound! Sun in Taurus and Moon in Pisces brings artistic reverie. Where we do not have the means to meet our artistic demands, we must apply some creative ingenuity. Today our moods will be bubbly, engaging, and eager to indulge our fantasies.

**Venus conjunct Mars** (occurring April 14 – 27) This conjunction brings together the feminine and the masculine in the sign of Pisces. Venus conjunct Mars in Pisces brings out a tendency towards active passivity, where masculine and feminine counterparts will be attempting to produce harmony with a submissive, or seemingly effortless, level of interaction. Not all attempts for love will be passive in nature, since Venus and Mars are conjunct on the cusp, at the 29 degree mark of Pisces, just one degree away from Aries. This conjunction puts us in touch with the power of love in action and active attraction. Here, we are easily seduced by love, particularly that of a spiritual or romantic nature, and we may become easily sucked in by temptation. This may serve as a good time to express love ardently and sincerely, and to receive love just as well. This is also a good time for an individual to get in touch with both the masculine and feminine aspects of the self, and to create peace between those active and passive parts of the personality. Venus and Mars conjunct in Pisces will bring a strong interest in art, music, dance, and many types of divine practice. While Venus and Mars are conjunct in Pisces, lovers will benefit strongly from the act of sharing and expressing their spiritual beliefs. This is a time of integration between the feminine and masculine forces – it is best done in stride and with care. Masculine expression has less of a chance here, while Mars is in the malleable, mutable waters of Pisces. However, Venus in Pisces is an exalted place for the pioneer of love, soothing the feminine approach to spiritual love with a great deal more grace and tact. This is a good time to empower love relationships with the greatest respect. This aspect will return on June 21, with Venus and Mars conjunct in Taurus.

# April 22nd Wednesday

| Moon in Pisces / Aries | PDT | EDT | |
|---|---|---|---|
| Moon conjunct Venus goes v/c | 6:28 AM | 9:28 AM | |
| Mars enters Aries | 6:44 AM | 9:44 AM | |
| Moon enters Aries | 7:08 AM | 10:08 AM | |
| Moon conjunct Mars | 7:09 AM | 10:09 AM | |
| Moon square Pluto | 12:55 PM | 3:55 PM | |
| Mercury square Jupiter | 5:52 PM | 8:52 PM | |
| Sun trine Pluto | 10:44 PM | 1:44 AM | (April 23) |

*Mood Watch*: For a short time this morning, the Pisces Moon goes void-of-course and there may be a tendency towards vagueness or apathy. Soon enough, the Moon enters Aries, and not long after, Mars (the ruler of Aries) also enters Aries. Here we go from cool to hot, hot, hot. Aries Moon activates our moods and gets us all stirred up. This is a good time to watch the temper, and to be aware of the potential for others to get hot under the collar, particularly since the Moon will be conjunct with Mars. Control those animal passions, but do not suppress them. Be patient, but don't play the martyr. Go with the flow – it's hot!

**Mars enters Aries** (Mars in Aries: April 22 – June 6) Mars, the planet of action and masculine drive and force, is at home in Aries, the sign it rules, where it initiates activities in the most forward and direct manner possible. Mars is the god of war in mythology; often Mars related experience is generated through our impulses, our anger and rage, our fear and compulsion, our need to confront and bring forth the primal force of energy and zeal that is our ability to take action – it's our spark of life. Mars now in Aries boosts the lives of Aries people and gives them both the energy and the incentive to take action in their lives, and there are undoubtedly heated matters going on in their lives as well. Mars' influence generates activity and heat which can often appear explosive under pressure. Aries people are reminded to keep a cool sense of control at all times, and to build on their crucible of energy with a direct sense of clarity and purpose. Aries folks can strike now while the iron is hot, but use caution: be aware of fires, potential accidents, and fevers. Capricorn and Cancer folks need to be especially cautious as Mars now squares to their natal

Sun sign, causing the events around them to seem personally abrasive and particularly maddening at times. Libra people may be aware of extreme fiery activity in their lives with Mars opposing their natal Sun sign. The other fire signs of the zodiac also may benefit. Leo and Sagittarius people are experiencing the favorable trine of Mars to their natal Sun signs; this gives our fire sign friends a boost of energy, some hot and some all too hot. Fire signs have within them the means to naturally identify with the forces of Mars activity in their lives. However, even when one is in one's element, the relentless spirit of Mars must be carefully tempered in people's busy lives, or they'll burn out. Mars in Aries places an emphasis on the courage, initiative, drive, energy, willpower, and strength necessary to take action. This kind of force forms the hot lava pools of *Pele* – the Hawaiian volcano goddess of fire, lightning, and dance (to name a few of her attributes). A lot goes on with Mars in Aries, so when the strain becomes too absorbing, remember to rest now and then.

**Mercury square Jupiter** (occurring April 18 – 25) Mercury in Taurus is square to Jupiter in Aquarius; this may be an especially difficult time to raise money for charities. Like last year, this year the travails of Mercury square Jupiter will affect us more frequently than usual due to the retrograde patterns of Mercury. It is no wonder the economic strife and uncertainty that has befallen us over the past year has forced us to discuss the complex matters of prosperity with repetitious difficulty. During this aspect it may be best to hold off on a job request, asking for a raise, or signing any binding contracts concerning long term investment and payment schedules. This aspect may bring discussions or complaints which revolve around the difficulties of getting funds or capital to grow, and it has a tendency to create expensive misunderstandings when it comes to large scale investments. It may be an especially tricky time to communicate during travels, and it may be best to double check travel schedules. Due to Mercury retrograde (May 6/7 – 30), this aspect will reoccur May 10 – 26, reaching its peak on May 20. It will also occur June 4 – 13, reaching its exact peak mark on June 10. This autumn, Mercury square Jupiter occurs November 4 – 10, reaching its exact peak on November 8 with Mercury in Scorpio.

**Sun trine Pluto** (occurring April 16 – 25) Positive, life altering changes are occurring, particularly in the lives of those Aries/Taurus cusp born people celebrating birthdays this year from April 16 – 25. These folks are currently undergoing the favorable trine aspect of Pluto to their natal Sun, bringing out experiences that involve transformation, and encounters with greater powers and with fate. It is always difficult to speculate just how the Pluto experience will manifest. For some of these birthday folks, the concept of receiving gifts and empowerment in the midst of fateful events may seem rocky and not particularly advantageous. Have no fear; this is a time to get in touch with your power, birthday Aries/Taurus! It is wise to remember Pluto moves slowly in our cosmos, and powerful encounters that seem deadly or harsh are actually a necessary process. Though unavoidable, matters involving fate can be positive, and the trine aspect does represent a gift being bestowed. Aries/Taurus birthday people, be grateful this is the trine aspect that brings power issues into your life in a more positive fashion with Pluto, and the work of destiny will bestow untold gifts this year. This is a time of positive transformation. Sun trine Pluto will reoccur August 17 – 26, reaching its exact aspect on August 23.

# April 23rd Thursday

**ờ**

**Moon in Aries**

| | PDT | EDT |
|---|---|---|
| Moon sextile Jupiter | 11:44 PM | 2:44 AM (April 24) |

*Mood Watch*: The Moon wanes darkly in Aries and, in general, our moods are met by our need for courage, self-reliance, and a logical course of action. People will need incentives, praise, and room for self-expression. Where these freedoms are not met, there will be oppression, conflict, and aggressive tension. The Sun in Taurus with a darkly waning Aries Moon often brings stubbornness and strife. On a positive note, these are the struggles that allow us to grow stronger and more independent. It's like this time of year – the young spring flowers are struggling to burst forth, and with this struggle comes absolute, unabashed beauty and strength.

# April 24th Friday

**Earth Day / NEW MOON in TAURUS**

**Moon in Aries / Taurus**

| | PDT | EDT |
|---|---|---|
| Venus enters Aries | 12:12 AM | 3:12 AM |
| Moon sextile Neptune goes v/c | 5:10 AM | 8:10 AM |
| Moon enters Taurus | 11:45 AM | 2:45 PM |
| Mercury sextile Uranus | 12:41 PM | 3:41 PM |
| Moon trine Pluto | 5:12 PM | 8:12 PM |
| Moon conjunct Sun | 8:21 PM | 11:21 PM |

Venus square Pluto begins (see May 2)

*"Our world faces a true planetary emergency. I know the phrase sounds shrill, and I know it's a challenge to the moral imagination"*
- Al Gore

*Mood Watch*: For a time this morning/afternoon the Moon will be void-of-course in Aries. During this time it is best to avoid potential confrontations or accidents. A little later, **New Moon in Taurus** (Moon conjunct Sun) emphasizes the acquisition of new possessions, or it could mean there is a need to restore, replenish, and maintain the old ones. Personal contentment counts with new possessions. Search for the value of what you need and want. This serves as a good time to clean the bad energy off misguided objects of power. It's Earth Day; New Moon in Taurus is exalted and calls to us to enjoy the beauty that surrounds us. Shut down the noise and go celebrate nature!

**Venus enters Aries** (Venus in Aries: April 24 – June 6) Now that Venus is direct (since April 17), it is currently entering Aries for the second time this year, since February 2. Now that Venus is no longer retrograde, the flow of love will come more easily, although still somewhat abruptly in the sign of Aries. For a recap on the influence of Venus in Aries, *see February 2*, when Venus, the planet of love, beauty, and the arts, first entered the detrimentally challenging position of Aries.

**Mercury sextile Uranus** (occurring April 21 – 26) Sensationalism may be played up in the news during this aspect. Mercury is in Taurus focusing talk, information and news on such practical matters as the value and cost of things, while Uranus is in Pisces, blowing all practicality right out of the water and stirring up chaos in the arts and in the world of our beliefs. Mercury sextile Uranus gives us the opportunity to freely speak our minds and to address the turmoil that exists in our lives. This aspect pops up a number of times this year, and well into next year, implying the need for sound communication around areas of disorder and commotion. Mercury sextile Uranus was non-exact in January, beginning on January 26 and ending before its fruition on February 1. Due to the next phase of Mercury retrograde (May 6/7 – 30), this aspect will reoccur on a couple of more occasions: first, May 13 – 24, reaching its exact aspect on May 20, and secondly, it will occur May 29 – June 12, reaching an exact aspect on June 9. Mercury sextile Uranus will begin to occur again on December 20, but due to Mercury's retrograde cycle beginning on December 26, it will not reach an exact peak until February 5, 2010. Mercury will be in Capricorn by late December, emphasizing the need for a voice with down-to-earth authority and command – a voice that will guide us in the midst of chaos.

# April 25th Saturday

| Moon in Taurus | PDT | EDT |
|---|---|---|
| Moon trine Saturn | 1:34 PM | 4:34 PM |
| Mercury square Neptune | 5:54 PM | 8:54 PM |

*Mood Watch*: The newly waxing Taurus Moon brings material focuses, a bustling energy in the marketplace, and a firm sense of enterprising gaiety. Moon trine Saturn brings a serious effort to accomplish goals and meet certain needs. All of this must be done at our own pace, and without the pressures of marauding salespeople. Many of us have a budget to consider. Moon in Taurus is an excellent time to tap into the true value of things.

**Mercury square Neptune** (occurring April 20 – 29) This aspect often brings difficulty in communications with the spirit world, and with understanding human spirituality and beliefs. As a result, talk and discussion concerning what we believe in and strive for may be greatly misunderstood. Neptune is in Aquarius, stirring up the issue of human divinity and the structure of humanity's beliefs in the confusing shifts of the Aquarian age. While Mercury in Taurus is squaring Neptune, pragmatic thought and divinity will be tested, and relaying information on these subjects may seem very difficult. Anticipate religious or belief related arguments and disputes. Deep subjects must not be treated lightly while Mercury squares Neptune. Due to Mercury retrograde (May 6/7 – 30), this aspect will reoccur May 13 – June 13, reaching a couple of peaks, May 20 and again on June 9. This aspect will reoccur for a final time this year, November 7 – 13, reaching its peak on November 11 with Mercury in Scorpio.

# April 26th Sunday

| Moon in Taurus / Gemini | PDT | EDT |
|---|---|---|
| Moon square Jupiter | 2:55 AM | 5:55 AM |
| Moon sextile Uranus | 5:43 AM | 8:43 AM |
| Moon square Neptune | 7:43 AM | 10:43 AM |
| Moon conjunct Mercury goes v/c | 8:41 AM | 11:41 AM |

| Mars square Pluto | 9:14 AM | 12:14 PM |
| Moon enters Gemini | 2:01 PM | 5:01 PM |
| Moon sextile Venus | 3:15 PM | 6:15 PM |
| Moon sextile Mars | 7:51 PM | 10:51 PM |
| Mercury-sextile-Venus-non-exact (occurring April 26 to May 1 – see below) | | |

♉

*Mood Watch*: After yesterday's ambitious shopping spree, some folks may feel their resources are somewhat tapped, as the Taurus Moon goes void-of-course for awhile. Overnight, the Moon was square to Jupiter, and the general course of many folk's moods may reflect the need to buckle the pocketbook. Later this afternoon/ early evening, as the Moon enters Gemini – talkative expressions of mood bring numerous details for us to think about. Curious and thoughtful moods will keep us talking.

**Mars square Pluto** (occurring April 18 - 30) Mars in Aries square Pluto in Capricorn brings recklessly domineering battles over the seemingly unchangeable realities of global power structures. Mars emphasizes all forms of action while Pluto represents the transformational powers of destiny. These two planets in the square position spell out the potential for trouble with regard to our actions. Strong disputes and war related action between generations, and among those of different cultures, are likely to occur. This aspect does imply a more likely time for an attack from groups seeking to take power, but with such attacks there will be struggles. These actions against or conflicts with higher powers are likely to backfire – it is best not to bluff those of a higher or unanticipated authority at this time, as taking action in an attempt to create a transformation may be very dangerous. This may be a particularly difficult time to fight addiction, disease, and war related stress – it is also the most crucial time not to give up the fight. Thankfully, this is the only time this year we will have to endure Mars square Pluto.

**Mercury-sextile-Venus-non-exact** (occurring April 26 – May 1) In a couple of days, Mercury sextile Venus will come within a few degrees of an exact sextile aspect. However, due to the fact that Venus went retrograde this month (see April 17), all too quickly this aspect begins to dissipate before it gets a chance to reach its peak. For the remainder of this month, the affects of Mercury sextile Venus are active. Mercury is in Taurus, bringing money matters, and other practical kinds of focuses, to the forefront of our relationships. Venus is in Aries, bringing ardent, courageous, and inspirational kinds of love and attractions. This is a good time to seek opportunity with matters of love and the arts. This aspect occurred January 24 – 27, reaching an exact peak on January 26, when Mercury was retrograde in Capricorn and Venus was in Pisces. This aspect also occurred February 21 – 27, reaching its peak on February 25 with Mercury in Aquarius and Venus in Aries. This aspect will return in full swing, July 30 – August 31, reaching its exact peak on two separate occasions; first on August 7 with Mercury in Virgo and Venus in Cancer, and secondly on August 28 with Mercury in Libra and Venus in Leo.

# April 27th Monday
**Moon in Gemini**         **PDT**      **EDT**

| Moon square Saturn | 3:11 PM | 6:11 PM |

*Mood Watch*: It's spring, the Moon is waxing in Gemini, and the Moon will be

111

square to Saturn on this Monday afternoon. This implies that it will be difficult for people to kick off the beginning of the work week with any resolve to get some work done. Good weather may cause this distraction, or interesting weather may also lead us away from our normal routines. Our moods may be put off – or encouraged – by gossip or an overly curious attitude. We may tend to make idle chatter, or engage in nervous conversation. If you're tired, coffee may not help, especially if you keep drinking it without proper nourishment. Whatever the case, this is a good time to take most conversations with a grain of salt. Nourish the nervous system with omega-3s and perhaps, tonight would be a good time to eat fish. Brain foods help the nervous edge of the Gemini Moon.

## April 28ᵗʰ Tuesday

| Moon in Gemini / Cancer | PDT | EDT |
|---|---|---|
| Moon trine Jupiter | 5:00 AM | 8:00 AM |
| Moon square Uranus | 7:28 AM | 10:28 AM |
| Moon trine Neptune goes v/c | 9:22 AM | 12:22 PM |
| Moon enters Cancer | 3:38 PM | 6:38 PM |
| Moon square Venus | 6:07 PM | 9:07 PM |
| Moon opposite Pluto | 8:51 PM | 11:51 PM |

*Mood Watch*: The Gemini Moon keeps us mentally active and bursting with details, but later in the morning/early afternoon, the void-of-course Moon begins. Our moods may suffer the tendency to mix up our facts, or to misinterpret the details of our lives. After a time of delays, mix ups, and confusion the world settles down as the Moon enters Cancer, bringing some definition to our emotions. This is a good time talk about how we feel, but don't expect fond affections, as the Moon square Venus tends to complicate matters. Later tonight, Moon opposite Pluto puts us in touch with the need to resolve power issues. There has been a lot on our minds lately, and the Cancer Moon is here to teach us about what we are feeling.

## April 29ᵗʰ Wednesday

| Moon in Cancer | PDT | EDT |
|---|---|---|
| Moon square Mars | 12:17 AM | 3:17 AM |
| Moon sextile Sun | 7:16 AM | 10:16 AM |
| Moon sextile Saturn | 4:54 PM | 7:54 PM |
| Sun trine Saturn begins (see May 5) | | |

*Mood Watch*: If someone reaches out to you, it sometimes means they trust you, or sometimes manipulative motivation is at work. When the Moon is in Cancer and someone is opening up to you, it is potentially dangerous to ignore them. Cancer Moon brings out our need for nurturing reassurance and, sometimes, motherly affection and advice is needed. It is an honor to be trusted by someone, and it is even more honorable when we do not break that trust. Sometimes we need to learn how to just listen, not judge, and give our advice only when it is asked of us. There are many ways to care, and since people are often complex, it may take awhile before we learn how to care in a way that is helpful. Don't buy guilt – it's far too expensive!

# April 30ᵗʰ Thursday

**Moon in Cancer / Leo**

| | PDT | EDT |
|---|---|---|
| Moon trine Uranus goes v/c | 9:45 AM | 12:45 PM |
| Mercury enters Gemini | 3:33 PM | 6:33 PM |
| Moon enters Leo | 5:55 PM | 8:55 PM |
| Moon sextile Mercury | 6:01 PM | 9:01 PM |
| Moon trine Venus | 10:01 PM | 1:01 AM (May 1) |

♉

*Mood Watch*: An awkward day is in store for us as the Cancer Moon turns void-of-course, and this brings the potential for a roller coaster ride of emotional ups and downs. Let it flow – there is nothing you can do to change it. Later, as the Moon enters Leo, playful moods bring relief. This is a good time to enjoy entertaining fun and to forget about the awkward day.

**Mercury enters Gemini** (Mercury in Gemini: April 30 – May 13) Mercury is the ruling planet of two astrological signs, Gemini and Virgo. When in Gemini, Mercury is known to increase our attention to detail and to cover a wide range of interesting topics. Mercury in Gemini directs and orchestrates information – like food for the brain – in an interesting and captivating way. Mercury in Gemini, the mutable air sign, is the best time to inspire a storyteller who is often looking for ways to make the story more interesting. Talk, discussion, stories, gossip, and the news media all generate flashes designed to captivate one's interest even if only for one moment. Mercury in Gemini brings out the two sides of every story. The well developed story has merit as a description of the course of our own existence. Pay heed to the message if the storyteller happens to be telling *your* story while Mercury is in Gemini. Mercury will go retrograde on May 6/7, causing it to return to the tail end of Taurus on May 13. By May 30, Mercury will go direct at the 22 degree mark of Taurus. On June 13, the forward moving Mercury returns to Gemini (June 13 – July 3) where it will keep us busily conversing and straightening out our misunderstandings from Mercury retrograde communications. For more information on Mercury retrograde through Gemini, see the section in the introduction about *Mercury retrograde periods*.

# May 1ˢᵗ Friday

**Beltane / May Day / FIRST QUARTER MOON in LEO**

**Moon in Leo**

| | PDT | EDT |
|---|---|---|
| Moon trine Mars | 5:43 AM | 8:43 AM |
| Moon square Sun | 1:44 PM | 4:44 PM |

*Mood Watch*: The expression of a **First Quarter Moon in Leo** (Moon square Sun) places our moods in states of playfulness, self indulgence, and the need for expression and adoration. Today's attractions tend to be towards those areas of life that we identify with the most. With the Sun in Taurus, the Moon in Leo is most likely expressed by the act of flashing around our best toys. Moods reflect on the contest of who has the best, the biggest, the shiniest, and the most expensive toys, cars, clothes, house and garden. Entertainment value and quality of presentation are just as important. Bonus points go out to those who not only have the finest trimmings, but know how to use what they have in an imaginative, original, and creative manner. Cool is always "in," and requires the assurance of the proper attitude.

Happy **May Day!** This is a traditional old world solar holiday, also known as **Beltane**. We have now reached the half-way mark – and the height – of the spring season. This holiday celebrates the dance of the Maypole and fertility, beauty, rapturous love, and the various kinds of youthful play and frolic appropriate to spring. The famous European *Green Man* with his mask of leaves, the rampaging goat-footed god *Pan* whose flutes thrill us with passion, and the mischievous *Khidr* of Islam who transcends form – all these (and many more) spirited, fervent, male archetypes – these are the lads who delight in the chase of the fair maiden. Persephone, Goddess of Greek myth, returns from Hades. She brings back the mirth of Venusian beauty and represents the fertility and the blossoming of the nurturing, life-sustaining plant world. May Day is a celebration of the fruition and beauty fond in nature. It represents the awakening of the passion and youthfulness in all of life. This time calls to us all to take joy in the fertilization of those parts of ourselves and our lives that need to be brought to fruition.

# May 2ⁿᵈ Saturday

| Moon in Leo / Virgo | PDT | EDT | |
|---|---|---|---|
| Venus square Pluto | 10:08 AM | 1:08 PM | |
| Moon opposite Jupiter | 11:24 AM | 2:24 PM | |
| Moon opposite Neptune goes v/c | 3:08 PM | 6:08 PM | |
| Moon enters Virgo | 9:37 PM | 12:37 AM | (May 3) |
| Moon square Mercury | 11:28 PM | 2:28 AM | (May 3) |

*Mood Watch*: The waxing Leo Moon engages us in the need for fun, theatrics, and entertainment. By this afternoon/evening however, the Leo Moon goes void-of-course. Self-oriented attitudes may put others off. Our moods may be spacey, preoccupied, and easily distracted. A simple case of forgetfulness may also be the crux of our lost moods. Later tonight, Moon in Virgo will help us to think more clearly and practically.

**Venus square Pluto** (occurring April 24 – May 7) Venus in Aries was retrograde (March 6 – April 17), which is why this aspect is occurring for a third time this year. The slower moving Pluto is now retrograde (April 4 – Sept. 11); nevertheless this aspect will reoccur for the fourth and final time this year, October 10 – 17, reaching its exact aspect on October 15, with Venus in Libra square Pluto in Capricorn. For a recap on this currently repeating story of Venus in Aries square Pluto in Capricorn, *see February 5*, when it first occurred this year.

# May 3ʳᵈ Sunday

| Moon in Virgo | PDT | EDT | |
|---|---|---|---|
| Moon trine Pluto | 3:02 AM | 6:02 AM | |
| Moon trine Sun | 10:03 PM | 1:03 AM | (May 4) |

*Mood Watch*: The Sun in Taurus in accompaniment with the waxing Virgo Moon brings practicality, resourcefulness, and a deep curiosity. Our Virgo Moon moods will encourage us to question, analyze, and doubt anything that can't be easily proved. The lunar aspects of the day are positive in nature, although one takes place overnight and the other occurs much, much later. This is a good time to partake in outdoor recreation, and to enjoy pets, plants, books, computers, puzzles, cleanliness, order, precision, and good conversations.

♉

# May 4ᵗʰ Monday
## Moon in Virgo

| | PDT | EDT |
|---|---|---|
| Moon conjunct Saturn | 12:08 AM | 3:08 AM |
| Moon opposite Uranus goes v/c | 6:30 PM | 9:30 PM |

*Mood Watch*: A waxing Virgo Moon Monday is good time to organize, apply communication skills, and to tend to practical needs. This is also a good time to clean, purify, and to chase away all imposing doubts with a thorough investigation. This is not the time to fear what may be lurking under a great pile of mess; it's only scary if you think it's scary, therefore, doubt, *doubt*! Once you've tended to the dirty deed, you'll feel a whole lot better. Tonight the Moon goes void-of-course, and by this time it may be wise to avoid tedious scrutiny. Beware of the tendency for people to be critical or extremely demanding. Circumvent petty arguments. Bathe.

# May 5ᵗʰ Tuesday
## Cinco de Mayo
## Moon in Virgo / Libra

| | PDT | EDT | |
|---|---|---|---|
| Sun trine Saturn | 2:34 AM | 5:34 AM | |
| Moon enters Libra | 2:51 AM | 5:51 AM | |
| Moon trine Mercury | 5:46 AM | 8:46 AM | |
| Moon square Pluto | 8:22 AM | 11:22 AM | |
| Moon opposite Venus | 11:20 AM | 2:20 PM | |
| Moon opposite Mars | 9:54 PM | 12:54 AM | (May 6) |

*Mood Watch*: The waxing Libra Moon atmosphere is studious, congenial, and interactive. The day will have its ups and downs, but most people will try to make the best of it. It will help to apply a loving and patient attitude when the boat is rocked. This is a good time to avoid excesses, to seek objectives, and to give some ample time to others to make decisions, deliberate, and plan events.

**Sun trine Saturn** (occurring April 29 – May 8) This aspect particularly affects Taurus people celebrating birthdays April 29 – May 8. This is a positive time for these Taurus folks to get a handle on their lives, and it may be easier for them to take on the responsibilities of life with fewer complications and less difficulty in the year to come. These birthday folks may notice more acceptable forms of control, responsibility and work occurring in their lives. Now is your time (birthday people) to successfully work on putting some structure into your life; the kind of structure you've needed and wanted awaits you in the coming year. It is possible that time (Saturn) is on your side to make that move you've wanted to make. This aspect last occurred January 5 – 14, and it reached its peak on January 11, affecting the birthday Capricorns of that time.

# May 6th Wednesday

## Moon in Libra

|  | PDT | EDT |  |
|---|---|---|---|
| Mercury goes retrograde | 10:01 PM | 1:01 AM | (May 7) |
| Moon trine Jupiter | 11:56 PM | 2:56 AM | (May 7) |

*Mood Watch*: Libra Moon often focuses our attention on partners and loved ones. It is also the Moon for getting some legal work done, especially the last will and testament, legislative bills and documents, and disputes over the disruption of peace. With so much on our minds, it certainly does not help that Mercury is going retrograde today (see below). What we need to focus on the most here is tolerance. Expect the worst and you're likely to be pleasantly surprised, particularly around midnight (PDT) / 3a.m.(EDT) when the joys of Moon trine Jupiter bring unabashed pleasure to our dreams and our blessed truths.

**Mercury goes retrograde** (Mercury retrograde: May 6/7 – 30) For the next week (until May 13), Mercury will be retrograde in one of the primary places it rules, Gemini. Mercury retrograde in Gemini is likely to bring negativity to gossipy communication, and there are likely to be numerous misunderstandings over minor details. Be on the lookout for frequent bouts of dyslexia, and other communication mistakes in such Gemini related activities as writing, speaking, journalism, and overall communications. During this time it will be best to attempt communications more than once or twice, and to be persistent as well as patient. On May 13, the retrograde Mercury will re-enter Taurus. Mercury retrograde in Taurus (May 13 – 30) may bring disputes over possessions, or over the necessity for practicality and economic viability. At first it may be difficult to sit through everyone's excuses and misinformation, but eventually there will be a logical explanation to Mercury related setbacks. For more information on Mercury retrograde, see the section in the introduction about *Mercury retrograde periods*.

# May 7th Thursday

*Full Moon Eve*

## Moon in Libra / Scorpio

|  | PDT | EDT |
|---|---|---|
| Moon trine Neptune goes v/c | 3:00 AM | 6:00 AM |
| Moon enters Scorpio | 9:48 AM | 12:48 PM |
| Moon sextile Pluto | 3:27 PM | 6:27 PM |

*Mood Watch*: The void-of-course Libra Moon may be trying for some folks, as there may be a tendency towards stubborn indecision. As the Moon enters Scorpio, the drama unfolds. This Full Moon Eve of Scorpio may bring all kinds of things – things like creative and dynamic action, subtle secrecy, issues of power and control, fear and loathing, torrid and soulful love-play, unexpected outbursts, and enigmatic and powerful moods in general. Consider yourself lucky – or especially tolerant – if your day does not turn out to fit any of these descriptions.

# May 8th Friday

## FULL MOON in SCORPIO

### Moon in Scorpio

|  | PDT | EDT |  |
|---|---|---|---|
| Moon sextile Saturn | 1:58 PM | 4:58 PM |  |
| Moon opposite Sun | 9:02 PM | 12:02 AM | (May 9) |

*Mood Watch*: **Full Moon in Scorpio** (Moon opposite Sun) reaches its peak tonight, and throughout the day our moods are – for lack of a better word – intensified. ♉ As this lunar fullness builds to a crescendo of emotional dramas, our emotional patterns are being played out in interesting ways. Intense desires – and what provokes them – reveal a lot about who we are and what we need to appease the satisfaction-hungry inner child. Silly entertaining fun, and off-the-cuff kinds of play and humor are good medicine. The Full Scorpio Moon is a good time for garden lovers to transplant flowers and shrubs as well as plant seeds. Safe physical exercises and activities are excellent avenues of release. Mercury has been retrograde since Wednesday – don't let communication mistakes get you down!

# May 9ᵗʰ Saturday

| Moon in Scorpio / Sagittarius | PDT | EDT | |
|---|---|---|---|
| Moon  square Jupiter | 9:04 AM | 12:04 PM | |
| Moon  trine Uranus | 10:13 AM | 1:13 PM | |
| Moon square Neptune goes v/c | 11:49 AM | 2:49 PM | |
| Moon  enters Sagittarius | 6:49 PM | 9:49 PM | |
| Moon  opposite Mercury | 9:30 PM | 12:30 AM | (May 10) |
| Sun square Jupiter begins  (see May 16) | | | |

*Mood Watch*: This morning we awaken with the post-Full Moon void-of-course in Scorpio. To many folks this could equate to an emotional hangover. As with any hangover, it must be nursed with care, given some space to relax – and it would be senseless to try to kick ourselves into gear prematurely. It is always wise to keep an eye out for danger and avoid precarious situations while the Moon is void-of-course in Scorpio. Later on, the Moon enters Sagittarius, and our energy levels and social awareness begin to move in a much more amicable direction. The Sagittarius Moon, although waning, is still very full and this is a good time to work off excess emotional baggage by becoming physically active or by exploring. Some genuine rest might also be appealing to some folks today, while some philosophical exploration will be sure to inspire.

# May 10ᵗʰ Sunday

**Mother's Day**

| Moon in Sagittarius | PDT | EDT | |
|---|---|---|---|
| Moon  trine Venus | 9:51 AM | 12:51 PM | |
| Moon  trine Mars | 10:59 PM | 1:59 AM | (May 11) |
| Sun square Neptune begins  (see May 16) | | | |
| Mercury square Jupiter begins  (see May 20) | | | |

" *My mother had a great deal of trouble with me, but I think she enjoyed it.* "  - Mark Twain (1835 – 1910)

\* *The Celestial Forecaster's editor (a mother of three) notes, "Ha! She enjoyed it when he grew up and moved out!"*

*Mood Watch*: Today's lunar aspects bring the potential for positive interaction. The Sagittarius Moon often brings optimism, stimulating encounters, generosity, and broadmindedness. This may be a good time to take some risks, to go beyond the usual bounds, and to seek some adventure. That said, if it's Mother that you're trying to please, make sure you listen to her needs. Read between the lines if you have to, but be sure not to pressure her into something more than extravagant. Mercury is retrograde and there may be a tendency for a lot of mixed messages. Actions usually speak louder than words and the important thing is to let Mom know you love her. If this is not an option and/or if Mother is no longer around to please, there's no reason why you can't indulge and nurture yourself. Every "inner child" needs a Mother and every Mother has an "inner child."

# May 11th Monday

| Moon in Sagittarius | PDT | EDT | |
|---|---|---|---|
| Moon square Saturn | 12:06 AM | 3:06 AM | |
| Moon sextile Jupiter | 8:33 PM | 11:33 PM | |
| Moon square Uranus | 9:24 PM | 12:24 AM | (May 12) |
| Moon sextile Neptune goes v/c | 10:55 PM | 1:55 AM | (May 12) |
| Sun sextile Uranus begins (see May 16) | | | |

*Mood Watch*: The Moon wanes in Sagittarius and our moods are likely to be introspective, philosophical, explorative, and creative. This time could bring out the broader picture of global activity, especially for those who are traveling. This may also be a good time to plan summer trips, or to take a new route to work for the sake of experiencing new discoveries. Finding the right fitness programs are also good things to consider during the Sagittarius Moon. Through most of the day, people's moods will be outgoing and somewhat accommodating.

# May 12th Tuesday

| Moon in Sagittarius / Capricorn | PDT | EDT |
|---|---|---|
| Moon enters Capricorn | 6:09 AM | 9:09 AM |
| Moon conjunct Pluto | 12:05 PM | 3:05 PM |

*Mood Watch*: The waning Capricorn Moon is not generally considered a good time to explore people's feelings. During Sun in Taurus and Moon in Capricorn, people tend to be staunch, distant, or preoccupied with their work. This may be the time to talk dollars and cents, to cover material matters, and to get some serious business done. This afternoon, Moon conjunct Pluto may be a time when people seem especially insensitive, or more likely, they may be somewhat manipulative and daunting with their attitudes. There are times when we must be frank about our situations and the waning Capricorn Moon acts as a buffer to separate emotional turmoil from the need to face important decisions.

# May 13th Wednesday

| Moon in Capricorn | PDT | EDT |
|---|---|---|
| Moon square Venus | 1:21 AM | 4:21 AM |
| Moon trine Saturn | 12:20 PM | 3:20 PM |
| Moon square Mars | 3:24 PM | 6:24 PM |
| Mercury enters Taurus | 4:51 PM | 7:51 PM |
| Sun conjunct Mercury begins (see May 18) | | |
| Mercury sextile Uranus begins (see May 20) | | |

*Mood Watch*: The Moon in Capricorn carries on for the second day in a row, and many people may feel that they are making some progress in business. It is best not

118

to push this progress too swiftly, as Mercury retrograde in Taurus (May 6 – 30) may have a bearing on communication mistakes, particularly in matters of business. This is a good time to be direct, but thorough, and take your time. Although we will feel as if we're making some progress with Moon trine Saturn, later in the day Moon square Mars could bring fiery conflict. Stick to your guns and don't make yourself vulnerable to potential advantage takers.

**Mercury enters Taurus** (Mercury in Taurus: May 13 – June 13) Retrograde Mercury re-enters Taurus today and will continue to go back through the late degrees of Taurus until May 30, when it goes direct at the 22 degree mark of Taurus. On June 13, the forward moving Mercury will re-enter Gemini once again, bringing it right back to the place where it is today. For more information on Mercury in Taurus, *see April 9*, when Mercury first entered Taurus this year. As for this time of Mercury retrograde in Taurus, occurring May 6 through May 30, see the introduction in the beginning of this book about *Mercury retrograde periods.*

# May 14ᵗʰ Thursday
**Moon in Capricorn / Aquarius**

| | PDT | EDT |
|---|---|---|
| Moon trine Sun | 6:34 AM | 9:34 AM |
| Moon sextile Uranus | 10:20 AM | 1:20 PM |
| Moon trine Mercury goes v/c | 5:58 PM | 8:58 PM |
| Moon enters Aquarius | 7:01 PM | 10:01 PM |
| Mercury square Neptune begins (see May 20) | | |

*Mood Watch*: Day three of the Moon in Capricorn brings continued focuses on diligence in work and in getting some things accomplished When goals or deadlines are not met, today's Moon sextile Uranus holds the potential for drastic measures to be taken. There will be persistent efforts at concentration and people may seem particularly serious at times. This evening, as the Moon trine Mercury goes void-of-course for an hour, amicable chatter brings a less likely time for concentrated effort. This is a time when communication, although positive in nature, could bring dicey results, particularly now that Mercury is retrograde (May 6 – 30). Tonight's Moon in Aquarius brings inquisitiveness with regard to science, technology, and the fixing of computer crashes.

# May 15ᵗʰ Friday
**Moon in Aquarius**

| | PDT | EDT |
|---|---|---|
| Moon sextile Venus | 6:16 PM | 9:16 PM |

*Mood Watch*: Waning Aquarius Moon events often require the scientific approach. This is a time when we may have to review and correct our tendencies towards stupidity and stubbornness. Sun in Taurus and Moon in Aquarius brings a strong desire on the part of many people to fix what is broken. If something is no longer practical, it is our human nature to find its purpose. This does not mean that you need to move the old cracked bathtub outside and turn it into a tacky shrub planter; there are ways to fix (or mask) old tubs in an aesthetically pleasing manner. The important thing is to apply ingenious solutions, and not to turn absolutely every undesirable dysfunctional item into garbage. The world is full of garbage and

119

humanity needs to find better solutions. The Aquarius Moon gives us the edge to be ingenious. Ask around, search the Internet, and find answers. Don't forget the old adage: "one man's junk is another man's treasure."

# May 16th Saturday

| Moon in Aquarius | PDT | EDT | |
|---|---|---|---|
| Sun  square Jupiter | 1:45 AM | 4:45 AM | |
| Sun  sextile Uranus | 6:08 AM | 9:08 AM | |
| Moon  sextile Mars | 8:24 AM | 11:24 AM | |
| Saturn goes  direct | 7:07 PM | 10:07 PM | |
| Sun  square Neptune | 10:05 PM | 1:05 AM | (May 17) |
| Moon  conjunct Jupiter | 10:46 PM | 1:46 AM | (May 17) |

*Mood Watch*: A busy day of significant aspects keeps us hoppin'. The waning Aquarius Moon gives our moods the edge to work through our problems. This is the time to work at staying on the ball, and if at all possible, be sure to try and get some peaceful rest when it's all said and done.

**Sun square Jupiter** (occurring May 9 – 19) This occurrence of Sun in Taurus square Jupiter in Aquarius will particularly affect those Taurus people celebrating birthdays May  9 – 19. This aspect creates difficulties and obstacles to the personal joy and prosperous welfare of these birthday folks. Getting ahead financially or just staying on top of current trends or financial shifts may be personally challenging right now, requiring persistence and determination. Taurus folks who are doing well financially may find this aspect is challenging their sense of what makes them happy, or that advancement in the world brings too much complexity and requires a lot of management. Though not all Taurus are living as prosperously as they may desire, they do have the ability to come through this and be much better for it. Obstacles create challenges, but do not necessarily dictate an end to efforts to improve our welfare. It is the Taurus personality (Sun) that is being challenged (square aspect) in matters of advancement (Jupiter), requiring Taurians to make do with less assistance than they had anticipated. This may be a time to redefine and redirect personal goals. Taurus birthday folks must reexamine what truly brings prosperity for them in their lives. Scorpio birthday folks, some of you are next in line to experience this Jupiter square to your natal sun. This aspect will reoccur November 3 – 13, reaching its exact aspect on November 10.

**Sun sextile Uranus** (occurring May 11 – 18) This occurrence of Sun sextile Uranus particularly affects those Taurus folks celebrating birthdays May 11 – 18. These birthday people are being given an opportunity to blow off some chaotic steam and to reach for qualities of freedom that may have been absent in their recent past. This will be your time to make radical breakthroughs, birthday Taurus; your natal Sun is currently sextile Uranus for a good reason – to find a liberating balance in the midst of the chaos. Once you've done this, you'll be ready to take the next step. Right now, there is no holding back, so go for it; discover your freedom. The victory of creative change will bring a more optimistic outlook on life. This aspect last occurred on January 9, covering the period of January 5 – 11, when the Sun was in Capricorn.

**Saturn goes direct** (Saturn direct: May 16, 2009 – Jan. 12, 2010) Saturn, which represents time, restriction, responsibility, and disciplinary acts, has been retrograde since December 31, 2008 and will go direct today until January 12 next year. Saturn retrograde often requires us to backtrack on many previous, as yet unfulfilled, obligations and disciplines. Since late December last year, Saturn retrograde has been a time of implementing, testing and correcting various types of security measures in our lives, and many sacrifices were made in order for us to feel a sense of completion and accomplishment. Today Saturn goes direct at the 14 degree mark of Virgo and will remain in Virgo until October 29 when it enters Libra. This is a good time to regenerate the discipline of our senses, to end destructive habits, particularly bad health practices, as well as to make new lifestyle choices and changes. As Saturn begins to move forward, this may be the time for Virgo folks to move forward towards positive endings and new beginnings as Virgo related focuses become society's priority.

Saturn in Virgo focuses on the power of research, statistics, accounting, communication and the dexterity of the mind. Here, our disciplines waver between qualities of cautious discrimination to sheer criticism. It also focuses on such Virgo-like matters as the quality and purity of one's environment, crafts, academic studies, agricultural disciplines, and systems analysis. Virgo says: "I analyze." While Saturn travels through Virgo, structure and discipline, when applied to analysis and forethought, brings magnanimous results. Here, there is no room for Virgo's ability to question or to cast doubt. Here, it is skill, persistence, and indefatigable management that will support grand feats of accomplishment for Virgo.

**Sun square Neptune** (occurring May 10 – 20) This occurrence of Sun square Neptune especially affects those Taurus people celebrating birthdays from May 10 – 20. Neptune, in the square position to these folk's natal Sun, brings a perception that obstacles are getting in the way of Spirit, the spiritual path, or the acknowledgment of one's beliefs. The challenge for these Taurus birthday folks is to overcome the doubts and confrontations that interfere with their beliefs. Over the next year, there will undoubtedly be some spiritual adjustments, and perhaps a change of belief is required for those encountering birthdays at this time. Taurus change? Never! Well, unless it suits them, of course. This aspect will reoccur November 9 – 18, reaching its exact aspect on November 15, when the Sun will be in Scorpio, affecting the lives and beliefs of some Scorpio people.

# May 17th Sunday
## LAST QUARTER MOON in AQUARIUS

| Moon in Aquarius / Pisces | PDT | EDT |
|---|---|---|
| Moon conjunct Neptune | 12:14 AM | 3:14 AM |
| Moon square Sun | 12:25 AM | 3:25 AM |
| Moon square Mercury goes v/c | 3:39 AM | 6:39 AM |
| Moon enters Pisces | 7:16 AM | 10:16 AM |
| Moon sextile Pluto | 12:51 PM | 3:51 PM |

*Mood Watch*: **Last Quarter Moon in Aquarius** (Moon square Sun) brings humanitarian focuses to the scope of our experience. A kind word or sympathetic ear has great healing power and oftentimes promotes peace. This Moon beckons us to find solutions, however temporary, to human problems, and it connects us with the dichotomies and ironies of the human experience. This is a time when the work of genius is ever present, but often goes undetected. Since the Last Quarter Moon takes place when the majority of us are asleep in North America, most of our moods will be focused through the qualities of the waning Pisces Moon. Pisces Moon brings an instinctive and reflective understanding of the course of today's events. This is a good time to tap into your creative and intuitive side.

# May 18th Monday

| Moon in Pisces | PDT | EDT |
|---|---|---|
| Sun conjunct Mercury | 3:01 AM | 6:01 AM |
| Moon opposite Saturn | 12:11 PM | 3:11 PM |

*Mood Watch*: The waning Pisces Moon moves our moods in mysterious ways. Many folks may find that they are less inclined to make a fuss. However, the exception to this prediction may come while the Moon is opposite to Saturn. There may be strong demands for some folks to meet deadlines, or to take matters more seriously than they will, or desire, to do. Waning Pisces Moon often brings out escapist tendencies in people.

**Sun conjunct Mercury** (occurring May 13 – 20) This conjunction will create a much more thoughtful, communicative and expressive year ahead for those Taurus folks celebrating birthdays May 13 – 20. This is your time (birthday Taurus) to record ideas, relay important messages, and pay close attention to your imaginative thoughts as they are touched by Mercury, creating the urge to speak and be heard. Birthday Taurus, your thoughts will reveal a great deal about who you are, now and in the year to come.

# May 19th Tuesday

| Moon in Pisces / Aries | PDT | EDT | |
|---|---|---|---|
| Moon conjunct Uranus | 8:54 AM | 11:54 AM | |
| Moon sextile Mercury | 10:37 AM | 1:37 PM | |
| Moon sextile Sun goes v/c | 2:41 PM | 5:41 PM | |
| Moon enters Aries | 4:29 PM | 7:29 PM | |
| Moon square Pluto | 9:37 PM | 12:37 AM | (May 20) |

*Mood Watch*: The waning Pisces Moon encourages us to play, dream, escape, and enjoy the arts. This morning's Moon conjunct Uranus may lead us to do radical or unusual things. Some examples of less desirable scenarios may include destructiveness, the abandonment of duties, or some may fall off the wagon. As Moon sextile Mercury occurs, this may be a good time to work through Mercury retrograde (May 6 – 30) by taking the opportunity to discuss details more thoroughly. Later today, when the Moon goes void-of-course, expect some delays, contingencies, or basic spacey attitudes. As the Moon enters Aries, our moods may become less patient or more self-oriented. Waning Moon in Aries is a good time to work on self-confidence, or on arrogance, whichever the case may be. Also, expect the potential for harsh attitudes when the Moon squares with Pluto.

# GEMINI                                                                    ♊

Key Phrase: "I THINK"
Mutable Air Sign
Ruling Planet: Mercury
Symbol: The Twins
May 20th through June 20th

## May 20th Wednesday
**Moon in Aries**

| | PDT | EDT | |
|---|---|---|---|
| Mercury square Neptune | 2:22 AM | 5:22 AM | |
| Sun enters Gemini | 2:51 PM | 5:51 PM | |
| Moon conjunct Venus | 8:21 PM | 11:21 PM | |
| Mercury square Jupiter | 8:45 PM | 11:45 PM | |
| Mercury sextile Uranus | 11:47 PM | 2:47 AM | (May 21) |

*Mood Watch*: Aries Moon encourages us to take a stand, and to take charge in areas of our lives where we have control. This is a time when people will be more prone to take the direct approach in matters. There is a stronger drive to create perfection, and many folks are more inclined to make an effort to banish old energies and create a newer, or more controllable, atmosphere. Through the use of proper channels, as well as an application of self-confidence, this can be achieved.

**Mercury square Neptune** (occurring May 14 – June 13) This aspect often brings difficulty in communications with the spirit world, and with understanding human spirituality and beliefs. Due to Mercury's current retrograde cycle (May 6/7 – 30), this aspect is occurring for the second time this year. While Mercury is retrograde, this aspect will have a confusing and difficult affect on our ability to communicate our beliefs. This must be the year for us to take extra precautions when attempting to communicate spiritual subjects. Mercury square Neptune would technically end on May 26, but due to the fact that Neptune goes retrograde on May 28 (while Mercury is still retrograde until May 30), this aspect starts right back up as soon as it ends, giving it a prolonged occurrence period, until June 13. During this particular period, Mercury square Neptune will reach another peak on June 9. This aspect will also occur next autumn (Nov. 7 – 13,) reaching its peak on November 11 with Mercury in Scorpio. For a recap on the story of Mercury in Taurus square Neptune in Aquarius, *see April 25*, when it first occurred this year.

**Sun enters Gemini** (Sun in Gemini: May 20 – June 20) Gemini people love to think. They're often thinking of ways to change the picture and to make it brighter and more detailed. The mutable and adaptable mind must be free to roam with different concepts and ideas that haven't been fully integrated into the big picture.

123

Gemini weaves tapestries of thought; great storytellers, Geminis are often articulate and eloquent speakers, captivating audiences with details and keen observations. Duality is the key factor that shapes the Gemini perspective, and there is always a need to explore the two sides of life.

**Mercury square Jupiter** (occurring May 10 – 26) Retrograde Mercury in Taurus is square to Jupiter in Aquarius. This aspect last occurred on April 22 and it's occurring for the second time this year while Mercury is currently retrograde (May 6/7- 30). Back on May 10, when this particular phase of Mercury square Jupiter began, the retrograde Mercury was at the 1 degree mark of Gemini beginning its square to Jupiter at the 25 degree mark of Aquarius; this has brought troubling and complex themes of absolute confusion over the minor, but important, details of money management. Also, costly confusion ensues in the areas of politics, science, and technology. Since Mercury moved back into Taurus on May 13, Mercury in Taurus has put a more stubborn and possessive tone to our communications, but the confusion around financial statistics is still in question while Mercury is retrograde, until May 29. This is an especially difficult time to communicate during travels and to receive accurate travel information. While Mercury is retrograde in Taurus and Jupiter is in Aquarius, this will be a very difficult time to successfully raise money for charities. This aspect will also occur on two more occasions this year; first, June 4 – 13, reaching its exact aspect on June 10. Next, it occurs November 4 – 10, reaching its exact position on November 8 with Mercury in Scorpio. For a recap on the story of how Mercury square Jupiter affects us, *see April 22*, when this aspect first reached its peak this year.

**Mercury sextile Uranus** (occurring May 13 – June 11) Due to Mercury's current retrograde process (May 6/7 – 30) this aspect is occurring for the second time this season, since April 24. Mercury, currently retrograde in Taurus, sextile Uranus in Pisces, is occurring for an extended period of time, and it's likely to cause communication mix-ups surrounding chaotic circumstances and unexpected conditions. This will be a time of misinterpretation with regard to our rebellious tendencies. Mercury sextile Uranus was also "non-exact" in January, beginning on January 26 and ending before its fruition on February 1. This aspect will reach its peak for the third time this year, with Mercury direct, reaching its exact peak on June 9. Mercury sextile Uranus will begin to occur again on December 20, but due to Mercury's retrograde cycle beginning on December 26, it will not reach an exact peak until February 5, 2010. For more information on Mercury sextile Uranus, *see April 24*, when this aspect first reached its peak.

# May 21st Thursday

**Moon in Aries / Taurus**

| | PDT | EDT | |
|---|---|---|---|
| Moon conjunct Mars | 8:20 AM | 11:20 AM | |
| Moon sextile Jupiter | 2:55 PM | 5:55 PM | |
| Moon sextile Neptune goes v/c | 3:34 PM | 6:34 PM | |
| Moon enters Taurus | 9:38 PM | 12:38 AM | (May 22) |
| Mars sextile Jupiter begins (see May 26) | | | |
| Mars sextile Neptune begins (see May 26) | | | |

*Mood Watch*: Today's first lunar aspect is Moon conjunct Mars, and this brings an active – rarin' to go – punch to the start of our day. Today marks the first *full day* of the Sun in Gemini and today's Aries Moon allows us to explore the newness of this time. Aries comes first, and our moods may be reflected in our need to handle matters expediently, and with a certain degree of executive flare. Beware of rudeness as the Moon goes void-of-course, as there may be a tendency for some people to put their foot in their mouth, particularly while Mercury is retrograde (May 6 – 30). Much later this evening, Moon in Taurus settles down our moods to look upon life in a much more practical and sensible way.

## May 22$^{nd}$ Friday

| Moon in Taurus | PDT | EDT | |
|---|---|---|---|
| Moon trine Pluto | 2:20 AM | 5:20 AM | |
| Moon trine Saturn | 10:48 PM | 1:48 AM | (May 23) |

*Mood Watch*: The blossoming days of spring are here! There are trines in our lunar aspects! There is a darkly waning Taurus Moon, but a Taurus Moon is exalted, and this is good. Here is a favorable time to apply wisdom and ingenuity with the material world, to seek out the value that is found in nature and in our treasured possessions. Sun in Gemini and Moon in Taurus is a good time to seek pleasures and to share them with others. Let the beauty of this time guide you to make resourceful and rewarding decisions.

## May 23$^{rd}$ Saturday

| Moon in Taurus / Gemini | PDT | EDT | |
|---|---|---|---|
| Moon conjunct Mercury | 2:46 PM | 5:46 PM | |
| Moon sextile Uranus | 5:05 PM | 8:05 PM | |
| Moon square Jupiter | 5:25 PM | 8:25 PM | |
| Moon square Neptune goes v/c | 5:48 PM | 8:48 PM | |
| Moon enters Gemini | 11:33 PM | 2:33 AM | (May 24) |

*Mood Watch*: The darkly waning Taurus Moon may bring stubborn moods at times, particularly as the Moon is conjunct with Mercury while Mercury remains retrograde in Taurus (May 6 – 30). The early evening may bring some hesitancy and many folks are not likely to cooperate with normal routines while the Moon sextile Uranus brings a strong desire for liberation. As the Moon squares with Neptune and goes void-of-course, the stubborn and vague among us will undoubtedly become even more stubborn and vague. Let it be – there's no forcing the bull to come out of the china shop till it's good and ready, otherwise there could be sheer disaster. Later, when the Moon enters Gemini, our moods may seem increasingly more profound and complex; it's a good time to rest

## May 24$^{th}$ Sunday
### NEW MOON in GEMINI

| Moon in Gemini | PDT | EDT | |
|---|---|---|---|
| Moon conjunct Sun | 5:10 AM | 8:10 AM | |
| Moon square Saturn | 11:46 PM | 2:46 AM | (May 25) |

*Mood Watch*: The **New Moon in Gemini** (Moon conjunct Sun) allows for new thoughts and ideas to flow, and new feelings about the way we are thinking will begin to emerge. New Moons are like clean slates. It's time to begin a process of strengthening and celebrating your energy and to plan new vistas for growth, particularly in the area of emotional wellbeing. Pay attention to those newer thoughts, ideas and caprices in the wind. This would be a good time to initiate a new round of creative writing or to apply a new mental discipline in a manner which will eventually become more personally beneficial. Making a new attempt at reaching out to an old friend or opening up communications with a new circle will bring great new insights to one's field of knowledge at this time.

# May 25ᵗʰ Monday
**Memorial Day, USA**

| Moon in Gemini / Cancer | PDT | EDT | |
|---|---|---|---|
| Moon sextile Venus | 6:32 AM | 9:32 AM | |
| Moon sextile Mars | 4:50 PM | 7:50 PM | |
| Moon square Uranus | 5:41 PM | 8:41 PM | |
| Moon trine Jupiter | 6:07 PM | 9:07 PM | |
| Moon trine Neptune goes v/c | 6:17 PM | 9:17 PM | |
| Moon enters Cancer | 11:58 PM | 2:58 AM | (May 26) |
| Venus conjunct Mars begins (see June 21) | | | |

*Mood Watch*: The Moon is newly waxing in Gemini. Sun and Moon in Gemini is a busy time for the mind and the engaging and communicative part of our beings. Things happen with the Sun and Moon in this placement and there is a strong underlining current urging us to take note of all those curious details of life as they go fluttering by faster than we can contain them. A childlike fascination fills the air and there will be an endless stream of chatter and babble. This evening, as the Gemini Moon goes void-of-course, our moods may be scattered, defused, or nervous at times. Let the trine of the Moon to Neptune ease your mind. Relax!

# May 26ᵗʰ Tuesday

| Moon in Cancer | PDT | EDT | |
|---|---|---|---|
| Moon opposite Pluto | 4:15 AM | 7:15 AM | |
| Mars sextile Jupiter | 8:19 PM | 11:19 PM | |
| Mars sextile Neptune | 9:36 PM | 12:36 AM | (May 27) |

*Mood Watch*: Sun in Gemini and Moon in Cancer is generally a positive combination. As new feelings emerge, they can be very revealing, since the Moon is very much at home in Cancer and our feelings don't usually lie to us during this time. While the not-so-ideal qualities of Mercury retrograde (May 6 – 30) continue to rattle our communications and our brains, let this Cancer Moon fill your heart with kindness, hope, and peace.

**Mars sextile Jupiter** (occurring May 21 – 29) Mars in Aries is sextile Jupiter in Aquarius. Swift and direct actions, when taken, have the opportunity to go profoundly far, may have a strong impact on humanity, and be very successful in the long run. Those who act on specific urges and impulses to achieve their heart's desire are more likely to make a breakthrough during this aspect. This is a time to make true efforts to promote career skills or to enhance a career move. Remember

– action is required; mere good intentions will get you nothing while this aspect is in full force. This is a good time to go adventuring and exploring while this year's only performance of Mars sextile Jupiter promotes opportunities.

**Mars sextile Neptune** (occurring May 21 – 29) Mars in Aries is sextile to Neptune in Aquarius. Personal initiative – when taken – brings the potential for a spiritual awakening in humanity. Mars sextile Neptune is a splendid time to *act* on our *beliefs*. This aspect brings the vitality of Mars' energy into a favorable position with the spirit-awakening influence of Neptune. This is a place where we can safely dump our anger and can potentially make a connection with a spiritual healing process. Those who act on their visions and the ceremonies of their particular belief systems will have an opportunity to connect with a very profound spiritual experience. This aspect makes the active work of artists, poets, and musicians into unique and very powerful statements about being in an endowed and sacred state of awareness. There is an irony at work with these two forces; Mars is active and masculine, while Neptune has a very nebulous and passive guise that affects our deeper inner sense of beliefs and spirit. When these two planets are placed in a favorable position to each other, personal spiritual breakthroughs can be made.

# May 27ᵗʰ Wednesday

**Moon in Cancer**

| | PDT | EDT |
|---|---|---|
| Moon sextile Saturn | 12:12 AM | 3:12 AM |
| Moon square Venus | 10:03 AM | 1:03 PM |
| Jupiter conjunct Neptune | 1:07 PM | 4:07 PM |
| Moon sextile Mercury | 1:38 PM | 4:38 PM |
| Moon trine Uranus | 6:24 PM | 9:24 PM |
| Moon square Mars goes v/c | 8:06 PM | 11:06 PM |
| Mars trine Pluto begins (see June 3) | | |

*Mood Watch*: This morning the youthfully waxing Cancer Moon envelops our moods with intuitive hunches and revealing perspectives about how we are feeling. Morning/afternoon affections may be compromised while the Moon is square to Venus. Moon sextile Mercury brings us a favorable opportunity to work through communication mix-ups. Moon trine Uranus allows us to kick up our heels a bit. Tonight, as the Moon goes void-of-course, defensive moods require a respite at this point and there are often barriers or lines of limitation drawn. Our guard is up while the Cancer Moon is void-of-course, and not much progress occurs as adjustments must be made for compulsive and – as some see it – confusing behavioral patterns.

**Jupiter conjunct Neptune** (occurring April 3 – Aug. 13) The conjunction of Jupiter and Neptune is a rare occurrence and it serves as an important time to morally and spiritually uplift our communities with an enthusiastic and generous effort. Jupiter represents expansion, prosperity, social advancement, opportunities towards growth – to name a few – while Neptune represents our experience with divine mystery and the spirit of our beliefs. Jupiter conjunct Neptune in Aquarius may be naturally drawing us to review our beliefs about humanity and the human spirit. This is a time of extraordinary expansion with inventions and technology (Jupiter in Aquarius), and we will take on a more expansive viewpoint of life's mysteries, the arts, and our belief in humanity and the role of science (Neptune in Aquarius). This conjunction brings on a number of initiations concerning commerce and our world economy; all of this is a reflection of the integration of our beliefs. Jupiter conjunct Neptune brings an excellent time to seek endowments for the arts, to support and assist those people who are facing addictions, and to work towards expanding spiritual programs, investments in social programs and, in particular, to seek and improve upon venues for religious practices and sacred ceremonies. Jupiter conjunct Neptune brings limitless possibilities for spiritual advancement in humankind. This is the time to put our money into the projects we believe we can use to most effectively help ourselves and others. During this time of Jupiter conjunct Neptune, be sure to invest in something that you have great faith in; the rewards will supersede the imagination. Tomorrow Neptune will go retrograde (May 28 – Nov. 4), this may slow down the process of empowering our beliefs, as we tend to contemplate the spiritual state of things rather than experience it directly. Jupiter will also go retrograde (June 15 – Oct. 12,) and the retrograde patterns of both Jupiter and Neptune will cause this conjunction to occur a second time this year – on July 10. Where there is belief, there will be room for change and expansion with Jupiter conjunct Neptune. This aspect will reach its peak for a third and final time this year on December 21, and covers the period of occurrence dates from October 30, 2009 – January 8, 2010.

# May 28ᵗʰ Thursday

| Moon in Cancer / Leo | PDT | EDT | |
|---|---|---|---|
| Moon enters Leo | 12:45 AM | 3:45 AM | |
| Moon sextile Sun | 1:24 PM | 4:24 PM | |
| Neptune goes retrograde | 9:30 PM | 12:30 AM | (May 29) |
| Venus sextile Neptune begins (see June 2) | | | |

*Mood Watch*: Undaunted, instinctual urges fill our moods as the Moon enters Leo. Here, our personal needs cry aloud for some unabashed fun and indulgence. Family and friends will also require some attention.

**Neptune goes retrograde** (Neptune retrograde: May 28 – Nov. 4) Like clock-work, every year the planet Neptune goes retrograde for about five months. Today Neptune goes retrograde in Aquarius. Neptune governs the spiritual dimensions and, when in Aquarius, it inspires a special interest in the spiritual development of humanity. Neptune harmonizes spiritual vibrations and represents intuition and higher feminine wisdom. While Neptune is retrograde, many of the spiritual issues that have come up in the last five to six months will reoccur. For the next five months, be aware of the frequency of escapist tendencies, and of the inclination to internalize deep-rooted spiritual matters. Being firm with your own spiritual center will allow for progressive spiritual growth, especially while Jupiter is conjunct with Neptune (see yesterday). Be careful not to blindly disrupt the core of another's belief system, nor to become ensnared by someone else's blindness with regard to your own beliefs during Neptune's retrograde months.

# May 29th Friday

**Moon in Leo**

| | PDT | EDT | |
|---|---|---|---|
| Moon square Mercury | 3:09 PM | 6:09 PM | |
| Moon trine Venus | 3:21 PM | 6:21 PM | |
| Moon opposite Neptune | 9:14 PM | 12:14 AM | (May 30) |
| Moon opposite Jupiter | 9:28 PM | 12:28 AM | (May 30) |
| Venus sextile Jupiter begins (see June 2) | | | |

II

*Mood Watch*: The waxing Leo Moon will bring joyous and playful moods with the Sun in Gemini. Frisky and flirtatious moods are likely to entice our spirit. Mercury is almost direct (see tomorrow), but we must remember that the worst time for communication mix-ups and misunderstandings occurs within a three day period of Mercury going into, or coming out of the retrograde period. That is why we must be especially careful of what we say and how we communicate while the Moon is square to Mercury. However, Moon trine Venus brings positive strength and might, as well as a favorable time for loved ones and friends to work things out. Later tonight, Moon opposite Neptune brings opportunities to enjoy fantasies and spiritual reverie. Finally, Moon opposite Jupiter brings generous and joyous moods. Tonight will be a fine time to enjoy the company of good friends.

# May 30th Saturday

**FIRST QUARTER MOON in VIRGO**

**Moon in Leo / Virgo**

| | PDT | EDT |
|---|---|---|
| Moon trine Mars goes v/c | 1:19 AM | 4:19 AM |
| Moon enters Virgo | 3:18 AM | 6:18 AM |
| Moon trine Pluto | 7:44 AM | 10:44 AM |
| Mercury goes direct | 6:22 PM | 9:22 PM |
| Moon square Sun | 8:22 PM | 11:22 PM |
| Sun square Saturn begins (see June 5) | | |

*Mood Watch*: There is a strong investigative curiosity at work with the Sun in Gemini and the Moon in Virgo. Tonight brings the **First Quarter Moon in Virgo** (Moon square Sun). Both of these Mercury ruled signs (Gemini and Virgo) emphasize the need to keep things flowing both on a logical and practical level of application, particularly when passing on information. The Moon is right in tune with today's astrological events, as it is especially significant that Mercury goes direct today, and one must be cautious and thorough with their details when communicating around this time. For now, we may find ourselves eager to communicate, but it may take a few days for communications to be relayed more clearly.

**Mercury goes direct** (Mercury direct: May 30 – Sept. 6/7) Since May 6/7, Mercury has been retrograde in the sign of Gemini, commonly causing problems and confusion when relaying information. In Gemini, the retrograde Mercury often causes communication mix-ups with regard to talk in general, discussions, stories, gossip, and news media information. This has undoubtedly been an especially difficult time for Gemini people or those with Mercury in Gemini. Now we can breathe a greatly needed sigh of relief as Mercury, the planet governing the realms of communication, becomes stationary and will soon begin to move forward. Take note that our faculties and manner of communicating will definitely improve within the next few days. Although perhaps not today – when the stationary Mercury often freezes communication efforts – but very soon, our communications will run more smoothly; this will be a good time to begin clearing up various misunderstandings occurring over the past few weeks. For more information on this recently completed phase of Mercury retrograde, see May 6/7. For more on Mercury retrograde patterns throughout this year, see the introduction on *Mercury retrograde periods*.

# May 31st Sunday

| Moon in Virgo | PDT | EDT |
|---|---|---|
| Moon conjunct Saturn | 5:38 AM | 8:38 AM |
| Mars enters Taurus | 2:18 PM | 5:18 PM |
| Moon trine Mercury | 7:32 PM | 10:32 PM |

*Mood Watch*: While the Moon is in Virgo our moods are rapidly affected by the need to be resourceful and precautionary. Virgo Moon encourages us to take care of practical matters and to find the time to mull things over for awhile. Tonight's Moon trine Mercury will help us to set matters straight in our minds.

**Mars enters Taurus** (Mars in Taurus: May 31 – July 11) Mars represents all modes of action. In the fixed earth sign of Taurus, Mars' action is particularly worked out through the physical realm, making this a primary time to work active energy through the body, or to take affirmative action in the physical world, moving or activating it to change. This is a time when many of us will take strong actions with our financial and material welfare. Mars (the ruler of Aries), is considered the detrimental position – while in Taurus – for the warrior planet. More than a few years ago, when Mars was in Taurus from July 27, 2005 to February 18, 2006, we were forced to take action with the physical world due to hurricane Katrina, which was followed by more hurricanes and immense fund raising efforts to resolve the mess they caused. Mars' energy enlivens such Taurus related activities as bargain hunting, buying and selling, bidding, investing, banking, decorating, and creating a practical work space. Mars in Taurus boosts the life energy of Taurus people and gives them the incentive to take action. Mars generates heat which can often appear explosive under pressure. Taurus people are reminded to keep a cool sense of control at all times and to be aware of the tendency towards temper tantrums when events get overheated. Taurus folks can strike while the iron is hot but they must use caution and be aware of fires and fevers. Aquarius and Leo folks also need to be especially cautious as Mars now squares to their natal Sun, causing actions around them to seem abrasive to them personally. Scorpios may be particularly aware of fiery activity in their lives at this time with Mars opposing their natal Sun.

# June 1st Monday

| Moon in Virgo / Libra | PDT | EDT |
|---|---|---|
| Moon opposite Uranus goes v/c | 1:33 AM | 4:33 AM |
| Moon enters Libra | 8:17 AM | 11:17 AM |
| Moon square Pluto | 12:51 PM | 3:51 PM |

*Mood Watch*: Through a portion of the morning, the waxing Moon in Virgo will be void-of-course. We are still trying to adjust to the recent phase of Mercury retrograde (May 6 – 30,) and with this comes some residual confusion and common mix-ups. In a couple of days, it will all pass completely. For some, this phase is crippling to the mind, but for most, it is just a common stage of trial and error. The Libra Moon portion of the day brings friendly and observant moods. Besides the effort to catch up on financial transactions, the start of a new month often brings renewed hope, inspiration, and a willingness to do things well. Today's Moon square Pluto may bring struggles while we try to cope with pressures and difficult transitions. For the most part, Sun in Gemini and Moon in Libra keeps us keen, interactive, and willing to handle whatever comes along.

# June 2nd Tuesday

**Moon in Libra**

| | PDT | EDT |
|---|---|---|
| Moon trine Sun | 6:26 AM | 9:26 AM |
| Venus sextile Neptune | 8:53 AM | 11:53 AM |
| Venus sextile Jupiter | 4:39 PM | 7:39 PM |
| Venus trine Pluto begins (see June 8) | | |

*Mood Watch*: Pleasant vibrations are in the air and today's lunar aspects are positive and upbeat. Sun in Gemini and Moon in Libra brings intelligent, congenial, and balanced moods. Our perspectives on life may seem a lot clearer today than recent days have shown. This is a good time to enjoy epicurean delights and good company.

**Venus sextile Neptune** (occurring May 28 – June 4) Venus in Aries brings love, attraction, beauty, and the nature of feminine expression into prominence. Neptune in Aquarius is a time to awaken human spirituality and to excel in creative expression through music, art, writing, etc. Spread this healing power around for all to share! This time also holds the potential for one to realize the profound beauty and the depths of which true love is capable. This aspect will reoccur December 17 – 22, reaching its exact aspect on December 20, when Venus will be in Sagittarius.

**Venus sextile Jupiter** (occurring May 29 – June 4) This aspect is currently reaching an exact peak for the third time this year. This is an excellent time to shower loved ones with gifts and compliments, to allow expansion to occur in love matters, and to take the next step towards enlivening and enhancing the beauty of life. Later this year, this aspect will also occur December 17 – 22, reaching its exact peak on December 20, with Venus in Sagittarius. For more information on Venus in Aries sextile Jupiter in Aquarius, *see February 16*, when it first occurred.

# June 3rd Wednesday

**Moon in Libra / Scorpio**

| | | |
|---|---|---|
| Moon trine Neptune | 9:05 AM | 12:05 PM |
| Moon trine Jupiter | 9:42 AM | 12:42 PM |
| Moon opposite Venus goes v/c | 11:01 AM | 2:01 PM |
| Moon enters Scorpio | 3:44 PM | 6:44 PM |
| Moon opposite Mars | 8:19 PM | 11:19 PM |
| Moon sextile Pluto | 8:23 PM | 11:23 PM |
| Mars trine Pluto | 9:36 PM | 12:36 AM (June 4) |

131

*Mood Watch*: Throughout the earlier part of the day, Moon in Libra continues to bring pleasant and amiable moods. As the Libra Moon goes void-of-course, our moods shift from pleasant to somewhat uncertain at times. The void Libra Moon is often a difficult time to deliberate and make decisions. Decide what you want to do *early this morning* and then stick to it, especially since most people are not likely to be very flexible. By afternoon/early evening, the Moon enters Scorpio, our moods will begin to intensify, and many people will become preoccupied with their hidden ambitions. This evening, mediocrity takes the back seat.

**Mars trine Pluto** (occurring May 27 – June 7) Mars is now in Taurus trine Pluto in Capricorn. Constructive, systematic, and practical action leads to positive, monumental, and powerful transformations. Actions taken now are more likely to have favorable results or to be influential with higher powers. This is a good time to resolve personal aggression directed towards the views and differences of another generation or established powers. This is also a good time for vital discoveries in the fight against diseases. Mars trine Pluto brings opportunity for favorable direct action that may well make a powerful and impressionable impact. Youthful or strong new influences will reach places of power, and a new generation will take many seats of power in political offices of the world. Mars, the god of war, and Pluto, the underworld god (or hell raiser), may actually be reaching some favorable kind of truce. This is the only time this aspect will occur this year.

# June 4th Thursday
**Moon in Scorpio**

| | PDT | EDT |
|---|---|---|
| Moon sextile Saturn | 8:44 PM | 11:44 PM |
| Mercury square Jupiter begins (see June 10) | | |

*Mood Watch*: Sun in Gemini and Moon in Scorpio brings curiosity and excitement. The waxing Scorpio Moon lights up the sky with anticipation, and sexual prowess may be evident. It is wise to guard yourself against foolishness and impetuous acts. In other words, use condoms when appropriate. Tonight's Moon sextile Saturn allows us to act responsibly, and it's a superb opportunity to educate others about being responsible. This is, after all, still spring, and the sounds of stray cats is a stiff reminder for us to mind our civil manner in the midst of excitement. On a Scorpio Moon, anything can happen!

# June 5th Friday
**Moon in Scorpio**

| | PDT | EDT |
|---|---|---|
| Sun square Saturn | 12:10 PM | 3:10 PM |
| Moon opposite Mercury | 1:57 PM | 4:57 PM |
| Moon trine Uranus | 6:17 PM | 9:17 PM |
| Moon square Neptune | 6:29 PM | 9:29 PM |
| Moon square Jupiter goes v/c | 7:18 PM | 10:18 PM |

*Mood Watch*: Today will be busy and exciting. During a waxing Scorpio Moon in the days of Gemini we tend to face challenges, find solutions, keep active, and we're likely to empower our moods with a fair dollop of passion. It is the Gemini in us that goes about the detail of placing the cherry on the top of that dollop of passion, and it is the Scorpio in us that snatches it away. With so much going on, there is always plenty to observe. Tonight, as the Moon goes void-of-course, be careful not to place yourself in a particularly vulnerable position, as victimization may run rampant.

**Sun square Saturn** (occurring May 30 – June 8) This occurrence of Sun square Saturn especially affects those Gemini born people who are celebrating birthdays May 30 – June 8. These folks may be experiencing some personal challenges such as impatience, loss of control, a poor sense of timing, or difficulty identifying with current obligations. The challenge is therefore to overcome those obstacles that intrude on one's control of discipline and accuracy. These challenges will pass, and for those folks who have uplifting and positive aspects occurring in their lives, these (Saturn square natal sun) challenges may seem insignificant. By October 29, Saturn will enter Libra, and the challenges of maintaining difficult disciplines will begin for people born on the Sagittarius/Capricorn cusp. Overall, these folks will have a good look at what really matters in life, and hopefully, they will honor and appreciate it. Saturn represents those things in life that we are willing to work for and maintain. Don't give up, Gemini birthday folks – conserve your energies and take losses and difficulties in stride! Through the tests, a stronger human being emerges to take on future tests with greater confidence and ability. Avoidance of responsibilities or hardships now will only make life more difficult later. This aspect will reoccur December 19 – 28, reaching its exact aspect peak on December 25, affecting the birthday Sagittarians and Capricorns of that time.

# June 6th Saturday
*Full Moon Eve*

| Moon in Scorpio / Sagittarius | PDT | EDT |
|---|---|---|
| Moon enters Sagittarius | 1:24 AM | 4:24 AM |
| Venus enters Taurus | 2:06 AM | 5:06 AM |
| Mercury sextile Uranus begins (see June 9) | | |

*Mood Watch*: Overnight the Moon enters Sagittarius and we have now arrived at the Full Sagittarius Moon Eve. This is an excellent time for us to explore, seek adventure, and contemplate or participate in travel. Global awareness is sparked, and philosophical views are running strongly. Sagittarius says: "I see." Seek vision!

**Venus enters Taurus** (Venus in Taurus: June 6 – July 31) Venus in Taurus is the time of an extraordinary attraction to beauty. Here in Taurus, Venus is at home nurturing us with sensual pleasure and enhancing our appreciation of nature and earthly bounty, as well as our appreciation for quality and specialty craftsmanship. Venus in Taurus brings out aesthetic awareness, and places a greater emphasis on the love of having valuable items, wealth, and abundance. Venus attracts and draws, and Taurus represents material acquisition and attainment. Taurus people will be touched by the need for love and affection in their lives as Venus crosses over their natal Sun. Now is the time to acquire, polish, clean, and beautify things that give a sense of truly having something. To create beauty around oneself is to enhance one's sense of wellbeing. Beauty, of course, varies according to the eye of the beholder. Simple pleasures are the best – an effort to enjoy the beauties of life is not necessarily expensive.

# June 7th Sunday

**FULL MOON in SAGITTARIUS**

| | PDT | EDT |
|---|---|---|
| Moon square Saturn | 7:35 AM | 10:35 AM |
| Moon opposite Sun | 11:12 AM | 2:12 PM |

Uranus-square-Pluto-non-exact (occurring from June 7 – June 23, 2009 – see below) - reaches various peaks from: 2012 – 2015

*Mood Watch*: The **Full Moon in Sagittarius** (Moon opposite Sun) brings new insights about life, and emotional energy runs very high throughout the day. For many, there is a tendency to go way out beyond the usual bounds and discover new territory as a matter of circumstance. How we chose to perceive and develop our understanding of this new territory has a lot to do with what stage in our life we have come to, and what kind of philosophy best suits our own individual needs.

**Uranus-square-Pluto-non-exact** (occurring June 7 – 23) This aspect is not your run-of-the-mill common occurrence! Oh no, this aspect has an irregular cycle of every 50 to 80 years, depending on the retrograde cycles of Uranus and Pluto. This main aspect involves two of the three outer planets, which are among the slowest moving in our solar system. Their interaction with each other affects *all* of human-kind, bringing unfathomable – and unpredictable – acts of chaos and transformation and complex changes, usually of historical proportions. Starting now, for just 17 days, we have the very first glimpse of Uranus square Pluto which takes years to develop, and will take a few more years to reach its ominous peak, as well as taking its good old time to fully dissipate. Take note: Uranus square Pluto is temporarily showing itself for the first time this century, and the events of the next 17 days will provide some major clues for the types of dramatic changes we can expect to encounter over the next decade.

Uranus is the outer planet that represents revolution, chaos, explosive energy, and big changes. Pluto is known as the underworld god, the one who tests and evaluates the stability of all things, and where there is weakness, Pluto removes or anni-hilates weakness with illness, famine, decay, and putrefaction. Pluto purifies or cleans away that which is dead and gone. Where Pluto traverses, permanent change occurs. Out of this transformation, an entirely different perspective will affect our understanding of how things work on the physical plane. In the square position, these two planets are a force to be reckoned with – and then some. This is the time to start paying attention to the signs.

This aspect last occurred in the early 1930s and won't return, after this next phase, until the early 2070s. The peak occurrence dates for Uranus square Pluto in this next phase are June 24, 2012, September 19, 2012, May 20, 2013, November 1, 2013, April 21, 2014, and March 17, 2015.

# June 8th Monday

**Moon in Sagittarius / Capricorn**

| | PDT | EDT |
|---|---|---|
| Moon square Uranus | 5:46 AM | 8:46 AM |
| Moon sextile Neptune | 5:51 AM | 8:51 AM |
| Moon sextile Jupiter goes v/c | 6:50 AM | 9:50 AM |
| Venus trine Pluto | 12:22 PM | 3:22 PM |
| Moon enters Capricorn | 12:59 PM | 3:59 PM |

134

| | | |
|---|---|---|
| Moon conjunct Pluto | 5:43 PM | 8:43 PM |
| Moon trine Venus | 6:13 PM | 9:13 PM |

Ⅱ

*Mood Watch*: The dwindling remains of yesterday's Full Sagittarius Moon energy builds insightful and philosophical reverie. However, our moods may be somewhat spacey or thoughtless while the Sagittarius Moon is void-of-course. This afternoon, the waning Capricorn Moon allows us to get a more grounded picture of how we might choose to profit from our insightful outlook

**Venus trine Pluto** (occurring June 2 – 11) Venus in Taurus is trine to Pluto in Capricorn. Practical beauty, the value of nature, and efforts to make the planet greener are enhanced and made stronger as we wade through the hardships of a vast landscape of irreversible change and transformation. Now is the time to let our ecological wishes be known, as those who are in positions of power are a little more likely to acknowledge the value of land preservation for the sake of delicate ecosystems. Beauty can be found in all aspects of existence. Venus trine Pluto represents a love or fascination for the workings of fate and power. This aspect often allows a breakthrough to occur for those who are under stress from hardship. There is hope yet that we will acquire an appreciation for the not-so-glamorous aspects of existence. This is also an aspect that allows for adoration and loving energy to flow more easily between generations, despite all the differences that have separated us in these fast changing times. This aspect will reoccur September 15 – 23, reaching its exact aspect on September 20.

# June 9ᵗʰ Tuesday

| Moon in Capricorn | PDT | EDT |
|---|---|---|
| Moon trine Mars | 1:43 AM | 4:43 AM |
| Mercury sextile Uranus | 2:42 PM | 5:42 PM |
| Mercury square Neptune | 2:50 PM | 5:50 PM |
| Moon trine Saturn | 8:10 PM | 11:10 PM |

*Mood Watch*: Sun in Gemini and Moon in Capricorn is an excellent time to multi-task with precision and focused effort. Here we are rarely hindered by uncertainty or emotionality. This is a time to make progress and to get some business done. Our moods will be purposeful and amicably serious. Don't waste the day: apply some effort towards serving needs, and by the end of the day, there will be a real sense of accomplishment.

**Mercury sextile Uranus** (occurring June 6 – 12) Due to last month's Mercury retrograde process (May 6/7 – 30), this aspect is occurring for the second time this season since April 24. Now that Mercury is no longer retrograde (since May 30), this aspect is likely to assist us in setting the records straight with regard to communication mix-ups that may have been prevalent during the past month's chaotic circumstances and unexpected conditions. Mercury sextile Uranus was also "non-exact" in January, beginning on January 26 and ending before its fruition on February 1. Mercury sextile Uranus will begin to occur again on December 20, but due to Mercury's retrograde cycle beginning on December 26, it will not reach an exact peak until February 5, 2010. For more information on Mercury sextile Uranus, *see April 24*, when this aspect first reached its peak.

135

**Mercury square Neptune** (occurring May 13 – June 13) This aspect often brings difficulty in communications with the spirit world, and with understanding human spirituality and beliefs. Due to last month's Mercury retrograde cycle (May 6/7 – 30) and Neptune's retrograde cycle (which began on May 28), this aspect is occurring for the third time this year. It will also reoccur in the autumn, November 7 – 13, reaching its peak on November 11 with Mercury in Scorpio. For a recap on the story of Mercury in Taurus square Neptune in Aquarius, *see April 25*, when it first occurred.

# June 10<sup>th</sup> Wednesday

**Moon in Capricorn**

| | PDT | EDT |
|---|---|---|
| Mercury square Jupiter | 8:30 AM | 11:30 AM |
| Moon sextile Uranus | 6:39 PM | 9:39 PM |
| Moon trine Mercury goes v/c | 8:31 PM | 11:31 PM |
| Sun square Uranus begins (see June 17) | | |
| Sun trine Neptune begins (see June 17) | | |

*Mood Watch*: Now that the working pace of midweek is established, the Capricorn Moon encourages many people to make better efforts, and inspires our moods to get focused on important matters and to perform significant tasks and duties. This time may also be tiring for some folks since this past weekend's Full Sagittarius Moon had many of us on the run during these busy days of Sun in Gemini. This is the time to set aside fears and worries by getting to work on the areas of life where we are able to make improvements and reduce some serious concerns. However, once the Moon goes void-of-course, try to take it easy.

**Mercury square Jupiter** (occurring June 4 – 13) Due to Mercury's latest retrograde period (May 6/7 – 30), this aspect is occurring for the third time this year while Mercury is currently direct. This is an especially difficult time to communicate during travels and to receive accurate travel information. This aspect will occur on one more occasion this year: November 4 – 10, reaching its exact aspect on November 8. For a recap on how Mercury square Jupiter affects us, *see April 22*, when this aspect first reached its peak.

# June 11<sup>th</sup> Thursday

**Moon in Capricorn / Aquarius**

| | PDT | EDT |
|---|---|---|
| Moon enters Aquarius | 1:52 AM | 4:52 AM |
| Moon square Venus | 12:43 PM | 3:43 PM |
| Moon square Mars | 6:47 PM | 9:47 PM |
| Sun trine Jupiter begins (see June 17) | | |

*Mood Watch*: Sun in Gemini and Moon in Aquarius is a great time to be innovative, clever, and to tap into some rich intelligence. That said, this may not be the day to make headway with friends, while the Moon is square to Venus, and later, while it is square to Mars, try not to rock the boat of friendship and partnership. Try to work matters out with others as best you can. Aquarius Moon puts us in touch with the many needs and foibles of humanity. Sometimes we must set emotions aside and address the real problems, the long term disruptions, and not just the immediate emotional responses and symptoms. If there is ever a time to sort through the details of our human dilemmas, Sun in Gemini and Moon in Aquarius is it. Meanwhile, try to have some fun too – we are, after all, only human.

Ⅱ

# June 12ᵗʰ Friday
**Moon in Aquarius**

|  | PDT | EDT |
|---|---|---|
| Moon trine Sun | 11:15 PM | 2:15 AM  (June 13) |

*Mood Watch*: Our intelligence – or lack of it – always stands out on an Aquarius Moon day, especially during the busy spring days of Sun in Gemini. The Aquarius Moon brings clever, innovative, and gifted perspectives. The Sun and Moon are in air signs, and this is the time to compile data and research, and to integrate it into spring projects and social endeavors. Aquarius Moon is a good time to socialize, work with large groups of people, and to learn about the things that get people excited. Experimental moods lead to amazing discoveries. This evening's Moon trine Sun brings harmonious intelligence. Use this time wisely: educate yourself.

# June 13ᵗʰ Saturday
**Moon in Aquarius / Pisces**

|  | PDT | EDT |
|---|---|---|
| Moon conjunct Neptune | 7:21 AM | 10:21 AM |
| Moon conjunct Jupiter | 8:33 AM | 11:33 AM |
| Moon square Mercury goes v/c | 2:03 PM | 5:03 PM |
| Moon enters Pisces | 2:31 PM | 5:31 PM |
| Moon sextile Pluto | 6:57 PM | 9:57 PM |
| Mercury enters Gemini | 7:45 PM | 10:45 PM |
| Mars trine Saturn begins  (see June 22) | | |

*Mood Watch*: Waning Moon in Aquarius leads our moods on a quest towards knowledge. On some level, the desire for a certain kind of freedom or personal breakthrough calls out to some folks. The restlessness of spring season stirs our hearts. People we haven't seen in some time are starting to come out in droves. With the Moon and Sun both in air signs, there will be a lot on our minds and much to talk about. Later in the day, as the Moon enters Pisces, our moods will exhibit numerous kinds of intuitive responses. In those areas of life where we have no proof, no substantial evidence, we must find our faith. No matter what you believe, there will always be times when you will need to trust in something or someone. Pisces Moon guides our intuition and very often, our strong hunches lead us to the right path.

**Mercury enters Gemini** (Mercury in Gemini: June 13 – July 3) Due to its last retrograde period (May 6/7 – 30), Mercury is entering Gemini for the second time this year since April 30. Mercury in Gemini directs and orchestrates information – like food for the brain – in an interesting and captivating way. For a recap on the story of how Mercury in Gemini affects our communications, *see April 30*, when Mercury first entered Gemini.

# June 14ᵗʰ Sunday

**Flag Day, USA**

| Moon in Pisces | PDT | EDT | |
|---|---|---|---|
| Moon sextile Venus | 6:33 AM | 9:33 AM | |
| Moon sextile Mars | 10:52 AM | 1:52 PM | |
| Moon opposite Saturn | 9:19 PM | 12:19 AM | (June 15) |

*Mood Watch*: Pisces Moon brings drifty and dreamy moods. Intuitive perception and creative desires emerge. Music, art, dance and wild abandon become choice focuses. More relaxed and less limiting environments of mood attract us. Spiritual continuity inspires us and the release of our emotions brings healing. Sun in Gemini and Moon in Pisces brings on bubbly and frivolous expressions of thought and mood. This is a good time to flirt, play, meditate, unwind, and enjoy the reverie and tranquility of the open waters.

# June 15ᵗʰ Monday

**LAST QUARTER MOON in PISCES**

| Moon in Pisces | PDT | EDT |
|---|---|---|
| Jupiter goes retrograde | 12:50 AM | 3:50 AM |
| Moon square Sun | 3:13 PM | 6:13 PM |
| Moon conjunct Uranus goes v/c | 6:17 PM | 9:17 PM |
| Venus trine Saturn begins (see June 21) | | |

*Mood Watch*: The **Last Quarter Moon in Pisces** (Moon square Sun) occurs today. The Pisces Moon influence brings a dreamy sort of atmosphere. A mysterious and enchanting quality of reflection is occurring, allowing the imagination to roam with consistent accuracy and touching the core of our beliefs. Waning Pisces Moon tends to keep us entranced by those areas of our life that bring depth and meaning. This is a good time to cleanse the spiritual cobwebs from our own lives. Reinforce personal fortitude with the strength to overcome addictions by using sheer will-power and belief in oneself.

**Jupiter goes retrograde** (Jupiter retrograde: June 15 – Oct. 12) The planet of expansion and prosperity now begins to recede back through the degrees of the zodiac today through October 12. The planet Jupiter itself does not go backwards; it is only the apparent shift in our orbital position to Jupiter that makes it appear this way. Most planets orbiting around the Sun eventually go into a retrograde pattern from our geocentric view of planetary movement. Jupiter in Aquarius (Jan. 5, 2009 – Jan. 18, 2010) brings prosperity and expansion to such areas of life as science, technology, politics, human resources, and research and development. This is a time when marketing strategies often employ the themes of new invention, consulting in specialty fields, human rights activism, and broadcasting. Jupiter retrograde is not the best time for the growth of large scale funds and investments, but it is a good time to meditate, and to observe carefully, what truly makes us happy in the realms of fortune seeking. A clearer sense of growth will occur through internal processing and through personal skill development. While Jupiter is retrograde, it is important to apply wisdom and caution in the economic area of our lives, and in our livelihood, so that we may see future growth.

138

# June 16th Tuesday

Ⅱ

**Moon in Pisces / Aries**

| | PDT | EDT |
|---|---|---|
| Moon enters Aries | 12:50 AM | 3:50 AM |
| Moon square Pluto | 4:54 AM | 7:54 AM |
| Moon sextile Mercury | 5:36 AM | 8:36 AM |
| Sun opposite Pluto begins (see June 23) | | |

*Mood Watch*: Sun in Gemini and Moon in Aries spells out fun. Sometimes the fun occurs at the expense of others, but for the most part, people are likely to carry out their own ambitions with an active fervor that will attract others. Flashy cars and spiffy outfits may be one way the Aries Moon spirit shows itself. However, the more spiritually engaged folks among us are likely to show their daring savvy by making eye contact and tipping their new summer hats. Whatever it takes, once your daily chores are performed, be sure to have fun!

# June 17th Wednesday

**Moon in Aries**

| | PDT | EDT |
|---|---|---|
| Sun trine Neptune | 3:45 AM | 6:45 AM |
| Sun square Uranus | 7:56 AM | 10:56 AM |
| Sun trine Jupiter | 7:28 PM | 10:28 PM |

*Mood Watch*: Aries Moon often brings out a spirit of competitiveness. The waning Aries Moon brings restlessness and forces numerous folks to rustle up some energy around special interest activities. Aries Moon encourages us to act on aggressive moods while we still have the volition and the courage to fight the battles that are calling to us. It is also a time to have some fun, and if you didn't get around to doing that during yesterday's Aries Moon, don't let this precious Aries Moon time go uncelebrated today.

**Sun trine Neptune** (occurring June 10 – 20) Something big is going on with Gemini birthday people today, with three solar aspects seeding the busy lives of our Gemini friends celebrating birthdays this week. It begins with Neptune; this occurrence of Sun trine Neptune particularly affects those Gemini people celebrating birthdays from June    10 – 20. These Geminis are experiencing the favorable trine aspect of Neptune to their natal Sun, bringing gifts of spiritual encounters and awareness, as well as a calming effect on life. This serves as a good time (particularly for these birthday folks) to seek visions, apply prayer and meditation, and to explore spiritual avenues and beliefs that are being presented. Unfortunately, this calming and spiritually fortifying aspect may be somewhat overshadowed by the simultaneous affects of Sun square Uranus (see below), which is also bringing tyrannical chaos into these birthday folks' lives. Still, bear in mind that Sun trine Jupiter brings the greatest potential for prosperous advancement for birthday Geminis (see below). Meanwhile, Sun trine Neptune ensures that the compulsory passive and kindly qualities of Neptune's influence will lead Gemini birthday people to be easily seduced by spiritually uplifting practices and sanctuaries. Gemini, the trine of Neptune to your natal Sun will assist you in finding the calm space in the eye of the storm. This aspect will reoccur October 10 – 19, reaching its peak on October 16 with the Sun in Libra.

**Sun square Uranus** (occurring June 10 – 20) This occurrence of Sun square Uranus particularly affects those Gemini people celebrating birthdays June 10–20. The square of Uranus to these Gemini folks' natal Sun brings a strong dose of unrestrained chaos and challenging events. This may be the year for you, Gemini birthday folks, to surrender to those aspects of life that are truly out of your control, and to concentrate more rationally on those facets of life over which you do have control. Sometimes the aftermath of Uranus influence is an improvement, but with the square aspect at work, it is likely these people will feel personally challenged. It is important to understand that some types of personal challenges are best left alone, while others must be confronted directly without causing destructive damage, particularly to oneself. On the other hand, birthday Gemini folks, if your life has no foundation, there is no point in holding on to the illusion of stability at this juncture of your sojourn. Albeit slowly, this aspect will pass in due time. Try to be detached from chaotic events as they occur, and the outcome will seem less costly. It is vital not to give rapid change too much resistance, lest you be subject to the reversals of trying to fight chaos with logic at a time when resistance is futile. Project the picture of peace and it will be there for you at the other end. This aspect will reoccur December 8 – 17, reaching its peak on December 14 with the Sun in Sagittarius.

**Sun trine Jupiter** (occurring June 11 – 20) This aspect brings those Gemini people celebrating a birthday from June 11 – 20 to a favorable natal solar position with relation to Jupiter. This will be a time of gifts and expansion for these birthday folks, and there are good times ahead for them in the coming year. This aspect will bring a better sense of what it means to expand and attain one's personal desire. Despite Sun square Uranus (see above), be sure to take the time right now (Gemini birthday people) to enjoy and appreciate life, which will definitely improve for those who are being given the gifts of joy this aspect often brings. Sun trine Jupiter will reoccur with the Sun in Libra, October 4 – 13, reaching its peak on October 10.

# June 18ᵗʰ Thursday

| Moon in Aries / Taurus | PDT | EDT |
|---|---|---|
| Moon sextile Neptune | 12:56 AM | 3:56 AM |
| Moon sextile Jupiter | 2:03 AM | 5:03 AM |
| Moon sextile Sun goes v/c | 2:33 AM | 5:33 AM |
| Moon enters Taurus | 7:19 AM | 10:19 AM |
| Moon trine Pluto | 10:58 AM | 1:58 PM |

*Mood Watch*: Early this morning, there may be some impatience in the air while the Aries Moon is void-of-course. Soon enough however, the Moon enters Taurus and reminds us to get a better handle on our physical world. The Moon is exalted in Taurus and this is a great time to bring practical, useful, and esthetically pleasing material goods into your life. The Moon also wanes in Taurus, and this means that it is just as essential to clean away items in your life that are no longer of use and appear to be taking up space. If you are one of the people who cannot appreciate the power of the statement, "less is more," then now's the time for you to seek an empty, clean, Zen atmosphere, and plant yourself in the center. If the emptiness that surrounds you doesn't enliven your senses then nothing ever will. Useless junk collects dust. Polish and clean your world and you will appreciate it a whole lot more. Taurus Moon is the time to determine what is valuable to you and what is not.

Ⅱ

# June 19ᵗʰ Friday

**Moon in Taurus**

| | PDT | EDT |
|---|---|---|
| Moon conjunct Venus | 6:00 AM | 9:00 AM |
| Moon conjunct Mars | 7:06 AM | 10:06 AM |
| Moon trine Saturn | 10:31 AM | 1:31 PM |

*Mood Watch*: Positive lunar aspects will most likely bring auspicious interaction on this waning Taurus Moon day. This is a time when we are most likely to connect with what we need and want, and to go out there and get it. On this last full day of the Sun in Gemini, the busy fervor of spring blossoms opens up our outlook on life. The waning Taurus Moon is a good time to review finances and to set financial matters straight. If that seems to be all you've been doing in these past couple of years of sharp economic decline, it is vitally important to stay focused on meeting financial goals and to find ways to enjoy simple pleasures to rewards those efforts.

# June 20ᵗʰ Saturday

**Summer Solstice (Begins Late - Pacific Daylight Time)**

| Moon in Taurus / Gemini | PDT | EDT | |
|---|---|---|---|
| Moon square Neptune | 3:59 AM | 6:59 AM | |
| Moon sextile Uranus | 4:21 AM | 7:21 AM | |
| Moon square Jupiter goes v/c | 5:01 AM | 8:01 AM | |
| Moon enters Gemini | 9:59 AM | 12:59 PM | |
| Sun enters Cancer | 10:45 PM | 1:45 AM | (June 21) |
| Moon conjunct Mercury | 11:50 PM | 2:50 AM | (June 21) |

*Mood Watch*: Early this morning, the Moon wanes in Taurus as it goes void-of-course. The dawn hours may generate some lazy or stubborn moods. The wise Solstice practitioners among us are most likely to choose to do their dawn saluta-tions to the Sun tomorrow instead of today. This is especially true since the Sun won't actually enter Cancer until late tonight and June 21ˢᵗ is considered the tradi-tional day of summer Solstice. By late morning/early afternoon, the Moon enters Gemini, and this is an excellent time to explore life's possibilities, to communicate about various details, and to begin the celebration of this exuberant time of Summer Solstice. This is the zenith time of the Sun, and in A. E. Waite's Tarot trump card, The Sun XIX, the image of youthful twins (a symbol of Gemini) are shown glee-fully dancing in the garden. The prophecy is clear: celebrate gleefully! HAPPY "SPRI-SUM" DAY! – See tomorrow's *Mood Watch* for an explanation.

**Sun enters Cancer** (Sun in Cancer: June 20 – July 22) This is the time when Summer Solstice enthusiasts are out celebrating old traditions and creating new ones while thanking the Sun for life and light. The dominion of the sign of Cancer is expressed by cardinal water, affecting people in deep and unconscious ways. Cancer people are extremely intuitive and often very psychic or perceptive. Cancers value and prize their deep emotional attachments and treasured memories and feelings. Cancer is a home oriented sign, and making the home a well-loved place calls out to us. Barbeques, home improvements, and other home based events are the focuses of many folks during the days of Sun in Cancer.

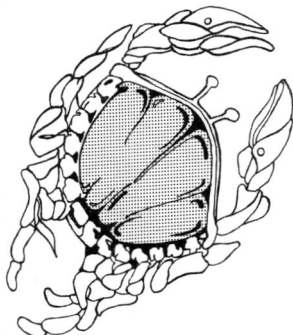

# CANCER

Key Phrase: "I FEEL"

Cardinal Water Sign

Ruling Planet: Moon

Symbol: The Crab

June 21th through July 22nd

# June 21st Sunday

**Traditional Summer Solstice (Solstice - Eastern Daylight Time) / Father's Day**

**Moon in Gemini**

| | | | |
|---|---|---|---|
| Venus conjunct Mars | 6:09 AM | 9:09 AM | |
| Moon square Saturn | 11:51 AM | 2:51 PM | |
| Venus trine Saturn | 11:30 PM | 2:30 AM | (June 22) |
| Mercury square Saturn begins (see June 26) | | | |

*Mood Watch*: *Happy Father's Day*! June 21st is traditionally known as Summer Solstice while yesterday was a partly spring and partly summer day. Yesterday, the early commencement of summer solstice encompassed the solar qualities of Gemini and Cancer, and this phenomenon could be referred to as a "spri-sum" day. Today, however, the sun is in Cancer for the entire day and that makes this the official first *full* day of summer. Despite some early morning seriousness, due to Moon square Saturn, Gemini Moon brings curious, talkative, and communicative moods. The Moon also wanes darkly, which brings depth and profoundness to our moods.

**Venus conjunct Mars** (occurring May 25 – June 30) This conjunction brings together the feminine and the masculine in the sign of Taurus. Venus conjunct Mars in Taurus brings out a tendency towards physical love and affection, where masculine and feminine counterparts will be attempting to produce harmony with an emphasis on luxury, comfort, and beautiful surroundings. This conjunction puts us in touch with the power of love in action and active attraction. Here, love is expressed in an amorous and demonstrative fashion. This is a good time to commit to practical and realistic endeavors with a partner and to bring stability to a relationship. This is also a good time for an individual to get in touch with both the masculine and feminine aspects of the self, and to create peace between those active and passive parts of the personality. While Venus (the ruler of Taurus and Libra) is at home in the sign of Taurus (see June 6), Mars (the ruler of Aries), is not at home here, and Taurus is considered the detrimental position for the warrior planet (see May 31 - Mars enters Taurus). This is a time of integration between the feminine and masculine forces – it is best done in stride and with care. Masculine expression has less of a chance here, while Mars is in the oppressive fixed earth sign of Taurus. Without the consent of our affection, love must not be forced in a physical manner, as there are ways and means to temper our love-play artfully. Venus in Taurus is a comfortable place for the pioneer of love, soothing the feminine approach to love with a great deal more sensibility, grace, and tact. This is a good time to empower love relationships with the greatest respect. This conjunction last occurred on April 21, when Venus and Mars were in Pisces on the cusp of Aries.

**Venus trine Saturn** (occurring June 15 – 25) Since Venus and Mars are currently conjunct in Taurus (see above) today's Venus trine Saturn will be followed by tomorrow's Mars trine Saturn. This brings a very timely quality to relationships, and raises the questions of commitment and devotion with regard to our active love connections. Fortunately, the trine aspect brings probabilities that are more positive in nature when it comes to the law of attraction. Today's aspect of Venus trine Saturn implies that there is a good possibility here for a happy ending. Venus in Taurus trine Saturn in Virgo brings an earthy, practical, and stable expression of love and commitment to love. Venus in Taurus (see June 6) emphasizes the need for a practical, financially sound commitment to the person or thing that holds the greatest attraction. Here is where we easily devote ourselves to what attracts us most. Where love and attraction have withstood the test of time, this aspect is bound to remind us of whom – and what – matters most. Venus trine Saturn often brings the gift of responsive and enduring love. This aspect may assist in bringing some peace to the structure or the closure of a love relationship. This is good time to initiate or enhance a love vow or oath, and to apply the values of devotion and responsive caring. Love is a gift and a responsibility. Genuine love, when given without expectations, will return naturally, bringing true love into your life. Use this time affectionately and wisely. It often makes an impression and it is the only time this beneficial aspect will occur this year.

# June 22nd Monday
## NEW MOON in CANCER

| Moon in Gemini / Cancer | PDT | EDT |
|---|---|---|
| Moon trine Neptune | 4:21 AM | 7:21 AM |
| Moon square Uranus | 4:46 AM | 7:46 AM |
| Moon trine Jupiter goes v/c | 5:19 AM | 8:19 AM |
| Mars trine Saturn | 7:44 AM | 10:44 AM |
| Moon enters Cancer | 10:11 AM | 1:11 PM |
| Moon conjunct Sun | 12:34 PM | 3:34 PM |
| Moon opposite Pluto | 1:21 PM | 4:21 PM |

*Mood Watch*: The **New Moon in Cancer** (Moon conjunct Sun) beckons to our moods to tune into newly emerging feelings about ourselves. The New Cancer

Moon invites fresh experience and brings new desires to nurture the child within and build up a fresh outlook on our home life. Cancer focuses on the nurturing strength of the mother. This is a good time to bring new things to the home and brighten up one's outlook with nurturing and uplifting moods and feelings.

**Mars trine Saturn** (occurring June 13 – 26) Detrimental Mars in Taurus trine Saturn in Virgo brings positive, although somewhat abrupt, breakthroughs in expediting the will to accomplish certain goals. Large scale projects can expect to move ahead. Our actions bring gifts with this aspect, provided there is an application of discipline and timing. At best, Mars trine Saturn provides a sense of good timing. Activities will be very physical, and decisive action will occur very quickly while these two planets are in earth signs. This may be a good time to apply diligent practice with one's favorite sport, especially those physical activities which demand precision and perfect timing. The timely gift of willpower and discipline brings rewards and positive results. To fully benefit from this aspect, one must use the energy (Mars) responsibly (Saturn). This is usually a time of harmonious transitions, when endings and new beginnings are easily merged. This aspect last occurred January 16 – 27, reaching its exact peak on January 24, when exalted Mars was in Capricorn.

# June 23rd Tuesday

| Moon in Cancer | PDT | EDT |
| --- | --- | --- |
| Sun opposite Pluto | 12:41 AM | 3:41 AM |
| Moon sextile Saturn | 11:43 AM | 2:43 PM |
| Moon sextile Mars | 1:00 PM | 4:00 PM |
| Moon sextile Venus | 2:15 PM | 5:15 PM |

*Mood Watch*: Today's lunar aspects to Saturn, Mars, and Venus are all in the sextile position and this brings positive opportunities to our work, and in our relationships with the masculine and feminine forces of the universe. The youthfully waxing Cancer Moon is a good time to incorporate new ways to nurture and reassure emotional concerns that may have cropped up in the last little while. Warmth and comfort are good.

**Sun opposite Pluto** (occurring June 16 – 26) The Sun is at the midsummer cusp of Gemini/Cancer, and for the first time in our lifetime, Sun in Cancer opposes Pluto in Capricorn. Late born Geminis and early born Cancer folks having birthdays from June 16 – 26 are undergoing the effects of Pluto being in a lengthy opposition to their natal Sun sign. Birthday folks, with Pluto in opposition to your identity, this is the time to accept transition, however overwhelming the circumstances. Persist in recognizing the empowering differences each generation embodies. Gemini folks born near the Cancer cusp – here's the good news: it won't be that much longer for Pluto to be in opposition to your natal Sun position. Since 1995, Pluto has been teaching Gemini people about the necessity of regeneration, and the shifting of the powers that be. Sun in Cancer opposite Pluto in Capricorn particularly affects early born Cancer birthday people, and they must begin to face the awakening challenges of transformation. These challenges may appear threatening and are often perceived as a painful process of loss and destruction.

144

Late Gemini and early born Cancer birthday folks, do not get hung up on high expectations of life or you are likely to burn out. These lessons are meant to be, so open up to the need for endurance and perseverance during this time – use wisdom as your guide. Survival counts! Use your senses and your sensibilities well, but do not resist the forces of great change. Surviving all this means the best of life is yet to come, as you will grow to appreciate life in a delightfully transformed way. This is also true for your opposites, the late born Sagittarians and early born Capricorns, who are feeling the conjunction of Pluto to their natal Sun.

# June 24ᵗʰ Wednesday

**Moon in Cancer / Leo**

| | PDT | EDT |
|---|---|---|
| Moon trine Uranus goes v/c | 4:24 AM | 7:24 AM |
| Moon enters Leo | 9:50 AM | 12:50 PM |

*Mood Watch*: This morning, the young Cancer Moon goes void-of-course for a number of hours, and this may cause tendencies towards emotionality, worry, fear, or guilt. Even if you think you're immune to such indulgences, there is a good chance that some of the people around you are encountering these things. The early part of the day is likely to go a whole lot more smoothly if you play along and express a little sympathy or some sensitivity. In turn, if you feel as though you are a victim of these moods, be sure to steer clear of insensitive oafs and situations that might exacerbate your condition. Soon enough, the Moon enters Leo, and most of the today brings the right time to engage with supportive family members and to escape into entertaining hobbies and personal projects. Leo Moon is the time to engage in the strength of personal willpower.

# June 25ᵗʰ Thursday

**Moon in Leo**

| | PDT | EDT |
|---|---|---|
| Moon sextile Mercury | 10:26 AM | 1:26 PM |
| Moon square Mars | 3:41 PM | 6:41 PM |
| Moon square Venus | 6:12 PM | 9:12 PM |
| Venus square Neptune begins (see July 1) | | |

*Mood Watch*: The earliest days of summer are here and the Moon is waxing in the sunny place of Leo. The first lunar aspect of the day, Moon sextile Mercury, brings an opportunistic time to communicate with others and to work out unresolved matters. If someone you know was foolish enough to choose yesterday morning's void-of-course Cancer Moon to break off an engagement, expect to see a lot more fuss and complexity over male and female problems this afternoon and evening, especially while the Moon is square to Mars and Venus. Leo Moon is generally a good time to seek entertainment, fun, and theatrical outlets, but the melodramas are not usually any fun if they're subjective. Leo's totem is the lion and there's always the Egyptian Lion Goddess, Sekhmet's way of handling it – bite off some heads! The *Celestial Forecaster's* Leo editor adds, "Then have a nice refreshing red beer with helpful herbal potions (Jagermeister will do!)" Let humor and keen prowess be your guide.

# June 26<sup>th</sup> Friday

| Moon in Leo / Virgo | PDT | EDT |
|---|---|---|
| Mercury square Saturn | 1:30 AM | 4:30 AM |
| Moon opposite Neptune | 4:34 AM | 7:34 AM |
| Moon opposite Jupiter goes v/c | 5:28 AM | 8:28 AM |
| Moon enters Virgo | 10:47 AM | 1:47 PM |
| Moon trine Pluto | 1:57 PM | 4:57 PM |
| Moon sextile Sun | 8:14 PM | 11:14 PM |
| Venus square Jupiter begins (see July 1) | | |

*Mood Watch*: The waxing Moon in Leo puts us in touch with our pride and our joy. There is pride in the self, pride in the family, and pride in the way we put our own signature on things. Strength, self assurance and vitality are worthy focuses, but as the Leo Moon goes void-of-course, some may mix up their pride with their sense of dignity. In the early part of the day, beware of the potential for egos to clash. People may become irritable if they're ignored. As the Moon enters Virgo, pragmatism and adaptability will enter into the spirit of our moods. Virgo Moon is a good time to be health conscious, altruistic, and to practice some discernment.

**Mercury square Saturn** (occurring June 21 – 27) Mercury in Gemini square Saturn in Virgo creates tension in communications. Under the influence of this aspect, the battle to maintain accurate or precise information may be strongly evident. There may also be a tendency for "foot-in-mouth disease" as people may say the wrong things at the wrong time. It is wise to use caution when attempting communications during Mercury square Saturn, especially concerning matters of time and timing. It is also wise to be careful not to misinterpret health related information. While Mercury is square to Saturn, beware of the tendency for people to make uninformed assumptions about the conclusion or outcome of important matters. This will also be an especially difficult time to inform people of the ending of things, or to inform someone of a death or to speak at a funeral – not that this task isn't already difficult enough! Mercury square Saturn will reoccur December 3 – 10, reaching its exact peak on December 7, when Mercury will be in Capricorn and Saturn will be newly in the sign of Libra (see Saturn enters Libra: Oct. 29).

# June 27<sup>th</sup> Saturday

| Moon in Virgo | PDT | EDT |
|---|---|---|
| Moon conjunct Saturn | 2:34 PM | 5:34 PM |
| Moon square Mercury | 7:34 PM | 10:34 PM |
| Moon trine Mars | 8:57 PM | 11:57 PM |

*Mood Watch*: Virgo Moon is a good time to be gentle, discreet, careful, and accurate. Since the past week may have had it's ups and downs with regard to people's attitudes, today's waxing Virgo Moon serves as a good time to focus on drawing the lines, particularly while the Moon is conjunct with Saturn. Later, Moon square Mercury may be a tricky time to try to talk matters through, but it may also be the most beneficial time to think carefully and discerningly through the complexity of those matters. Later tonight, Moon trine Mars brings positive energy and courageous moods. Perhaps, after a day of deliberation, we will find the happy medium.

# June 28th Sunday

**Moon in Virgo / Libra**

| | PDT | EDT |
|---|---|---|
| Moon trine Venus | 1:05 AM | 4:05 AM |
| Moon opposite Uranus goes v/c | 8:26 AM | 11:26 AM |
| Moon enters Libra | 2:25 PM | 5:25 PM |
| Moon square Pluto | 5:40 PM | 8:40 PM |
| Mercury trine Neptune begins (see July 1) | | |
| Mercury trine Jupiter begins (see July 1) | | |
| Mercury square Uranus begins (see July 1) | | |
| Venus sextile Uranus begins (see July 1) | | |
| Mars square Neptune begins (see July 6) | | |
| Mars square Jupiter begins (see July 6) | | |

*Mood Watch*: Unless you're into kick boxing, Sunday is usually a kicked back sort of day for most people, but today there is definitely something in the air that seems far from kicked back; in fact, *kicked over* might be the more appropriate term. As the Virgo Moon opposes Uranus and goes void-of-course, chaos ensues. Some folks are likely to be querulous, fussy, servile, petty, fault-finding, prudish, modest, self-doubting, interfering, obsessive, and skeptical – you get the idea. It's no wonder; have a look at the incredibly long list of significant aspects that are beginning to occur, with many of them set to strike on the busiest celestial day of the year, July 1. As the Moon enters Libra, our moods are met with the need for some peace, diplomacy, and some balance. Libra Moon brings solace to those who need some civilized logic.

# June 29th Monday

**FIRST QUARTER MOON in LIBRA**

**Moon in Libra**

| | PDT | EDT |
|---|---|---|
| Moon square Sun | 4:29 AM | 7:29 AM |

*Mood Watch*: The Sun is in Cancer emphasizing activities of the home, the world of our feelings, and the need to preserve our emotional attachments; the **First Quarter Moon in Libra** (Moon square Sun) encourages us to harmonize with our partners and friends. This is the Moon that brings out a wide range of focuses on the need to create balance in various kinds of relationships, particularly those of a close nature. It's time to make adjustments, especially during so much celestial activity in the air (see July 1)!

# June 30th Tuesday

**Moon in Libra / Scorpio**

| | PDT | EDT |
|---|---|---|
| Moon trine Mercury | 10:03 AM | 1:03 PM |
| Moon trine Neptune | 2:11 PM | 5:11 PM |
| Moon trine Jupiter goes v/c | 2:59 PM | 5:59 PM |
| Moon enters Scorpio | 9:19 PM | 12:19 AM (July 1) |

*Mood Watch*: A number of trines with the Moon in Libra will bring a good chance for a pleasant day. That said, later in the day/evening the Libra Moon goes void-of-course, causing a tendency for confusion and indecision. By the time the Moon enters Scorpio, we begin to feel the power of an extraordinary day of aspects, set to take place tomorrow. These aspects are already in effect, and the best thing we can do is decrease the amount of complexity in our lives and simplify our schedules for the next week or so. Otherwise, brace yourself.

# July 1st Wednesday

## Canada Day

| Moon in Scorpio | PDT | EDT | |
|---|---|---|---|
| Uranus goes retrograde | 12:38 AM | 3:38 AM | |
| Moon sextile Pluto | 12:41 AM | 3:41 AM | |
| Venus square Neptune | 1:00 PM | 4:00 PM | |
| Mercury trine Neptune | 1:47 PM | 4:47 PM | |
| Moon trine Sun | 4:48 PM | 7:48 PM | |
| Mercury trine Jupiter | 6:34 PM | 9:34 PM | |
| Mercury square Uranus | 7:12 PM | 10:12 PM | |
| Venus square Jupiter | 9:24 PM | 12:24 AM | (July 2) |
| Venus sextile Uranus | 10:41 PM | 1:41 AM | (July 2) |
| Mercury opposite Pluto begins (see July 4) | | | |
| Mars sextile Uranus begins (see July 7) | | | |

*Mood Watch*: Today tops the 2009 chart as far as the most significant aspects occurring in one day. This much can be said about the Moon being in Scorpio: it allows us to tap intuitively into the intensity of it all and to handle it. Without further adieu, pay attention to the pending dialog as there will be a lot for our moods to assimilate.

**Uranus goes retrograde** (Uranus retrograde: July 1 – Dec. 1) Uranus, the outer planet representing revolution, chaos, explosive energy, and big changes, now appears to turn back through the zodiac in the sign of Pisces. Since March 10, 2003, Uranus in Pisces has been stirring up a revolution in religion, music, the arts, poetry, psychic research, occultism, movie making and plays. Outer planets move slowly, and this one will take five months to backtrack only four degrees before it moves forward once again. Uranus influences chaos and volatile or abrupt energies, and inspires the need for change and breakthroughs in the pursuit of freedom. When retrograde, the influence of Uranus teaches us to handle uncertainty, particularly internal chaos. Many aspects of chaos tend to be sporadically repeated until the boundaries of restriction loosen enough so we can move more freely. Uranus retrograde is a time when humanity as a whole must backtrack over their revolutionary practices in order to make breakthroughs in the long run. Uranus liberates, although for some people the retrograde process may seem to be excessively inhibiting, particularly if one's surroundings do not allow for much freedom. For rebels, contemplation and internalization bring greater inner strength. While Uranus is retrograde, be sure to set a standard for a certain degree of freedom in your life, so that you can stop and smell the flowers this summer and into the days of autumn. Don't let this valuable time of the year slide by without allowing your inner rebel to kick up his or her heels once in awhile. Freedom is a worthy thing to claim.

**Venus square Neptune** (occurring June 25 – July 4) Venus in Taurus square Neptune in Aquarius brings earthy pleasures, love, and expressions of beauty and femininity into a place where they run up against the obstacles represented by the

148

higher, more refined goddess image that humanity expects. A conflict of beliefs about womanhood is common with this aspect, and sometimes women, artists, and very attractive people are placed on high pedestals. Despite this, the human element usually leads them to certain error and they suffer great delusions. It is here that beauty suffers a spiritual conflict. The expectation and conditioning of others has created a false image of beauty, and the person on whom it is imposed is likely to be suffocated by the beliefs of others. With Venus square Neptune, what we want is challenged by what we know is best for us. Consequently, it may be difficult for some people to make a personal connection with spiritual attractions. Beliefs concerning love matters may be tested. Despite the conflicts, this is a time to rise to the challenge of believing in love and loving your own choice of spiritual path. As for the art of love, the influences of this aspect are not as harsh for those who understand that true beauty is found in the core of feminine wisdom, and that magnetic attraction goes beyond temporal beauty. This aspect will reoccur November 21 – 29, reaching its exact aspect peak on November 26 with Venus in Scorpio.

**Mercury trine Neptune** (occurring June 28 – July 3) Mercury in Gemini trine Neptune in Aquarius brings thoughtful discussions and intuitive knowledge. Communicate about spiritual needs with helpful counsel and receive gifts of renewed faith in your own beliefs. Accept that some messages are there to spiritually uplift you. This is a superb aspect for discussing personal philosophies and metaphysical subjects, and a good time to communicate with the spirit world. Mercury trine Neptune brings gifts of encouraging news from Spirit. Out of the upheaval will come a much needed boon during this very busy day of numerous planetary aspects. Those who are open to communication and prayer will have a spiritual channel attuned to their hearts and minds where peace and tranquility can be found. Mercury trine Neptune will reoccur October 20 – 26, reaching its exact aspect on October 24, with Mercury in Libra.

**Mercury trine Jupiter** (occurring June 28 – July 3) This most favorable aspect brings good news of expansion and prosperity to those who are open to broadening their awareness. Ask and you shall have! Mercury in Gemini trine Jupiter in Aquarius inspires thoughtful and clever communication which can lead to career breakthroughs, adventure, great achievements, happiness and wellbeing. This is an excellent time to learn new skills which will improve one's livelihood and better one's outlook. This is also a great time for salespeople to make sales. Since Jupiter is in Aquarius, this is a favorable time to launch fundraisers for charities. Mercury brings news, while Jupiter brings wealth and prosperous change. Mercury trine Jupiter is often considered to be an advantageous time to advertise and put information out there, and to ask for a job or a loan. Look openly for opportunity when sharing information, and promote yourself and your capabilities. This aspect will reoccur October 16 – 22, reaching its exact aspect on October 20 with Mercury in Libra.

**Mercury square Uranus** (occurring June 28 – July 3) As a general rule, this aspect creates excessive disruptions in communications. Mercury in Gemini square Uranus in Pisces brings communications, talks, discussions and news that may appear troubled and challenged by unusual or explosive circumstances. It is also possible that important news of a radical nature will be obscured by sensationalism or overlooked as insignificant. Mercury in the sign of Gemini emphasizes the need to communicate about absolutely everything, while Uranus in the sign of Pisces emphasizes the need to deal with the revolutionary processes of beliefs, religion, and spiritual matters. The two focuses are creating a tension between people as they discuss their beliefs. Religious debates bring out the two sides of an issue repeatedly. Be careful what you say and how you say it; stirring up chaos can sometimes cause disruptive damage that is not really necessary and, in this case, may be a contributing factor that costs some folks their jobs or something else important to them. This aspect will reoccur on one more occasion this year, November 26 – December 2, reaching its exact position on November 30 with Mercury in Sagittarius.

**Venus square Jupiter** (occurring June 26 – July 4) As if it isn't already bad enough with several significant aspects occurring today, including Venus square Neptune (see above), Venus is also square to Jupiter. This brings love and feminine awareness (Venus) into difficulty (the square aspect) with regard to both spiritual (Neptune) and material (Jupiter) matters. Venus in Taurus square Jupiter in Aquarius brings a love for comforting beauty and affection which may be challenged by the need to handle escalating economic obligations or social debts. Our experiences of beauty and affection may be tested by the difficulty of attracting or acquiring prosperity. Some might say that the act of appreciating beauty is a form of prosperity in itself. Unfortunately, this aspect may create an obstacle to acknowledging the expenses incurred by our attractions and love-needs. This aspect reminds us that something more than love's blindness is required in order for us to fully realize our riches and the value of what we care about most. Venus square Jupiter will reoccur November 18 – 26, reaching its exact aspect on November 23, with Venus in Scorpio.

**Venus sextile Uranus** (occurring June 28 – July 3) Venus in Taurus sure is busy today, with much ado about love, beauty and the need for luxurious affection. First Venus is square to Neptune, then it is square to Jupiter, and to top it off, Venus sextile Uranus stirs up our affections with a great deal of unbelievable chaos. The sextile aspect of Venus to Uranus brings possibilities in love that can go beyond the usual bounds. Venus in Taurus sextile Uranus in Pisces often means that natural beauty takes on a radical or unusual kind of expression. Eccentric love may erupt with this aspect. Venus sextile Uranus can encourage us to break useless tendencies and habits, and also may bring an opportunity for love related matters to transcend the restriction of unmet personal desires. This is the only time this aspect will occur this year.

# July 2nd Thursday

| Moon in Scorpio | PDT | EDT | |
|---|---|---|---|
| Moon sextile Saturn | 5:11 AM | 8:11 AM | |
| Moon opposite Mars | 6:34 PM | 9:34 PM | |
| Moon square Neptune | 11:38 PM | 2:38 AM | (July 3) |

*Mood Watch*: The Moon has a way of being in the right place at the right time when it comes to checking the astrological temperature of our moods. Today's waxing Scorpio Moon teaches us how to cope with pressures, such as the pressures of yesterday's long winded celestial aspects. The busy whirlwind of activity still abounds, and today's lunar aspects suggest we still have a long haul of activity to encounter and work our way through. Scorpio says: "I create," or "I desire." This is a good time to create an understanding that works for you, and to place your hopes on your heart's desire, no matter how dire or exciting life's predicaments may seem. Sun in Cancer and Moon in Scorpio is generally an emotional time for us, and it allows us to authentically purge our transformative and unrelenting souls. Tomorrow will be crazy in the USA; if you don't want to deal with bank machine charges, crazy traffic lines, and bustling marketplaces, prepare for the madness today!

# July 3rd Friday

| Moon in Scorpio / Sagittarius | PDT | EDT |
|---|---|---|
| Moon square Jupiter | 12:18 AM | 3:18 AM |
| Moon trine Uranus | 12:32 AM | 3:32 AM |
| Moon opposite Venus goes v/c | 3:03 AM | 6:03 AM |
| Moon enters Sagittarius | 7:10 AM | 10:10 AM |
| Mercury enters Cancer | 12:18 PM | 3:18 PM |

*Mood Watch*: For awhile this morning, the void-of-course Scorpio Moon may feel like an emotional hangover. This morning might not be a good time to partake in the crazy void-Moon traffic during the commencement of the long weekend of the US holiday. In many places throughout North America, including Canada which is still recuperating from a crazy Canada Day (July 1), there is a powerful spirit of restlessness. Once the Moon enters Sagittarius, the full extent of bustling travelers and beefed-up marketplaces can be felt. Some are poised to serve and make a buck, while others are determined to get away, even if only for a short escape. Sagittarius Moon brings out the adventurer in us, but if you're not interested in getting caught up in the hubbub of entrepreneurs, fortune-hunters, or buccaneers, take swift measures to buckle down in a quiet place with plenty of food on hand.

Mercury enters Cancer (Mercury in Cancer: July 3 – 17) The shift in communications turns our attention from an emphasis on details and logic (Mercury in Gemini) to a focus on feelings and senses (Mercury in Cancer). This is a time when many people will appear to intuit their way through conversations. Thoughts may blend with mood as the emphasis on emotional expression takes the stage. As Mercury goes through the sign of Cancer, take special note of a tendency for people to talk more specifically about their feelings, defenses, and the need to be nurtured. Mercury in Cancer makes some people more intuitive to the thoughts of others, and this may be an easier time to interpret people's thoughts by observing their emotional body language. Through Cancer, thoughts and communications are shaped by the course of our complex world of emotions.

# July 4ᵗʰ Saturday

Independence Day, USA

| Moon in Sagittarius | PDT | EDT |
|---|---|---|
| Mercury opposite Pluto | 8:28 AM | 11:28 AM |
| Moon square Saturn | 4:43 PM | 7:43 PM |
| Sun sextile Saturn begins (see July 9) | | |

*"America is a young country with an old mentality. "*
– George Santayana (1863 – 1952) - US (Spanish-born) philosopher

***Mood Watch***: Today's vibrantly waxing Sagittarius Moon will bring strong philo-sophical perspectives and moods. It would be wise to apply caution and to act espe-cially responsibly while the Moon is square to Saturn. Sagittarius says: "I see," and today's overall activities call for vision and creative effort to enjoy this valuable summer time.

**Mercury opposite Pluto** (occurring July 1 – 5) For the first time in our lifetime, Mercury in Cancer opposes Pluto in Capricorn. Emotional perspectives of the intense and grotesque aspects of the news may be emphasized, causing horror, fascination, realization, and for some people, a kind of triumph as well. The news highlights power issues and the ensuing struggles for a breakthrough. This aspect will only be evident for a short time, but the long term affects for some folks may be unforgettable. Mind boggling awareness abounds now as the need to comprehend awakening powerful issues comes through in our thoughts and discussions.

# July 5ᵗʰ Sunday

| Moon in Sagittarius / Capricorn | PDT | EDT | |
|---|---|---|---|
| Venus enters Gemini | 1:22 AM | 4:22 AM | |
| Moon sextile Neptune | 11:17 AM | 2:17 PM | |
| Moon sextile Jupiter | 11:45 AM | 2:45 PM | |
| Moon square Uranus goes v/c | 12:17 PM | 3:17 PM | |
| Moon enters Capricorn | 7:07 PM | 10:07 PM | |
| Moon conjunct Pluto | 10:28 PM | 1:28 AM | (July 6) |

***Mood Watch***: The morning starts out brightly and on an encouraging note with the positive lunar aspects. Just as the long US holiday began with traffic on the void-of-course Moon, today's long void-of-course Moon in Sagittarius will bring no relief. Hang in there; while the Moon remains void for more than seven hours, expect delays, spacey moods, and a tendency for people to go out of the usual bounds, or to get lost. Later tonight, the Moon in Capricorn will bring a diligent spirit to cap our evening affairs. Our moods and actions will tend to be resourceful, disciplined, concentrated, and unwavering. This is a good time to try to get some rest.

**Venus enters Gemini** (Venus in Gemini: July 5 – 31) Venus, the influence of love, magnetism and attraction now enters Gemini, the personification of duality. Love desires may be split and suffer from ambivalence and schisms. Gemini people will focus more intently on personal attractions and love related matters, while Sagittarius folks may be overwhelmed by love concerns as Venus opposes their natal Sun. Virgo and Pisces people are also likely to feel affection related chal-lenges or difficulties in their life as Venus squares their natal Sun positions. Librans and Aquarians will find things a little easier. With Venus in Gemini, there is an attraction to writing, speaking about, and recording extraordinary experiences and stories, especially about beauty and love. Gossip and talk about love matters will be especially prevalent. Venus in Gemini shows us the two sides of love – the giving and the taking. As attractions appear more diverse, concerns may arise among those with a jealous nature. Love related changes are rampant – to some it's a challenge, while for others, it's a breath of fresh air.

# July 6th Monday

*Full Moon Eve*

| Moon in Capricorn | PDT | EDT |
|---|---|---|
| Moon opposite Mercury | 6:35 AM | 9:35 AM |
| Mars square Neptune | 7:42 AM | 10:42 AM |
| Mars square Jupiter | 1:47 PM | 4:47 PM |

*Mood Watch*: The Full Moon Eve is upon us and while the Moon is full in Capricorn, David Bowie's lyrical term "serious moonlight" describes it all. After all, David Bowie is a Capricorn! Full Capricorn Moon activities tend to be serious, profound, goal conscious, astute, and enterprising. Capricorn Moon reminds us to act in a conscientious way, to be practical and aware, particularly when it comes to knowing one's limitations. This is quite odd to think about when the Full Moon is so often associated with lunacy and craziness. Capricorn is in the opposite position to the Moon's home base, Cancer, and yet, sometimes opposites create the perfect balance. Capricorn is a cardinal sign and so is Cancer. In between Cancer and Capricorn falls the cardinal sign Libra which concentrates our energies on the need for balance. Somewhere between pragmatism and lunacy, the Full Capricorn Moon strikes a perfect balance. Don't let the pending lunar eclipse impede on your sensibilities.

**Mars square Neptune** (occurring June 28 – July 10) Heated activities run into obstacles concerning the work of Great Spirit and the fulfillment of spiritual harmony. Mars is in Taurus and there may be a physical disruption that intrudes on or impedes our spiritual level of experience. Martial forces are bursting through temples, belief systems, and holy moments. Active aggression occurs around spiritual groups and religious institutions, often targeting the belief systems of others. Mariners at sea may run into challenging storms. This aspect also brings the potential for accidents and temper tantrums, especially with regard to opinions about substance abuse and sacred matters. It is important not to get so wrapped up in the spiritual side of things that physical world realities, such as fire, are overlooked. Angry outbursts are likely to affect sacred land or the personal territory of spiritual sentiment. While Mars square Neptune occurs, it is best to anticipate confrontations concerning moral or spiritual issues. As this aspect passes, it will be easier to put spiritual beliefs and practices back on course without much conflict or interference. Meanwhile, stay aware and ready to deal with whatever comes along.

**Mars square Jupiter** (occurring June 28 – July 10) Fortunately, this is the only time Mars square Jupiter occurs this year. As it occurs, various activities are met with the obstacles of economic oppression and shortfall. This is a very difficult time to excel in business endeavors, especially in actively trading markets. This aspect warns us that there will be trouble when approaching the job market aggressively. Trying to make progress using headstrong attitudes and unwarranted self-confidence might impede progress. This aspect brings no-nonsense demands or increases in our workload. Mars in Taurus suggests the need for aggressive business tactics and banking adjustments, which are likely to become expensive while Mars is square to Jupiter. Jupiter is in Aquarius, focusing on the expansion of wealth through science, technology, and social development (see Jupiter enters Aquarius: Jan. 5). The square aspect of these two planets creates a challenging dynamic in the struggle to grow economically. Expect to work a lot harder and perhaps a lot longer in order to smooth the rough edges of the financial empire while Mars in Taurus squares Jupiter in Aquarius.

# July 7th Tuesday
**FULL MOON in CAPRICORN – Penumbral Lunar Eclipse**

| Moon in Capricorn | PDT | EDT |
|---|---|---|
| Mars sextile Uranus | 12:48 AM | 3:48 AM |
| Moon opposite Sun | 2:21 AM | 5:21 AM |
| Moon trine Saturn | 5:45 AM | 8:45 AM |

*Mood Watch*: The **Full Moon in Capricorn** (Moon opposite Sun) occurs overnight. The Full Moon always suggests a time of celebration, and the earthy Capricorn expression focuses on the accomplishment of goals through the application of persistence and diligence. The gold is in your integrity and work. This morning the Full Capricorn Moon will be trine to Saturn – Saturn being the planet that rules Capricorn – and this brings an excellent time to focus on accomplishing and setting important goals that will eventually bring satisfaction.

**Penumbral Lunar Eclipse:** Every year there are at least two lunar eclipses, this year there are four, and today brings the second one. The first penumbral lunar eclipse occurred on February 9. The next penumbral lunar eclipse occurs on August 5, and the final eclipse – a partial lunar eclipse – occurs on December 31. A lunar eclipse occurs when the Earth moves between the moon and the sun, blocking the light that reflects off the moon's surface back to Earth. The darkness of a "penumbra" varies gradually from total darkness at one edge to full brightness at the other. Darkness is the key, as there tends to be the common belief that the casting of a shadow upon the Moon brings darker than average moods. Some view this as mere superstition while others may base this belief on their personal experiences. A lunar eclipse with the Moon in Capricorn may bring earthquakes around this time, or some other kind of earth shattering event. There may also be a death of a notable figure. Capricorn says: "I use"; this is a good time to beware of manipulative characters or those who might take advantage of unwitting victims.

**Mars sextile Uranus** (occurring July 1 – 9) Mars in Taurus is sextile to Uranus in Pisces. Systematic forces of combat (Mars in Taurus) have the potential (the sextile aspect) to create mysterious kinds of chaos in unanticipated ways (Uranus in Pisces). Mars governs all activities and forces of action. Uranus governs the element of surprise, change, and liberation. The sextile aspect brings opportunity, and puts this stubborn but practical Mars energy into a position of arousing and

154

igniting the explosive, unpredictable and chaotic energies of Uranus. Both of these planets are charged with forceful energy and vitality as well as being violent and unsettled at times. Masculine forces are forging ahead abruptly and loudly right now. The overall qualities of Mars sextile Uranus are very fiery, although not necessarily completely destructive. It is important to look for the opportunity and potential in all sources of raw masculine energy. This aspect last occurred Jan. 16 – 25, reaching its exact peak on January 22 with Mars in Capricorn.

# July 8th Wednesday

| Moon in Capricorn / Aquarius | PDT | EDT |
|---|---|---|
| Moon sextile Uranus | 1:08 AM | 4:08 AM |
| Moon trine Mars goes v/c | 2:42 AM | 5:42 AM |
| Moon enters Aquarius | 8:03 AM | 11:03 AM |
| Moon trine Venus | 4:06 PM | 7:06 PM |
| Sun conjunct Mercury begins (see July 13) | | |

*Mood Watch*: For a temporary period during the morning, the void-of-course Capricorn Moon may encumber our sensibilities. Soon enough, however, the Moon enters Aquarius and although it now wanes, it is still quite full. A full, but waning, Aquarius Moon brings thought provoking insights. People may seem either very ingenious or downright moronic. Brilliance takes all forms and shapes. This is no time to shut down and give into human stupidity. Later today, Moon trine Venus brings affectionate moods, and artistic endeavors may come off particularly brilliant or profound. Experiment! Today, anything is possible.

# July 9th Thursday

| Moon in Aquarius | PDT | EDT |
|---|---|---|
| Sun sextile Saturn | 12:09 AM | 3:09 AM |
| Mercury sextile Saturn begins (see July 11) | | |

*Mood Watch*: Today the waning Aquarius Moon does not complicate matters with aspects to other planets. It is simply an Aquarius Moon; however, this statement is misleading as there is nothing simple about an Aquarius Moon. This is a time when eccentricity and ingenuity abound to keep our moods interesting and unpredictable. This is a good time to look for the loopholes in daily routines, and to look for an innovative way to see things differently. It may also be a time when acts of stupidity are particularly annoying. Stick with the smart people.

**Sun sextile Saturn** (occurring July 4 – 11) This occurrence of Sun sextile Saturn particularly affects those Cancer people celebrating birthdays between July 4 – 11, helping them focus their energy and disciplines with greater clarity throughout the year. As Saturn enters the sextile aspect to the natal Sun of these Cancer people, they will have a greater sense of making progress through discipline, and they may very well begin to see the rewards of their diligent labor in the coming year. This is only true, however, as long as they apply themselves to their work and maintain a vigilant and persistent effort to master personal discipline and training. Birthday Cancer folks of this time must remember: greater control comes with genuine effort. This aspect will reoccur November 20 – 26, reaching its exact aspect peak on November 24 with Sun in Sagittarius and Saturn in Libra.

155

# July 10th Friday

| Moon in Aquarius / Pisces | PDT | EDT | |
|---|---|---|---|
| Jupiter conjunct Neptune | 2:11 AM | 5:11 AM | |
| Moon conjunct Jupiter | 12:41 PM | 3:41 PM | |
| Moon conjunct Neptune | 12:44 PM | 3:44 PM | |
| Moon square Mars goes v/c | 7:16 PM | 10:16 PM | |
| Moon enters Pisces | 8:43 PM | 11:43 PM | |
| Moon sextile Pluto | 11:47 PM | 2:47 AM | (July 11) |

*Mood Watch*: Sun in Cancer and Moon in Aquarius bring bubbly and eccentric moods. For the most part, people are curious, engaging, and fair-minded. The USA's *Declaration of Independence* (written by politicians, philosophers, astronomers, and astrologers) was signed with the Sun in Cancer and the Moon in Aquarius. This allowed for a strong, loyal, innovative, and devoutly home-based country. Let the pioneering spirit of the day bring new frontiers to your way of experiencing life. Let originality and keenness of mind prevail. As the Moon goes void-of-course, give it a rest, and as the Moon enters Pisces, let intuition be your guide.

**Jupiter conjunct Neptune** (occurring April 3 – Aug. 13) Jupiter conjunct Neptune in Aquarius brings limitless possibilities for spiritual advancement in humankind. Due to the retrograde patterns of Jupiter and Neptune this year, this rare-occasion event is reaching its peak for the second time during its occurrence dates. For a recap on the story of this fascinating conjunction between Jupiter and Neptune, *see May 27*, when it first occurred this year. This conjunction will reach its peak for a third and final time this year on December 21, and covers the period of occurrence dates from October 30, 2009 – January 8, 2010.

# July 11th Saturday

| Moon in Pisces | PDT | EDT |
|---|---|---|
| Moon square Venus | 10:43 AM | 1:43 PM |
| Mercury sextile Saturn | 6:55 PM | 9:55 PM |
| Mars enters Gemini | 7:55 PM | 10:55 PM |

*Mood Watch*: This morning's waning Pisces Moon brings a penchant for hypersensitivity, especially while Moon square Venus makes it difficult for artists to work their creative drive into something more pleasing. In general, it may be difficult to let go of the things to which we are attached, or to harmonize with ease. As the day continues, the Pisces Moon envelops our moods with vague inclinations, a deep curiosity, and a subtle quality of perception. Later, Moon sextile Saturn brings the need for clarity, commitment, and it requires a better look at where to draw the lines. Pisces Moon is famous for opening up our spiritual interests.

**Mercury sextile Saturn** (occurring July 9 – 12) Mercury in Cancer is sextile Saturn in Virgo. Mercury in Cancer requires accurate but sensitive communications over vital subjects. Meanwhile, Saturn in Virgo demands prudent and carefully analyzed measures with regard to setting up perimeters and implementing rules. This tends to be a time when struggles and difficulties are discussed, and people draw collective conclusions on how best to handle their problems or responsibilities. This is an opportunistic aspect for communicating work skills, particularly with regard to home related tasks and chores. Make use of it while the opportunity is here. Mercury sextile Saturn will reoccur November 14 – 18, reaching its peak on November 16 with Mercury in Sagittarius and Saturn in Libra.

**Mars enters Gemini** (Mars in Gemini: July 11 – Aug. 25) Mars, the planet of war, energy, action, and force will focus its attention through Gemini, the sign of thinking, communicating, and duality. Gemini people will experience heated thoughts, challenges with anger and fevers, and will most likely endure extended surges of energy and strength. When the energy is harnessed, action manifests as oral or written communications – and all of these expressions will have a fiery and inspired flare. As a general rule, Mars in Gemini helps to stimulate and activate dual perspectives, making it easy to see and understand both sides of a heated discussion while making it more difficult to take sides. Forces may seem scattered and restless for some people at this time. Other people will find that Mars in Gemini sharpens the perception and insight, and these people will stand out through their clear outspokenness. This is a good time to avoid being talked into fighting other people's battles – watch out for smooth talking recruiters.

# July 12ᵗʰ Thursday

| Moon in Pisces | PDT | EDT |
|---|---|---|
| Moon opposite Saturn | 7:24 AM | 10:24 AM |
| Moon trine Mercury | 9:57 AM | 12:57 PM |
| Moon trine Sun | 1:28 PM | 4:28 PM |
| Sun trine Uranus begins (see July 18) | | |

*Mood Watch*: Despite the evident pressures of this morning's Moon opposite Saturn, Pisces Moon gives no boundaries to the scope of feelings. The imagination is strong and feelings are absorbed from all around. A little later, communications are favorable with the Moon trine Mercury. Throughout the day, the Moon in Pisces brings imaginative, poetic and deeply feminine images to the forefront of our emotional awareness. The waning Pisces Moon can be a time when the desire to escape from reality is strong. As Moon wanes, it brings a greater necessity for the closure and dissipation of emotional climaxes that have occurred in the past couple weeks. Pisces Moon brings out our need to quench thirsts, connect with aquatic life forms, and release feelings through art and music. Addictive or compulsive behavior is also strong at this time.

# July 13ᵗʰ Monday

| Moon in Pisces / Aries | PDT | EDT |
|---|---|---|
| Moon conjunct Uranus goes v/c | 1:02 AM | 4:02 AM |
| Moon sextile Mars | 9:46 AM | 12:46 PM |
| Moon square Pluto | 10:28 AM | 1:28 PM |
| Sun conjunct Mercury | 7:15 PM | 10:15 PM |
| Mercury trine Uranus begins (see July 16) | | |

*Mood Watch*: First there are the early morning hours of the void-of-course Pisces Moon, where we encounter some spacey, and mystifying, escapist tendencies. Then we experience the turbo-charged energy of the Aries Moon. The coffee, and even the decaf, spins our moods into hyper-drive as we charge into the early part of the day under the influence of Moon sextile Mars. The dramas and the power-plays thickly coat the atmosphere of our moods, while Moon square Pluto reminds us of the supremacy of life's unyielding transitions. The waning Aries Moon keeps us busy as we charge into – and out of – the bold and intrepid urgency of life itself.

**Sun conjunct Mercury** (occurring July 8 – 16) This conjunction will create a much more thoughtful, communicative and expressive year ahead for those Cancer folks celebrating birthdays July 8 – 16. This is your time (birthday Cancer) to record ideas, relay important messages, and pay close attention to your imaginative thoughts as they are touched by Mercury, creating the urge to speak and be heard. Birthday Cancer, your thoughts will reveal a great deal about who you are, now and in the year to come.

## July 14th Tuesday

| Moon in Aries | PDT | EDT |
|---|---|---|
| Moon sextile Venus | 2:37 AM | 5:37 AM |

*Mood Watch*: Today's waning Moon in Aries sets the tone for many people to push their way through traffic and shopping lines, and to focus on themselves and their own interests. While some are assured they know exactly what they want, others seem baffled at the tenacity and the fortitude behind the push and drive of selfish desires. Selfhood is okay to sport around and we are a self-oriented culture, feeling our way through to find our identities and maintain our egos with some sort of dignity. We're doing okay as long as we are not completely oblivious to the needs of others. This is indeed a time when selfhood is touched upon, and our general moods are based on our own personal needs as well as those pushy or powerful enough to come first! Avoid butting heads if that's not what you're willing to do. For some folks however, head-butting is common practice.

## July 15th Wednesday

**LAST QUARTER MOON in ARIES**

| Moon in Aries / Taurus | PDT | EDT |
|---|---|---|
| Moon square Sun | 2:52 AM | 5:52 AM |
| Moon square Mercury | 6:17 AM | 9:17 AM |
| Moon sextile Jupiter | 7:30 AM | 10:30 AM |
| Moon sextile Neptune goes v/c | 8:06 AM | 11:06 AM |
| Moon enters Taurus | 3:28 PM | 6:28 PM |
| Moon trine Pluto | 6:02 PM | 9:02 PM |
| Venus square Saturn begins (see July 21) | | |

*Mood Watch*: We now come to the **Last Quarter Moon in Aries** (Moon square Sun). Obstacles occur between one's emotions and one's sense of personal identity due to the square aspect. This Moon in Aries expression of mood has very little trouble manifesting new energies. Last Quarter Moon requires disengaging from intensified emotional energy. Dropping problems with the ego becomes the key to this moon. One cannot change the stubbornness and selfishness of others, but one can make a difference by setting the right example individually. Be true to yourself.

# July 16th Sunday

**Moon in Taurus**

| | PDT | EDT |
|---|---|---|
| Mercury trine Uranus | 12:33 AM | 3:33 AM |
| Moon trine Saturn | 11:03 PM | 2:03 AM (July 17) |

*Mood Watch*: The waning Taurus Moon tempers our sense of ambition. As a general rule, the Taurus Moon puts us in touch with our sensibilities. It can also bring laziness, stubbornness, materialism, and a superficial need for a sense of security. The waning Taurus Moon is an excellent time to focus on cleaning up our environment, and to beautify our surroundings with some good, old-fashioned, practical, hands-on care.

**Mercury trine Uranus** (occurring July 13 – 17) Mercury, emphasizing the transmission of news and information, is now in the favorable trine position to Uranus, representing disruption and chaos. This aspect brings news of disorder and calamity which (through the trine aspect) represents a gift, probably one of freedom or a break in the mundane routine. There are many premature or radical breakthroughs waiting in the wings, and Mercury trine Uranus often brings news of these discoveries. Mercury is in Cancer trine to Uranus in Pisces. Talk will be generated about changes in our belief structures and in the arts. Catch phrases, or radical concept statements and ideas, are often born under this aspect, and are more easily absorbed. Mercury trine Uranus also allows for brilliant concepts to shine through and be worded in a way that radically makes sense. This is a good time to record thoughts and appreciate brilliant thinking. This aspect will reoccur November 7 – 13, reaching its peak on November 11 with Mercury in Scorpio.

# July 17th Friday

**Moon in Taurus / Gemini**

| | PDT | EDT |
|---|---|---|
| Moon sextile Sun | 11:44 AM | 2:44 PM |
| Moon square Jupiter | 11:52 AM | 2:52 PM |
| Moon square Neptune | 12:41 PM | 3:41 PM |
| Moon sextile Uranus goes v/c | 1:46 PM | 4:46 PM |
| Mercury enters Leo | 4:07 PM | 7:07 PM |
| Moon enters Gemini | 7:40 PM | 10:40 PM |
| Moon sextile Mercury | 8:16 PM | 11:16 PM |
| Mercury sextile Mars begins (see July 20) | | |

*Mood Watch*: The Moon wanes in Taurus. The early part of the day may seem like a particularly trying time to try to schlep around physically encumbering material wares, especially while the Moon is square to Jupiter and Neptune. This afternoon, Moon sextile Uranus brings the void-of-course phase of the Moon. Confusion and chaos may distress our Taurus Moon responsiveness, and obstinacy may arise. Later, as the Moon enters Gemini, our moods become more flexible, and we may be in a better position to benefit from a clarifying discussion – or two. Gemini Moon gives us the incentive to work our way through the thickness of grave details.

**Mercury enters Leo** (Mercury in Leo: July 17 – Aug. 2) Mercury in Leo is an excellent time to effectively write or perform screenplays and comedy. When Leo the lion speaks, it's a penetrating sound! Mercury in Leo puts the focus of information, news and discussions on entertainment, personal interests, and connection

159

with families. This is the time when many kids are turning to – or away from – family in an effort to find answers. They seek answers they can live with, answers about determining self-identity as well as survival skills. This is a time when do-it-yourself themes and self-help information assist us to respond to our individual needs. Mercury in Leo is a time when the mind establishes, reaffirms and maintains a self-created identity. Connections with Leos will come easily as expressed thoughts become more colorful and dramatic, and communications shift toward charismatic interplay. Self-expression and soulful fortitude will be more evident in our communications while Mercury is in Leo.

# July 18ᵗʰ Saturday

| Moon in Gemini | PDT | EDT | |
|---|---|---|---|
| Moon conjunct Mars | 3:03 AM | 6:03 AM | |
| Sun trine Uranus | 5:35 PM | 8:35 PM | |
| Moon conjunct Venus | 9:05 PM | 12:05 AM | (July 19) |

*Mood Watch*: Gemini Moon puts the focus of our moods on communicating and receiving information. Activities revolve around writing, speeches, conversations, and secretarial duties. On the surface a lot of the information sifts past our ears, through seemingly meaningless detail, and eventually more significant, more useful and practical information is attained.

**Sun trine Uranus** (occurring July 12 – 21) This occurrence of Sun trine Uranus favorably affects our Cancer friends celebrating birthdays July 12 – 21. It puts the radical forces of Uranus in the favorable trine position to the natal Sun of these Cancer folks. This is the time for these birthday people to make the breakthrough. Don't hold back, Cancer folks; chaos is here to stay for awhile, and the apparent madness occurring in your lives is there for a reason. Let the experience be positive as long as this aspect brings gifts. Expect restless desires for freedom and a heart-felt need to break out of your personal prison. These challenges are a necessary part of Cancer folks' growth patterns, and the resultant changes are positive in nature, though on the surface they may seem harsh and overbearing. Freedom knocks loudly and the course of change for these people is inevitable in the next year. The trine aspect bestows gifts of triumph, and this could be a good time to let chaos be the force that brings freedom. This aspect will reoccur November 8 – 17, reaching its exact aspect peak on November 14, and will affect the Scorpio birthday people of that time.

# July 19ᵗʰ Sunday

| Moon in Gemini / Cancer | PDT | EDT | |
|---|---|---|---|
| Moon square Saturn | 1:37 AM | 4:37 AM | |
| Moon trine Jupiter | 1:06 PM | 4:06 PM | |
| Moon trine Neptune | 2:07 PM | 5:07 PM | |
| Moon square Uranus goes v/c | 3:11 PM | 6:11 PM | |
| Moon enters Cancer | 8:50 PM | 11:50 PM | |
| Moon opposite Pluto | 10:57 PM | 1:57 AM | (July 20) |

*Mood Watch*: Gemini Moon teaches us about handling multiple details. While most of us are asleep in North America, Moon square Saturn keeps our dreams full of intense labors and it punctuates our need to deal with our responsibilities. For the most part, today will be an outgoing and pleasant day with the Moon in the trine position to Jupiter and Neptune. However, as the Moon squares with Uranus and goes void-of-course, expect the potential for some explosive chaos. It's the close of the weekend, and those summer holiday travelers may be the reason for numerous accidents and traffic jams through the more congested thoroughfares. Tonight, as the Moon enters Cancer, intuitive reflection will give our moods a clearer perspective on the events of the day.

# July 20ᵗʰ Monday

**Moon in Cancer**

| | PDT | EDT |
|---|---|---|
| Mercury sextile Mars | 4:32 PM | 7:32 PM |

*Mood Watch*: A certain degree of moodiness is to be expected on this Cancer Moon Monday. After all, the Moon now wanes darkly towards tomorrow's New Moon, which also brings a total solar eclipse. In the midst of darkness there is a demand on our psyche to find inner strength. Don't let the dark clouds ruin your picnic! Rejoice in the trials of life, for therein you will find triumph and hidden glory. There's great truth in the saying, "it's always darkest before the dawn." Blow off these temporary blues and give it a jazzy tempo!

**Mercury sextile Mars** (occurring July 17 – 22) Mercury sextile Mars brings opportunities that can be recognized, received, communicated and acted upon. Mercury in Leo is sextile Mars in Gemini. News or information, particularly with regard to family members, may lead to the taking of immediate action. Mercury in Leo emphasizes talk and discussions that revolve around personal needs and the family. Mars in Gemini brings thoughtful and intellectually stirring activities. Family oriented deliberation leads to effective action, often with a dual purpose. Applying active communication has the potential for a very favorable outcome. This aspect will return on two more occasions this year, first, September 25 – October 8, reaching its peak on September 30. Secondly, it reaches another peak on October 4 with Mercury in Virgo and Mars in Cancer.

# July 21ˢᵗ Tuesday

**NEW MOON in CANCER – Total Solar Eclipse**

| Moon in Cancer / Leo | PDT | EDT |
|---|---|---|
| Moon sextile Saturn | 1:56 AM | 4:56 AM |
| Venus square Saturn | 1:05 PM | 4:05 PM |
| Moon trine Uranus | 2:51 PM | 5:51 PM |
| Moon conjunct Sun goes v/c | 7:34 PM | 10:34 PM |
| Moon enters Leo | 8:27 PM | 11:27 PM |

*Mood Watch*: The **New Moon in Cancer** (Moon conjunct Sun) beckons to our moods to tune into the latest feelings about ourselves, and particularly, our homes. The New Cancer Moon invites new experience and brings fresh desires to nurture the child within and build up a brighter outlook on our home life. Cancer focuses on the nurturing strength of the mother. This is a good time to bring new things to the home and brighten up one's outlook with nurturing and uplifting moods and feelings.

**Total Solar Eclipse:** In the sign of Cancer, this Eclipse brings an emphasis on controversies rooted in our feelings and emotional core. For some, the ability to have clear feelings may seem overshadowed, but it must be remembered that this is only a brief shadow. Eclipses are believed to threaten the lives and liberty of leaders and special figures in society. The cardinal water sign of Cancer in the ecliptic state often influences hurricanes, floods, storms, and drought. This is the time to reassure those who are undergoing emotional dramas and to be patient with emotional outbursts. The last Eclipse (a Lunar Eclipse) occurred on July 7. Every time there is a Solar Eclipse, there is always a Lunar Eclipse within two weeks. This Eclipse duo will have another Eclipse pair at the opposite time of year: *see January 26 & February 9.* Although this may not feel like a particularly easy time for starting anew, the Solar Eclipse touches our lives with a fluid and accepting kind of assertiveness to move through the greatest obstacles. Beware of the tendency for some people to lean towards substance abuse, depression, and emotional instability. Consult the Internet for the times and locations for viewing this year's total Solar Eclipse, as many sights show a real-time view of this event.

**Venus square Saturn** (occurring July 15 – 24) Venus in Gemini is square to Saturn in Virgo. It may be difficult to engage in romance, particularly when communicating, as it might seem that something is always getting in the way of basic pleasures. Perhaps it is best not to get bent out of shape over some people's need to create restrictions in order to protect their own sense of security while love related troubles are being worked out. No matter how much one prioritizes a focus on love, it is still likely to be misinterpreted on some level during Venus square Saturn. Love related dramas may be taken too seriously. The basic expression of love will flow more easily without the limitations of expectations or demands, though this advice may not work so well when it comes to making excuses. Give it your best, keep singing the praises of love and applying the law of attraction, but expect some challenges and limitations nonetheless. This aspect will return December 24 – 31, reaching an exact square on December 28 with Venus in Capricorn and Saturn in Libra.

# LEO

Key Phrase: "I WILL"

Fixed Fire Sign

Ruling Planet: Sun

Symbol: The Majestic Lion

July 22nd through August 22nd

# July 22nd Wednesday

**Moon in Leo**

| | PDT | EDT |
|---|---|---|
| Moon sextile Mars | 8:04 AM | 11:04 AM |
| Sun enters Leo | 9:35 AM | 12:35 PM |
| Moon conjunct Mercury | 11:58 AM | 2:58 PM |
| Venus trine Jupiter begins | (see July 26) | |
| Venus trine Neptune begins | (see July 27) | |

*Mood Watch*: The Moon newly waxes in Leo, and it's a great place for the Moon to get us in the mood for the pending days of the Sun in Leo. This is the time to recharge your batteries, to indulge in your favorite activities, and to get in tune with family, and friends. Leo Moon is the time to seek leisurely endeavors, to ease up on overwhelming work tasks and, if need be, delegate parts of your heavy workload to someone you trust. If you don't have people you trust and your life is not set up that way, perhaps it's time to start training others to assist you. This may be the time for you to address issues of trust. If you've been burnt through trust maybe it's time to get back on the horse and try again. If you fail to give yourself a break and to trust others, you are choosing a very beastly way of life. Leo the lion is proud and trusting. A time comes when we all must learn to trust, whether we need to trust colleagues, friends, professional help, or most of all – ourselves. This includes trusting your own judgment; you'll need to trust that if you want to feel confident and move past life's hardships.

**Sun enters Leo** (Sun in Leo: July 22 – Aug. 22) Leo, the sign ruled by the Sun, fills the season with strong, instinctive fervor and deep, fiery desire. Leo focuses on will, identity, truth, selfhood, integrity, pride, and strength. Yours is a lustful time of year, Leo, and your totem, the lion, is one of the most self-assured of the zodiac's symbols. Sun in Leo focuses our attention on Sun related frolic and play, outdoor activities for children and families, and the entire entertainment industry. This is the time for self-development and fulfillment. Leo says, "I Will," and it is important for a Leo to be expressive in the act of will. The Leo part within us must remember with a true affirmation of will we can have *anything* we want – we just can't have *everything*. Choose what is true to the self!

# July 23rd Thursday

**Moon in Leo / Virgo**

| | PDT | EDT | |
|---|---|---|---|
| Moon sextile Venus | 4:34 AM | 7:34 AM | |
| Moon opposite Jupiter | 11:56 AM | 2:56 PM | |
| Moon opposite Neptune goes v/c | 1:28 PM | 4:28 PM | |
| Moon enters Virgo | 8:23 PM | 11:23 PM | |
| Moon trine Pluto | 10:24 PM | 1:24 AM | (July 24) |
| Venus square Uranus begins | (see July 28) | | |

*Mood Watch*: Sun and Moon in Leo bring the potential for humorous interaction, kindness, and playfulness. However, as the Moon opposes Jupiter, some folks may be feeling overwhelmed by financial troubles, or they may get the feeling that too much progress is occurring all at once. This afternoon, Moon opposite Neptune brings a void-of-course Leo Moon and our moods may be spacey, forgetful, preoc-cupied, and self-absorbed. Laziness may set in for some folks and the strong need for a relaxing break may be tugging at our heart strings. Tonight's Virgo Moon brings a better time to think matters through.

# July 24th Friday

| Moon in Virgo | PDT | EDT |
|---|---|---|
| Moon square Mars | 10:45 AM | 1:45 PM |

*Mood Watch*: Virgo Moon gives us the impetus to work through complexity. While the Moon is square to Mars, many folks may feel challenged by health related problems. Rage may occur with regard to our addictions or overindulgences. There may be difficulty in the effort to muster up some strength and to deal with matters head-on. Quite simply, the Virgo Moon is here to give us the incentive to handle complications with some tact, precision, and order. This is a good time to seek pragmatic solutions. Steer clear of critical or pedantic sarcasm and cruelty. Extreme defensiveness is just a sign of insecurity. Virgo analyzes but that doesn't mean we must find fault and nitpick the efforts of others. This is a good time to clean up your act.

# July 25th Saturday

| Moon in Virgo / Libra | PDT | EDT | |
|---|---|---|---|
| Moon conjunct Saturn | 3:12 AM | 6:12 AM | |
| Moon square Venus | 10:02 AM | 1:02 PM | |
| Moon opposite Uranus goes v/c | 4:14 PM | 7:14 PM | |
| Moon enters Libra | 10:26 PM | 1:26 AM | (July 26) |

*Mood Watch*: The Virgo Moon emphasizes our need to purify, cleanse, and clean up our surroundings. This is a good time to execute good health practices, and to seek gentle kindness, especially while the Moon is square Venus, and people tend to be less than pleasant. The waxing Virgo Moon motivates us to find order and logic in the way we choose to handle matters. As the Moon opposes Uranus, it then goes void-of-course. This is a time when our moods may be challenged by criticism, self-doubt, or the inclination to be argumentative. A quiet night at home may be the way to go, but if you've got big plans, try not to let people's overly inquisitive criticisms get to you.

# July 26th Sunday

| Moon in Libra | PDT | EDT | |
|---|---|---|---|
| Moon square Pluto | 12:30 AM | 3:30 AM | |
| Moon sextile Sun | 4:42 AM | 7:42 AM | |
| Moon trine Mars | 4:24 PM | 7:24 PM | |
| Venus trine Jupiter | 9:07 PM | 12:07 AM | (July 27) |
| Mercury opposite Jupiter begins | (see July 30) | | |

*Mood Watch*: The Moon waxes in Libra, a time when our moods are oriented towards an accommodating, congenial, and friendly manner. For the most part, today's aspects are relatively positive in nature. Somewhere the birds are singing, the sky is blue, and people are getting along. As the philosopher, Mick Jagger – born on this day in 1943 – once said: "You can't always get what you want." Libra plays the diplomat, but many folks know that diplomacy is just a sneaky way of tricking the people into thinking that they're getting what they want. Diplomacy doesn't always make friendships work. Sometimes we need to be honest, to ask for what we *need* and not necessarily what we *want*. That's why it's very important to remember Sir Mick's counter charge: "...but if you try sometime, you just might find, you get what you need." Although they are few and far between, the honest and well loved diplomats will generally get what they need.

**Venus trine Jupiter** (occurring July 22 – 29) Valuable and inspiring gifts of love and affection come with this aspect. Love (Venus) is harmoniously placed with prosperity and opportunity (Jupiter). Venus in Gemini trine Jupiter in Aquarius brings intelligent love and affection, and flirtatious and lighthearted expressions of beauty which may lead to unusual – but very humane and conscientious – encounters with richness and prosperity. This is a great time to give gifts of love, and for many, it offers an expansive outlook of love's power. Getting ahead in life, in this case, has everything to do with appreciating and loving those areas of life in which we want to expand and prosper. A positive outlook can indeed help make this happen. This year we will be graced with the presence of this delicious tango of Venus and Jupiter again from October 23 – 31, reaching its exact aspect peak on October 28 with Venus in Libra.

# July 27ᵗʰ Monday

| Moon in Libra | PDT | EDT | |
|---|---|---|---|
| Moon sextile Mercury | 7:47 AM | 10:47 AM | |
| Moon trine Jupiter | 5:28 PM | 8:28 PM | |
| Moon trine Venus | 7:36 PM | 10:36 PM | |
| Moon trine Neptune goes v/c | 7:53 PM | 10:53 PM | |
| Venus trine Neptune | 10:51 PM | 1:51 AM | (July 28) |
| Mercury opposite Neptune begins (see July 31) | | | |
| Venus opposite Pluto begins (see August 1) | | | |

*Mood Watch*: The waxing Libra Moon is likely to bring very pleasant and congenial moods while the Moon is lined up with a monopoly of favorable aspects, particularly all those nice trines. Tonight's void-of-course Moon may bring some indecisiveness, making the late night an especially good time to kick back and relax.

**Venus trine Neptune** (occurring July 22 – 30) Venus in Gemini is trine Neptune in Aquarius. This brings detail oriented feminine love right in harmony with ingenious kinds of spiritual expression. Artistic endeavors will shine with spiritual brilliance. This aspect brings calmness and tranquility that are vitally needed, particularly in love related matters, and especially while Venus is square Uranus *(see tomorrow)*. When coming from a place of love, it is easier to draw down a spiritual enhancement of that love with Venus trine Neptune. Enjoying beauty is a way to acquire gifts of the spirit world. This is a good time to actively engage in peaceful, pleasurable, and spiritual love. This aspect will reoccur October 28 – November 5, reaching its exact aspect peak on November 2 with Venus in Libra.

# July 28th Tuesday
## FIRST QUARTER MOON in SCORPIO

| Moon in Libra / Scorpio | PDT | EDT |
|---|---|---|
| Moon enters Scorpio | 3:56 AM | 6:56 AM |
| Moon sextile Pluto | 6:03 AM | 9:03 AM |
| Venus square Uranus | 1:38 PM | 4:38 PM |
| Moon square Sun | 3:00 PM | 6:00 PM |

*Mood Watch*: The **First Quarter Moon in Scorpio** (Moon square Sun) arouses our moods in deep and impassioned ways. Throughout today, this waxing quarter Moon of Scorpio persists to bring our moods to a strange and intense level of existence. Get in touch with your creative and imaginative side, and celebrate your passion.

**Venus square Uranus** (occurring July 23 – 31) Venus, the planet that governs love and magnetism, is square Uranus, the planet of chaos and disruption. It may be difficult for love (Venus) to flourish in a spontaneous and carefree fashion. Venus in Gemini is square to Uranus in Pisces. Some folks are likely to become too easily affronted by radical or explosive kinds of magnetism. This influence may be testing the power of love to withstand the chaos of extremes and sudden change. Venus square Uranus will reoccur December 14 – 22, reaching its exact position on December 19 with Venus in Sagittarius.

# July 29th Wednesday

| Moon in Scorpio | PDT | EDT |
|---|---|---|
| Moon sextile Saturn | 4:04 PM | 7:04 PM |

*Mood Watch*: Waxing Scorpio Moon calls to our passionate center. The Sun is in Leo, the Moon is in Scorpio, drama of some sort is bound to happen. Energy rises to the occasion. Scorpio Moon focuses our energies on the need for a positive and uplifting outlook. Physical exertion will help to defuse intense emotions. Spirit releases a death cry, hunger is satiated, and peace is restored. Sales and thefts soar high in the market place. Today's Moon sextile Saturn will help us to determine where, or how, to draw the lines.

# July 30th Thursday

| Moon in Scorpio / Sagittarius | PDT | EDT |
|---|---|---|
| Moon square Mercury | 1:08 AM | 4:08 AM |
| Moon square Jupiter | 1:30 AM | 4:30 AM |
| Mercury opposite Jupiter | 3:38 AM | 6:38 AM |
| Moon square Neptune | 4:30 AM | 7:30 AM |
| Moon trine Uranus goes v/c | 5:54 AM | 8:54 AM |
| Moon enters Sagittarius | 1:10 PM | 4:10 PM |
| Mercury trine Pluto begins (see August 3) | | |
| Mercury sextile Venus begins (see August 7) | | |

*Mood Watch*: For those who find themselves sorely awake after a particularly restless night, that was the Scorpio Moon, busily undergoing strong lunar aspects and delving into the deep caverns of our heartstrings. This morning and afternoon may be disorienting at times while the Moon is void-of-course. Later, the Moon in

Sagittarius gives us the eagle-eye view of our moods. Our perception will seem to grow clearer and more astute.

♌

**Mercury opposite Jupiter** (occurring July 26 – 31) Mercury in Leo is opposite to Jupiter in Aquarius bringing very overwhelming, entertaining, and personal observations about the advancement of science and humanity's aspirations. We may find ourselves bartering for things that cannot be sold. An economic shift may bring financial or political awareness, and the incessant chatter which fills the airwaves has a further effect on the sharp movements occurring in the stock market. This aspect also focuses news on the opulent lifestyles of the rich and famous, as people find themselves unable to stop talking about their financial situation or their need for advancement, a raise, or an income. Wealth is highlighted, and there is considerable debate as to what wealth really represents. Most of the time wealth is an illusion, and people really don't know what they're talking about when they make assumptions about the apparent well being of others. As class separation continues, it is a time of acute concern in this realm. This short-lived aspect only occurs once this year.

# July 31ˢᵗ Friday

| Moon in Sagittarius | PDT | EDT |
|---|---|---|
| Mercury opposite Neptune | 12:47 AM | 3:47 AM |
| Moon trine Sun | 5:51 AM | 8:51 AM |
| Moon opposite Mars | 4:21 PM | 7:21 PM |
| Venus enters Cancer | 6:27 PM | 9:27 PM |
| Mars square Saturn begins (see August 10) | | |

*Mood Watch*: It's the last day of the week – and month – on a waxing Sagittarius Moon day. A lively and outgoing kick to our moods makes this a particularly active day. Sun in Leo and Moon in Sagittarius gives many folks the incentive to explore, see the sights and to tap into creative energy.

**Mercury opposite Neptune** (occurring July 27 – Aug. 1) Mercury opposite Neptune makes us acutely aware of discussions concerning religious beliefs. Beliefs go beyond the physical to the metaphysical realms, where information is accessed and spiritual fortification occurs. It is wisest to be clear on one's own beliefs, and not to put oneself in a position of having to defend or expose those beliefs before a pack of merciless critics. Spiritual growth and enlightenment are not easy things to relay in conversation, and during this aspect it may seem particularly overwhelming for some folks to try to communicate effectively, or to comprehend what others are trying to communicate about spiritual matters. This opposition only occurs once this year.

**Venus enters Cancer** (Venus in Cancer: July 31 – Aug. 26) Venus now enters the nurturing sign of Cancer, an appropriate place for the expression of love and affection. It invites those with rocky love relationships to patch things up, and to do so with more heart and less uncertainty. Venus will be in Cancer today through August 26, encouraging our affections and affinities to be carefully placed and nurtured. When attractions occur, they will have a lasting impression and will seem very strong and emotionally sound. Venus in Cancer brings out a love for such things as the ocean, leisurely aquatic sports, motherly care and expression, and all varieties

167

of nurturing. While Venus travels over their natal Sun, those folks born in the sign of Cancer will be especially aware of their love life and their needs for pleasure.

# August 1st Saturday
**Lammas / Lughnassad**

| Moon in Sagittarius | PDT | EDT | |
|---|---|---|---|
| Moon square Saturn | 3:44 AM | 6:44 AM | |
| Moon sextile Jupiter | 12:27 PM | 3:27 PM | |
| Moon sextile Neptune | 4:02 PM | 7:02 PM | |
| Venus opposite Pluto | 4:35 PM | 7:35 PM | |
| Moon square Uranus | 5:31 PM | 8:31 PM | |
| Moon trine Mercury goes v/c | 10:42 PM | 1:42 AM | (August 2) |

*Mood Watch*: The Sagittarius Moon puts us in the mood to explore. Today brings us to the solar holiday of *Lammas* and we have now reached the halfway mark of summer. The word *Lammas* comes from the term loaf-mass and it traditionally represents the first harvest of corn. The Druids call this festival holiday Lughnasadh, a time dedicated to Lugh, the Celtic Sun god whose name means "shining one." Just as the first crops are cut, this time represents a sacrifice, for Lugh was killed, but he came back to life. After Summer Solstice (June 21) the Sun's light begins to die, and rebirth occurs at Winter Solstice (December 21). Lammas takes place when the crops are thirsty and the green traces of spring have long gone. The fields become strawlike and golden. The Green Man of spring (May 1/Beltane) has been transformed, and he now appears to us as a straw figure popularly known as The Wicker Man or Jack Straw. Although the Sun's light dies away, the life of the Sun is retained in the living harvest. Let unwanted worries and fears die with the Sun King, and reaffirm the picture of self with the promise of the life contained in the harvest of seeds. Collect seeds of wisdom and contemplate in the heart of summer what part of you must die, and what part must be sustained and preserved through the impending autumn and winter, until it can be reborn at Solstice. Celebrate life in the bounty of the summer harvest.

**Venus opposite Pluto** (occurring July 27 – Aug. 4) For the first time in our lifetime, Venus in Cancer opposes Pluto in Capricorn. The love we feel for home, and those places from which we draw a nurturing spirit (Venus in Cancer) will be diametrically opposed to those elements and conditions of life that transform our homes and home-life into something more career based (Pluto in Capricorn). Matters concerning love, beauty, and affection may be overwhelmed by powerful forces or unforeseeable twists of fate. These fateful forces may be intruding somehow on the objects or people we love and admire. This could include just about any kind of scenario – from being shattered over the loss of a loved one, to a terminal disease, to the process of learning how to fully accept and support some kind of total transformation of a loved one. Some people find it difficult to support loved ones through severe kinds of hardship, yet now is the time to offer support to them, despite the opposing forces that appear too harsh or overwhelming. This aspect may well bring on an acute awareness of the desire that some have for power, and the need to have power over loved ones. No one, no matter how powerful, can justifiably tell us what we love, who we love, or how we are to love. Deep in our hearts dwells the truth.

When the going gets tough, look to your heart!

♌

# August 2nd Sunday

**Moon in Sagittarius / Capricorn**

| | PDT | EDT |
|---|---|---|
| Moon enters Capricorn | 1:08 AM | 4:08 AM |
| Moon conjunct Pluto | 3:16 AM | 6:16 AM |
| Moon opposite Venus | 4:26 AM | 7:26 AM |
| Mercury enters Virgo | 4:07 PM | 7:07 PM |

*Mood Watch*: The strongly waxing Moon in Capricorn brings serious moods, and there is a greater effort to handle big jobs and responsibilities. Today's focuses will be largely work oriented, but since today is Sunday, this morning's aspect of Moon opposite Venus is likely to bring a strong focus on the need for pleasure and leisurely comforts. Today may be the time to work on a thesis or to clean out the garage, especially since the Capricorn Moon gives us the impetus to work through tedious chores that require our focus and attention.

**Mercury enters Virgo** (Mercury in Virgo: Aug. 2 – 25) Virgo is a most advantageous place for Mercury – the place where it both rules and is exalted. Mercury in Virgo brings clarity to our plan for the coming events of autumn. It also puts the focus of talk on such issues as computers, budgets, systems analysis, harvesting, accounting, filing, and organizing. Mercury in Virgo brings out the skeptical and analytical side of every argument and topic of discussion, keeping us on our toes. Overall, this is a great time for communications, research, and strategic planning. Due to next month's retrograde cycle of Mercury (Sept. 6/7 – 29,) it will be in Virgo a couple of times this year, reentering the tail end of Virgo on September 17.

# August 3rd Monday

**Civic Holiday, Provincial Day, Canada**

**Moon in Capricorn**

| | PDT | EDT |
|---|---|---|
| Mercury trine Pluto | 7:11 AM | 10:11 AM |
| Moon trine Saturn | 5:07 PM | 8:07 PM |
| Sun sextile Mars begins (see August 17) | | |

*Mood Watch*: In Canada, today brings the continuation of a long holiday weekend. Nevertheless, the Capricorn Moon keeps many folk's minds on work, achievements, and meeting goals. Some folks feel stuck, wishing they didn't have to work, but the call of duty is compelling us to stay focused. For everyone, this is a good time to apply discipline, and to center on what needs to be done. There will be many more days of summer to enjoy.

**Mercury trine Pluto** (occurring July 30 – Aug. 5) Mercury in Virgo trine Pluto in Capricorn brings the message of hope. Mercury in Virgo gives a very methodical, discriminating and meticulous expression to our methods of communication. Mercury trine Pluto brings greater definition to the meaning of fate, and allows us to more easily communicate about the power struggles occurring collectively around the world. Mercury is the communications tower that transmits information. Pluto's disruptive energy is focusing our attention on such issues as contagious diseases, senseless crime, misunderstandings between cultures, facing up to addiction, and

169

many other painful realities. This is a good time to express encouraging words and reinforce the troubled people of our world with a sense of hope. This aspect last occurred April 7 – 12, reaching its exact peak on April 10.

# August 4th Tuesday
*Full Moon Eve*

| Moon in Capricorn / Aquarius | PDT | EDT |
|---|---|---|
| Moon sextile Uranus goes v/c | 6:21 AM | 9:21 AM |
| Moon enters Aquarius | 2:07 PM | 5:07 PM |

*Mood Watch*: Serious, but lazy, moods captivate our morning focuses as the Capricorn Moon goes void-of-course. Not being able to get things done could make this a frustrating or confusing time, and this may be a tricky time to stay focused. The Moon is building up towards fullness and sometimes the high volume of activity stretches us thin. By afternoon/early evening, the Moon enters Aquarius and we may be confronted with unusual kinds of thoughts. Some folks may seem overly idealistic, while others may be especially brilliant – perhaps even hard to follow. Aquarius Moon brings out the absurd in some folks. On the other hand, this may be a time of amazing breakthroughs, rebel rousing fun, or deep thought. Go with the flow – the Moon is full!

# August 5th Wednesday
**FULL MOON in AQUARIUS – Penumbral Lunar Eclipse**

| | PDT | EDT |
|---|---|---|
| Moon opposite Sun | 5:54 PM | 8:54 PM |
| Mars trine Jupiter begins (see August 13) | | |

*Mood Watch*: The **Full Moon in Aquarius** (Moon opposite Sun) enlivens our senses with the need to apply clarity and definition. The mood of the day is likely to be blanketed in bizarre and unusual occurrences, and it's often focused on modern technological breakthroughs and invention. People may seem idealistic and generous in some respects of this lunar expression, or out of hand and downright unrealistic in others. This is a good time to celebrate knowledge.

**Penumbral Lunar Eclipse:** In Aquarius, this eclipse brings an emphasis on the needs of humanity and the systems by which mankind operates. This may be a time of technological glitches or vicarious breakthroughs. There may also be some form of inspiration or liberating change as a result of intense scrutiny at the way systems operate. For some, the act of thinking comprehensively may be overshadowed by the lunar eclipse energy. This is a good time to pace ourselves. A lunar eclipse occurs when the Earth moves between the moon and the sun, blocking the light that reflects off the moon's surface back to Earth. Every year there are at least two lunar eclipses, this year there are four. Today brings the third of the four lunar eclipses. The other penumbral lunar eclipses occurred on February 9 and July 7. The final eclipse – a partial lunar eclipse – occurs on December 31. The darkness of a "penumbra" varies gradually from total darkness at one edge to full brightness at the other. Darkness is the key, as there tends to be the common belief that the casting of a shadow upon the Moon brings darker than average moods. Some view this as mere superstition while others may base this belief on their personal experiences.

♌

# August 6ᵗʰ Thursday

| Moon in Aquarius | PDT | EDT |
|---|---|---|
| Moon trine Mars | 1:11 AM | 4:11 AM |
| Moon conjunct Jupiter | 12:46 PM | 3:46 PM |
| Moon conjunct Neptune goes v/c | 5:19 PM | 8:19 PM |

*Mood Watch*: Today we are left with a lot of food for thought. There will be much to contemplate and a lot to process now that we are in the post-full Moon stages of the month. This is a good time to harness our newest inclinations and to implement an experimental way of living life. Sometimes we have to add a new routine in order to determine what's missing in our lives. Sometimes, extraction brings better awareness. Aquarius Moon makes us curious to see how we respond to change. Sometimes experimentation brings relief, and sometimes it doesn't. Either way, the curiosity is what drives us. Later, as the Moon goes void-of-course, it may be wise to stop experimenting, as technical equipment tends to break down more easily during this lunar expression.

# August 7ᵗʰ Friday

| Moon in Aquarius / Pisces | PDT | EDT |
|---|---|---|
| Moon enters Pisces | 2:33 AM | 5:33 AM |
| Moon sextile Pluto | 4:29 AM | 7:29 AM |
| Moon opposite Mercury | 6:34 PM | 9:34 PM |
| Moon trine Venus | 6:39 PM | 9:39 PM |
| Mercury sextile Venus | 8:55 PM | 11:55 PM |
| Saturn opposite Uranus begins (see September 15) | | |

*Mood Watch*: The Pisces Moon is still rather full, but it is definitively waning, and this means our moods will be deeply preoccupied, introspective, and also, very bubbly and engaging at times. Today's lunar aspects bring regenerative, communicative, and pleasant experiences.

**Mercury sextile Venus** (occurring July 30 – Aug. 31) Mercury in Virgo sextile Venus in Cancer teaches us of the necessity to speak up cautiously and discriminately for our needs, particularly for nurturing and endearing kinds of love and affection. This aspect focuses talk and discussion on the things in life we are most attracted to and touched by. The sextile aspect of Mercury to Venus brings hope and good possibilities for our love needs. This is a good time to speak up for the things and the people of our lives – those things and people whom we treasure. This aspect occurred earlier this year from January 24 – 27, reaching an exact peak on January 26, when Mercury was retrograde in Capricorn and Venus was in Pisces. It also occurred February 21 – 27, reaching its peak on February 25 with Mercury in Aquarius and Venus in Aries. Mercury sextile Venus was non-exact in April, beginning on April 26 and ending before its fruition on May 1. During this occurrence cycle of Mercury sextile Venus, it will reach an exact peak once again on August 28 with Mercury in Libra and Venus in Leo.

171

# August 8th Saturday
**Moon in Pisces**

| | PDT | EDT |
|---|---|---|
| Moon square Mars | 4:13 PM | 7:13 PM |
| Moon opposite Saturn | 6:26 PM | 9:26 PM |
| Mars trine Neptune begins (see August 17) | | |
| Sun opposite Jupiter begins (see August 14) | | |

*Mood Watch*: The Pisces Moon is a complex and very mutable one, and our moods can move in all sorts of directions. This means we may have a difficult time staying focused, but at the same time, we are taking in a number of multifaceted perceptions. This is no time to underestimate the degree to which others perceive what's going on. Moon square Mars and Moon opposite Saturn are two lunar aspects that often force us to deal with life's complexities. Nothing can be forced very easily during a waning Pisces Moon. This Moon is teaching us about the necessity to go with the flow and to skip past the anger, denial, bargaining, and depression. The name of today's game is: acceptance. In due time, we may use our perceptiveness to determine a better plan of action.

# August 9th Sunday
**Moon in Pisces / Aries**

| | PDT | EDT |
|---|---|---|
| Moon conjunct Uranus goes v/c | 5:44 AM | 8:44 AM |
| Moon enters Aries | 1:22 PM | 4:22 PM |
| Moon square Pluto | 3:09 PM | 6:09 PM |

*Mood Watch*: This morning the Pisces Moon conjuncts with Uranus and goes void-of-course. The chaos is likely to bring spacey moods throughout the morning and into the afternoon. As the Moon enters Aries, our moods are energized, more integral, and a great deal more courageous. This comes just in time to deal with life's more permanent complexities as the Moon squares with Pluto. This is a good time to utilize incentives, to face problems head-on, and to internalize, as well as contemplate, our initiatives with a great deal more clarity.

# August 10th Monday
**Moon in Aries**

| | PDT | EDT |
|---|---|---|
| Moon square Venus | 10:47 AM | 1:47 PM |
| Mars square Saturn | 5:16 PM | 8:16 PM |
| Mars square Uranus begins (see August 18) | | |

*Mood Watch*: Sun in Leo and Moon in Aries emphasize the power of selfhood. The complexity of our need for pleasure is addressed with the Moon square Venus. This is indeed a time when selfhood is touched upon, and our general moods are based on our own personal needs, as well as the needs of those who are pushy or powerful enough to come first! Avoid butting heads if that's not what you're looking for, since it's very easy to do on a waning Aries Moon.

**Mars square Saturn** (occurring July 31 – Aug. 16) Mars is in Gemini and Saturn is in Virgo where activities are divided, and probably overly discussed, due to tedious and complex tasks that have critical deadlines. This aspect is known for creating confrontations between offensive and defensive forces, and is usually not a good time to start a new enterprise, particularly in the fields of communications and broadcasting while Mars and Saturn are square to each other in the two signs ruled by Mercury. When deploying forces in battle, this aspect often brings fiery and sometimes tragic endings. It is wise to proceed with extra caution. For some, this could be a time of accidents or tragic endings. This may be an especially difficult time to muster the strength to finish up projects, or to end affairs amicably. Fortunately, this is the only time that Mars will square Saturn this year.

# August 11ᵗʰ Tuesday

| Moon in Aries / Taurus | PDT | EDT | |
|---|---|---|---|
| Moon trine Sun | 1:02 AM | 4:02 AM | |
| Moon sextile Mars | 4:43 AM | 7:43 AM | |
| Moon sextile Jupiter | 7:55 AM | 10:55 AM | |
| Moon sextile Neptune goes v/c | 1:02 PM | 4:02 PM | |
| Moon enters Taurus | 9:48 PM | 12:48 AM | (August 12) |
| Moon trine Pluto | 11:26 PM | 2:26 AM | (August 12) |
| Sun opposite Neptune begins (see August 17) | | | |

*Mood Watch*: Favorable lunar aspects bring numerous opportunities. If we act on our brazen incentives we are likely to encounter positive results. However, it is best to act on these incentives early today as this afternoon's waning Aries Moon goes void-of-course, and this tends to bring false starts and rudeness. Expect the potential for delays, traffic jams, and irritable moods. Later tonight, Moon in Taurus tempers our moods with desires for pleasure, comfort, and relaxation.

# August 12ᵗʰ Wednesday

| Moon in Taurus | PDT | EDT |
|---|---|---|
| Moon sextile Venus | 11:29 PM | 2:29 AM |
| Mercury conjunct Saturn begins (see August 17) | | |

*Mood Watch*: The waning Taurus Moon is a superb time to focus on relaxation, leisurely pleasures, and comforting summer activities. The waning Moon is an introspective time, and yet Taurus is the place of exaltation for the Moon. This combination brings the potential for harmony and peace, especially since the only lunar aspect, Moon sextile Venus (set to occur much, much later tonight) brings an opportunistic time to engage in pleasurable and loving feelings. We are poised to encounter a number of busy lunar aspects tomorrow, but today the Moon compels us to be calm, to work on our composure and, most of all, to enjoy life!

# August 13ᵗʰ Thursday

| LAST QUARTER MOON in TAURUS | PDT | EDT |
|---|---|---|
| Moon trine Mercury | 2:13 AM | 5:13 AM |
| Mars trine Jupiter | 9:29 AM | 12:29 PM |
| Moon trine Saturn | 11:11 AM | 2:11 PM |
| Moon square Sun | 11:53 AM | 2:53 PM |
| Moon square Jupiter | 1:43 PM | 4:43 PM |
| Moon square Neptune | 7:00 PM | 10:00 PM |
| Moon sextile Uranus goes v/c | 8:16 PM | 11:16 PM |
| Mercury square Mars begins (see August 25) | | |

*Mood Watch*: The Moon starts the day pleasantly, with so many trine aspects, but as the day progresses, we will have a lot of things to work through with so many square aspects. The **Last Quarter Moon in Taurus** (Moon square Sun) focuses the general course of our moods on creating some sense of order in our financial situations, and encourages the need for creature comforts and esthetically pleasing or luxurious surroundings. There is often a focus on cleaning up and/or selling various useful artifacts that have collected in our lives. The Last Quarter Taurus Moon often inspires the activities of yard sales, auctions and flea markets. This is a good time to transform one's atmosphere into a more useful and practical working order. Letting go of attachment to material things that have bogged one down with too much maintenance or disruptive costs may very well be the best move, and if ever there is a time to do this, it is during the Last Quarter Moon of Taurus. Certain kinds of sacrifice produce some very remedial freedom.

**Mars trine Jupiter** (occurring Aug. 5 – 17) Mars is in Gemini activating a strong focus on details, communications, thought processes, and placing an all-around emphasis on the power of success. Jupiter is in Aquarius, expanding our economic growth through scientific awareness, technology, and extraordinary types of skills. Act on opportunities as they arise, and set visions and dreams into a feasible plan that holds the potential for favorable actions to occur. The drive to create some expansion of our livelihood involves resourceful awareness. Mars activates and stirs action, while Jupiter represents not only economy and advancement, but our sense of philosophic and visionary awareness as well. For some people this aspect brings gifts of inheritance; for all of us it brings opportunities for growth. Mars trine Jupiter allows us to activate a stronger, more intelligent grasp of our domain, and gives many folks the extra energy and spark to boost their sense of achievement and advancement. This most auspicious aspect only occurs once this year, so it will be best to take advantage while the action is, potentially, the most lucrative.

# August 14ᵗʰ Friday
**Moon in Taurus / Gemini**

| | PDT | EDT |
|---|---|---|
| Moon enters Gemini | 3:24 AM | 6:24 AM |
| Sun opposite Jupiter | 10:52 AM | 1:52 PM |

*Mood Watch*: Early this morning, the waning Moon enters Gemini. Sun in Leo and Moon in Gemini bring a playful, thoughtful, and interesting day for our moods. This is a good time to enjoy theater, entertainment, and personal hobbies, especially through writing, speaking, and communicating our thoughts. Gemini Moon is a great time to share ideas and, particularly while the Sun is in Leo, to be creative while hamming it up.

**Sun opposite Jupiter** (occurring Aug. 8 – 17) Leo birthday people, celebrating birthdays from August 8 – 17, are experiencing the opposition of Jupiter to their natal Sun. This brings an acute awareness of the shifts in personal economic conditions and issues, for better or worse. There is a strong personal awareness,

174

or perhaps an obsession, at work to obtain a sense of wealth, joy, and wellbeing. The need for peace in the shifting economy of these times is strong for these Leo birthday folks. Use your best techniques, birthday Leo, to abstain from impulse buying or credit card use. Governing your expenditures with wisdom instead of impetuosity will assuredly bring you around to the place you know you need to be. While it all comes at you at an overwhelming pace, remember this, Leo – you can have (just about) anything you want – you just can't have *everything*. This aspect only occurs once this year.

# August 15ᵗʰ Saturday

| Moon in Gemini | PDT | EDT | |
|---|---|---|---|
| Moon square Mercury | 11:38 AM | 2:38 PM | |
| Moon square Saturn | 3:13 PM | 6:13 PM | |
| Moon trine Jupiter | 4:45 PM | 7:45 PM | |
| Moon sextile Sun | 7:11 PM | 10:11 PM | |
| Moon conjunct Mars | 7:55 PM | 10:55 PM | |
| Moon trine Neptune | 10:06 PM | 1:06 AM | (August 16) |
| Moon square Uranus goes v/c | 11:17 PM | 2:17 AM | (August 16) |
| Venus sextile Saturn begins (see August 19) | | | |

*Mood Watch*: The Moon wanes in Gemini and with it comes a somewhat complex sort of day. It is complex due to the fact that the day begins with a couple of square aspects to the Moon. It is also complex by virtue of the mental acuity that is required to sort out the many details of a Gemini Moon time. By afternoon/evening, Moon trine Jupiter brings a jovial, celebration oriented, and generous time for our moods. The hot days of summer are in full swing, and in some places it's extremely hot, making it difficult to cool down, even in the night hours as Moon conjunct Mars impresses us with hot attitudes. Let the final say of the Moon trine Neptune bring a positive spirit, an all accepting spirit that allows us to calm ourselves, as well as our Gemini Moon thoughts.

# August 16ᵗʰ Sunday

| Moon in Gemini / Cancer | PDT | EDT |
|---|---|---|
| Moon enters Cancer | 6:12 AM | 9:12 AM |
| Moon opposite Pluto | 7:34 AM | 10:34 AM |
| Mercury opposite Uranus begins (see August 21) | | |

*Mood Watch*: This morning our busy and mentally taxing moods begin to fade as the void-of-course Gemini Moon enters Cancer. The waning Cancer Moon is a good time to tidy up the home, to make the home more comfortable and inviting, and to nurture emotional drama with loving care and nourishment. Cancer Moon always brings up our maternal instincts, particularly when we need them most. Don't fall prey to fears, worries, or negative feelings; fight these things with courage, confidence, and positive thoughts. This is the way of the strong Mother Moon, to encourage our hearts with the generous gracefulness that keeps us sound.

# August 17th Monday

| Moon in Cancer | PDT | EDT |
|---|---|---|
| Sun sextile Mars | 3:57 AM | 6:57 AM |
| Mercury conjunct Saturn | 8:14 AM | 11:14 AM |
| Sun opposite Neptune | 1:54 PM | 4:54 PM |
| Moon conjunct Venus | 2:10 PM | 5:10 PM |
| Moon sextile Saturn | 4:51 PM | 7:51 PM |
| Moon sextile Mercury | 5:33 PM | 8:33 PM |
| Mars trine Neptune | 6:28 PM | 9:28 PM |
| Venus trine Uranus begins (see August 22) | | |
| Sun trine Pluto begins (see August 23) | | |
| Mars opposite Pluto begins (see August 26) | | |

*Mood Watch*: It's a moody Monday, teaming with busy aspects. Fortunately, positive lunar aspects are here to encourage us, and so is the waning Cancer Moon. Although we are likely to be somewhat temperamental at times, this is quite understandable, as our moods are the defense mechanism that keeps us guarded while there are so many astrological aspects taking place. Go with the flow.

**Sun sextile Mars** (occurring Aug. 3 – 23) Sun sextile Mars brings a surge of favorable energy and activity into our lives, particularly enlivening the lives of those Leos, and cusp born Virgos, celebrating a birthday from August 3 – 23. There are opportunities at work, which must be acted upon in order for all of this extra energy to pay off. There may also be a lot of anguish or pressure with regard to self-image, and the heat stirred up by this experience requires direction and assertiveness. Now is the time for Leo birthday folks to take action, to get in shape, and to build up their energy and strength. This is the only time this solar aspect will occur with Mars this year.

**Mercury conjunct Saturn** (occurring Aug. 12 – 20) Mercury conjunct Saturn will bring talk about the need to put an end to the useless or unwanted components of our lives. It will focus our thoughts on the areas of life that have reached limitations, or where timely new beginnings – or endings – are occurring. When occurring in Virgo, this conjunction implies that strong rules or guidelines will be established with regard to business communications, and also health related restrictions and disciplines will be communicated. There is a discerning quality at work with Mercury conjunct Saturn, making this conjunction a very good one for speakers and writers to inspire, initiate and capture vital thoughts. News concerning the end of a cycle is likely to occur. Examples include retirement announcements, job loss, and possibly even the news of a notable death. Overall, Mercury conjunct Saturn tends to bring out a strong tone of seriousness in communications. There is a restriction, a discipline, a carefully considered emphasis of thoughts placed on our communications; and there is a serious intent to get the word across in no uncertain terms. Governments and corporations may make new and restrictive proclamations for order. There is the strong implication at work that we must be seriously responsible for what we say, particularly around authority and in official public statements. "Anything you say can and will be used against you..." Due to the retrograde cycle of Mercury coming up next month (Sept. 6/7 – 29), this conjunction will repeat on September 22 with Mercury retrograde, and again on October 7 with

176

Mercury direct.

**Sun opposite Neptune** (occurring Aug. 11 – 20) This occurrence of Sun opposite ♌ Neptune especially affects those Leo people celebrating birthdays from August 11 – 20. Neptune in opposition to these folks' natal Sun brings a strong awareness of Spirit, the spiritual path, and the acknowledgment of one's beliefs. The challenge facing these Leo birthday folks is to confront and overcome all disruptive personal doubts that cause them to question the practice of believing. These people will be imminently aware this year of the vast shifts in spiritual beliefs, and they may feel quite overwhelmed by the confusion and fluctuations of their own spiritual awareness. This is no surprise – it is occurring for numerous people at this time – Leos will just experience it more directly. This is the time to go to a personal sanctuary of choice and tune into Spirit.

**Mars trine Neptune** (occurring Aug. 8 – Aug. 22) Mars in Gemini trine Neptune in Aquarius brings intelligent, spiritually enhanced, and uplifting kinds of energy. This aspect creates an active trend to empower our beliefs. This will be an active time of obtaining spiritual gifts and helpful guidelines from the spirit world. Mars guarantees activities will occur, and with Neptune in the trine position, these activities will be favorably stirred up with spiritual and psychic awareness. This serves as a good time to initiate creative and imaginative spiritual practices and ceremonies, and to empower the personal outlook and spiritual wellbeing.

# August 18ᵗʰ Tuesday

| Moon in Cancer / Leo | PDT | EDT |
|---|---|---|
| Moon trine Uranus goes v/c | 12:08 AM | 3:08 AM |
| Moon enters Leo | 6:56 AM | 9:56 AM |
| Mars square Uranus | 7:24 PM | 10:24 PM |

*Mood Watch*: This morning we may find ourselves shaking off a bit of an emotional hangover while the Moon is void-of-course in Cancer. However, soon enough the Moon enters Leo, and our moods will become brighter, more cheery, although still somewhat introspective as the Moon wanes darkly. We will have a lot to process after yesterday's long bout with numerous aspects. Leo Moon gets us up and running. This is a good time to connect with friends, family, or to simply enjoy personal hobbies, pleasures, and leisurely endeavors. That said, it is important to apply caution while Mars reaches its peak square with Uranus (see below).

**Mars square Uranus** (occurring Aug. 10 – 23) Mars square Uranus is sometimes tyrannical, and is never an aspect to be underestimated. Masculine fortitude and the enigmatic force of chaos are in a volatile and difficult phase of expression when Mars is square to Uranus. This aspect was suspiciously present when the December 26, 2004 tsunami disaster of the century swept the Indian Ocean. Today, Mars is in the sign of Gemini and while it squares to Uranus; the resulting tensions may cause a schism in the forces of offensive and defensive action. While Uranus is in Pisces, chaos abounds in the sacred territory of our beliefs. The events of Mars square Uranus do not always predictably yield natural disasters, but unfortunately they are often the catalyst for difficult human trials. This aspect is like a pressure cooker; it may seem dormant at first, but if not carefully handled, the aftermath can be a real

177

mess! It is wise to completely avoid extremely risky undertakings that may rock the boat of fiery activity during Mars square Uranus. This is no time to step into the eye of the storm, or the rapidly diminishing waters of the shoreline! Fortunately, this is the only time this aspect will occur this year.

# August 19th Wednesday

| Moon in Leo | PDT | EDT | |
|---|---|---|---|
| Venus sextile Saturn | 3:10 AM | 6:10 AM | |
| Moon opposite Jupiter | 5:10 PM | 8:10 PM | |
| Moon opposite Neptune | 10:59 PM | 1:59 AM | (August 20) |

*Mood Watch*: Sometimes the darkly waning Moon in Leo brings a tendency towards summer laziness. Early tomorrow morning brings the New Leo Moon to its fruition. Much of today we are building our awareness towards new elements of self recognition. This is a good time to work on raising self-esteem. Image comes from within and is generated by the sheer magnitude of the will – it can come from no other than the self. Everyone has room to grow if they take time to apply some self-respect and discipline.

**Venus sextile Saturn** (occurring Aug. 15 – 21) Venus in Cancer sextile Saturn in Virgo brings the security of nurturing and reassuring expressions of love which are being amicably shared between lovers and friends. Venus emphasizes the vibrations of love, magnetism, and beauty, and while in Cancer, it brings an emphasis on the need for a peaceful retreat or a stable home environment. Saturn's influence emphasizes the awareness of time, responsibility, and dedication; while this planet is in Virgo, it inspires the need for a wholesome diet and good health practices, outdoor recreation, and relaxing hobbies. Saturn reminds us that beauty is temporary but with proper maintenance, it can also be preserved. This is a good time to capture a glimpse of beauty that will leave a lasting mark. This aspect will reoccur November 30 – December 5, reaching its exact aspect peak on December 4, with Venus in Sagittarius, and Saturn newly in Libra (see Oct. 29).

# August 20th Thursday

**NEW MOON in LEO**

| Moon in Leo / Virgo | PDT | EDT |
|---|---|---|
| Moon sextile Mars | 1:28 AM | 4:28 AM |
| Moon conjunct Sun goes v/c | 3:01 AM | 6:01 AM |
| Moon enters Virgo | 7:00 AM | 10:00 AM |
| Moon trine Pluto | 8:16 AM | 11:16 AM |
| Mercury square Pluto (August 26) | | |

*Mood Watch*: The **New Moon in Leo** (Moon conjunct Sun) is a time of personal discovery. Leo is the optimist, and the New Leo Moon brings positive new perspectives to personal goals, as well as inspiring a new outlook on the personal image. The Moon is void-of-course in Leo before most of us are in full swing, but unfortunately, the void Moon factor keeps us predominately lazy. By morning, the very new Virgo Moon dominates today's stage. This is a good time to implement and establish healthier eating routines and apply some organization.

178

# August 21st Friday

♍

**Moon in Virgo**

| | PDT | EDT | |
|---|---|---|---|
| Mercury opposite Uranus | 4:47 AM | 7:47 AM | |
| Moon conjunct Saturn | 6:23 PM | 9:23 PM | |
| Moon sextile Venus | 11:28 PM | 2:28 AM | (August 22) |

*Mood Watch*: Purity and cleanliness are the keys to a newly waxing Virgo Moon. Our moods will tend to be cautious, careful, and for some, perhaps shy and retiring. This is a good time for us to review our resources, to check on our earth-friendly green footprint, and to work towards preventing a wasteful or expensive course of action. Virgo says: "I analyze," and this is a good time to do just that.

**Mercury opposite Uranus** (occurring Aug. 16 – 24) Mercury in Virgo opposes Uranus in Pisces. Explosive events under discussion are testing our ability to trust or be convinced. Many will approve openly but will still maintain a healthy dose of skepticism. Ideas may seem bigger than life, and talk seems to focus on concepts which have not been fully grasped, but appear to be presented with assured confidence. Shocking or liberating statements tend to come out with this aspect. There is an acute awareness of the need to speak out for freedom, and the dialogue may appear sharp; radical and sometimes vulgar language may erupt. Outrageous claims and verbal presumptions made at this time may bring fiery or irrational flare-ups in discussion groups and chat rooms. This is a really good time to watch your mouth. Due to the next phase of Mercury retrograde (Sept. 6/7 – 29), this aspect will reoccur on two more occasions; covering the period from September 16 – October 7, it first reaches its peak on September 23 with Mercury retrograde, and secondly, it reaches another peak on October 4 with Mercury direct

# VIRGO

Key Phrase: " I ANALYZE "

Mutable Earth Sign

Ruling Planet: Mercury

Symbol: The Virgin

August 22nd through

September 22nd

# August 22nd Saturday

**Moon in Virgo / Libra**

| | PDT | EDT |
|---|---|---|
| Moon opposite Uranus | 12:55 AM | 3:55 AM |
| Moon conjunct Mercury | 2:34 AM | 5:34 AM |
| Moon square Mars goes v/c | 4:44 AM | 7:44 AM |
| Moon enters Libra | 8:12 AM | 11:12 AM |
| Moon square Pluto | 9:29 AM | 12:29 PM |
| Venus trine Uranus | 4:31 PM | 7:31 PM |
| Sun enters Virgo | 4:38 PM | 7:38 PM |

179

*Mood Watch*: Early this morning the youthful Moon waxes, and it's just ahead of the Sun as it goes void-of-course in Virgo. This morning is a good time to avoid being overly critical. It may also be a difficult time to get organized. When the Moon enters Libra, our emotional patterns are likely to shift towards a much more accommodating and congenial spirit. This will be helpful to us as the Moon squares with Pluto and forces us to reconcile with the trials of our transformations. This afternoon, the Sun enters Virgo, a transformation that reminds us that summer is passing quickly. Meanwhile, the Libra Moon focuses our attention on partnerships, relationships, and our civil duties to protect those we love. A studious flare puts many in the mood to address the pending days of school and new work routines. Those who are in denial will balance their emotional force-field with plans to make the most of summer while it's still happening.

**Venus trine Uranus** (occurring Aug.17 – 25) Venus in Cancer is trine Uranus in Pisces. Tender hearted and motherly kinds of love and attraction will make positive breakthroughs in matters of belief and believing. Venus trine Uranus brings a favorable attraction to revolutionary concepts. This is a time of freedom fighters and rebel love, and youth is easily attracted to the spirit of rebellion. Dangerous love and taking chances become common occurrences. This aspect creates an attraction to the unusual, yet it allows a harmony to exist in love related matters while chaotic occurrences are taking place. Love at first sight is explosive at this time, but not necessarily long lasting. This aspect will reoccur November 21 – 28, reaching its exact aspect peak on November 25 with Venus in Scorpio.

**Sun enters Virgo** (Sun in Virgo: Aug. 22 – Sept. 22) Virgo's key phrase is "I analyze," and the pragmatic spirit of Virgo examines all avenues of life. It is just like Virgo to pick everything apart, detail by detail, and yet Virgo strives to get as much of an overview of the whole picture as possible. Virgo questions, Virgo doubts, and Virgo demands proof. The Mercury ruled mutable sign of earth is keen, sharp-witted, and not so quick to believe any sort of random information, unless it's painstakingly researched by some reputable sources. Virgo will question the source every time. Virgos are famous for their ability to count, calculate, and measure everything that must be accounted for, which is why Virgo is chosen to watch over the vital and bountiful harvest season.

# August 23rd Sunday

**Moon in Libra**

| | PDT | EDT |
|---|---|---|
| Sun  trine Pluto | 11:19 AM | 2:19 PM |
| Moon  trine Jupiter | 8:01 PM | 11:01 PM |

*Mood Watch*:  The youthfully waxing Libra Moon brings out the need for balance. If there is no balance, there is no peace. It's quite simple: for those of you who have indulged in your pleasures far too much, today is the day to make an effort to face up to unfinished work. Autumn is not that far away; do something constructive today and you'll feel the incentive to keep going. As for those who deserve a break and need to stop and smell the flowers, put down that work project – today is your day to relax, enjoy the fruits of summer, and unwind. Equilibrium is the name of the game. This is the time to tip the scales in your favor.

180

**Sun trine Pluto** (occurring Aug. 17 – 26) Positive, life-altering changes are occurring in the lives of Leo and Virgo cusp born people celebrating birthdays this year ♍ from August 17 – 26 . They are currently undergoing the favorable trine aspect of Pluto to their natal Sun, bringing out experiences that involve transformation and encounters with greater powers and fate. It is always difficult to speculate just how the Pluto experience will manifest itself. Have no fear; this is a time to get in touch with your power, birthday Leos and Virgos! Pluto moves slowly in our cosmos, and powerful encounters that seem deadly or harsh are actually a necessary part of the process. Matters involving fate can be positive, and the trine aspect does represent a gift being bestowed – however unlikely it may seem. Be grateful this trine brings power issues into your life in a more positive fashion, leading to positive transformation. Finding out how to benefit from this power is a big part of discovering Pluto's gifts. This aspect last occurred April 16 – 25, reaching its exact peak on April 22, affecting some of the Aries/Taurus cusp born folks.

# August 24ᵗʰ Monday

| Moon in Libra / Scorpio | PDT | EDT |
|---|---|---|
| Moon trine Neptune | 3:09 AM | 6:09 AM |
| Moon square Venus | 7:54 AM | 10:54 AM |
| Moon trine Mars goes v/c | 11:11 AM | 2:11 PM |
| Moon enters Scorpio | 12:17 PM | 3:17 PM |
| Moon sextile Pluto | 1:37 PM | 4:37 PM |
| Moon sextile Sun | 3:41 PM | 6:41 PM |

*Mood Watch*: Our morning moods address the need to feel balanced, harmonious, and objective. As the Moon goes void-of-course, indecision leaves us somewhat spaced out, but only for a short time. As the Moon enters Scorpio, the energy intensifies and our moods will be more prone to seek excitement, thrills, and stimulation. The waxing Scorpio Moon is never dull.

# August 25ᵗʰ Tuesday

| Moon in Scorpio | PDT | EDT |
|---|---|---|
| Mars enters Cancer | 10:15 AM | 1:15 PM |
| Mercury enters Libra | 1:20 PM | 4:20 PM |
| Mercury square Mars | 9:03 PM | 12:03 AM (August 26) |

*Mood Watch*: The Scorpio Moon is always a good time to get in the mood to handle great shifts in energy. This is particularly true with the shift of Mars entering Cancer and Mercury entering Libra (see below). Additionally, Mercury square Mars is an active – but trying – time for our communications (see below). If there is anything that will help us deal with these changes, Scorpio Moon will. Try to take it easy, and go with the flow.

**Mars enters Cancer** (Mars in Cancer: Aug. 25 – Oct. 16) The fiery drive of force, Mars, now focuses the spirit of action on such Cancerian activities as nurturing and mothering. Mars in Cancer also emphasizes a focus on the home, household improvement or remodeling – possibly even a move to a new home or making the adjustments following a big move. Cancer represents large bodies of water such as the oceans and great lakes, and while Mars is in Cancer, marine activities are

181

emphasized. Military ships will be preparing for battle tests and strategic training. Aquatic sports may become highly popular. Mars in Cancer represents the defenses of the emotions and the tender aspects of our being that we strive so hard to protect. Mars is a natural protector and defender but is also quite capable of offensive attack. Cancer people especially need to be aware of the potential for emotional flare ups, particularly with regard to the home. While Mars is in Cancer, Cancer born people are stirred up with a lot of heat and activity in their lives. Too much worry or fear is likely to lead to some serious anger and defensiveness. Be aware of the potential for heat, fire, and fevers, Cancer folks. Use this energy in your life to keep the flow moving, and to create to your heart's content!

**Mercury enters Libra** (Mercury in Libra: Aug. 25 – Sept. 17) Mercury in Libra aligns us with diplomacy, tact, and the need to connect with friends and loved ones. Libra is the cardinal autumn sign that emphasizes balance and adjustment. Today through September 17, Mercury in Libra will bring a focus on harmonizing with others and preparing for the pending change of the seasons. This is a good time for people to communicate by gathering important information, as our decision making process kicks into high gear. Due to the retrograde pattern of Mercury this September (Sept. 6/7 – 29), Mercury will be in Libra for a couple of cycles this year, and it will also return to Virgo (Sept. 17 – Oct. 9). Mercury will begin its second cycle in Libra through a good portion of October (Oct. 9 – 28). For more information on Mercury retrograde in Libra, see the section in the introduction about *Mercury retrograde periods.*

**Mercury square Mars** (occurring Aug. 13 – Sept. 8) Mercury in Libra is square to Mars in Cancer. Diplomatic thinking creates complications, and indecisiveness or conflict occurs around some activities. Under the influence of this aspect, it is not a good time to lose one's temper. Be especially careful to watch what you say, preferably thinking before you speak; words can be easily taken the wrong way. This aspect stimulates arguments and mental blocks concerning the actions of others (Mercury in Libra in the square position to Mars) and could easily lead to verbal destruction in the home (Mars in Cancer). Mercury square Mars makes it difficult for some to justify their actions or explain why they take a certain stand in life. Refrain from making risky comments, and be careful not to misinterpret information as being hostile or personal. Remember, during this complex time of Mercury square Mars, not to shoot the messenger. During its occurrence dates, this aspect will reach an exact peak again on September 3, right at the point that Mercury will be slowing to a stationary position, and then it will begin its retrograde cycle on September 6/7. This aspect will repeat for a third time, October 27 – November 4, reaching its exact peak on November 1 with Mercury in Scorpio and Mars in Leo.

# August 26th Wednesday

| Moon in Scorpio / Sagittarius | PDT | EDT |
|---|---|---|
| Moon square Jupiter | 2:15 AM | 5:15 AM |
| Moon sextile Saturn | 5:25 AM | 8:25 AM |
| Mercury square Pluto | 9:11 AM | 12:11 PM |
| Venus enters Leo | 9:11 AM | 12:11 PM |
| Moon square Neptune | 10:21 AM | 1:21 PM |

182

| | | | |
|---|---|---|---|
| Moon trine Uranus goes v/c | 11:35 AM | 2:35 PM | |
| Mars opposite Pluto | 1:34 PM | 4:34 PM | |
| Moon enters Sagittarius | 8:16 PM | 11:16 PM | |
| Moon trine Venus | 9:27 PM | 12:27 AM | (August 27) |
| Moon sextile Mercury | 10:35 PM | 1:35 AM | (August 27) |

♍

*Mood Watch*: The waxing Scorpio Moon prepares us for a number of astrological aspects. Emotions are running strong, and so is the course of events. As the Moon goes void-of-course, it is wise not to let your defenses down. In fact, you may notice that defensiveness, suspicion, and intensity are on the rise. It's no wonder; between the void Scorpio Moon and the busy astrological atmosphere, keeping a good guard up is essential. Later, as the Moon enters Sagittarius, a more positive and upbeat outlook on life will encourage our moods. Sagittarius is a good time to make – or plan – a get-away, even if only a brief one. Keep it simple.

**Mercury square Pluto** (occurring Aug. 20 – 30) This is the second time Mercury square Pluto is occurring this year, and for the first time in our lifetime, Mercury in Libra is square to Pluto in Capricorn. Procrastinating and vacillating thoughts make it difficult to communicate with those of another generation. This is a particularly difficult time to deal with burdensome issues and discuss them in a manner that relieves tension. Mercury square Pluto often brings harsh and sometimes fatal news. Talk revolves around the corruption of superpowers and the setbacks caused by this corruption. This may be a particularly difficult time to discuss matters involving permanent change. Mercury square Pluto occurred for the first time this year March 24 – 28, reaching its exact peak on March 27 with Mercury in Aries. For some, this may seem harsh now, but it could seem even worse by the time this aspect repeats, September 13 – 20, reaching its peak on September 17, with Mercury retrograde (Sept. 6/7 – 29). Discussions occurring around difficult matters of fate will seem a little less harsh when we come full circle with this aspect, as it repeats for the last time this year, October 5 – 12, reaching its peak on October 10 with Mercury direct.

**Venus enters Leo** (Venus in Leo: Aug. 26 – Sept. 20) Venus in Leo brings out the more playful side of love. It also brings out the desire for more sophisticated and elaborate types of art and aesthetics. Venus represents the expression of love and affection; it is the influence of magnetism, beauty, and of feminine refinement. In the sign of Leo, Venus brings out desires and needs for personal attention. Magnetism is one of Leo's most endearing traits, and it is this magnetism that brings what Leos want most: loving attention. The entertainment industry will be highlighted as music, poetry, art, singing and acting are all enhanced with heartfelt expression. Leos will be more aware of their need for love. The love of looking good, having the best, and being the best is alluring to the ego. Wild lust will abound and the love of fantasies will be enhanced. Love affairs may be torrid and dramatic, while affections, when first initiated, can seem very ardent and sincere. One might be hesitant to believe that a too-good-to-be-true relationship is actually occurring. On the other hand, if it doesn't feel harmonious, it may be because the love affair is more focused on the demands and needs of just one person. Leo demands a lot of affection and, when Venus comes into play, the need for attention sometimes outweighs the need to reciprocate that attention. It is always wise not

183

to have expectations in love matters and to be sure that the joys of exchanging love are balanced.

**Mars opposite Pluto** (occurring Aug. 17 – 31) Mars in Cancer opposes Pluto in Capricorn, stirring up emotional activities in the home over career related transformations. This aspect activates big changes. Oppositions have a strong impact. Combine that fact with two strong planetary influences, Mars and Pluto – the outcome often involves swift, martial transformation. This aspect may create conflict between generations, and between those with diametrically opposed cultures. Now that Pluto is in Capricorn, a serious transformation directly affects leaders and those who have an effect on the economy. This is a time to be vigilant and guarded. Expect swift, permanent changes during this time of Mars opposite Pluto.

# August 27th Thursday
FIRST QUARTER MOON in SAGITTARIUS    PDT
EDT

| | | |
|---|---|---|
| Moon square Sun | 4:42 AM | 7:42 AM |

*Mood Watch*: **First Quarter Moon in Sagittarius** (Moon square Sun) allows our moods to be adaptable and responsive to the situations that arise. Likely interests include sports events, adventure, vision quests, and philosophical perspectives. While the Virgo Sun reminds us to budget our resources for the changing season ahead, the Sagittarius Moon reminds us to reach out there while the brilliant beauty of summer is still occurring. Adventure and hope abound. Sagittarius says: "I see" – make use of the vision and take the time to *see beyond*.

# August 28th Friday

| Moon in Sagittarius | PDT | EDT | |
|---|---|---|---|
| Mercury sextile Venus | 6:24 AM | 9:24 AM | |
| Moon sextile Jupiter | 12:11 PM | 3:11 PM | |
| Moon square Saturn | 4:44 PM | 7:44 PM | |
| Moon sextile Neptune | 9:11 PM | 12:11 AM | |
| Moon square Uranus goes v/c | 10:26 PM | 1:26 AM | (August 29) |

*Mood Watch*: Our moods now shift towards a restless inquisitiveness and visionary awareness as the Sagittarius Moon waxes. Sports and outdoor activities are emphasized, and there is a need to push beyond the usual bounds and explore. Moon in Sagittarius puts the emphasis on such endeavors as travel and vision quests. With this visionary process comes the desire to expand.

**Mercury sextile Venus** (occurring July 30 – Aug. 31) Mercury in Libra sextile Venus in Leo teaches us of the necessity to speak up intelligently for our needs, particularly for personally entertaining, as well as for family related kinds of love and affection. Also, Mercury in Libra emphasizes communications which revolve around issues of companionship and marriage, while Venus in Leo emphasizes the necessity for affections to be heartfelt and family compatible. This is a good time to harmoniously explore opportunities and new possibilities, when discussing family matters and personal needs. This aspect focuses talk and discussion on the

184

things in life we are most attracted to and touched by. The sextile aspect of Mercury to Venus brings hope and good prospects for our love needs. This is a good time to speak up for the things and the people of our lives – those things and people whom we treasure. This aspect occurred earlier this year from January 24 – 27, reaching an exact peak on January 26, when Mercury was retrograde in Capricorn and Venus was in Pisces. It also occurred February 21 – 27, reaching its peak on February 25 with Mercury in Aquarius and Venus in Aries. Mercury sextile Venus was non-exact in April, beginning on April 26 and ending before its fruition on May 1. During this occurrence cycle of Mercury sextile Venus, it also reached an exact peak on August 7 with Mercury in Virgo and Venus in Cancer.

# August 29th Saturday
**Moon in Sagittarius / Capricorn**

| | PDT | EDT | |
|---|---|---|---|
| Moon enters Capricorn | 7:44 AM | 10:44 AM | |
| Moon conjunct Pluto | 9:09 AM | 12:09 PM | |
| Moon opposite Mars | 1:00 PM | 4:00 PM | |
| Moon square Mercury | 2:11 PM | 5:11 PM | |
| Moon trine Sun | 9:51 PM | 12:51 AM | (August 30) |

*Mood Watch*: While the dwindling remains of the void-of-course Sagittarius Moon keep us somewhat spaced out or feeling a bit lost, the Capricorn Moon settles in soon enough, and with this comes a clearer conscience. The Capricorn Moon brings focused and serious moods, but there may be a tendency for many folks to pay little attention to how they are actually feeling. After a busy week of astrological events, many of us are content to get on with life, to stop dramatizing our emotions, and to get on with practical matters.

# August 30th Sunday
**Moon in Capricorn**                PDT          EDT

*Mood Watch*: There are no lunar aspects complicating our moods today. While the Moon waxes in Capricorn, some very practical and easy-going moods make this a good time to get things done. Sun in Virgo and Moon in Capricorn is a superb time to clean up your surroundings, tend to unfinished business, and to catch up in those areas of life where the physical world needs some extra work. There is always something that needs to be done, even if that means taking the time to rest and relax. Practical and stoic moods can bring dry humor.

# August 31st Monday
**Moon in Capricorn / Aquarius**

| | PDT | EDT |
|---|---|---|
| Moon trine Saturn | 6:11 AM | 9:11 AM |
| Moon sextile Uranus goes v/c | 11:08 AM | 2:08 PM |
| Moon enters Aquarius | 8:42 PM | 11:42 PM |

*Mood Watch*: The morning starts out well with the Moon trine Saturn on a Capricorn Moon day. At first there is a sense of control, but by the time the Moon goes void-of-course, all of that changes. People may seem somewhat indifferent towards – or unwilling to get too excited about – numerous things during the late afternoon and well into the evening, with special occasions being the exception. Even under the circumstances of special occasions, there may be an underlying boredom or inability for many folks to appreciate the course of the way things are going throughout the day. Progress is often slowed due an unwillingness to perform duties at optimum levels. Melancholic behavior and sheer laziness may be contagious under the void Capricorn Moon, and it may be helpful to defuse negative attitudes with positive affirmations. Mundane tasks may seem a lot more tedious than expected, and there may be a tendency to abandon chores and tasks altogether. Capricorn is an awkward place for the Moon to begin with, but the void-of-course factor may bring apathetic attitudes to make the best of our moods. Hang in there; tonight's Aquarius Moon will bring a better sense of closure for the day.

# September 1st Tuesday

**Moon in Aquarius**

| | PDT | EDT |
|---|---|---|
| Moon trine Mercury | 6:21 AM | 9:21 AM |
| Moon opposite Venus | 11:27 AM | 2:27 PM |

*Mood Watch*: Innovative and thoughtful moods kick off this new month with the Sun in Virgo and the Moon in Aquarius. Thoughts and ideas will be unusual and inspired, especially while the Moon trines with Mercury. However, as the Moon opposes Venus this morning/afternoon, we must be careful not to overwhelm our loved ones with strange ideas. This also may be a wild time to get our sense of harmony under control. For the most part, Moon in Aquarius is a good time to enjoy social outings and appreciate the late summer with our most inspired friends and comrades as the Moon waxes towards its fullness in the next few days.

# September 2nd Wednesday

**Moon in Aquarius**

| | PDT | EDT | |
|---|---|---|---|
| Moon conjunct Jupiter | 12:25 PM | 3:25 PM | |
| Moon conjunct Neptune goes v/c | 10:18 PM | 1:18 AM | (September 3) |

*Mood Watch*: The Moon in Aquarius waxes strongly as it brings a focus on knowledge and learning new skills. This is a time of fairs, social endeavors, conventions, as well as philanthropic and fund raising events. The beginning of September is always such an amazingly busy time for many folks in North America. The Aquarius Moon gives us the impetus to handle big puzzles, and to take on large events. The feeling of expansion occurs while the Moon conjuncts with Jupiter. Get in touch with your sense of prosperity!

# September 3rd Thursday

*Full Moon Eve*

**Moon in Aquarius / Pisces**

| | PDT | EDT |
|---|---|---|
| Moon enters Pisces | 8:57 AM | 11:57 AM |
| Mercury square Mars | 9:09 AM | 12:09 PM |
| Moon sextile Pluto | 10:17 AM | 1:17 PM |
| Moon trine Mars | 8:38 PM | 11:38 PM |

*Mood Watch*: Rich delights abound on this Full Moon Eve. Pisces Moon draws many people to the heart of their beliefs and needs. Addictive tendencies may cause some folks to bear the risk of overindulgence. The creative process of performing and enjoying music and fine art is a superb way to celebrate this Moon. Full Moon Eve in Pisces is a mystical time that brings strong psychic inclinations and a wide range of emotional expression and insights.

**Mercury square Mars** (occurring Aug. 13 – Sept. 8) For the second time during its occurrence dates, Mercury in Libra is reaching an exact square to Mars in Cancer. As it turns around the Sun, Mercury is about to become stationary, and it will almost seem as if communications are at a standstill during the following week. Mercury will go retrograde soon (September 6/7), which is why this aspect is reaching a peak for the second time during this cycle. Those who are undergoing conflict with others may do best to give the deadly silent treatment, rather than repeatedly give insults and verbal abuse which is common with this aspect. It could be awhile, at least until Mercury goes direct (September 29), before currently erupting conflicts caused by some people's words and actions are smoothed over. This aspect will repeat for a third time, October 27 – November 4, reaching its exact peak on November 1 with Mercury in Scorpio and Mars in Leo. For a recap on the story of what's going on with Mercury square Mars, *see August 25.*

# September 4th Friday

| FULL MOON in PISCES | PDT | EDT |
|---|---|---|
| Moon opposite Sun | 9:02 AM | 12:02 PM |

*Mood Watch*: The **Full Moon in Pisces** (Moon opposite Sun) brings out the psychic in everyone. People can be very sensitive, and as a result, some people express themselves in very artistic or perhaps nonsensical manners. Enchantment sets the stage for Full Pisces Moon activity early in the day. Dance, music, and art are often activities of the Full Pisces Moon. Imaginations will run wild today and anything is possible. Pisces says: "I believe," and while the Moon is full in Pisces, it is vitally important to carry our beliefs wisely, as destructive tendencies may bring us down if we're not careful. This will also be a time to watch out for low self-esteem or substance abuse.

# September 5th Saturday

| Moon in Pisces / Aries | PDT | EDT |
|---|---|---|
| Moon opposite Saturn | 6:45 AM | 9:45 AM |
| Moon conjunct Uranus goes v/c | 9:52 AM | 12:52 PM |
| Moon enters Aries | 7:14 PM | 10:14 PM |
| Moon square Pluto | 8:30 PM | 11:30 PM |

*Mood Watch*: The Moon in Pisces now wanes, but it is still quite full. Psychic impressions and intuition will run strongly today. This morning, it may be overwhelming to try to handle too many responsibilities with the Moon opposing Saturn. As the Moon goes void-of-course, it may be wise to hold off on expectations, as people tend to be very spacey during the void Pisces Moon. Most of the day there will be apathetic attitudes, so expect at least one thing: unpredictability. Later this evening as the Moon enters Aries, our moods may become slightly impatient, and

187

many folks may appear somewhat self-absorbed. This is a busy time of year and many people are engaged in setting up new projects in preparation for autumn. Aries Moon taps into our need to get things going. Soon though, we will be met with perplexity as Mercury begins its retrograde process (see tomorrow).

# September 6th Sunday

| Moon in Aries | PDT | EDT | |
|---|---|---|---|
| Moon opposite Mercury | 7:00 AM | 10:00 AM | |
| Moon square Mars | 9:24 AM | 12:24 PM | |
| Moon trine Venus | 9:13 PM | 12:13 AM | (September 7) |
| Mercury goes retrograde | 9:45 PM | 12:45 AM | (September 7) |
| Venus opposite Jupiter begins (see September 11) | | | |

*Mood Watch*: There is alertness in our step as we greet the day. First, Moon opposes Mercury, and our minds will be attentive and full. Then, the Moon squares with Mars and the complexity of our sojourn into the day will require firm action and strength. The Moon wanes in Aries and our moods will be prone to decisiveness, motivation, and straightforwardness. Later tonight there will be kindness in our hearts. In the midst of what seems like a relatively positive day, there is a cloud of uncertainty. The cloud's name is Mercury retrograde. Such clouds are common, as they occur three times a year, and last up to three weeks. For some, this phenomenon is hardly noticeable, particularly for the astute among us. However, many folks will be teaming with doubt, criticism, and confusion while Mercury is retrograde in Virgo. The plot thickens, so brace yourself.

**Mercury goes retrograde** (Mercury retrograde: Sept. 6/7 – 29) Hold on to your thinking caps – today Mercury goes retrograde in Libra, and it will also be retrograde in Virgo (Sept. 17 – 29). Mercury retrograde in Libra will likely cause numerous miscommunications between friends and among partners. Negotiations among friends and marital partners may be confusing and frustrating, and it may be especially difficult to make decisions. With Mercury retrograde in Libra (Sept. 6/7 - 17,) peace talks among diplomats may seem useless, and cancellations and postponements of court cases and judicial processes may be prevalent. On September 17, the retrograde Mercury will reenter Virgo where it is likely to raise quite a bit of doubt – or skepticism – with regard to the accuracy of our calculations, information, and basic communications. Try to give speakers a decent chance before jumping all over their words. Interruptions and tensions are likely to occur during discussions. A key to getting through the Mercury retrograde period is to be attentive to important details, to inquire often, and to listen carefully. For more on Mercury retrograde, see the section in the introduction about *Mercury retrograde periods*.

# September 7th Monday

**Labor Day, USA / Labour Day, Canada**

| Moon in Aries | PDT | EDT |
|---|---|---|
| Moon sextile Jupiter | 7:16 AM | 10:16 AM |
| Moon sextile Neptune goes v/c | 5:11 PM | 8:11 PM |

*Mood Watch*: The month is fully underway with Labor Day now upon us. The

188

Aries Moon keeps us vigilant, determined, and headstrong to meet the demands of our needs. This morning's Moon sextile Jupiter gives us the opportunity to count our blessings. This evening, as the Aries Moon goes void-of-course, it will be wise to hold off on the tendency to race around in vain, unless – for some reason – you enjoy going around in circles. Between Mercury newly retrograde and the Moon void-of-course, it would be a good idea to refrain from rudeness or hot-temperedness. Also, beware of the possibility that others may get caught up in this trend.

## September 8th Tuesday

**Moon in Aries / Taurus**

| | PDT | EDT |
|---|---|---|
| Moon enters Taurus | 3:17 AM | 6:17 AM |
| Moon trine Pluto | 4:30 AM | 7:30 AM |
| Moon sextile Mars | 7:37 PM | 10:37 PM |

*Mood Watch*: Taurus Moon has a grounding affect. Sun in Virgo and Moon in Taurus focuses our attention on finances, the need for resources, and a myriad of material concerns. The waning Taurus Moon stirs a heartfelt awareness of what we have, what we have lost, and what we hope to gain. This is a good time to tend to practical needs in a methodical and carefully thought out manner.

## September 9th Wednesday

**Moon in Taurus**

| | PDT | EDT | |
|---|---|---|---|
| Moon square Venus | 9:46 AM | 12:46 PM | |
| Moon trine Sun | 10:24 AM | 1:24 PM | |
| Moon square Jupiter | 1:34 PM | 4:34 PM | |
| Moon trine Saturn | 10:43 PM | 1:43 AM | (Sept. 10) |
| Moon square Neptune | 11:26 PM | 2:26 AM | (Sept. 10) |

*Mood Watch*: Moon is in Taurus it is said to be "exalted," an ideal time to get in tune with the earth and our bodies. This morning, Moon square Venus may be a difficult time to get along easily with loved ones. Desired assets may be hard to attain or maintain while the Moon squares with Jupiter. Taurus Moon reminds us to take thorough care of our worldly possessions, before the damaging elements of time and neglect take care of them first. Sun in Virgo and Moon in Taurus demand prudent and practical measures to gain satisfaction. Try to tackle physical tasks while moving with ease, and seek beauty – therein lies your pleasure.

## September 10th Thursday

**Moon in Taurus / Gemini**

| | PDT | EDT |
|---|---|---|
| Moon sextile Uranus goes v/c | 12:16 AM | 3:16 AM |
| Moon enters Gemini | 9:16 AM | 12:16 PM |
| Moon trine Mercury | 6:49 PM | 9:49 PM |
| Sun conjunct Saturn begins (see September 17) | | |
| Venus opposite Neptune begins (see September 15) | | |

*Mood Watch*: The morning may start out with a stubborn quality of mood, particularly while the Taurus Moon is void-of-course. As the Moon enters Gemini, our moods will be a great deal more thoughtful, detail oriented, and filled with chatter. To some, it is useless and idle chatter, particularly while Mercury is retro-

189

grade (Sept. 6/7 – 29). However, there is hope. Be persistent and vigilant to keep a watchful eye on details, schedules, and changes. Gemini Moon reminds us to communicate, over and over again. That's the best way to move through Mercury retrograde. Tonight, as the Moon trines with Mercury, use this opportunity to turn the idle chatter into constructive communication. Reiterate on plans, ideas, and complex situations. Do this and all will be well.

## September 11th Friday
### LAST QUARTER MOON in GEMINI

| | PDT | EDT |
|---|---|---|
| Venus opposite Jupiter | 12:54 AM | 3:54 AM |
| Pluto goes direct | 9:58 AM | 12:58 PM |
| Moon trine Jupiter | 5:57 PM | 8:57 PM |
| Moon square Sun | 7:15 PM | 10:15 PM |
| Moon sextile Venus | 7:42 PM | 10:42 PM |
| Sun opposite Uranus begins (see September 17) | | |

*Mood Watch*: The **Last Quarter Moon in Gemini** (Moon square Sun) brings talkative moods and informative interaction. People will have a lot on their minds today and intellectual pursuits are emphasized. This is the time to enjoy games, puzzles, and social conversations. Mercury may be retrograde, but we can still have fun!

**Venus opposite Jupiter** (occurring Sept. 6 – 13) Venus in Leo brings a love for elaborate entertainment and the regal touch in the arts. It also focuses on a love for the self, for personal needs, and for the family. Meanwhile, the retrograde Jupiter in Aquarius focuses on the need for scientific and technological advancement. It also focuses on the funding of charities, and those areas of our lives where we share common goals for society and our human rights. Venus opposite Jupiter brings on a significant awareness of the dynamics of attraction and wealth. During this aspect, many folks will find themselves torn between the need to focus on the self verses the need to help the less fortunate of our communities. Custody battles are hard fought under these circumstances. The process of overcoming personal loss requires a great deal of effort to attain the healing power of love. Money related tests and troubles in relationships are often a factor under this aspect. Venus opposite Jupiter increases awareness of the need for joy in relationships.

**Pluto goes direct** (Pluto direct: Sept. 11, 2009 – April 6, 2010) After the long – but common – retrograde period of Pluto (April 4 – September 11), the planet of transformation now moves into a smooth, direct pattern for the rest of the year. Since April, Pluto has been going back through the earliest degrees of Capricorn. Now that it is direct, with Pluto at the zero degree mark of Capricorn, we can better acknowledge the evolution of humankind's condition in order to survive and adapt to the challenges that are occurring on planet Earth. This transformation emphasizes consciousness, without which we would not be. This is not a time to take life for granted; rather, it is a time to participate in making life better by consciously transforming fear into determination and despair into belief in oneself. Pluto in Capricorn (since 2008) inspires a new journey where we build a new world for ourselves and for the generations to come.

# September 12ᵗʰ Saturday

♍

| Moon in Gemini / Cancer | PDT | EDT |
|---|---|---|
| Moon square Saturn | 3:37 AM | 6:37 AM |
| Moon trine Neptune | 3:45 AM | 6:45 AM |
| Moon square Uranus goes v/c | 4:29 AM | 7:29 AM |
| Moon enters Cancer | 1:18 PM | 4:18 PM |
| Moon opposite Pluto | 2:26 PM | 5:26 PM |
| Moon square Mercury | 8:40 PM | 11:40 PM |

*Mood Watch*: This is a good day to laugh. It's a time to laugh at the way confusion and chaos put us so thoroughly into a tailspin. Don't laugh at the expense of others; be sure to let them in on the joke. The void-of-course Gemini Moon and Mercury retrograde is a funny combination. Don't expect anyone to make much sense, or know what they're doing. It's a joke, remember? Laughter is the best way to approach these minor debacles. If you're surrounded by humorless slave-drivers, brace yourself, and pat yourself on the back for finding a way to see the humor in your own private way. As the Moon enters Cancer, emotionality is to be expected, especially as the Moon opposes Pluto. Sometimes life is fraught with drama. Later, when the Moon is square to Mercury, don't get caught up in trying to explain the joke. Everyone knows a joke is no longer funny the minute you have to explain it. A cool composure is all that's required. A good cry might be good, too.

# September 13ᵗʰ Sunday

| Moon in Cancer | PDT | EDT |
|---|---|---|
| Moon conjunct Mars | 9:09 AM | 12:09 PM |
| Mercury square Pluto begins (see September 17) | | |

*Mood Watch*: The Cancer Moon wanes. The only lunar event today, Moon conjunct Mars, puts us in touch with the need to let out anguish, frustration, or just to let out whichever feelings seem especially active. This is also a time to take action, to act on the volition of our hearts. Cancer Moon drives our emotions to the surface and allows us to review them, particularly since our feelings are always in a state of change. This is a time when our feelings don't lie, unless we've mastered the art of rejecting the truth. This is a time to let the feelings flow and then let them go. Don't hold on to guilt, fear, or worries – let them go! You'll feel a whole lot better once you do. If you're feeling good, and don't feel the necessity to go through this drill, consider yourself fortunate this time. Cancer Moon will put you through this drill again, and if you are good at embracing the truth, then you're certainly evolving. If not, it's back to the drill. Cancer Moon is not all that complicated!

# September 14ᵗʰ Monday

| Moon in Cancer / Leo | PDT | EDT |
|---|---|---|
| Moon sextile Sun | 1:49 AM | 4:49 AM |
| Moon sextile Saturn | 6:41 AM | 9:41 AM |
| Moon trine Uranus goes v/c | 6:57 AM | 9:57 AM |
| Moon enters Leo | 3:38 PM | 6:38 PM |
| Moon sextile Mercury | 8:21 PM | 11:21 PM |
| Saturn square Pluto begins (see November 15) | | |

*Mood Watch*: It's a blue Monday. No, not a blue Moon, but a blue Monday. The waning Cancer Moon is void-of-course. Mercury is retrograde (Sept. 6/7 – 29). It's Monday. The combination can be rough for some people. If it's not rough for you, it doesn't mean that others aren't going through something. As long as you're aware of this, you have no need to let it spoil your day! Hang in there. Tonight brings a better time as the Moon enters Leo. People will be more prone to working things out with family and friends, or they are very likely to seek out entertainment and fun. Moon sextile Mercury may bring some relief to our minds; it's a good time to talk.

# September 15ᵗʰ Tuesday

**Moon in Leo**

| | PDT | EDT | |
|---|---|---|---|
| Saturn opposite Uranus | 5:51 AM | 8:51 AM | |
| Venus opposite Neptune | 2:36 PM | 5:36 PM | |
| Moon opposite Jupiter | 9:50 PM | 12:50 AM | (Sept. 16) |
| Venus trine Pluto begins (see September 20) | | | |

*Mood Watch*: The waning Leo Moon brings playful and feisty moods. The onslaught of emotional ups and downs the past couple of days has come to a close. If you're still holding onto stuff, the waning Leo Moon is a good time to lean on friends and family, or to work on bettering your personal needs. No one knows you better than you do, and if someone does, perhaps it's time you paid some more attention to yourself. The waning Leo Moon makes us introspective. This is a very bold move for a sign such as Leo, as it tends to project outwardly.

**Saturn opposite Uranus** (occurring Aug. 7 – Oct. 3) Saturn in Virgo opposite Uranus in Pisces brings doubt, criticism and strong discernment with regard to an acute awareness of explosive endings occurring on the planet. This aspect is a big one that has reached its peak – off and on – in a repeating pattern since last year's US election, November 4. Revolution will be evident, and catastrophic natural disasters may also be evident. For a recap on the story of this very important aspect, now occurring for the second time this year, *see February 5*, when it last reached its peak.

**Venus opposite Neptune** (occurring Sept. 10 – 18) Venus in Leo is opposing Neptune in Aquarius. What we are attracted to may be opposed to what we (or others) believe in. Selfishness conflicts with philanthropy. Wild and instinctual expressions of love and beauty are at odds with universal beliefs. This aspect brings an awareness of the dichotomy between fashion's feminine archetypes versus a natural or spiritual expression of femininity. The feminine spirit needs to be free and connect with a more divine image of womanhood; however, the goddess that lives within may seem distant or hard to reach. Nonetheless, the feminine parts of the spirit (Venus) are being made acutely aware of the divine parts of the spirit (Neptune) in one way or another. The opposition of Venus to Neptune may seem like an overwhelming time to try to make a spiritual connection with large groups of people, especially through the mediums of art, music, and theater. There may be a desire to create a spiritual refuge or retreat – an attractive, sensual, and aesthetically pleasing sanctuary. This opposition only occurs once this year.

192

# September 16th Wednesday

♍

| Moon in Leo / Virgo | PDT | EDT |
|---|---|---|
| Moon opposite Neptune | 7:36 AM | 10:36 AM |
| Moon conjunct Venus goes v/c | 9:10 AM | 12:10 PM |
| Moon enters Virgo | 4:55 PM | 7:55 PM |
| Moon trine Pluto | 6:01 PM | 9:01 PM |
| Sun conjunct Mercury begins (see September 20) | | |
| Mercury conjunct Saturn begins (see September 22) | | |
| Mercury opposite Uranus begins (see September 23) | | |

*Mood Watch*: The Sun is in Virgo and the Moon is in Leo, but unfortunately, the waning Leo Moon will be void-of-course for almost eight hours. There are ways to take advantage of a void-of-course Moon, and while it is void in Leo, our predominate mood tendencies will be geared towards introspective reflection. The downside of this Moon will resemble a preoccupation with personal needs, thoughts, and desires. Many folks may seem self oriented, or concerned more about family and friends than about work and civil duties. That's okay if you have the luxury of focusing on yourself, but not everyone does. Today's lunar aspects are positive in general, and as the Moon enters Virgo, a strong emphasis will be placed on the need to think things through. While the Sun and Moon are both in the Mercury ruled sign, Virgo, three new aspects to Mercury are beginning today. Mercury is currently retrograde (Sept. 6/7 – 29) causing us to reiterate on a number of points previously communicated.

# September 17th Thursday

| Moon in Virgo | PDT | EDT |
|---|---|---|
| Sun opposite Uranus | 2:41 AM | 5:41 AM |
| Mercury square Pluto | 4:44 AM | 7:44 AM |
| Sun conjunct Saturn | 11:22 AM | 2:22 PM |
| Moon sextile Mars | 4:21 PM | 7:21 PM |
| Mercury enters Virgo | 8:25 PM | 11:25 PM |
| Sun square Pluto begins (see September 23) | | |

*Mood Watch*: The Moon is waning darkly in the Mercury ruled sign, Virgo, and Mercury is currently retrograde (Sept. 6/7 – 29). There is a whole lot of complexity at work. While the retrograde Mercury stands poised at the brink of the Virgo/Libra cusp, it would not be surprising if people's communication skills seem melancholic, indifferent, or confused. This is a good time to try to encourage others to keep a stiff upper lip, to fight depression, and to battle doubt and disparity with hope and non-judgmental parity. Desperate people really need help today, and this is the time to take them seriously. Meanwhile, don't despair yourself; recognize this dark time for what it is and allow the dark shadow to pass over you, not through you. It's always darkest just before the New Moon. The balsamic phase of the pending New Moon brings insight and wisdom.

**Sun opposite Uranus** (occurring Sept. 11 – 20) This occurrence of Sun opposite Uranus particularly affects Virgos celebrating birthdays September 11 – 20. The opposition of Uranus creates an acute awareness of the revolutionary forces in one's life. There will undoubtedly be a lot of chaos, and the challenge (in part) may be to

193

accept the rebel within you, and to persevere through the drastic and edgy discord. This is the time to go with the flow of unusual and unpredictable occurrences. It's also a good time to learn the Tao of chaos, and to understand that this awakening force is enlivening a sense of freedom. The only alternatives are to break through, or to break down if one resists. Survival counts; use your senses and your sensibilities well but do not resist the forces of great change. In its opposition to Virgo, Uranus in Pisces will both challenge and strengthen our Virgo (birthday) friends to live a life of freedom. This may be particularly difficult given the fact that (since Sept. 2007) Virgos have been facing the traverses of Saturn through their natal sun sign. Uranus opposite the Virgo Sun teaches Virgo the value in allowing for a greater range of possibilities. This will be an exciting and, at times, exhausting year ahead for these Virgo folks.

**Mercury square Pluto** (occurring Sept. 13 – 20) The retrograde Mercury in Libra is square to Pluto in Capricorn. Procrastinating and vacillating thoughts make it especially difficult to communicate with those of another generation, or to discuss hardships and matters of fate in a constructive manner – especially while Mercury is retrograde (Sept. 6/7 – 29). This aspect will repeat one more time, October 10, with Mercury direct. For more information on this currently repeating peak performance of Mercury square Pluto, *see August 26*, when it last occurred.

**Sun conjunct Saturn** (occurring Sept. 10 – 20) This occurrence of Sun conjunct Saturn in Virgo especially affects those Virgo people celebrating birthdays September 10 – 20. These birthday people are experiencing a perfect time to focus on change. Saturn is also reminding you birthday folks to take charge of your life more responsibly, and to recognize the importance of your limitations. Maybe it's time for an overhaul, Virgo – at least until certain areas of your life become more comfortable again. Saturn is urging you to connect with a sound dose of responsibility that fits your lifestyle and energy level. This may be the time to tune into the body and give it what it needs, and to deal succinctly with health matters. This year, it may be best for these birthday Virgos to incorporate a healthy exercise and diet routine that is fun and effective. Don't be so hard on yourself either, Virgo; try to remember to reward yourself throughout this year with each measure of your progress – it's good for the soul. Make up for lost time, and apply some self-love and nurturing to your renewed self-discipline. Hang in there and keep up the work, birthday folks, and don't be so glum; the tedious work in which you are now immersed will bring you genuine rewards later on. Note: Saturn has been in Virgo since September 2, 2007, and now is a considerable distance (24 degrees) through this constellation; Saturn will enter Libra this year on October 29.

**Mercury enters Virgo** (Mercury in Virgo: Sept. 17 – Oct. 9) Virgo is a most advantageous place for Mercury – the place where it both rules and is exalted. Today, the retrograde Mercury is moving back into the late degrees of Virgo. On September 29, Mercury will go direct at the 21 degree mark of Virgo. For more information on Mercury retrograde through the sign of Virgo, see the introduction on *Mercury retrograde periods*. For a review of Mercury in Virgo, *see August 2*, when it first entered Virgo this year.

# September 18th Friday

♍

NEW MOON in VIRGO

| Moon in Virgo / Libra | PDT | EDT |
|---|---|---|
| Moon opposite Uranus | 9:25 AM | 12:25 PM |
| Moon conjunct Saturn | 10:17 AM | 1:17 PM |
| Moon conjunct Sun | 11:45 AM | 2:45 PM |
| Moon conjunct Mercury goes v/c | 4:56 PM | 7:56 PM |
| Moon enters Libra | 6:26 PM | 9:26 PM |
| Moon square Pluto | 7:34 PM | 10:34 PM |

*Mood Watch*: **New Moon in Virgo** (Moon conjunct Sun) invites us to start all over again with the growing process of our feelings. This Moon calls to our feelings to apply a new form of skepticism, a new way of analyzing, and to apply caution. How about a new way of accounting or a new set of health practices? Finding new resources is often a common practice during the New Virgo Moon. This is the time to organize and prepare for the autumn season, a time when making adjustments is essential. New Virgo Moon assists us to prepare for the changes that occur in the physical world.

# September 19th Saturday

**Rosh Hashana**

| Moon in Libra | PDT | EDT |
|---|---|---|
| Moon square Mars | 8:45 PM | 11:45 PM |

*Mood Watch*: Autumn Equinox is just a few days away, and today's Libra Moon, which is ever so new, now opens the porthole to autumn moods. It may be sunny out, or even hot. Some folks may not be willing to give up their white pinstripes or their Panama boater hats. The solar light dips its rays aggressively through our windows and casts prismatic lights through the crystals that are there to capture them. The heat of late summer is often seasoned with a distinctive autumn breeze. This is the time to place ourselves in the equilibrium of the forces, to put balance into our lives. This is the day to prepare for what's coming.

# September 20th Sunday

| Moon in Libra / Scorpio | PDT | EDT | |
|---|---|---|---|
| Moon trine Jupiter | 1:00 AM | 4:00 AM | |
| Sun conjunct Mercury | 3:04 AM | 6:04 AM | |
| Venus enters Virgo | 6:32 AM | 9:32 AM | |
| Moon trine Neptune goes v/c | 11:44 AM | 2:44 PM | |
| Venus trine Pluto | 7:57 PM | 10:57 PM | |
| Moon enters Scorpio | 9:53 PM | 12:53 AM | (September 21) |
| Moon sextile Pluto | 11:05 PM | 2:05 AM | (September 21) |
| Moon sextile Venus | 11:24 PM | 2:24 AM | (September 21) |

*Mood Watch*: It's an eventful day of celestial activities and, unfortunately, the Libra Moon will go void-of-course for just over ten hours. Whereas the Libra Moon would customarily assist us to create numerous adjustments throughout the day, the void Libra Moon tends to bring a great deal of indecision, indolence, and procrastination. Nonetheless, Libra Moon activity also brings congenial, equitable,

195

and graceful moods. Just don't expect to hear – or see – a whole lot of logic in the course of interacting with others. As the Moon enters Scorpio our moods will be better suited to get a handle on life's little dramas.

**Sun conjunct Mercury** (occurring Sept. 16 – 21) This conjunction will create a much more thoughtful, communicative and expressive year ahead for those Virgo and Libra folks celebrating birthdays September 16 – 21. This is your time (birthday Virgo/Libra) to record ideas, relay important messages, and pay close attention to your imaginative thoughts as they are touched by Mercury, creating the urge to speak and be heard. Birthday people, your thoughts will reveal a great deal about who you are, now and in the year to come.

**Venus enters Virgo** (Venus in Virgo: Sept. 20 – Oct. 14) Venus now enters the sign of Virgo, where love and attraction are highlighted with such Virgo-like traits as shyness, prudence, purity, and virginal beauty. While Venus is in Virgo, the expression of love and beauty will be analyzed and reflected upon, and love related activities are more often reserved or calculated than they are acted upon. Venus in Virgo is referred to as "the fall," a less ideal position for Venus and a time when disappointment in love matters may be felt by some folks. Keep faith in your affections, despite the cooling of passions.

**Venus trine Pluto** (occurring Sept. 15 – 23) For the first time in our lifetime, Venus in Virgo is trine to Pluto in Capricorn. Venus trine Pluto is certainly exciting – with fate, power, love, and intensity at work! This aspect represents a love or fascination occurring with regard to the work of fate as well as power. Venus in Virgo emphasizes our love for cleanliness, purification, and good health practices, and while Venus is trine to Pluto, there is a strong appeal among the various generations, and among influential powers, to apply more care and effort to organize and implement greater health practices. Venus trine Pluto allows a breakthrough to occur for those who have trouble accepting the work of fate. This aspect allows loving energy to flow more easily between generations. Love triumphs over all, especially with Venus trine Pluto. This is a great time to let love cure the pain. This aspect last occurred June 2 – 11, reaching its exact peak on June 8.

# September 21st Monday
## Moon in Scorpio / *No Exact Aspects*

*Mood Watch*: This last day of summer comes on a Monday. To many, the days of summer seem to have already ended. By the time September steps into its third week, many North Americans have been fully acclimated to the pending fall's demanding schedule, and to the regiment of school studies. This doesn't mean that we aren't still prone to daydream and sneak back into some summer activities, especially when and where the weather's still good for outdoor activity. Today's Scorpio Moon reminds us of the necessity to transform ourselves. Wherever passions exist, we will be drawn to them, especially today.

# LIBRA                                                    ♎

Key Phrase: "I BALANCE"
Cardinal Air Sign
Ruling Planet: Venus
Symbol: The Scales
September 22nd through October 22nd

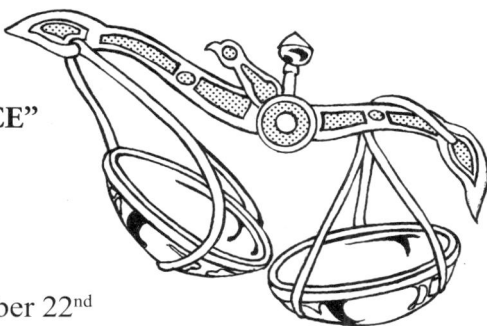

## September 22nd Tuesday

Autumnal Equinox

| Moon in Scorpio | PDT | EDT |
|---|---|---|
| Mercury  conjunct Saturn | 2:09 AM | 5:09 AM |
| Moon  trine Mars | 4:17 AM | 7:17 AM |
| Moon  square Jupiter | 6:03 AM | 9:03 AM |
| Sun  enters Libra | 2:18 PM | 5:18 PM |
| Moon  square Neptune | 5:44 PM | 8:44 PM |
| Moon  trine Uranus | 6:12 PM | 9:12 PM |
| Moon  sextile Mercury | 7:06 PM | 10:06 PM |
| Moon  sextile Saturn goes v/c | 8:33 PM | 11:33 PM |

**Mood Watch**: The last hours of summer burn through the a.m. hours, and by afternoon, the Sun will be in Libra. While the Moon is in Scorpio, we will be ready to handle change, however subtle or intense the change may be. Autumn Equinox is a time to make adjustments, and the Scorpio Moon guarantees that we will do it with fervor. It is always wise to stay on the up and up, to keep track of our valuables, our strengths, and our vulnerabilities, but this is often especially so during the Scorpio Moon, and particularly while it is void-of-course later tonight.

**Mercury conjunct Saturn** (occurring Sept. 16 – 25) Retrograde Mercury conjunct Saturn will bring confusing talk about the need to put an end to the useless or unwanted components of our lives. Due to the current phase of Mercury retrograde (Sept. 6/7 – 29), this conjunction is occurring for the second time this year. For a review of the influence of Mercury conjunct Saturn, *see August 17*, when it first occurred. This conjunction will start reoccurring in just a few days (Sept. 28 – Oct. 10,) and will reach its next peak on October 7 with Mercury direct.

**Sun enters Libra** (Sun in Libra: Sept. 22 – Oct. 22) It's the magical time of Autumnal Equinox. This time of year calls to us to reach out to each other and create a support system and a network of helpful friends to prepare for the busy season ahead and the darker and colder days yet to come. The Sun now enters Libra, a Venus ruled sign that focuses our attention on the power of teamwork and partnership. The key phrase for Libra is, "I balance," and the key to Libra's happiness comes with a sense of balance. Another factor to take into account for our Libran friends is the perpetual state of adjustment required to meet that balance. Libra could therefore easily say, "I adjust." The cornucopia of life is full of expressions of harmony and beauty. Libra focuses on libraries and accesses data and knowledge, particularly concerning law. May this new autumn season be pleasurable and fruitful for you and all your loved ones!

# September 23rd Wednesday

| Moon in Scorpio / Sagittarius | PDT | EDT |
| --- | --- | --- |
| Moon enters Sagittarius | 4:43 AM | 7:43 AM |
| Moon sextile Sun | 5:55 AM | 8:55 AM |
| Sun square Pluto | 7:22 AM | 10:22 AM |
| Mercury opposite Uranus | 8:39 AM | 11:39 AM |
| Moon square Venus | 12:15 PM | 3:15 PM |

*Mood Watch*: Sagittarius Moon allows us to open up and to travel outside our usual perspectives on life. This gives us a bird's eye view, or at least a different view, of our situations in life. Sagittarius Moon is a classic time to draw our attention to things like sports, travel, and projects that connect us with the world outside.

**Sun square Pluto** (occurring Sept. 17 – 26) This occurrence of Sun square Pluto particularly affects those Virgo and early born Libra cusp people celebrating birthdays from September 17 – 26. For them, Pluto squaring their natal Sun brings disruptive changes and many challenges to overcome, such as the pain of loss and the severity of transformation. These tests often involve illness, irreparable damage, and dramatic life changes. Trying to hold onto the regrets and the pain of the past will only bring greater destruction later. This is the time to persevere through the obstacles of hardship. The hardships that are taking place now will resurface again in time, and that necessitates finding methods of release and of attitude adjustment in order to survive the anxiety and stress. Take it one day at a time, and do not let fear and worry rule you. Know you are not alone in facing these challenges. Move steadily through the required transformation, as stagnation and fear will only bring extended suffering. This aspect also occurred during the same date range in March (March 17 – 26), reaching its exact peak on March 23, especially affecting the Pisces/Aries birthday people of that time.

**Mercury opposite Uranus** (occurring Sept. 16 – Oct. 7) Retrograde Mercury in Virgo opposes Uranus in Pisces. This is a really good time to watch your mouth. Communication errors could be catastrophic at this time. Due to the current phase of Mercury retrograde (Sept. 6/7 – 29), this aspect is occurring for the second time this year. For a review of the influence of this aspect, *see August 21*, when it first occurred. During these occurrence dates, this aspect will reach another peak on October 4 with Mercury direct.

# September 24th Thursday

| Moon in Sagittarius | PDT | EDT |
| --- | --- | --- |
| Moon sextile Jupiter | 2:55 PM | 5:55 PM |
| Mars trine Uranus begins (see October 4) | | |

*Mood Watch*: Methuselah lived nine hundred years, but as it says in the song, "*it ain't necessarily so.*" Some would theorize this is just a myth, but did anyone consider the possibility that they were talking about nine hundred *lunar cycles*, and *not* solar *years*? If this was true, Methuselah lived 69.2 solar years, and that's much more believable. All kinds of misnomers can take place in the translation. The Moon is in Sagittarius today, and philosophical questions like this one are likely to be entertained. Our moods will be interested, curious, and theoretical at times, but beware of the fact that Mercury is still retrograde (Sept. 6/7 – 29), and this is a time when all kinds of misinformation will lead us to be philosophical.

# September 25th Friday
## FIRST QUARTER MOON in CAPRICORN

| Moon in Sagittarius / Capricorn | PDT | EDT | |
|---|---|---|---|
| Moon square Mercury | 1:30 AM | 4:30 AM | |
| Moon sextile Neptune | 3:35 AM | 6:35 AM | |
| Moon square Uranus | 3:58 AM | 6:58 AM | |
| Moon square Saturn goes v/c | 7:15 AM | 10:15 AM | |
| Moon enters Capricorn | 3:19 PM | 6:19 PM | |
| Moon conjunct Pluto | 4:44 PM | 7:44 PM | |
| Moon square Sun | 9:50 PM | 12:50 AM | (September 26) |
| Mercury sextile Mars begins (see October 4) | | | |

*Mood Watch*: This morning the waning Moon in Sagittarius goes void-of-course, and our moods may be easily distracted as many folks may tend to stray away from their usual routines or get caught up in a series of delays. By afternoon/early evening, the **First Quarter Moon in Capricorn** (Moon square Sun) strongly emphasizes the need for serious labor. Some staunch determination is required. There is a steadily mounting concern to achieve a notable level of accomplishment or completion in projects, particularly after the slow progress of the earlier part of the day. The harvest ripens and the physical labor force of the world is hard at work. The pending October festivals and banquets require a tremendous amount of preparation. People's moods are greatly moved by the acknowledgement of merits. The need to hunt for a steady job, a marketing edge, or a secure investment keeps us vigilant and focused. Punctuality in business is stressed. Some may feel isolated by constant work and no play. No one likes feeling rushed, particularly when high standards must be met.

# September 26th Saturday

| Moon in Capricorn | PDT | EDT |
|---|---|---|
| Moon trine Venus | 6:00 AM | 9:00 AM |
| Moon opposite Mars | 7:23 AM | 10:23 AM |
| Moon trine Mercury | 11:35 AM | 2:35 PM |
| Moon sextile Uranus | 4:20 PM | 7:20 PM |
| Moon trine Saturn goes v/c | 8:33 PM | 11:33 PM |

*Mood Watch*: If there is ever a time to be constructive, focused, and to get things done, the waxing Capricorn Moon is often the best time to do it. It's a splendid day to actively get a handle on unfinished projects. Moon trine Venus brings pleasurable moods. Moon opposite Mars is a good time to get completely motivated to become active, but also a good time to beware of the potential for accidents. Moon trine Mercury brings a superb time to communicate, organize, and share information, but beware of the potential for communication related setbacks while Mercury is retrograde (Sept. 6/7 – 29). Moon sextile Uranus is the right time to wind down the focuses of being in work-mode, and to kick up your heels and seek some recreational freedom. Tonight, Moon trine Saturn is a good time to review responsibilities, goals, and deadlines, but be careful not to attempt strenuous types of work, especially since the Moon will be void-of-course at this point, a good time to take it easy. It's also an important time to plan on taking it easy for the whole rest of the weekend, as tomorrow's endless void-of-course Moon will make it difficult to get much done at all, or to discuss plans and goals very constructively. This is especially true while Mercury is retrograde.

# September 27th Sunday
## Moon V/C in Capricorn / *No Exact Aspects*

*Mood Watch*: We might as well just call this a *void-of-course day*. If you must, blame it on the Moon! That said, the stars incline, but they do not compel us – or dictate to us what we can and can't do. What does this tell us about the mood of the day? People may tend to be overly serious, or frustrated about their plans not happening on time. Some may seem downright poker-faced, unaffected, and disinterested about your explanation of what it says in the *Celestial Forecaster*. To each his own. In fact, you may well discover that this common saying is the apt term for today's moods – to each his own. No one is likely to be especially patient, accommodating, or useful to your needs. Capricorn says, "I use," and it's a use and be used world sometimes. Don't let it get you down! If someone you know is having a birthday today, it's *their* day – let them have the benefit of the doubt.

# September 28th Monday
## Yom Kippur
### Moon in Capricorn / Aquarius

| | PDT | EDT |
|---|---|---|
| Moon enters Aquarius | 4:06 AM | 7:06 AM |
| Moon trine Sun | 4:12 PM | 7:12 PM |

*Mood Watch*: The especially long void-of-course Capricorn Moon finally comes to an end early this morning. A scientific approach to life captures our moods. This is a time when we are more likely to be understanding, perceptive, and spontaneous. Life's little surprises will seem more interesting. Sun in Libra and Moon in Aquarius is a good time to think matters through. This may be somewhat necessary since Mercury is about to go direct (see tomorrow) and this tends to be a time when communications seem to stand still. It will be a few days yet before connections and exchanges will go smoothly. For now, the Aquarius Moon is a good time to accept humanity's foibles, and to look for comforting and humorous metaphors to describe the unusual way in which life unfolds.

# September 29th Tuesday

| Moon in Aquarius | PDT | EDT |
|---|---|---|
| Mercury goes direct | 6:14 AM | 9:14 AM |
| Moon conjunct Jupiter | 3:25 PM | 6:25 PM |

**Mood Watch**: Sun in Libra and Moon in Aquarius is a time to officiate and clarify the terms of our life with education, law, documentation, and research. A busy shuffle rustles through the halls of large institutions. Waxing Aquarius Moon puts the spotlight on such focuses as science, charities, and humanitarian based causes and issues. Unusual and eccentric people are spurred towards exposing their creative genius. The general mood is outgoing and eccentric. Meanwhile, Mercury is shifting, and ignorance is bliss. Human foibles happen.

**Mercury goes direct** (Mercury direct: Sept. 29 – Dec. 26) Since September 6/7, Mercury has been retrograde in the signs of Libra and Virgo, commonly causing communication glitches and confusion when relaying information. In Libra, the retrograde Mercury often causes communication mix-ups with regard to making decisions, arranging social affairs, harmonizing relationships, and when attempting to make compromises. Mercury retrograde in Virgo has caused important information and data to undergo a tailspin. Now we can breathe a greatly needed sigh of relief as Mercury, the planet governing the realms of communication, becomes stationary and will soon begin to move forward. Take note that our faculties and manner of communicating will definitely improve within the next few days. Although perhaps not today, when the stationary Mercury often freezes communication efforts, but very soon our communications will run more smoothly; this will be a good time to begin clearing up various misunderstandings occurring over the past few weeks. For more information on this recently completed phase of Mercury retrograde, see September 6. For more on Mercury retrograde patterns throughout this year, see the introduction on *Mercury retrograde periods*.

# September 30th Wednesday

| Moon in Aquarius / Pisces | PDT | EDT | |
|---|---|---|---|
| Moon conjunct Neptune goes v/c | 4:33 AM | 7:33 AM | |
| Moon enters Pisces | 4:25 PM | 7:25 PM | |
| Moon sextile Pluto | 5:55 PM | 8:55 PM | |
| Mercury sextile Mars | 11:28 PM | 2:28 AM | (October 1) |

**Mood Watch**: Technical problems? Are there social idiosyncrasies and entanglements? Has humanitarian decency gone out the door? Are those who are pretending to know just making the problem worse? Does Mercury still seem retrograde to you? Relax; the Moon is void-of-course in Aquarius all day, for nearly twelve hours! Much of today's chaos will require some acceptance. We are all engaged in a learning process. Some must learn to listen, others must learn to keep the politics out of the personal realm, and most of us must learn to simply be more patient when the system doesn't work. The setbacks of the void Aquarius Moon often revolve around issues of knowledge and know-how. The mistakes we make are a factor of our learning process. Take this time to learn from the mistakes.

**Mercury sextile Mars** (occurring Sept. 25 – Oct. 8) Mercury in Virgo sextile Mars in Cancer brings informative messages of heartfelt triumphs and actions. Emotional responses to discussions are sure to keep our communications buzzing along swiftly. Mercury is still in a somewhat stationary, or slower moving position, as it has only recently gone direct since yesterday, and it may take a couple of days for communications to run smoothly. However, this aspect insures that communications will move quickly. Mercury sextile Mars presents opportunities which can be received, recognized, communicated and acted upon. News or information may lead to immediate action. It's an advantageous time to apply one's word with a full backing of action for a very favorable outcome. Mercury sextile Mars last occurred on July 20, with Mercury in Leo and Mars in Gemini. During these occurrence dates, this aspect will also reach another peak on October 4.

# October 1ˢᵗ Thursday

**Moon in Pisces**                                    **PDT**          **EDT**
Moon opposite Venus                          8:07 PM        11:07 PM

*Mood Watch*: The decadent days of October have arrived, and the strongly waxing Pisces Moon draws many people to the heart of their beliefs. Addictive tendencies bring the risk of overindulgence. Our moods drift into and out of a series of flowing and changing images and impressions. As the Moon travels through Pisces, a mystical and timeless element of perception captivates our moods. Bubbly, artistic, enchanting, and dreamy moments allow us to access a hidden sanctuary where the soulful or prayerful part of ourselves is unleashed. Today many folks will be drawn towards the need to seek out a favorite space or refuge, something far from the mundane. Let this be the place that recharges the batteries and allows the faith to be renewed.

# October 2ⁿᵈ Friday

**Moon in Pisces** / *Full Moon Eve*          **PDT**          **EDT**
Moon opposite Mercury                       12:07 PM        3:07 PM
Moon trine Mars                                 12:31 PM        3:31 PM
Moon conjunct Uranus                          3:01 PM        6:01 PM
Moon opposite Saturn goes v/c              8:28 PM        11:28 PM
Mars sextile Saturn begins (see October 12)

*Mood Watch*: Young nephew Merlin, age 12, was asked to write about the Full Moon Eve with the Moon in Pisces. He writes, "This will be an eventful day. Whoever is having (or going to) a party, I suggest that they don't have (too many) drinks." What fun is a party without drinks? Merlin knows that when adults overdo the drinks, they can get pretty obnoxiously silly. He's quite smart that way. Today he turns 14. Hopefully, he will be able to apply his own advice. The tricky thing about the influence of a strongly waxing Moon in Pisces is the necessity to apply moderation. It's okay to enjoy strong substances, but without moderation, the Pisces Moon has a way of over accentuating the strength of their affects. One could be easily seduced into overindulgence. Today's lunar aspects are rough and ready to drive this point home. Just be sure not to drink and drive, and be on the lookout for aggressive drivers who might be drunk, on drugs, or emotionally out of control. Today also marks the birthday of the late great legends, Groucho Marx, and Mohandas K. Gandhi. Great minds don't always think alike, but these Libran folks definitely believed in peace. ♎

# October 3rd Saturday
## FULL MOON in ARIES

| Moon in Pisces / Aries | PDT | EDT | |
|---|---|---|---|
| Moon enters Aries | 2:19 AM | 5:19 AM | |
| Moon square Pluto | 3:48 AM | 6:48 AM | |
| Moon opposite Sun | 11:09 PM | 2:09 AM | (October 4) |

*Mood Watch*: The **Full Moon in Aries** (Moon opposite Sun) reaches its peak much later tonight and charges our spirits with an extra dose of energy. All the high pomp and hype of this time comes to a crescendo and is marked with the burning and willful force of Aries Moon activity. A warrior spirit touches us all, particularly with regard to the personal challenges in our lives. Be prepared for headstrong attitudes and potential rudeness. There will also be a great deal of confidence, enthusiasm, and a pioneering spirit. This is a good time to celebrate and to enjoy the fruits of our labors. Shine on Harvest Moon!

# October 4th Sunday

| Moon in Aries | PDT | EDT | |
|---|---|---|---|
| Mercury sextile Mars | 4:25 AM | 7:25 AM | |
| Moon sextile Jupiter | 10:26 AM | 1:26 PM | |
| Mercury opposite Uranus | 1:59 PM | 4:59 PM | |
| Mars trine Uranus | 6:36 PM | 9:36 PM | |
| Moon sextile Neptune | 10:35 PM | 1:35 AM | (October 5) |
| Moon square Mars goes v/c | 10:45 PM | 1:45 AM | (October 5) |
| Sun trine Jupiter begins (see October 10) | | | |
| Venus opposite Uranus begins (see October 9) | | | |

*Mood Watch*: The post-Full Aries Moon now wanes and our incentive to promote speedy reactions begins to settle. The impetuous edge and straightforward tenacity of our moods begins to dissipate, and today it slows down to a much more steady and far less hurried pace. All the while, the cardinal fire heat of strong intent and the drive that urges us onward is ever present throughout the day.

**Mercury sextile Mars** (occurring Sept. 25 – Oct. 8) Mercury in Virgo sextile Mars in Cancer brings pragmatic chatter over heartfelt actions. Due to last month's phase of Mercury retrograde (Sept. 6/7 – 29), this aspect is occurring for the third and final time this year. This aspect first occurred July 17 – 22, reaching its exact peak on July 20. During these occurrence dates, this aspect also reached its peak on September 30. For a review of the influence of Mercury sextile Mars, *see September 30*, when it last occurred with Mercury in Virgo and Mars in Cancer.

**Mercury opposite Uranus** (occurring Sept. 16 – Oct. 7) Mercury in Virgo opposes Uranus in Pisces. Explosive and radical statements are getting the run around once more. Due to last month's phase of Mercury retrograde (Sept. 6/7 – 29), this aspect is occurring for the third and final time this year. For a review of the influence of this aspect, *see August 21*, when it first occurred.

**Mars trine Uranus** (occurring Sept. 24 – Oct. 10) Mars in Cancer trine Uranus in Pisces brings heated activities concerning very sensitive emotional matters, as well as the radical tendencies that are seen in art and spiritual practices. It is through this aspect that emotional breakthroughs may occur. This is a battle that arrives on an apparently emotional level, with the two planets in water signs. Then it turns into explosive and radical events, creating a long run of favorable gifts and triumphs due to the congenial nature of the trine aspect. Since when is destructive macho energy favorable? These particularly masculine planets are tempered in the feminine watery signs. Watch, meditate and observe; the answers are out there. This is a good time to tackle the breakdown of unwanted barriers that stifle the human spirit from evolving in chosen ways. Mars trine Uranus is bound to create fire somewhere, and the heat often can be worked to our advantage. In the triumph mode, Mars trine Uranus creates fireworks of celebration. There is a certain sense of truly being alive with regard to home life, the demand for spiritual freedom and rights, and the need to bring an artistic form of relief to those who have experienced the challenge of emotional and spiritual battles. This is the only time this aspect will reoccur this year.

# October 5th Monday

**Moon in Aries / Taurus**

| | PDT | EDT |
|---|---|---|
| Moon enters Taurus | 9:32 AM | 12:32 PM |
| Moon trine Pluto | 11:00 AM | 2:00 PM |
| Mercury square Pluto begins (see October 10) | | |

*Mood Watch*: The start of the day may seem like a sketchy one. Our general moods may be somewhat impatient, impetuous, or thoughtless. As the Moon enters Taurus, a much more practical, constructive, and persevering quality of mood allows us to drum up some positive attitudes. Moon trine Pluto will help us to create an optimistic approach to handle big problems and challenging projects. Although the Moon wanes and people may seem slightly more introspective, Taurus is the exalted place for the Moon – a good time to focus on creating pleasure, security, and to establish some workable routines to carry us through the week.

# October 6th Tuesday

**Moon in Taurus**

| | PDT | EDT |
|---|---|---|
| Moon square Jupiter | 4:18 PM | 7:18 PM |
| Moon trine Venus | 9:55 PM | 12:55 AM (October 7) |

*Mood Watch*: The Moon is in Taurus and the Sun is in Libra. Both Taurus and Libra are ruled by the planet Venus. This emphasizes the need for the security and balance of love. It also puts the emphasis on the need for pleasure, kindness, and beauty. This afternoon/evening Moon square Jupiter may challenge our sense of generosity, and some folks may seem challenged by their financial situation or the difficulties of balancing funds. Perhaps there is something that holds you back from enjoying life to the fullest? Once and awhile, everyone struggles with their sense of fulfillment. True love takes more than money. As for Venus, much

204

later tonight it will be trine with the Moon. This is a superb time to meditate, and reflect upon, on the power of love.

♎

# October 7ᵗʰ Wednesday

| Moon in Taurus / Gemini | PDT | EDT | |
|---|---|---|---|
| Moon sextile Uranus | 3:59 AM | 6:59 AM | |
| Moon square Neptune | 4:04 AM | 7:04 AM | |
| Moon sextile Mars | 6:30 AM | 9:30 AM | |
| Moon trine Mercury | 9:09 AM | 12:09 PM | |
| Moon trine Saturn goes v/c | 10:18 AM | 1:18 PM | |
| Moon enters Gemini | 2:46 PM | 5:46 PM | |
| Mercury conjunct Saturn | 11:30 PM | 2:30 AM | (October 8) |
| Venus conjunct Saturn begins (see October 13) | | | |
| Venus sextile Mars begins (see October 13) | | | |

***Mood Watch***: At first, we seem to be on a roll while handling matters, as the day starts out busily constructive. However, as the Taurus Moon goes void-of-course, it is trine with Saturn. Just when we are feeling like we're on the ball, a feeling of laziness, stubbornness, or self-indulgence sets us apart from optimal performance. Despite this, there is still an effort to get things done. Nevertheless, for a number of hours in the afternoon, some people may seem tired, distracted, or dull-witted. As the Moon enters Gemini, the clouds of the void Taurus Moon begins to dissipate. People's minds may seem to work better, and there will be a lot of communication about the course of today's affairs. Gemini Moon brings curiosity, observance, and adaptability.

**Mercury conjunct Saturn** (occurring Sept. 28 – Oct. 10) Mercury conjunct Saturn will focus our thoughts on the areas of life that have reached limitations, or where timely new beginnings – or endings – are occurring. Due to last month's phase of Mercury retrograde (Sept. 6/7 – 29), this conjunction is occurring for the third and final time this year. For a review of the influence of Mercury conjunct Saturn, *see August 17*, when it first occurred.

# October 8ᵗʰ Thursday

| Moon in Gemini | PDT | EDT |
|---|---|---|
| Moon trine Sun | 6:27 PM | 9:27 PM |
| Moon trine Jupiter | 8:41 PM | 11:41 PM |

***Mood Watch***: Sun in Libra and Moon in Gemini bring an interesting time of intellectual pursuits, witty humor, and congenial interaction. This is an excellent time to strategize and socialize. Today's lunar aspects are positive, upbeat, and they invite us to share joy with others. This is a good time to engage in teamwork, focus on research, and to make inquiries. A lot can be learned today. Why not choose some interesting people to interact with and to get some helpful ideas? Everyone needs support. Give a little, inquire, and learn something!

# October 9th Friday

| Moon in Gemini / Cancer | PDT | EDT |
|---|---|---|
| Moon square Venus | 7:23 AM | 10:23 AM |
| Moon square Uranus | 8:04 AM | 11:04 AM |
| Moon trine Neptune | 8:14 AM | 11:14 AM |
| Moon square Saturn | 2:52 PM | 5:52 PM |
| Venus opposite Uranus | 3:00 PM | 6:00 PM |
| Moon square Mercury goes v/c | 6:34 PM | 9:34 PM |
| Moon enters Cancer | 6:47 PM | 9:47 PM |
| Moon opposite Pluto | 8:17 PM | 11:17 PM |
| Mercury enters Libra | 8:43 PM | 11:43 PM |

*Mood Watch*: The waning Gemini Moon keeps us on the up and up intellectually, but since the Moon wanes, we may tend to be a lot more introspective, particularly with the early morning's lunar square aspects. Complexity forces us to mull things over. As the Moon trines with Neptune, our moods blend with life's complexities and the feeling of acceptance rings true. This afternoon, Moon square Saturn reminds us of the need to juggle impending deadlines and limitations. This evening, as Moon square Mercury occurs, there may be conflict in the way we think or communicate with others. The Gemini Moon goes void-of-course and swiftly enters Cancer. Here, our feelings begin to surface in more affirmative ways. Change brings different feelings.

**Venus opposite Uranus** (occurring Oct. 4 – 11) Venus in Virgo opposes Uranus in Pisces. Prudent love is tested by radical beliefs. Conflict may surface as love relationships are tested by fundamental differences of belief or by drug related problems. On the up side, exciting and unusual kinds of pleasure bring radical new awareness. On the down side, this type of love is explosive in nature, creating radical obsessions – some healthy and some not. Although they are often short lived, this aspect allows for unusual, exciting, and torrid love affairs. This is a good time for artists to make breakthroughs and for eccentric expressions of affection. Issues of freedom are likely to be raised in love related disputes. Strong psychic connections will occur more rapidly, invoking hypersensitivity that could easily get out of hand. No matter how you look at it, issues of love are surely being activated with a broadening sense of awareness.

**Mercury enters Libra** (Mercury in Libra: Oct. 9 – 28) Due to its last retrograde period (Sept. 6/7 – 29,) Mercury is entering Libra for the second time this year since August 25. Mercury in Libra directs and orchestrates information – like food for the brain – in a harmonious and engaging way. For a recap on the story of how Mercury in Libra affects our communications, *see August 25*, when Mercury first entered Libra.

# October 10th Saturday

| Moon in Cancer | PDT | EDT |
|---|---|---|
| Sun trine Jupiter | 1:38 AM | 4:38 AM |
| Mercury square Pluto | 11:42 AM | 2:42 PM |
| Venus square Pluto begins (see October 15) | | |
| Sun trine Neptune begins (see October 16) | | |

*Mood Watch*: A couple of planetary aspects are occurring, and a couple of aspects are just beginning. However, there are no specific lunar aspects on this waning Cancer Moon day. Our moods will be unpredictable, but they will be easily defined nonetheless. Cancer Moon puts us in touch with how we feel. This does not necessarily mean that we will be moody, but we will probably require some extra care and nourishment to stay on the ball.

**Sun trine Jupiter** (occurring October 4 – 13) Libra people celebrating a birthday from October 4 – 13 are undergoing a favorable natal solar position with relation to Jupiter. This will be a time of gifts and expansion for these birthday folks, and there are good times ahead for them in the coming year. This aspect will bring a better sense of what it means to expand and attain one's personal desire. Be sure to take the time right now, Libra birthday people, to enjoy and appreciate life. Despite the fact that Saturn is about to enter Libra (see Oct. 29), and control issues or responsibilities may become demanding for some Librans, life will definitely improve for those Libra birthday people who are being given the gifts of joy that the natal Sun trine Jupiter aspect often brings. This aspect last occurred June 11 – 20, reaching its peak on June 17, when the Sun was in Gemini.

**Mercury square Pluto** (occurring Oct. 5 – 12) Mercury in Libra is square to Pluto in Capricorn. Procrastinating and vacillating thoughts make it especially difficult to communicate with those of another generation, or to discuss hardships and matters of fate in a constructive manner. Due to Mercury's retrograde cycle last month (Sept. 6/7 – 29,) this aspect is reaching a peak for the fourth and final time this year. For more information on this currently repeating peak performance of Mercury square Pluto, *see August 26.*

# October 11th Sunday
## LAST QUARTER MOON in CANCER

| Moon in Cancer / Leo | PDT | EDT | |
|---|---|---|---|
| Moon square Sun | 1:55 AM | 4:55 AM | |
| Moon trine Uranus | 11:20 AM | 2:20 PM | |
| Moon sextile Venus | 3:43 PM | 6:43 PM | |
| Moon conjunct Mars | 6:02 PM | 9:02 PM | |
| Moon sextile Saturn goes v/c | 6:36 PM | 9:36 PM | |
| Moon enters Leo | 10:02 PM | 1:02 AM | (October 12) |

*Mood Watch*: Very early this morning we come to the **Last Quarter Moon in Cancer** (Moon square Sun). The emotional concerns surfacing now require that extra bit of nurturing and understanding. Feelings must surface at times throughout the day, particularly this evening as the Moon goes void-of-course. This is a good time to practice patience and to lend a listening ear. However, don't get caught up in allowing others to bend your ear if you feel like they are being manipulative or wasting your precious time. In group situations, it is wise to be patient, and to practice kind and cool composure. Much later, as the Moon enters Leo, bold self-expression and alertness entice our moods to be playful and friendly.

207

# October 12ᵗʰ Monday

**Columbus Day, USA  / Thanksgiving Day, Canada**

| Moon in Leo | PDT | EDT | |
|---|---|---|---|
| Moon sextile Mercury | 3:43 AM | 6:43 AM | |
| Mars sextile Saturn . | 1:51 PM | 4:51 PM | |
| Jupiter  goes direct | 9:35 PM | 12:35 AM | (October 13) |

*Mood Watch*: The waning Moon in Leo brings moods of self-assurance and confidence. Waning Leo Moon is a good time to encourage the people around us by acknowledging them with compliments and praise for their recent accomplishments. A small compliment can go a long way to reassure people their efforts are not in vain. Credit where credit is due, but by all means, give credit! Leo Moon is a great time for family gatherings. Happy Thanksgiving, Canada!

**Mars sextile Saturn** (occurring Oct. 2 – 17) Mars in Cancer sextile Saturn in Virgo only occurs once this year. This is an active time for establishing cleanliness in the home. During this aspect, actions create opportunities, provided there is an application of discipline and timing. Those who are affected by this aspect may feel noticed now. Diligently practice your favorite sport, especially those physical activities that demand precision and perfect timing. Offensive and defensive forces tend to work harmoniously with this aspect. Movement and the application of energy (Mars), plus responsibility and awareness of limitation (Saturn) allow the timely qualities of completion and new beginnings to occur. Mars sextile Saturn may be a good time to start a new enterprise, and is an especially opportunistic time to practice control or discipline. This would be the time to end a bad habit or to work to accomplish a goal.

**Jupiter goes direct** (Jupiter direct: Oct. 12, 2009 – July 23, 2010) Since June 15, Jupiter has been retrograde in the sign of Aquarius. Let us celebrate as the planet Jupiter moves forward! Jupiter represents skill, fortune, luck, wealth, expansion, wellbeing, and joviality; it's also associated with advancement, prosperity, opportunity, fulfillment, and inheritance. The process of Jupiter retrograde is sometimes difficult for systems, and for the predictability of economic growth, such as business and market control. Jupiter has been in Aquarius since January 5, emphasizing advancements in such Aquarius related things as science, technology, and humanitarian projects. Jupiter engages one with a sense of happiness and fulfillment. Now that Jupiter goes direct, advancement goes from an internalized process to an externalized process, which is how Jupiter operates best. Blessed are the Aquarius people, as the prosperity planet, Jupiter, has been and will continue to be sweeping through Aquarians' personal realm, giving them the opportunities and tools for growth needed to advance, and also bestowing a sense of joy. Next year will be Piscesians' year to identify with prosperity and happiness, as Jupiter enters the sign of Pisces on January 17, 2010.

# October 13th Tuesday

**Moon in Leo**

| | PDT | EDT |
|---|---|---|
| Moon opposite Jupiter | 3:06 AM | 6:06 AM |
| Venus conjunct Saturn | 3:51 AM | 6:51 AM |
| Moon sextile Sun | 8:37 AM | 11:37 AM |
| Venus sextile Mars | 11:30 AM | 2:30 PM |
| Moon opposite Neptune goes v/c | 2:20 PM | 5:20 PM |

Ω

*Mood Watch*: Dear Reader, the keyword for today is *affection*. While a couple of Venus aspects are at work (see below) the waning Leo Moon brings out our needs for affection, attention, warmth, kindness, and friendliness. What are you doing here? Get out into the world and spread some infectious affection, but first, don't forget to read about those aspects of Venus. Fond Best Regards, Your Affectionate Astrological Author. P.S. – The Moon goes void-of-course this afternoon/early evening, so beware of forgetfulness and beastly moods.

**Venus conjunct Saturn** (occurring Oct. 7 – 15) Venus and Saturn are conjunct in Virgo at the 28 degree mark, which makes it the cusp of Virgo and Libra. This creates subtly affectionate, communicative, and serious bonding between loved ones. This conjunction brings a favorable time to apply discipline in the arts and in love related matters. Venus conjunct Saturn represents our commitment and responsibility to the people we love and care about. It may also indicate there is a strong timely quality about love matters taking place, or that love matters are undergoing a restriction, or possibly even closure of some kind. This conjunction can go either way on the positive-negative scale, since the loving attraction of Venus can be either encouraged or thwarted by the responsible, serious, and limiting discipline of Saturn's energy. This is the only time Venus will be conjunct with Saturn this year.

**Venus sextile Mars** (occurring Oct. 7 – 16) Now the two planets of yin and yang are back for a third time in the opportunistic sextile position. Today's Venus in Virgo and Mars in Cancer will bring shy and virginal attractions, and home oriented displays of heroism and worthiness. It is here that feminine (Venus) and masculine (Mars) forces have an opportunity (the sextile aspect) to support each other. At this time, many vital love matters are being stirred and are bringing numerous opportunities. This aspect last occurred January 7 – Feb. 24, reaching one exact peak on January 24 with Venus in Pisces and Mars in Capricorn. It also reached a second peak on February 18, with Venus in Aries and Mars in Aquarius.

# October 14th Wednesday

**Moon in Virgo**

| | PDT | EDT |
|---|---|---|
| Moon enters Virgo | 12:45 AM | 3:45 AM |
| Moon trine Pluto | 2:20 AM | 5:20 AM |
| Venus enters Libra | 3:46 PM | 6:46 PM |

*Mood Watch*: The Moon wanes in Virgo. This is a time when we tend to become technical, critical, meticulous, and in need of some organization. When the Moon is in the Mercury-ruled sign of Virgo, it's a good time to clean up, apply some extra physical care and hygiene, and to take precautions not to catch other people's

209

cold and flu viruses. Fall season is slipping into the more challenging days of wet, stormy, and cold days here in North America. The Virgo Moon gives us the wherewithal to prepare for and handle the challenges of this time.

**Venus enters Libra** (Venus in Libra: Oct. 14 – Nov. 7) Venus enters Libra and now the course of magnetism, affection and feminine perception begins to focus on harmonizing and balancing relationships, marriages, and friendships. Venus will be in Libra today through November 7, stimulating our Libra friends with a strong sense of affection, and focusing our love relationships towards the goal of creating a more harmonized and balanced state of being. Venus is at home in Libra, and brings out a love of libraries, of scholarly works, and there is a greater attraction to large bodies of information. Venus in Libra emphasizes the love of books, education, law and order, friends and loved ones, and particularly a love and desire for balance wherever possible. As autumn continues, our nesting instincts grow deeper, and relationships that aren't stable enough to undergo the responsibilities and tests of winter are likely to break off, as Venus in Libra strives to apply diplomacy as tactfully as possible. As for the delicacy of love matters, in order to settle on the best choices and decisions possible, Libra strives hard to apply a great wealth of knowledge, common law, history, and helpful information with regard to relationships. Attraction is a mystery; Libra seeks to decode the mystery.

# October 15th Thursday

| Moon in Virgo | PDT | EDT |
|---|---|---|
| Venus  square Pluto | 10:21 AM | 1:21 PM |
| Moon  opposite Uranus | 4:32 PM | 7:32 PM |

*Mood Watch*: This Virgo Moon day kicks off the mid-month with pragmatic efforts and inquiries. Many folks seem to be well informed about matters and, when they are not, they are anxious to get to the bottom of their inquiries. Virgo Moon activities often give us something to think about, but we must be careful not to get caught up in a tendency to judge, doubt, or scrutinize too much. The Moon opposite Uranus brings especially chaotic moods. There is no point in analyzing what you're feeling. Practice kindness; it's the best deal!

**Venus square Pluto** (occurring Oct. 10 – 17) For the fourth time this year, Venus square Pluto occurs. However, this one is different; for the first time in our lifetime, Venus in Libra is square Pluto in Capricorn. The diplomatic, peaceable, cooperative and naturally harmonious side of our affections (Venus in Libra) is likely to take a pretty good beating, while a seemingly major transformation is occurring on a physical level (Pluto in Capricorn). Our concepts of beauty may be challenged as the corruption of superpowers prompts action which threatens or alters the beauty and pleasure in our lives. Venus square Pluto usually involves such difficulties as loss or death of a loved one, the obstacles of rejection, and general oppression for those aspects of life to which we are undeniably attached and which we hold dear. If something of this nature is occurring for you, it is best to recognize that love will triumph in every dimension, despite the pain of separation, or the disease and strife of the beloved. Be both strong and gentle in matters of love. Let the obstacles of love's pain become the building blocks of a better outlook, and a stronger love will

210

supersede these current trials of the heart. This aspect is a little more merciful at this time, with Venus in its home sign, Libra; that is, it's much more merciful than it was earlier this year, with Venus in the detrimental position of Aries. Due to Venus retrograde (March 6 – April 17), this aspect formerly occurred on three separate occasions, on February 5, April 3, and May 2, when Venus was in Aries.

♎

# October 16th Friday

| Moon in Virgo / Libra | PDT | EDT | |
|---|---|---|---|
| Moon conjunct Saturn | 12:55 AM | 3:55 AM | |
| Moon sextile Mars goes v/c | 3:18 AM | 6:18 AM | |
| Moon enters Libra | 3:29 AM | 6:29 AM | |
| Moon square Pluto | 5:09 AM | 8:09 AM | |
| Moon conjunct Venus | 6:56 AM | 9:56 AM | |
| Mars enters Leo | 8:32 AM | 11:32 AM | |
| Sun trine Neptune | 5:46 PM | 8:46 PM | |
| Moon conjunct Mercury | 10:23 PM | 1:23 AM | (October 17) |
| Mercury trine Jupiter begins (see October 20) | | | |
| Sun square Mars begins (see October 29) | | | |

**Mood Watch**: In the earliest hours, a busy set of lunar aspects and activity brings a somewhat restless awakening. The Moon enters Libra and we have now reached the dark phase of the lunar cycle. Change is definitively in the air. The Sun and Moon are both in Libra. This is the time to deliberate and to examine the best course of action to create a balance. Libra says: "I balance," and there is no point in waiting for the imbalances of your life to bring you down. Now is the time to take measures to secure a firm sense of stability.

**Mars enters Leo** (Mars in Leo: Oct. 16, 2009 – June 6/7, 2010) Mars will be in Leo for the remainder of the year and, since it will go retrograde (Dec. 20), it will stay in Leo for a good portion of 2010 – until June 6/7. Leo is a fearless place for the planet Mars; sheer action is stimulated and animated here. For the next eight months, Leo people will have a lot of extra energy and some of them will be forced to reckon with their temper. Leo folks, be creative with this extra energy while you have it. In the meantime, while traveling through Leo, Mars will go into the square position to the signs Taurus and Scorpio. Taurus and Scorpio people may have an exhausting – or accident prone – time. They may also need to steer clear of heated disputes, particularly with Leos. Aquarius people may be overwhelmed by brazen activity in their lives while Mars opposes their natal Sun. Mars in Leo generally brings positive and fortifying energy to the scope of all action. It's a good time to get in touch with one's instincts and to activate personal willpower.

**Sun trine Neptune** (occurring Oct. 10 – 19) This occurrence of Sun trine Neptune particularly affects those Libra people celebrating birthdays October 10 – 19. These Librans are experiencing the favorable trine aspect of Neptune to their natal Sun. This brings gifts of spiritual encounters and awareness, as well as a calming effect on one's life. It also serves as a good time (particularly for these birthday folks) to seek visions, apply prayer and meditation, and to explore spiritual avenues and beliefs that are being presented. This aspect last occurred June 10 – 20, reaching its peak on June 17, when the Sun was in Gemini.

# October 17th Saturday

**NEW MOON in LIBRA**

| | PDT | EDT | |
|---|---|---|---|
| *- Hecate's Moon* | | | |
| Moon trine Jupiter | 9:01 AM | 12:01 PM | |
| Moon trine Neptune | 8:27 PM | 11:27 PM | |
| Moon conjunct Sun goes v/c | 10:34 PM | 1:34 AM | (October 18) |

*Mood Watch*: The **New Moon in Libra** (Moon conjunct Sun) is a time of reaffirming and harmonizing our relationships with friends and partners, as well as a time of new friendship while autumn activities create a new working environment for many people. New rules also set the standard for how to create a more harmonious environment in the days of autumn. This Moon places an emphasis on laws, the courts, the litigation process, custody battles, and the like. Justice comes when there is peace, but this is not always found in the courts. The rest of the world will pretty much do what it has always done since the beginning of time, and not all matters are individually controllable. In order to begin anew, the New Libra Moon reminds us to seek peace within.

*Hecates's Moon:* Some may say that *"Hecate's Moon"* is the New Moon in Scorpio, others may say it's the New Moon closest to *All Hallows (Halloween / October 31st)*, others still may say its the New Moon of October that represents Hecate's Moon. As for this *New Moon of Hecate* – New in Libra – by a narrow margin this is the closest New Moon to All Hallows, and it's the New Moon of October. Hecate is the Wiccan goddess of the underworld who leads us through death towards a cycle of rebirth. She guides the lost souls to their final destiny, and can be called on at this time to guide those who have passed on, especially those who have met their end in a demeaning and challenged way, such as violent death or suicide. Hecate cures the ills that surround death. To honor her, take eggs, black bread, and beer to a Y-shaped path or road where an old tree stands. Give this offering to her and ask her to oversee the souls who have died that we want to see safely through to the other side. Honor her with respect – she is a serious and powerful spirit to call up, and no immature or insincere request will be granted by this goddess of the dark moon. If the wind kicks up or you receive a chill on the back of your neck, fear not; that's the spirit of Hecate confirming her presence. She will not hurt you as long as you respect her. If you would prefer to honor Hecate on the New Moon in Scorpio, this occurs on November 16.

# October 18th Sunday

**Moon in Libra / Scorpio**

| | PDT | EDT |
|---|---|---|
| Moon enters Scorpio | 7:23 AM | 10:23 AM |
| Moon square Mars | 9:10 AM | 12:10 PM |
| Moon sextile Pluto | 9:10 AM | 12:10 PM |

*Mood Watch*: At first, the void-of-course Libra Moon brings indecisive moods. As the morning progresses, the Moon steps into Scorpio, and our moods will begin to become more vibrant, fervent, and passionate. The Moon squares with Mars at the same time as it is in the sextile position to Pluto. Through the complexity of our actions comes the hope for overcoming trials and tribulations. The Scorpio Moon is here to guide us in an instinctual, resilient, and wholehearted manner. The bigger the test, the greater the victory. Arm yourself with vigilant passion and all will be well – and perhaps – heroic!

Ω

## October 19th Monday

**Moon in Scorpio**

| | PDT | EDT |
|---|---|---|
| Moon square Jupiter | 2:17 PM | 5:17 PM |

*Mood Watch*: The newly waxing Moon in Scorpio brings the need for warmth, acceptance, mental relaxation, and objectivity. Perhaps it would be wise to engage in some physical exertion in order to defuse emotional intensity. Some definite rest will be needed for those who have been feeling sick or run down. This is no time to push the envelope. This afternoon's Moon square Jupiter brings challenges to our sense of joy and prosperity. Challenges can always be worked out, and there is no reason to spread, or be affected by, less than prosperous feelings. This may also be a good time to watch the pocketbook, and to take precautions against theft. Scorpio Moon brings all kinds of possibilities, and with this comes many ways to handle life. Find your prosperity!

## October 20th Tuesday

**Moon in Scorpio / Sagittarius**

| | PDT | EDT |
|---|---|---|
| Moon trine Uranus | 1:36 AM | 4:36 AM |
| Moon square Neptune | 2:14 AM | 5:14 AM |
| Moon sextile Saturn goes v/c | 11:58 AM | 2:58 PM |
| Moon enters Sagittarius | 1:50 PM | 4:50 PM |
| Mercury trine Jupiter | 2:49 PM | 5:49 PM |
| Moon trine Mars | 5:52 PM | 8:52 PM |
| Sun sextile Pluto begins (see October 24) | | |
| Mercury trine Neptune begins (see October 24) | | |

*Mood Watch*: The waxing Scorpio Moon brings subtle complexity, and we may experience some very intuitive moods throughout the morning. For less than a couple of hours this afternoon, the Moon will be void-of-course, and this is a good time to apply caution, and to avoid suspicion or irritability. As the Moon enters Sagittarius, our moods may become more positive. Explorative moods and open-mindedness bring creativity.

**Mercury trine Jupiter** (occurring Oct. 16 – 22) Mercury gets the message out there, the trine aspect brings gifts and positive breakthroughs, and Jupiter brings prosperity. This most favorable aspect brings good news of expansion and prosperity to those who are open to broadening their awareness. Ask and you shall have! Mercury in Libra trine Jupiter in Aquarius brings harmonious communications which can lead to a gold mine of happiness and wellbeing. Since Jupiter is in Aquarius, this is a favorable time to launch fundraisers for charities. It's an excellent time to learn new skills which will improve one's livelihood and better one's outlook. This is also a great time for salespeople to make sales, and for people to advertise and put information out there. For some folks, Mercury trine Jupiter is an advantageous time to ask for a job or a loan, or to provide a service which may have a bearing on a potential promotion. Look openly for opportunity when sharing information, and promote yourself and your capabilities. This aspect last occurred on June 28 – July 3, reaching its exact peak on July 1, when Mercury was in Gemini.

# October 21st Wednesday

| Moon in Sagittarius | PDT | EDT | |
|---|---|---|---|
| Moon sextile Venus | 5:11 AM | 8:11 AM | |
| Moon sextile Jupiter | 10:46 PM | 1:46 AM | (October 22) |

*Mood Watch*: The closing days of the Sun in Libra bring positive and upbeat moods. Today's lunar aspects are very promising, with the Moon sextile to Venus early this morning and, much later, the Moon sextile Jupiter also brings the potential for positive vibrations. This is a good time to spread happiness while it is particularly infectious. Sun in Libra and Moon in Sagittarius brings stability and expansion. A new outlook can change everything. Change is always occurring, but it is best experienced when a positive outlook is applied. Don't wait for all this good stuff to come to you; here's your chance to make it happen! Explore, enjoy, and be merry!

# SCORPIO

Key Phrase: " I  CREATE " or

"I DESIRE"

Fixed Water Sign

Ruling Planet: Pluto

Symbol(s): The Scorpion,

The Eagle, and The Phoenix

October 22nd through

November 21st

# October 22nd Thursday

| Moon in Sagittarius / Capricorn | PDT | EDT | |
|---|---|---|---|
| Moon sextile Mercury | 3:47 AM | 6:47 AM | |
| Moon square Uranus | 10:33 AM | 1:33 PM | |
| Moon sextile Neptune | 11:19 AM | 2:19 PM | |
| Moon square Saturn | 10:14 PM | 1:14 AM | (October 23) |
| Moon sextile Sun goes v/c | 11:39 PM | 2:39 AM | (October 23) |
| Moon enters Capricorn | 11:40 PM | 2:40 AM | (October 23) |
| Sun enters Scorpio | 11:43 PM | 2:43 AM | (October 23) |

*Mood Watch*: Enthusiastic moods will brighten our outlook as the waxing Sagittarius Moon invites us to explore all avenues of possibility. If we are astute and willing to watch for the signs, a vision can be magnified with a positive affirmation. Perfect and empower that vision. A sincere effort to achieve will dutifully follow a clear vision. Sun in Libra and Moon in Sagittarius is a good time to live by example,

214

and to apply the old motto; "think globally, act locally." In these days of internet and reality television, our global message to the world spreads more rapidly and widely than we think. One person's small voice is nothing to be underestimated. Sagittarius Moon invites us to share our visions with the global community. ♏

**Sun enters Scorpio** (Sun in Scorpio: Oct. 22 – Nov. 21) This time of year, like the Scorpio personality, creates an air of mystery and mysticism. This is a time when people are more likely to focus on their hidden agendas and their need to get in touch with their own passion. Scorpio focuses our attention on the most important events of life: birth, sex, death and regeneration or transformation, as this sign is ruled by the underworld god known as Pluto. Scorpio represents the powers of hidden meaning, the need for secrecy, and the deeper psychologically ensnaring struggles with the self-destructive nature of humans and beasts. The totem of the sign of Scorpio is classically the desert arachnid known as the scorpion. The scorpion sting can kill; this is the violent or criminal side of the Scorpio personality. There are other totems – the Eagle and the Phoenix. These higher aspects of the Scorpio personality relate to the eagle's ability to observe from very far away and see a larger and more objective picture of life while noting all the details essential to life itself. The Phoenix totem represents the ability to rise above the burning rays of the sun as a transformed and enlightened being. Pushing through and surviving the perilous difficulties and dangers of life is practically a personality trait of the sign of Scorpio. The Scorpio archetype demands some respect. Scorpios are often stereotyped for having a desire to live richly and often dangerously. There is always the vast and more esoteric version, too – the way of spirit, the mystical and spiritual path, or the acknowledgment of one's own truth.

# October 23rd Friday
## Moon in Capricorn

| | PDT | EDT | |
|---|---|---|---|
| Moon conjunct Pluto | 1:51 AM | 4:51 AM | |
| Moon square Venus | 10:44 PM | 1:44 AM | (October 24) |
| Venus trine Jupiter begins (see October 28) | | | |

*Mood Watch*: A couple of shifts have occurred since late last night; the Moon entered Capricorn and the Sun entered Scorpio. A much more serious set of moods have cropped up. This is a good time to focus on making some headway with projects and tasks. The Capricorn Moon keeps us busily working on securing our environment, meeting certain goals, and observing our deadlines and obligations. This is a good time to take care of business, as many people will be responsive to the necessity to get things done. This may not be the time to try to open up hidden emotions. Sometimes it is wiser to let emotional responses come out when they're good and ready. Capricorn Moon is not usually a constructive time to delve into emotional complexity.

215

# October 24ᵗʰ Saturday

| Moon in Capricorn | PDT | EDT | |
|---|---|---|---|
| Sun  sextile Pluto | 2:57 AM | 5:57 AM | |
| Mercury  trine Neptune | 9:55 AM | 12:55 PM | |
| Moon  sextile Uranus | 10:27 PM | 1:27 AM | (October 25) |

*Mood Watch*: The waxing Capricorn Moon is a good time to focus on career moves, and the emphasis of our moods is placed on the need to excel, and to improve one's lifestyle. This is the time to get practical about the later days of autumn. What's likely to stand out now is unfinished business. This is the time to prepare for storms, the colder weather, and the expenses of the holiday seasons ahead. The days of Scorpio become more intense as November approaches. The Capricorn Moon gives us what it takes to address big concerns.

**Sun sextile Pluto** (occurring Oct. 20 – 26) The Sun, now just one degree into Scorpio, is sextile Pluto, which is newly in Capricorn since last year. This brings opportunities that appear both vast and demanding to Libra and Scorpio cusp born people who are celebrating birthdays October 20 – 26. These birthday people are experiencing the sextile aspect of their natal sun to Pluto, giving them opportunities to take charge, to step into positions of power, and to accept and embrace permanent change in their lives. These are powerful transformations which provide opportunities to embody what has been learned from the personal trials of the past. Go thee forth and conquer, master Librans and Scorpions! Persist with diligence to resolve the conflicts of your life with self-respect and assurance. Your time to triumph is always available when your will to achieve is balanced by knowledge and hard work. This holds true for all signs of the zodiac. This aspect occurred earlier this year, February 16 – 23, reaching its peak on February 21 with the Sun in Pisces.

**Mercury trine Neptune** (occurring October 20 – 26) Mercury in Libra trine Neptune in Aquarius brings diplomacy in speech, and it also brings intuitive and uplifting knowledge. Communicate about spiritual needs with helpful counsel and receive gifts of renewed faith in your own beliefs. Recognize that some messages are there to spiritually uplift you. This aspect last occurred June 28 – July 3, reaching its exact peak on July 1.

# October 25ᵗʰ Sunday

### FIRST QUARTER MOON in AQUARIUS

| Moon in Capricorn / Aquarius | PDT | EDT | |
|---|---|---|---|
| Moon  square Mercury | 1:37 AM | 4:37 AM | |
| Moon  trine Saturn goes v/c | 11:14 AM | 2:14 PM | |
| Moon  enters Aquarius | 12:07 PM | 3:07 PM | |
| Moon  square Sun | 5:42 PM | 8:42 PM | |
| Moon  opposite Mars | 9:29 PM | 12:29 AM | (October 26) |

*Mood Watch*: Much of this morning Capricorn Moon brings serious moods, and for nearly an hour, the void-of-course Moon sets the tone for some serious confusion. Fortunately, this all turns around quickly as the Aquarius Moon uplifts our moods in studious ways. We have now reached the **First Quarter Moon in Aquarius**

216

(Moon square Sun). Waxing Aquarius Moon puts the spotlight on eccentric and unusual breakthroughs of humankind. Controversial subjects are strongly at work. At this time we are often aware of great shifts of energy, and the Aquarius Moon will assist our moods to meet and formally address humanity's newest challenges. ♏

# October 26ᵗʰ Monday
**Moon in Aquarius**

| | PDT | EDT | |
|---|---|---|---|
| Moon trine Venus | 6:46 PM | 9:46 PM | |
| Moon conjunct Jupiter | 11:39 PM | 2:39 AM | (October 27) |
| Mercury sextile Pluto begins (see October 28) | | | |
| Sun conjunct Mercury begins (see November 5) | | | |

*Mood Watch*: The waxing Aquarius Moon brings philanthropic moods. People will tend to be generous, open-minded, engaging, and at times, unconventional. This evening, Moon trine Venus brings the greatest potential for loving and pleasurable moods. Sun in Scorpio and Moon in Aquarius means anything is possible. In fact, the impossible is often a concept that is broadly entertained. Much, much later tonight, Moon conjunct Jupiter puts us in touch with our joy and our need to expand and grow in prosperous ways.

# October 27ᵗʰ Tuesday
**Moon in Aquarius**

| | PDT | EDT |
|---|---|---|
| Moon conjunct Neptune | 12:09 PM | 3:09 PM |
| Mercury square Mars begins (see November 1) | | |

*Mood Watch*: The waxing Aquarius Moon is a splendid time to focus on science, invention, research, systems analysis, charity work, and technology. A curious and innovative quality of outlook captures our moods. This is a good time to socialize with intellectuals, to examine new possibilities for your life, and to engage in something unusual or mind expanding. This afternoon's Moon conjunct Neptune brings open-mindedness, spiritual moods, and a firm grasp of the need for some peace and tranquility.

# October 28ᵗʰ Wednesday
**Moon in Aquarius / Pisces**

| | PDT | EDT |
|---|---|---|
| Moon trine Mercury goes v/c | 12:21 AM | 3:21 AM |
| Moon enters Pisces | 12:44 AM | 3:44 AM |
| Mercury enters Scorpio | 3:08 AM | 6:08 AM |
| Moon sextile Pluto | 3:10 AM | 6:10 AM |
| Moon trine Sun | 11:36 AM | 2:36 PM |
| Venus trine Jupiter | 7:01 PM | 10:01 PM |
| Mercury sextile Pluto | 8:53 PM | 11:53 PM |
| Venus trine Neptune (see November 2) | | |

*Mood Watch*: The waxing Pisces Moon brings romantic, artistic, musical, and poetic moods. For the most part, today's aspects are positive and cheerful. If the weather isn't wet, $H_2O$ is on the rise nonetheless, as our moods are sure to be watery, malleable, and mutable by nature. This is a good time to spread seeds, and lots of them – there are seeds of life, seeds of hope, and seeds of promise. Sun in

Scorpio and Moon in Pisces brings deep emotional reverie, intuitive perception, and creative spark. From this spark we get inspiration, warm sensitivity, and an all around good day to celebrate life's buoyant and regenerative qualities.

**Mercury enters Scorpio** (Mercury in Scorpio: Oct. 28 – Nov. 15) Mercury in Scorpio is often a time when communications are veiled in secrecy, and talk revolves around matters of intensity and sensitivity. Passionate issues are communicated with creativity and intuition. This is also a time to be aware that a sharp tongue may easily cause a violent or challenging reaction. It is through this medium of Mercury in the sign of Scorpio that the expression of communications is seemingly fearless, obstinate, reckless, and passionate. From indecent babble to the subtle perfection of clear articulation, discussions frequently deliver a powerful punch. Not only our words but also our appearance, mannerisms and attitudes all send out the message of who we are. The mask we choose for the grand masquerade of autumn's darkening days teaches us much about ourselves.

**Venus trine Jupiter** (occurring Oct. 23 – 31) Love (Venus) is harmoniously placed with prosperity and opportunity (Jupiter). Venus in Libra trine Jupiter in Aquarius brings engaging companionship and affection that inspires open-minded and innovative means for discovering joy and prosperity. Under this influence, love may grow and expand in adventurous and unexpected ways. This is a great time to give gifts of love and, for many people, it offers an expansive outlook. Without love in your life and a love for what you are doing, an expanding empire will eventually lose its luster. Venus trine Jupiter reminds us fortune can be realized with simple aesthetics and quality moments. This aspect last occurred July 22 – 29, reaching its exact peak on July 26 with Venus in Gemini.

**Mercury sextile Pluto** (occurring Oct. 26 – 30) This aspect brings an opportunity for us to get the message across to people in strong positions of power and authority. Mercury is newly in Scorpio (see above), focusing discussions on matters of birth, sex, death, and transformation. Pluto in Capricorn is forcing us to acknowledge our resources and to use them wisely. Mass media may well be entranced by news concerning world superpowers and/or challenging power issues. This is an opportunistic time to reach out to those of another generation and make an attempt to communicate something vital. This aspect last occurred March 7 – 11, and it reached its peak on March 10 with Mercury in Pisces.

# October 29th Thursday

| Moon in Pisces | PDT | EDT | |
|---|---|---|---|
| Sun square Mars | 12:55 AM | 3:55 AM | |
| Saturn enters Libra | 10:09 AM | 1:09 PM | |
| Moon conjunct Uranus goes v/c | 9:54 PM | 12:54 AM | (October 30) |

*Mood Watch*: Sun in Scorpio and Moon in Pisces is always a good time to intuit the big changes. The Pisces Moon hones in on our sensitivity levels and tells us what's going on in the unseen parts of our conscience. Today's big change of Saturn entering Libra (see below) prepares us for a shift in our responsibilities. As Saturn moves into a new sign, the Pisces Moon gives us the ability to move swiftly through multiple moods.

218

**Sun square Mars** (occurring Oct. 17 – Nov. 3) This aspect particularly affects those Scorpio born people celebrating birthdays this year from October 17 – November 3. ♏ It creates the illusion that obstacles are constantly getting in the way of the actions (and will) of these people. This may be a time when harnessing energy seems like a chore. It may serve as a good time for these people to lighten up on their expectations of themselves for awhile, and not let such setbacks get in the way of enjoying life. Relax! In time, it will be easier once again to get your personal goals and your willpower into a state of action. The year ahead may bring difficulty when it comes to relating to various events, particularly warlike events, as they occur. This may be an accident prone time in the lives of these birthday folks. Since this year may bring the tendency for accidents and mistakes, this will be a good time for these birthday folks to learn a great deal about how to pace themselves and to work through the obstacles in order to perfect personal visions and goals.

**Saturn enters Libra** (Saturn in Libra: October 29, 2009 – April 7, 2010 *and* July 21, 2010 – October 5, 2012) Saturn in Libra demands even-tempered and civil measures with regard to setting up perimeters and implementing rules. Approximately every 2 to 2.5 years, depending on the retrograde periods, Saturn enters a new zodiac sign. However, in this case, Saturn traverses through Libra for an extended period of nearly three years and, fortunately, Saturn is in the place of "exaltation" here in the sign of Libra. Saturn rules Capricorn, and the constellation Libra just happens to be in the challenging square position to where Saturn is customarily at home. In Libra, Saturn works hard.

With the exception of the period of April 7 – July 21, 2010, when the retrograde Saturn will return to the late degrees of Virgo, for the next three years, the expression of Saturn in Libra focuses our disciplines in such Libra related places and activities as politics, the judicial system, court related duties, law, mediation, libraries, teaching, dress design, the arts – including culinary arts – music, and the literary sciences. Saturn probably hits hardest in the realm of relationships where it also focuses our disciplines. It puts us in touch with our limitations in such Libra related subjects as marriage –common-law marriage included – friendship, social clubs, and in all kinds of relationships in general. Saturn tests the stability of all things, and in the peace-loving, harmony seeking realm of Libra, tests are not especially easy on relationships. The test of time, and often sacrifice, determines the strength and outcome of various types of relationships.

Saturn's travels through Libra may place disciplinary actions or restrictions on all kinds of laws, peace talks, and civil rights. Time itself is at a premium, since there will often be no time to ponder, deliberate, vacillate, procrastinate, barter, bluff or stall, as most diplomats are so prone to do. The allotted time to consider very important matters will often seem ineffectual, causing certain aspects of this planetary traversal to appear highly unfair. Saturn represents the demarcation of events and time; therefore, beginnings and endings mark our course in ways that just might seem unfair at times, but Saturn related activity pays no mind to the argument of what's fair. There just might not be enough time to put an end to certain kinds of suffering if it relies strictly on the scheduling and execution of court decisions. Our tests of time must be addressed with diligence and an unending supply of patience and determination with Saturn in the realm of Libra.

## SATURN'S RECENT HISTORY IN VIRGO

During the time of Saturn in Virgo, September 2, 2007 – October 29, 2009, it has been important to recognize and to empower the structure of our economic condition and of the communications that have shaped our views in this realm. Focuses such as accounting, systems analysis, secretarial duties, and the apparent condition of the healthcare field have all been subject to Saturnian kinds of restriction. Virgo people will not deny the past couple of years have been a time of hard work for them, but also a time when their disciplines have allowed them to claim a greater sense of control over their lives. While there has been no way for Virgos to avoid taking on responsibilities and to face personal limitations, by now a more dignified and confident level of discipline and achievement can be claimed by Virgo people. Take it easy, Virgo folks, and congratulations – this particular Saturn influence is now completed! Now the master of discipline and focus, Saturn, wends its way through the sign of Libra. In the next few years to come, lawful, deliberate, conciliatory, and diplomatic efforts will be the backbone of structure while Saturn is in Libra.

## WHAT SATURN REPRESENTS

Saturn's influence represents the times in our lives when we take authority and responsibility for something. It represents commitment. Saturn makes us realize that sometimes we are driven to make choices we do not want to make, and sometimes we are forced to participate in a system with which we don't agree. In our quest to perform our true will and to accomplish important goals, we are beset by obstacles, challenged by difficulty, and overwhelmed by the unpredictable factors of a vastly changing world. Saturn is the planet which gives us the edge to proceed with clarity and focus. It is also our protection mechanism, our lock-and-key to the issues in our lives on which we choose to work, determining when and how these matters are to be unlocked, handled, and completed. Saturn represents those areas in life where we earnestly work to focus and concentrate our energies; it is where we manage and maintain some control.

Ahhh, Saturn. So much to do about Saturn. This is the planet that puts us in touch with reality, and challenges us to apply discipline and a sense of limitation if we are to stay on course enough to survive. Saturn is the great teacher and the grim reaper all in one. Saturn is where the line is drawn in every chapter of the story of our lives. Beginnings and endings occur when Saturnian experiences penetrate our lives. There is a hard edge to creating new disciplines as well as giving up old ones. Saturn reflects time constantly and doesn't skip a beat. Time waits for no one, not even Librans, so this is your time, Libra folks, to get your sense of timing in gear and to do what you do best.

## HOW SATURN IN LIBRA AFFECTS LIBRANS

Saturn in Libra imposes greater responsibility and work on our Libra friends for the next few years while Saturn is transiting the Sun sign of Libra people. This may be the time for Librans to connect with their work and to use their talents to achieve goals that are important to them. Libras will need to make it through and succinctly handle many completion processes, and they may pass some significant milestones in the next couple of years. There will be a strong inclination to put an end to trifling imbalances, and Libra people will be busily focused on such challenging things as learning to identify with their career or work, working in a timely or limited manner, making final decisions, completing goals, organizing, weeding out superfluous relationships – and social affairs – that are a waste of time, and handling important responsibilities. Libra, the scales of justice, the diplomat, mediator, arbitrator, and peace maker will be put to the working test of setting up perimeters and territorial lines in an ever changing environment. Librans must create their own guidelines and set their own standards of what kind of work they will do and how much it will be worth to them. This is a very important time for Librans – a time of work and career related establishment or closure, and it is an important time in their marital and family life, too.

## HOW SATURN IN LIBRA WORKS IN OUR SOCIETY

Discipline and the act of setting limits will now be emphasized in such Libra related things as the judicial system, law enforcement, and the world of marriage and marital relationships. Libra represents the development of structure through law, and the preservation of the power and unique qualities of cultural and artistic pursuits.

While Saturn is in Libra, many work contracts will be based on people's diplomacy skills, their capabilities for harmonizing with others, as well as their tactfulness in tight situations. One might expect that with Saturn in Libra, disciplinary measures and carefully planned teamwork will mean serious business for competitive companies. Saturn in Libra may play a strong role in society's influence on what takes place in the world of justice. Libra represents our relationship with the laws, our law practices, and our capacity to enforce our laws. Over the next three years, more strict disciplines may be applied with regard to how we care for and gauge our laws, particularly our marital laws. Saturn is the teacher that instills guidelines and allows us to create new structure and a new foundation upon which to stand at a time when we are dealing with the crumbling remains of dysfunctional situations or behavior which might threaten our wellbeing. In Libra, the influences of Saturn place a great deal of emphasis on teamwork, compromise and, of course, responsibility in relationships. It is here that limitations will be firmly placed in the confines of how various kinds of relationships are established and conducted.

## THE DOWN SIDE OF SATURN IN LIBRA

Saturn's travels through Libra may well place disciplinary limitations or boundaries on some of the negative Libra-like things such as critical or hard driving perfectionism, procrastination, indolence, inconsistency, gullibility, excessive opulence, vacillation, or indecisive behavior. Obsessive-compulsive behavior is likely to be extremely obvious and not so easy to hide, as the demand for proper civil conduct and a more congenial effort to apply discipline does not allow for comfortable wallowing and blatant selfishness.

## THE UP SIDE OF SATURN IN LIBRA

Saturnian structure and concentration of effort will be reflected in a positive way through such Libra-like things as balance, adjustment, affection, articulation, sincerity, admiration, congeniality, dependability, accuracy, resourcefulness, scrupulousness, kindness, carefulness, and scholarly precision. Kind-hearted efforts will have a serious message, and on the positive side, there will be a more communal, harmonizing, and intelligent approach to work. More serious efforts in law enforcement, relationships, and marital affairs will bring a greater respect for the quality of our lives. Responsible and caring intent, along with well-balanced efforts will be the cutting edge tools for Libra's accomplishments while Saturn travels through Libra.

SATURN'S SQUARING AND OPPOSING AFFECTS ON THE CARDINAL SIGNS OF THE ZODIAC:

Now the cardinal signs of the zodiac go into a disciplinary mode as Saturn goes through the cardinal sign of Libra. Cancers and Capricorns will experience Saturn's squaring affect to their natal Sun signs over the next few years. They must learn to pace themselves and to be aware that Saturn squaring their natal Sun will bring career and work related tests, challenges, and difficulties. These people may have a great deal of doubt about their ability to identify with the work they are doing. Cancer and Capricorn people will need to be more focused on cleaning up unfinished business, solving repetitive problems, and they will be undergoing tedious kinds of work. This is the time to face personal limitations and find a way to work with them or around them. It's an opportunity for these folks to gain a real sense of accomplishment and mastery over the inevitable challenges that life brings.

Saturn in Libra will be opposing the cardinal sign of Aries, creating a more acute awareness of personal responsibilities on the part of our Aries friends. The work levels and disciplines in Aries' lives will be trying and overwhelming at times, and occasional bouts of exhaustion will inconvenience Aries. This is not a time for Aries folks to set themselves up with heavy commitments or workloads in the next few years ahead; the test of the days ahead will prove to be demanding enough. Aries people must learn to pace themselves and most of all, to be patient with their careers and work related focuses.

SATURN'S TRINE AFFECTS ON THE AIR SIGNS OF THE ZODIAC:

Saturn in the air sign of Libra will be trine to the other air signs of the zodiac, Aquarius and Gemini. This will activate and stimulate Aquarius and Gemini people's abilities to identify with the need for order and structure in their lives. They will experience a greater sense of ease in applying their work and creating more structure or discipline where they need it.

SATURN'S SEXTILE AFFECTS ON THE FIRE SIGNS – SAGITTARIUS AND LEO:

Sagittarius and Leo people are likely to experience more career or work opportunities, and get a better grasp on their personal disciplines, as Saturn goes through a sextile to their natal Sun signs. These people must act on their disciplines in order to find these opportunities and get results.

SATURN'S PERSONAL EFFECTS:

Saturn represents ability (responsibility), Sun represents identity (willingness). When Saturn transits a person's Sun sign, the tests they endure affect how they identify with the manner in which disciplines, responsibilities, and structures work in their lives – but it does *not* necessarily test their actual abilities. In order to find out how a person's actual abilities are being tested, the current transits of Saturn may be compared to the position of a person's natal Saturn in the birth chart. If a person's natal Saturn is afflicted in the chart, anything from health to career may ♏ be affected. Afflictions may be overcome, and that is the purpose of facing them and working through them. In the transits of Saturn to people's Sun signs, the main thing that stands out is their need to identify with what they are doing, usually in terms of career, work or responsibilities. Cancer and Capricorn people may encounter trouble identifying with their work in the next couple of years due to the square of Saturn to their natal Sun signs, but this doesn't necessarily mean that they won't accomplish goals and create structure in their lives. It just simply means that they will probably struggle with their own personal seal of approval with regard to their work. There may also be an inability for them to identify with their work, or they may have a difficult time accepting constructive forms of criticism as to how they are personally handling their work.

Saturn is there to remind us of the work required to deal with the harsh realities of life. When the work is done, our efforts are often rewarded with a sense of real accomplishment, as long as we act responsibly toward the things in life that really matter to us and that are actually posing a threat or needing attention. Libra says: "I balance." While Saturn travels through Libra, structure and discipline, when applied to peacemaking in relationships, brings magnanimous results. Here, there is no room for Libra's ability to vacillate or to be indecisive. Here, it is patience, skill, persistence, and indefatigable management that will support grand feats of accomplishment for Libra.

# October 30ᵗʰ Friday

**Moon in Pisces / Aries**

| | | PDT | EDT | |
|---|---|---|---|---|
| Moon | enters Aries | 10:55 AM | 1:55 PM | |
| Moon | opposite Saturn | 11:07 AM | 2:07 PM | |
| Moon | square Pluto | 1:19 PM | 4:19 PM | |
| Moon | trine Mars | 11:48 PM | 2:48 AM | (October 31) |
| Jupiter conjunct Neptune begins (see December 21) | | | | |

*Mood Watch*: This morning we awaken to the void-of-course Moon in Pisces. For awhile there, our moods are likely to be spacey, unrealistic, and vague, or over-emotional. As the Moon enters Aries, our moods shift over to a much more headstrong and rambunctious quality of expression. Aries says: "I am," and a much more self-assertive, self-motivated, and self-involved phase of moods can be expected. Today's lunar aspects indicate that, at times, people may seem bossy, pushy, or overly assertive. Once in awhile, certain individuals need to assert their independence. They need to know that they can do things on their own. Although we often depend on each other, there are times when we must learn how to rely solely on ourselves. The waxing Aries Moon time is a prime candidate for those – once in awhile – realizations.

# October 31ˢᵗ Saturday

**All Hallows (Halloween) / Samhain / Witches' New Year**

**Moon in Aries**

| | | PDT | EDT |
|---|---|---|---|
| Moon | sextile Jupiter | 7:45 PM | 10:45 PM |

223

*Mood Watch*: Happy, upbeat, and ambitious moods are unleashed as the waxing Aries Moon sets the tone for this fabled and well loved time of Halloween. Courageous and determined attitudes set the stage for a great deal of fun. Tonight's only aspect, Moon sextile Jupiter brings the potential for adventurous and generous moods.

*Happy Halloween! Happy Witches' New Year!* The slumber of the plant and animal world will deepen, and the crops and seeds of the fields will take their rest with the promise of returning as new growth in the spring. This is the time to honor the dead and invite the beloved spirits of our ancestors to join in our celebrations. Some believe from sunset until dawn, the spirits of our deceased loved ones are able to roam the earth and converse with the living. This is a particularly important time to speak aloud the names of those who have passed away (especially within the past year) and to honor them with the food, drink and song they enjoyed during their lifetime; following old traditions will awaken the memories of these loved ones. Don't forget to set a token plate of food and drink aside at mealtime in their honor.

Daylight Saving Time ends tomorrow. Don't forget to turn all clocks and timepieces back one hour this evening before hitting the sack. Tomorrow we begin Standard Time; at 2:00 a.m. on November 1st Daylight Saving Time ends coast to coast in North America.

# November 1st Sunday
**All Saints Day / Day of the Dead** – *Full Moon Eve*
**DAYLIGHT SAVING TIME ENDS**
*Turn clocks back one hour at 2:00 a.m.*

| Moon in Aries / Taurus | PST | EST |
|---|---|---|
| Moon opposite Venus | 1:57 AM | 4:57 AM |
| Moon sextile Neptune goes v/c | 5:28 AM | 8:28 AM |
| Moon enters Taurus | 4:44 PM | 7:44 PM |
| Mercury square Mars | 4:50 PM | 7:50 PM |
| Moon trine Pluto | 7:05 PM | 10:05 PM |

*Mood Watch*: Even though we've lost an hour, we'll get it back next spring. In the meantime, it's a good thing many folks are able to sleep in on this Sunday morning, especially since yesterday's ambitious Aries Moon has led us to this morning's rude and hot-tempered void-of-course phase of the Moon. If you aren't able to sleep in this morning, you'll have to learn to pace yourself today. There's only so much energy to go around, and some people may appear tired, cranky, and irritable. Impatience is the most likely culprit of today's estranged moods. Tonight's Taurus Moon will help change things, as more grounded and pleasant moods can be expected. Despite the ups and downs of mood, this is *All Saints Day (a.k.a. The Day of the Dead)* and it is a highly revered and celebrated time. The *Day of the Dead* is celebrated in Mexico by enthusiasts of the Mayan and Aztec cultures. Colorful altars with decorative skulls, photos of the dead, and symbols of death all adorn the streets. Dramatic and colorful events will occur, and despite the lunar void, these festive moods will undergo playful and charismatic expressions.

**Mercury square Mars** (occurring Oct. 27 – Nov. 4) Mercury in Scorpio is reaching

224

an exact square to Mars in Leo. Those who are undergoing conflict with others may find that such activities as secrecy, verbal abuse and deceptive chatter will lead to certain destruction and complex kinds of discord. This aspect is repeating for a third time this year and formerly occurred with Mercury in Libra and Mars in Cancer on August 25, and again on September 3. Refrain from making risky comments, and be careful not to misinterpret information as being hostile or personal. Remember, during this complex time of Mercury square Mars, not to shoot the messenger.

♏

# November 2nd Monday
## FULL MOON in TAURUS

| Moon in Taurus | PST | EST |
|---|---|---|
| Moon square Mars | 6:40 AM | 9:40 AM |
| Moon opposite Mercury | 8:03 AM | 11:03 AM |
| Moon opposite Sun | 11:12 AM | 2:12 PM |
| Venus trine Neptune | 3:21 PM | 6:21 PM |

*Mood Watch*: The **Full Moon in Taurus** (Moon opposite Sun) invites us to celebrate the beauty and the perfection of the valuable elements of the earth, and brings appreciation for the beauty in nature. The Taurus totem is the bull, and in its splendor, the bull is a marvelous and classically stubborn creature of habit. This Full Moon reminds us to take the time to enjoy and create beauty around us, and to indulge a little bit in some luxurious pleasures or leisure time. For those who realize the importance of celebrating planet Earth, now is the time to reflect on what you do have and how it is that these physical gifts of Earth can be enjoyed. Ask Mother Moon to bring you what you need and she will teach you how to sow for the harvest of your desire.

**Venus trine Neptune** (occurring Oct. 28 – Nov. 5) Venus in Libra trine Neptune in Aquarius enhances spiritual love. This aspect brings well balanced and generous kinds of love into harmony with a very ingenious kind of spiritual expression. It delivers a calmness and tranquility that are vitally needed, and there is a greater potential to create a spiritually enhanced atmosphere. Wherever there is spiritual turmoil, Venus trine Neptune helps to ease our woes with a support network of feminine kindness. Visiting or meditating upon sacred places and favorite sanctuaries brings visions and inner wisdom. Peaceful, pleasurable, and spiritual love is possible with this aspect, which last occurred July 22 – 30, reaching its exact peak on July 27 with Venus in Gemini.

# November 3rd Tuesday

| Moon in Taurus / Gemini | PST | EST | |
|---|---|---|---|
| Moon square Jupiter | 12:05 AM | 3:05 AM | |
| Moon sextile Uranus | 8:55 AM | 11:55 AM | |
| Moon square Neptune goes v/c | 10:03 AM | 1:03 PM | |
| Moon enters Gemini | 8:52 PM | 11:52 PM | |
| Moon trine Saturn | 9:52 PM | 12:52 AM | (November 4) |
| Sun square Jupiter begins (see November 10) | | | |

*Mood Watch*: If you didn't sleep so well last night and money is all you can think about this morning, there's a good chance you've been seduced by yesterday's full

Taurus Moon. Last night's Moon square Jupiter probably didn't help your financial outlook too much either. Perhaps you spent a lot of money on something you really needed and now you're paying the price – and feeling the chaos. Don't worry; you took care of something you needed and bills or no bills, what you now have will serve you for a long time to come. Autumn expenses often seem steep. Don't sweat the small stuff, as we all have our ups and downs in the financial world. Today's long post-full void-of-course Taurus Moon is bound to bring financial worry, laziness, stubbornness, bull-headedness, and insecurity. This is no time to be real hard on yourself or others. Give it awhile. Once the Moon enters Gemini, the logic and the details will all begin to fall into place.

# November 4th Wednesday

| Moon in Gemini | PST | EST |
|---|---|---|
| Neptune goes direct | 10:10 AM | 1:10 PM |
| Moon sextile Mars | 11:55 AM | 2:55 PM |
| Mercury square Jupiter begins | (see November 8) | |

*Mood Watch*: Today brings much to think about. Many folks will be active with their communications. Waning Gemini Moon also keeps us introspectively thoughtful. Today's only lunar aspect, Moon sextile Mars, brings an active time of *doing* as well as thinking. When we act on our thoughts, it means that we are often in sync with those thoughts. Thoughts in themselves are active little creatures, and to *act* on thoughts is a confirmation of will. As is says in *Liber Librae (The Book of Balance)* of the *Equinox* series, *1909*: "Act passionately; think rationally; be Thyself." This is a superb meditation for the Sun in Scorpio and the Moon in Gemini.

**Neptune goes direct** (Neptune direct: Nov. 4, 2009 – May 31, 2010) Neptune resumes a direct-moving course after five months (since May 28) of being retrograde. This will regenerate our spiritual and intuitive work and facilitate our development. Neptune is in Aquarius, influencing the flow of the Aquarian age and the evolutionary processes of belief systems. Neptune is the master of illusion, while Aquarius demands scientific proof. As Neptune proceeds further into Aquarius, we will learn to achieve a higher and freer sense of spiritual awareness – a sense that something divine is occurring, even though it cannot be explained in mortal terms. Since the late 20th century, Neptune has been in Aquarius filling our belief systems with a great deal of knowledge, and by April 2011, the planet of spiritual peace and serenity returns to its home base in Pisces, where our spiritual experience is infused with adaptable and inspiring believability. Neptune's calming and forgiving nature will help us to let go of malicious and non-productive thoughts, and will melt away cold-heartedness. A good meditation, when sincerely applied, helps to discharge our emotional baggage. Frequently invoke the spiritually uplifting meditations that work for you. This practice will lead you to a positive and regenerative place in your own spiritual evolution. Neptune moving direct allows us to move freely forward, using divine wisdom and our spiritual aspirations as guides.

# November 5th Thursday

| Moon in Gemini / Cancer | PST | EST |
|---|---|---|

| | PST | EST | |
|---|---|---|---|
| Sun conjunct Mercury | 12:02 AM | 3:02 AM | |
| Moon trine Jupiter | 3:33 AM | 6:33 AM | |
| Moon square Uranus | 11:52 AM | 2:52 PM | |
| Moon trine Neptune | 1:03 PM | 4:03 PM | |
| Moon trine Venus goes v/c | 7:47 PM | 10:47 PM | |
| Moon enters Cancer | 11:42 PM | 2:42 AM | (November 6) |

Venus sextile Pluto begins  (see November 8)

ℳ

*"Act passionately; think rationally; be Thyself."* - Liber Librae (The Book of Balance) of the Equinox series, 1909

**Mood Watch**: A busy time of multi-tasking, handling chaos, seeking a quiet refuge (even if only in your mind) – this tends to be the way of things with today's lunar aspects while the Moon is in Gemini. Tonight, Moon trine Venus brings amicable and pleasant moods, but by this time people are tired of conversing and observing the details of their atmosphere. Simple brainless activity will be the most valuable activity at the close of the evening.

**Sun conjunct Mercury** (occurring Oct. 26 – Nov. 10) This aspect will create a much more thoughtful, communicative and expressive year ahead for those Scorpio folks celebrating birthdays October 26 – November 10. This is your time (birthday Scorpios) to record ideas, relay important messages, and pay close attention to your imaginative thoughts as they are touched by Mercury, creating the urge to speak and be heard. Birthday Scorpio, your thoughts will reveal a great deal about who you are, now and in the year to come.

# November 6ᵗʰ Friday

**Moon in Gemini**

| | PST | EST |
|---|---|---|
| Moon square Saturn | 1:04 AM | 4:04 AM |
| Moon opposite Pluto | 2:08 AM | 5:08 AM |

**Mood Watch**: Long before daybreak, the Moon enters Cancer. Sun in Scorpio and Moon in Cancer is generally a very elusive, watery, emotional, and instinctual time. The rainy parts of North America just got even more rainy. An emotional emphasis seems to jump out of every form of interaction, even the casual kinds. Mother Moon is at home in Cancer, and many folks associate the home with mother. The archetypical mother focuses on nourishment, contentment, comfort, and safety. Where these are not, the motherly instinct tends to gnaw at the subconscious part of the soul. It beckons us to show care and compassion. Under traumatic circumstances, today's lunar aspects and atmosphere can be especially dramatic. The solution is simple: do as a loving and caring mother would do. Tender care works wonders. A listening ear and a lot of tissues may be all it takes.

# November 7ᵗʰ Saturday

**Moon in Cancer**

| | PST | EST |
|---|---|---|
| Moon trine Sun | 1:10 AM | 4:10 AM |
| Moon trine Mercury | 3:32 AM | 6:32 AM |
| Moon trine Uranus goes v/c | 2:26 PM | 5:26 PM |
| Venus enters Scorpio | 4:23 PM | 7:23 PM |

Mercury trine Uranus begins  (see November 11)
Mercury square Neptune begins  (see November 11)

227

*Mood Watch*: Today's moods are likely to bring some very positive, albeit emotional, results. Sun in Scorpio and Moon in Cancer is a good time to work through emotional trauma. The Moon is trine three times over, a lucky and auspicious set of mood shifts. However, the last trine aspect, Moon trine Uranus, also brings the void-of-course Moon. Radical tears must flow. This evening would be a good time to let it all out, and to nurture the soul with healthy and delicious comfort foods, warm and uplifting storybooks, and a comforting bubble bath.

**Venus enters Scorpio** (Venus in Scorpio: Nov. 7 – Dec. 1) The planet Venus, which influences matters of love, beauty, art, and attraction, now moves through Scorpio, bringing out deep and passionate levels of love's expression. While Venus is in Scorpio, we may feel preoccupied with themes of birth, sex, death and rebirth, and transformation. Magnetism runs strong with Venus in Scorpio, and love affairs are often torrid and well hidden. Sometimes the dark side of our love and our hidden fears surface while Venus is in Scorpio; this forces us to come clean about these feelings, and to take strong measures to ensure the power of our love. Venus is in detriment in the sign of Scorpio. This may be a time to work out anxiety, fear, mourning, and emotional stress relating to love. Sex is a common outlet under this type of stress. Love with passion is an empowering thing, but it is wise to ensure the experience does not hinder the wellbeing of those who are close to you. The intensity of Scorpio love can sometimes overwhelm loved ones. Love shines best when it is mutually expressed.

# November 8th Sunday

| Moon in Cancer / Leo | PST | EST | |
|---|---|---|---|
| Moon enters Leo | 2:22 AM | 5:22 AM | |
| Moon square Venus | 3:21 AM | 6:21 AM | |
| Moon sextile Saturn | 4:06 AM | 7:06 AM | |
| Mercury  square Jupiter | 6:42 AM | 9:42 AM | |
| Moon conjunct Mars | 8:21 PM | 11:21 PM | |
| Venus  sextile Pluto | 9:34 PM | 12:34 AM | (November 9) |
| Sun trine Uranus begins  (see November 14) | | | |

*Mood Watch*: Moon square Venus kicks off the early morning, and our moods may seem less than pleasant, or even challenged by the things and people we love. Despite this, the Leo Moon brings warmth and courage. The waning Leo Moon is a good time to connect with personal needs, family, and friends. Moon sextile Saturn helps us to put the day in order, and to do what is necessary to stabilize our lives. Tonight, Moon conjunct Mars brings active feelings. Leo Moon brightens our hearts in the darkening days of autumn.

**Mercury square Jupiter** (occurring Nov. 4 – 10) Mercury in Scorpio is square to Jupiter in Aquarius. Information that is veiled in secrecy is likely to be exposed in the most unexpected way to an unsuspecting public. With this aspect it is best to beware of negative views that discourage prosperous growth, as deceptive words, lies, and even the truth, are easily misconstrued on a much larger scale. During this aspect it may be best to hold off on a job request, asking for a raise, or signing any binding contracts concerning long term investment and payment schedules. It may be an especially difficult time to communicate during travels, and it may be best to double check travel schedules. This aspect has a tendency to create expensive misunderstandings when it comes to large scale investments. This may also be a difficult time to raise money for charities. Dig harder and investigate more thoroughly the details associated with long term investments. This aspect occurred on three former occasions this year, on April 22, May 20, and June 10, with Mercury in Taurus.

**Venus sextile Pluto** (occurring Nov. 5 – 10) This time last year, Pluto was revisiting Sagittarius for the final time in our lifetime and Venus was in Libra undergoing its final sextile position to Pluto in Sagittarius. Today, Venus is in Scorpio focusing on the need for swift, passionate, attentive, and urgent responses in love matters. Venus in Scorpio is now in the sextile position to Pluto in Capricorn for the first time in our lives. This aspect is most useful for those who command an element of love and passion for their work or career, and it allows them to optimize beauty in the course of their efforts. Opportunity knocks, and here, true beauty bridges the gap between generations. There was a time when Pluto, the god of the underworld, seized Persephone who was a symbol of youth, fertility and Venusian beauty. Many have viewed this myth as a power play on the part of the underworld king. Others view it as the well understood destiny of Beauty and the Beast. Venus sextile Pluto may bring exceptional breakthroughs in relationships. Sometimes the death of a power figure occurs, and the love of that figure is empowered by the impact of their fate. This may be the place where we discover the true power of love. Sometimes this aspect helps us to recognize the devotion of our loved ones, to see the acceptance of the difficulty and hardship that comes with their devotion. This is a good time to recognize and acknowledge the efforts of loved ones. Through this, greater devotion will shine. This aspect may allow someone to find true love by virtue of some unexpected twist of fate. It is here that the beauty and the beast surprise us when, through some form of trial or sacrifice, harmony and strength in love can be found. This aspect occurred at the beginning of the year, Dec. 31, 2008 – Jan. 6, 2009, reaching its peak on January 4, when Venus was in Pisces.

# November 9th Monday

LAST QUARTER MOON in LEO

| | PST | EST |
|---|---|---|
| Moon square Sun | 7:56 AM | 10:56 AM |
| Moon opposite Jupiter | 9:41 AM | 12:41 PM |
| Moon square Mercury | 12:56 PM | 3:56 PM |
| Moon opposite Neptune goes v/c | 6:43 PM | 9:43 PM |
| Sun square Neptune begins (see November 15) | | |

*Mood Watch*: Today, people will want to be entertained and to get their minds on enjoying life. We now come to the **Last Quarter Moon in Leo** (Moon square Sun). When the Moon is waning in Leo, it urges us to take special care of ourselves as well as the children in our life. Projects of interest are sometimes considered children as well. If there is a hobby of special interest to you, take the time to brighten and enliven this work which represents your own talent and self-reflection. Throughout the working (or playing) day, jokes will fly, toys of special interest will be admired and moods will reflect childlike frolic and revel. If you're serious about not being distracted by such playfulness perhaps a quiet workspace is the key. If you must

229

work with others, allow the frivolity to flow; the work will get done but the child in everyone has to play now and then. Tonight the Moon goes void-of-course and it may be difficult to keep track of things.

# November 10ᵗʰ Tuesday

| Moon in Leo / Virgo | PST | EST |
|---|---|---|
| Moon enters Virgo | 5:30 AM | 8:30 AM |
| Moon trine Pluto | 8:11 AM | 11:11 AM |
| Sun square Jupiter | 10:41 AM | 1:41 PM |
| Moon sextile Venus | 11:31 AM | 2:31 PM |

*Mood Watch*: Out of the foggy and clouded mist of the void-of-course Leo Moon, our self-absorbed morning moods will swiftly shift as the Moon enters Virgo. The Virgo Moon leads us to question what we are doing, to ponder, analyze, deliberate, and communicate about what's going on. This is a good time to be resourceful and thorough, or the boss is likely to decisively prod us strongly in this direction. Why not beat 'em to it? Anticipate what needs to be done and do it! Today, sharpness and keenness will get you some good bonus points.

*Sun square Jupiter* (occurring Nov. 3 – 13) This occurrence of Sun in Scorpio square Jupiter in Aquarius will particularly affect those Scorpio people celebrating birthdays November 3 – 13. This aspect creates difficulties and obstacles to the personal joy and prosperous welfare of these birthday folks. Getting ahead financially or just staying on top of current trends or financial shifts may be personally challenging right now, requiring persistence and determination. Scorpio folks who are doing well financially may find this aspect is challenging their sense of what makes them happy, or that advancement in the world brings too much complexity and requires a lot of management. Though not all Scorpios are living as prosperously as they may desire, they do have the ability to come through this and be much better for it. Obstacles create challenges, but do not necessarily dictate an end to efforts to improve our welfare. It is the Scorpio personality (Sun) that is being challenged (square aspect) in matters of advancement (Jupiter), requiring Scorpios to make do with less assistance than they had anticipated. This may be a time to redefine and redirect personal goals. Scorpio birthday folks must reexamine what truly brings prosperity for them in their lives. This aspect occurred earlier this year, May 9 – 19, reaching its peak on May 16, affecting the birthday Taurus folks of that time.

# November 11ᵗʰ Wednesday

**Veteran's Day, USA / Remembrance Day, Canada**

| Moon in Virgo | PST | EST | |
|---|---|---|---|
| Mercury trine Uranus | 3:37 AM | 6:37 AM | |
| Moon sextile Sun | 3:29 PM | 6:29 PM | |
| Mercury square Neptune | 4:11 PM | 7:11 PM | |
| Moon opposite Uranus | 8:57 PM | 11:57 PM | |
| Moon sextile Mercury goes v/c | 11:13 PM | 2:13 AM | (November 12) |

*Mood Watch*: It's poppy day. Not the poppies that grow in the fields of summer, but the plastic poppies worn on the lapels of veterans. The waning Virgo Moon brings a spirit of communication, curiosity, and many will be analyzing their feelings about war, their memories of battle, and their outlook on life's ongoing struggles over human conflict. Virgo Moon is a time when we tend to deliberate, and try to put things into perspective. Everyone has a different perspective, especially those who have served in wars. Mercury trine Uranus and square Neptune (see below,) may not help to ease our critical, disbelieving, and scrutinizing Virgo Moon ways. This is a time to ease the mind with some of the more gentle qualities of Virgo; seek relaxing hobbies, healthy and nutritious foods, kindness, gentleness, altruism, subtlety, and discernment.

**Mercury trine Uranus** (occurring Nov. 7 – 13) Mercury in Scorpio is trine to Uranus in Pisces. This combination stirs up an intelligent, compelling and awakening thought process, one that is usually well defined. This is a good time to record your thoughts and delight in brilliant thinking and information. Much of this brilliant thinking may seem like propaganda or information with a radical twist. Catch phrases, radical concept statements and ideas are often born under this aspect. Sensationalism, or matters of censorship, may be emphasized. Mercury in Scorpio dredges up important topics such as birth, sex, death, and the regenerative force realized through overcoming illness. Uranus is in Pisces, creating radical change in areas of addiction, the arts, music, psychology, and religion. This aspect last occurred July 13 – 17, reaching its peak on July 16 with Mercury in Cancer.

**Mercury square Neptune** (occurring Nov. 7 – 13) This aspect often brings a struggle to communicate with regard to the spirit world and human spirituality. Efforts to explain our beliefs may be especially challenging. Neptune is in Aquarius, stirring up issues around human divinity and humanity's beliefs in this confusing and changing period of the dawning age. While Mercury in Scorpio is squaring Neptune, dramatic kinds of thought will be challenged, particularly with respect to issues that concern divine experience (birth, sex, death); relaying this information may seem all the more difficult with this aspect. Anticipate religion related arguments and disputes. Deep subjects must not be treated lightly while Mercury squares Neptune. This aspect last occurred on three former occasions, April 25, May 20, and June 9 with Mercury in Taurus.

# November 12ᵗʰ Thursday

| Moon in Virgo / Libra | PST | EST |
|---|---|---|
| Moon enters Libra | 9:22 AM | 12:22 PM |
| Moon conjunct Saturn | 11:53 AM | 2:53 PM |
| Moon square Pluto | 12:12 PM | 3:12 PM |
| Venus square Mars begins (see November 19) | | |

*Mood Watch*: The morning may have its querulous, petty, and fault-finding qualities while the Moon is void-of-course in Virgo. As the Moon enters Libra, our moods shift over to a much more congenial and cooperative quality of expression. The waning Libra Moon focuses our attention on the need for justice, truth, fairplay, and balance. Our minds will be full of activity and ready to face some of the more serious aspects of what is occurring around us. This is a time when teamwork and calculated effort will bring some of the larger problems we face into a much more controllable level of tolerance. Sun in Scorpio and Moon in Libra rocks! You

231

will find a lot less apathy on the battlegrounds of today's events as heartfelt collaboration brings relief.

# November 13ᵗʰ Friday

**Moon in Libra**

| | PST | EST |
|---|---|---|
| Moon sextile Mars | 6:51 AM | 9:51 AM |
| Moon trine Jupiter | 6:28 PM | 9:28 PM |

*Mood Watch*: Today's lunar aspects are positive and cheerful. The waning Libra Moon brings internal balance, and where there has been turmoil, the truth comes out. Waning Libra Moon sometimes confronts us with our imbalances. This is a superb time to focus on the areas of life that have been put off the longest. For whatever reason, something important has been swept under the carpet; now's the time to shake the fabric and vacuum away the ancient stardust. The world turns and it also travels through space. There is no reason to avoid the old matter, for you too must revolve and change for the better. If something old is still haunting you, this means it's still important to you, and it's still unresolved. Face it now, while the core of those old dust bunnies can still be recognized. Libra Moon is a great time to consolidate lost friendships, make peace, and clear the air.

# November 14ᵗʰ Saturday

**Moon in Libra / Scorpio**

| | PST | EST |
|---|---|---|
| Moon trine Neptune goes v/c | 3:10 AM | 6:10 AM |
| Moon enters Scorpio | 2:24 PM | 5:24 PM |
| Moon sextile Pluto | 5:26 PM | 8:26 PM |
| Sun trine Uranus | 5:40 PM | 8:40 PM |
| Mercury sextile Saturn begins (see November 16) | | |

*Mood Watch*: As we approach mid-month, we seek middle ground through the persuasion of the Libra Moon. Today's Libra Moon wanes darkly, will be void-of-course throughout the day, and its cardinal nature compels us to seek level ground. It is likely that many of us will venture off the beaten track despite our need to remain centered. For most of the day, progress is slowed down by a persistent drive to get things just right. The act of weighing and measuring, judging and deliberating, as well as the attempt to balance out the situations that arise, will probably become more of an ordeal than a practical process. Void Libra Moons commonly bring indecision. As the Moon enters Scorpio, there will be a deeper perception of the various situations of life. A darkly waning Scorpio Moon, also known as the *balsamic* phase of the Moon, brings strong emotional depth.

**Sun trine Uranus** (occurring Nov. 8 – 17) This occurrence of Sun trine Uranus favorably affects our Scorpio friends celebrating birthdays November 8 – 17. It puts the radical forces of Uranus in the favorable trine position to their natal Sun. It is time for these people to make a breakthrough. Don't hold back, birthday Scorpios; chaos is here to stay for awhile. Let the experience be positive as long as this aspect brings gifts. Expect restless desires for freedom and the need to break out of your personal prison. Freedom knocks loudly, and the course of change is inevitable in the coming year. Change is necessary for growth. These influential changes are positive in nature, though on the surface they may seem harsh. Birthday people, the apparent madness occurring in your life is there for a reason. You will find a clearer picture in the long run by keeping up the good fight to preserve your inspiration, intelligence, and Scorpio passion. The trine aspect gives gifts of triumph, and this may be a good time to let chaos be the force that brings freedom. This aspect last occurred July 12 – 21, reaching its peak on July 18, affecting the birthday Cancer folks of that time.

# November 15th Sunday

| Moon in Scorpio | PST | EST |
|---|---|---|
| Saturn square Pluto | 7:20 AM | 10:20 AM |
| Moon conjunct Venus | 7:41 AM | 10:41 AM |
| Moon square Mars | 2:03 PM | 5:03 PM |
| Sun square Neptune | 3:10 PM | 6:10 PM |
| Mercury enters Sagittarius | 4:28 PM | 7:28 PM |

Mars-opposite-Jupiter-non-exact (occurring from November 15 to December 12 – see below)

*Mood Watch*: While there is so much strong celestial activity in the wings, the darkly waning Scorpio Moon takes flight in our moods. The Prince of Cups is a Scorpio character in the Tarot cards. In the *Thoth* deck, he is depicted as one who flies upon an eagle aloft the mist of the fixed waters. He is obsessed with power, subtlety, secrecy, and craft. However, he is also generous, often wise, and sensitive to attraction. The darkly waning Scorpio Moon frequently draws his kind of energy. We are interested in mystery, powerful circumstances, and if this all seems too esoteric for you, perhaps it is a very influential lawyer who has caught your attention. Caution calls to us under the conditions we now face. Scorpio Moon gives us what we need to face this time.

**Saturn square Pluto** (occurring Sept. 14, 2009 – Sept. 16, 2010) This is a large and long winded aspect that challenges and awakens us to address big transformations. Saturn and Pluto are both in cardinal signs (Libra and Capricorn) bringing lawfully sanctioned and physically enduring kinds of permanent change. When Saturn was in the challenging *opposite* aspect to Pluto back in August/September 2001, we all felt the brunt of some serious trials through the events of 9/11 and all that followed. It was not until April 26, 2003 that the Saturn opposite Pluto aspect came to an end of its cycle. In August 2007 and April 2008, the favorable *trine* aspect of Saturn and Pluto occurred, bringing us a temporary reprieve of more easily handling the trials of permanent change, as well as some long awaited rewards of our hard work and persistence during the difficult trials and transformations that the Saturn opposite Pluto tests demanded back in 2001. Through the events of Saturn opposite Pluto, the security guidelines we've created for ourselves, and to which we've adhered as a result of those events, have created a new foundation to sustain us. However, now the *square* aspect of Saturn and Pluto creates grave new difficulties that will force us to reconcile some age-old problems between the generations. For the next year to come, and for sometime in the aftermath, the tests of hardship are challenging us to face some serious rounds of devastating change; these are permanent, unrelenting, and difficult types of change that will definitively mark this period as a new century turning point.

233

Now that Saturn and Pluto are spending this time in the unfavorable square position to one other, it is up to us to determine how we will survive and grow stronger through this current transformation process. This is a time for us to apply a careful approach to lawmaking, and for us to be cautious with our sense of control, particularly with regard to the current channels of power occurring in the world at large. It is through the square aspect that we will take great pains in our efforts to redefine our responsibilities and to shift our goals and priorities to suit the rapidly changing ways of the 21$^{st}$ century. The trials that we will encounter will dramatically shape our ideas of how power works, and we will eventually acquire the knowledge and the survival tools to see us through this difficult time. Restrictive laws and corruption in corporate circles point to struggle that is being played out on the world stage through this aspect. Saturn in Libra brings oppression in judicial affairs while Pluto in Capricorn transforms the ways in which we go about the attainment of power. Limitations are likely to be imposed on numerous kinds of relationships while Saturn is in the square position to the harsh and unrelenting forces of Pluto. This aspect is likely to bring great change in our attitudes, especially with regard to how we adapt to the structure of our rapidly changing environment within the confines of its stringent laws.

**Sun square Neptune** (occurring Nov. 9 – 18) This occurrence of Sun square Neptune especially affects Scorpio people who are celebrating birthdays November 9 – 18. Neptune in the square position to these birthday folks' natal Sun brings a sense of obstacles getting in the way of Spirit or the acknowledgement of spiritual beliefs. The challenge for these Scorpio birthday folks is to overcome the interfering doubts and confrontations. This especially applies to overcoming those extremely dangerous and destructive addictive tendencies. Remember, Scorpio, spiritual lessons do not have to be life threatening! Over the next year, there will undoubtedly be some spiritual adjustments, and perhaps a change of belief is required. This aspect last occurred May 10 – 20, reaching its peak on May 16, affecting the Taurus birthday people.

**Mercury enters Sagittarius** (Mercury in Sagittarius: Nov. 15 – Dec. 5) Mercury, the planet of communication, information, and news is traveling through the sign of Sagittarius. New perspectives are bound to come up. News is always more philosophical and visionary when Mercury is in this sign. Word travels fast and further than expected. Sagittarius is the challenging "detrimental" place for Mercury, and this is a time when Mercury's greatest weapon – words – are best communicated with carefully considered diplomacy. People will be increasingly curious to know what is happening in the world, and to be more aware of global perspectives. Mercury in Sagittarius offers an opportunity to share your vision of a better world with others, and also brings adventure to the world of communications.

**Mars-opposite-Jupiter-non-exact** (occurring Nov. 15 – Dec. 12) Since Mars will go retrograde on December 20, this aspect does not actually reach its peak, nonetheless it is still actively affecting us, and it comes within a three degree orb. Heated activities and those areas of life where we wage battles (Mars) are at odds with our economic welfare and outlook (Jupiter). Mars in Leo opposes Jupiter in Aquarius. This aspect may bring family squabbles over personal needs, and there may also be a lot of economic shifts with regard to matters concerning human rights. Initiatives, when activated, will quickly come up against high levels of curiosity coupled with overwhelming market demands. This aspect brings an abrupt awareness of economic oppression or shortcomings. Fortunes may be mishandled due to unanticipated or accidental circumstances. For some, there may be an overwhelming surge of prosperity that cannot be handled without additional help. While Mars is opposed to Jupiter, active forces are diametrically opposed to expansive fortitude, and sometimes our anger is spurred due to a lack of flow or growth in our economic resources. This is a very busy time to attempt to excel in business endeavors, especially in actively trading markets. While Mars is opposing Jupiter it is wise to remember that when you're roused to anger, you must take heed not to "bite the hand that feeds you."

# November 16th Monday
## NEW MOON in SCORPIO

| Moon in Scorpio / Sagittarius | PST | EST | |
|---|---|---|---|
| Moon  square Jupiter | 1:03 AM | 4:03 AM | |
| Moon  trine Uranus | 7:57 AM | 10:57 AM | |
| Moon  square Neptune | 9:41 AM | 12:41 PM | |
| Moon  conjunct Sun goes v/c | 11:14 AM | 2:14 PM | |
| Mercury  sextile Saturn | 9:00 PM | 12:00 AM | (November 17) |
| Moon  enters Sagittarius | 9:22 PM | 12:22 AM | (November 17) |

*Mood Watch*: **New Moon in Scorpio** (Moon conjunct Sun) marks the regenerative point of the New Moon – and the sign of Scorpio just happens to represent the phenomenon of regenerative force and transformation. The New Moon in Scorpio focuses on a rebirthing process for our emotional body, and this is the time when we are sure to address the proverbial skeletons in our emotional closet. New Moon in Scorpio encourages us to regenerate our hopes while transforming our fears into a courageous and renewed outlook for ourselves. This is the time to take bold steps to defeat undesirable emotional patterns and fear mechanisms. New Scorpio Moon casts new light on our ability to overcome pain and suffering. This is a good time to avoid being around abusive or violent people as the Scorpio Moon will be void-of-course most of the day and night. The moon known as *Hecate's Moon* always occurs around the new moon of the witches' New Year holiday. To some people this Moon occurs today, with the New Moon in Scorpio, and to some folks this occurred during the last New Moon on October 17 – see this date for details.

**Mercury sextile Saturn** (occurring Nov. 14 – 18) Mercury in Sagittarius is sextile to Saturn in Libra. Philosophical viewpoints bring the potential for opportunities when it comes to applying judicial disciplines and the rules and regulations of the courts. Opportunities are now available to assist us in communicating vital information in a more organized and pragmatic fashion. This aspect gives people an opportunity to learn vital lessons concerning boundaries, limitations, responsibilities and timely completion. This is a favorable aspect to discuss where to set up boundaries and how to implement security systems, and to teach people about handling responsibilities and disciplines. This aspect last occurred July 9 – 12, reaching its peak on July 11 with Mercury in Cancer sextile Saturn in Virgo.

235

# November 17th Tuesday

| Moon in Sagittarius | PST | EST | |
|---|---|---|---|
| Moon sextile Saturn | 12:52 AM | 3:52 AM | |
| Moon conjunct Mercury | 1:23 AM | 4:23 AM | |
| Moon trine Mars | 11:41 PM | 2:41 AM | (November 18) |

*Mood Watch*: The newly waxing Moon in Sagittarius brings optimism and an outgoing spirit. The feeling of renewed hope is upon us. This is a good time to engage in philosophical conversation and to share ideas. This Moon enlivens our moods towards a congenial, cooperative and flexible expression of service. Keep an eye out for opportunity. Exploration and a little bit of risk taking is highlighted. This is a time when our moods are more prone to consider a greater number of possibilities and alternatives. Good food, travel, plays, and research are all strong Sagittarius Moon focuses.

# November 18th Wednesday

| Moon in Sagittarius | PST | EST |
|---|---|---|
| Moon sextile Jupiter | 10:10 AM | 1:10 PM |
| Moon square Uranus | 4:51 PM | 7:51 PM |
| Moon sextile Neptune goes v/c | 6:46 PM | 9:46 PM |
| Venus square Jupiter begins (see November 23) | | |

*Mood Watch*: Extraterrestrial activities have been tearing through the celestial highway of our experience. No, not alien invaders, although anything is possible with the types of activity that have recently occurred. Out of a myriad of deep thoughts, strong actions, and both lunar and other planetary influences, we have reached a place of philosophical reverie. The newly waxing Sagittarius Moon sets the mood for the need to question and explore new avenues of thought. More to the point, it is a new *vision*, or outlook on life, that we seek. Today will be a good day to invite philosophical perspectives, examine new ways to coexist with chaos, and to enhance and broaden perspectives on life through travel and exploration. Later, our moods will seem rather spacey as the Moon goes void-of-course. This is nothing new, as the Sagittarius Moon often sends us out beyond the usual realms.

# November 19th Thursday

| Moon in Sagittarius / Capricorn | PST | EST |
|---|---|---|
| Venus square Mars | 12:22 AM | 3:22 AM |
| Moon enters Capricorn | 7:01 AM | 10:01 AM |
| Moon conjunct Pluto | 10:38 AM | 1:38 PM |
| Moon square Saturn | 11:07 AM | 2:07 PM |

*Mood Watch*: The day may seem to start off rather spacey with the void-of-course Moon in Sagittarius. As the Moon enters Capricorn, our moods tend to be more practical, grounded, and on the level. Today's lunar aspects suggest conflict, the need to purge, and there may be times when the workload seems grueling and endless. Capricorn Moon doesn't give us much time to mull over our feelings. The drive of the mountain goat is determined, loyal, and stoic. However, there are

236

better points to consider. Capricorn's humor is subtle and simple, but hilarious ♏ once you get the joke. If you stop to observe carefully, there is a distinguished, profound, and entertaining quality to our moods. Success brings long lasting happiness. Today's moods may seem narrow-minded, but the success of your hard driven efforts will be sweet. Hang in there.

**Venus square Mars** (occurring Nov. 12 – 22) Venus in Scorpio is square to Mars in Leo. Beware of the jealousy and the fierce competition that these planets in these signs will tend to create. Venus square Mars creates tension and obstacles between the forces of love and the forces of defense. The archetypal images of Venus and Mars are largely that of feminine and masculine counterparts, and this aspect may bring stress between people in love relationships. The pain of separation or the sorrow of unrequited love may be a symptom of this time, as the rocky boat of romance is due to have some notable ups and downs. On the other hand, the difficulties of these tests may strengthen the power of love and, although it is sometimes very difficult to endure love related conflicts, it is also a necessary process to ensure the authenticity of our love experience.

# November 20th Friday

**Moon in Capricorn**                        PST            EST
Moon sextile Venus                          3:21 PM       6:21 PM
Sun sextile Saturn begins  (see November 24)

*Mood Watch*: Although the close of the workweek still has many of us hard at it, today's Capricorn Moon is a lot less severe than yesterday's hard driving lunar energy. We are now completing the final days of the Sun in Scorpio and the final third of autumn season is about to commence. To many folks in North America, it may already seem like winter. The Scorpio days prepare us for the intensity of the late autumn. Where unusually mild weather continues, fears of global warming strike the airwaves. Today's Capricorn Moon brings disciplined, goal conscious, responsible moods. Wherever we feel we have an obligation to straighten out myths, fears, and the feeling of hopelessness, our efforts will bring optimism and show the way towards solving big problems. Meanwhile, today also brings the potential for pleasantries, especially with Moon sextile Venus.

# SAGITTARIUS

Key Phrase: "I SEE" or

" I  PERCEIVE "

Mutable Fire Sign

Ruling Planet: Jupiter

Symbol: The Centaur

November 21st through

December 21st

# November 21st Saturday
## Moon in Capricorn / Aquarius

| | | |
|---|---|---|
| Moon  sextile Uranus | 4:28 AM | 7:28 AM |
| Moon  sextile Sun goes v/c | 7:04 PM | 10:04 PM |
| Moon  enters Aquarius | 7:10 PM | 10:10 PM |
| Sun  enters Sagittarius | 8:22 PM | 11:22 PM |
| Moon  trine Saturn | 11:51 PM | 2:51 AM | (November 22) |
| Mercury trine Mars begins  (see November 26) | | |
| Venus trine Uranus begins  (see November 25) | | |
| Venus square Neptune begins  (see November 26) | | |

***Mood Watch***: Today will feel as if many of us are on a roll. Great feats of accomplishment have been occurring while the Moon has been waxing in Capricorn these past couple of days. There's no harm in continuing to take big strides while many of us are busily tending to our responsibilities and our goals in life. The waxing Capricorn Moon is a handy time to do this, and even though some folks may feel tired at this stage in time, the sense of making some headway feels good to most of us. Capricorn's old adage, "I use," is not always helpful to the sensitive folks among us. It's a use and be used world sometimes. If we were able to be entirely independent, we wouldn't have Capricorns around. There is nothing wrong with creating structure and stability that will benefit others as well as yourself. Later tonight, the Aquarius Moon takes the adage one step further: "I know." With knowledge, we can do anything – we can even break down the structure of faulty legislation, false hopes, and the pretentious abuses of misuse. Every sign of the zodiac creates a balance in its own way.

**Sun enters Sagittarius** (Sun in Sagittarius: Nov. 21 – Dec. 21) Sun in Sagittarius represents the final laps of autumn and the shortest days of the solar year. The Sagittarius expression, "I see," opens our eyes to some new discoveries during this time. This mutable fire sign achieves visionary awareness by reaching out into the world of possibilities, the stars, and beyond. The Sagittarius time of year – often thought of as being early winter – is actually still fall season, and sees to the closing

238

of autumn by putting to sleep the last of the restless foliage in preparation for the pending winter's great slumber. Sun in Sagittarius days bring a focus on prosperity. Jupiter is the ruling planet of Sagittarius and inspires Sagittarians to excel, expand, and prosper. As the holidays begin and the Christmas season unfurls, the pressure to consume elaborate foods and purchase gifts, while keeping the great economic wheel turning, can be monumental for absolutely everyone. We are often required to pull together an outstanding number of social events and personal expenditures. The concept of prosperity has been tested to the extremes each time this season unfolds; it is, therefore, very important to get back to the basics of what one identifies as prosperous. The true challenge for many of us will be met when we finally reach out towards the higher vision of what prosperity really means. Sun in Sagittarius serves as a good time to direct the forces of vision and inspiration towards attaining a sense of wealth and wellbeing. Tiny Tim (of Charles Dickens fame) was a character who was not disappointed by the lack of food on his table Christmas day; he recognized the sacredness of sharing the company of his loved ones. Don't let the complications of the expectations of others spoil your own sense of attainment and satisfaction with life itself and with the people you have the privilege to share it with. Simple pleasures can bring prosperous joy. Sagittarius emphasizes travel, sports, and philosophy – all those things that require adaptable enthusiasm. There are many ways of seeing and many directions in which to look.

## November 22nd Sunday

| Moon in Aquarius | PST | EST |
|---|---|---|
| Moon sextile Mercury | 5:20 PM | 8:20 PM |

*Mood Watch*: The waxing Aquarius Moon inspires us to take on mounting tasks with brilliance and admirable confidence. The recent sweep of days with the Moon in Capricorn brought an onslaught of work conscious efforts. The Aquarius Moon alters our perspectives of life by tapping into our awareness to find intelligent ways to decrease our workload. Technology is one way we have learned to do this, and other ways can be found in the ingenuity of raising funds to help less fortunate people. We may also find ways to help ourselves, and to rebuild our financial losses and our lost credibility. Aquarius Moon builds morals, strengthens the human spirit, and entices us to examine new ways to see outside the proverbial box. Aquarius Moon brings consciousness raising glory. If you're puzzled about how to raise consciousness, seek it through research and conversation, especially while the Moon is sextile to Mercury. Opportunity comes to those who seek it.

## November 23rd Monday

| Moon in Aquarius | PST | EST |
|---|---|---|
| Moon opposite Mars | 2:38 AM | 5:38 AM |
| Moon square Venus | 11:30 AM | 2:30 PM |
| Moon conjunct Jupiter | 11:44 AM | 2:44 PM |
| Venus square Jupiter | 2:02 PM | 5:02 PM |
| Moon conjunct Neptune goes v/c | 7:35 PM | 10:35 PM |

*"Honk, Honk"* – Harpo Marx (1888 – 1964)

*Mood Watch*: In his book, *The Psalms of a Heretic*, the poet Munir Hanafi once

239

wrote: " *I ran through the forest, felt like the wind, then went to the city and over a coffee couldn't remember a tree.*" He entitled that poem, *Asleep*. The Sun is in Sagittarius, encouraging us to get out there, explore, and experience what's beyond. The Moon is in Aquarius, putting us in touch with our human nature and our intelligence. Just because we're intelligent doesn't mean we aren't asleep. Why would a city coffee preoccupy us so much that we would fail to remember something so profound as a forest setting, or even one monumental tree? Today there are a few lunar aspects poised to rudely awaken us, to cause conflict over the things we love and are attached to, and to bring obsession over our need to excel and prosper. It's no wonder the Aquarius Moon brings unusual or eccentric feelings about ourselves. We are unique and conquering. We are also feeble and small. Choose wisdom; remember a tree, and take it easy on the caffeine.

**Venus square Jupiter** (occurring Nov. 18 – 26) Venus in Scorpio square Jupiter in Aquarius brings a love for torrid and responsive affections that may be interrupted or challenged by the need to handle such costly economic pursuits as social obligations, systems analysis, computer sciences, and charity. Love relationships complicated by difficult money issues may be prevalent. Don't let money matters spoil the beauty of loving affection, but expect the strong possibility that this might well be the case with others. This aspect reminds us that something more than love's blindness is required in order for us to fully realize our riches and the value of what we care about most. Venus square Jupiter last occurred June 26 – July 4, reaching its exact peak on July 1, when Venus was in Taurus.

# November 24th Tuesday
## FIRST QUARTER MOON in PISCES

| Moon in Aquarius / Pisces | PST | EST |
|---|---|---|
| Sun sextile Saturn | 7:34 AM | 10:34 AM |
| Moon enters Pisces | 8:07 AM | 11:07 PM |
| Moon sextile Pluto | 12:07 PM | 3:07 PM |
| Moon square Sun | 1:38 PM | 4:38 PM |

*Mood Watch*: The **First Quarter Moon in Pisces** (Moon square Sun) often brings our hearts and minds to a peaceful place. A spacey, dreamy sort of consciousness leads to strong psychic awareness. While the first quarter Moon is in Pisces, calming kinds of music, art, and poetry will fill us with inspiration, intuition, and hope. Unhappy people are likely to turn to intoxicants to escape their troubles. Passive, cheerful, and kind sentiments will be greatly appreciated. Deep meditation and spiritual practices will empower the imagination.

**Sun sextile Saturn** (occurring Nov. 20 – 26) This occurrence of Sun sextile Saturn particularly affects Scorpio and Sagittarius cusp born people celebrating birthdays November 20 – 26, helping them focus their energy and discipline with greater clarity throughout this year. As Saturn traverses the sextile aspect to the natal Sun of these Scorpio and Sagittarius people, there is a sense of making progress through discipline, and they may very well begin to see the rewards of their diligent labor in the coming year. This is only true as long as they apply themselves to their work, and maintain a vigilant and persistent effort to master personal discipline and training. For the birthday folks of this time, greater control comes with genuine effort. This aspect last occurred July 4 – 11, reaching its peak on July 9, presenting better opportunities and allowing more control in the lives of some Cancer folks.

# November 25th Wednesday

**Moon in Pisces**

| | PST | EST |
|---|---|---|
| Moon square Mercury | 2:37 PM | 5:37 PM |
| Venus trine Uranus | 7:00 PM | 10:00 PM |

*Mood Watch*: The Sagittarius Sun brings exploration and bounty in our step, and it also emphasizes the need for vision and perceptive awareness. The waxing Pisces Moon brings psychic inclinations, intuitiveness, and there is often an unwitting responsiveness to the feelings and thoughts of others. This is a time of hypersensitivity to drugs and alcohol. It is also a time of finely attuned emotions and bubbly expressions of thought. The mutable signs of Sagittarius and Pisces will keep us flexible, artistic, and energetic. While the Moon is square to Mercury however, it may be wise to be cautious when communicating, as hypersensitivity may lead many people to easily misinterpret others, or to take complex kinds of thoughts the wrong way. Keep it simple!

**Venus trine Uranus** (occurring Nov. 21 – 28) Venus in Scorpio is trine Uranus in Pisces. Passionate love and attraction will allow people to make breakthroughs in relationships and in artistic disciplines. Venus trine Uranus brings a favorable attraction to revolutionary concepts. Harmony can exist in love related matters even while chaos is occurring. This is a time of freedom fighters, rebel love, and attraction to the unusual. Youth is attracted to and more highly susceptible to rebellion during this aspect. Dangerous love and taking chances become common occurrences. Love at first sight is explosive at this time, but not necessarily long lasting. This aspect last occurred August 17 – 25, reaching its peak on August 22 with Venus in Cancer.

# November 26th Thursday

**Thanksgiving Day, USA**

**Moon in Pisces / Aries**

| | PST | EST | |
|---|---|---|---|
| Moon conjunct Uranus | 5:08 AM | 8:08 AM | |
| Moon trine Venus goes v/c | 6:16 AM | 9:16 AM | |
| Mercury trine Mars | 6:53 AM | 9:53 AM | |
| Venus square Neptune | 4:15 PM | 7:15 PM | |
| Moon enters Aries | 7:09 PM | 10:09 PM | |
| Moon square Pluto | 11:07 PM | 2:07 AM | (November 27) |
| Mercury sextile Jupiter begins | (see November 29) | | |
| Mercury square Uranus begins | (see November 30) | | |

*Mood Watch*: It's a good thing that the Sun and Moon are in mutable signs. This will help us to be flexible, adaptive to various situations, and capable of accepting whatever comes along. Thanksgiving Day is an important holiday to many Americans. It may also be a difficult time for families, especially complex families with unconventional histories, divorces, and cross cultural origins. The Pisces Moon will be void-of-course throughout most of the day and well into the evening. This Moon notoriously brings spacey, vague, and nebulous feelings to the fore-

241

ground of our moods. It may be difficult to negotiate situations, to synchronize a get-together, and to get people to pay attention long enough to point them in the right direction. If you're planning a big family gathering, try to keep matters as simple as possible, and most of all, do not get hung up on high expectations! This is a time for bubbly expressions of gaiety, a nonchalant outlook, and easy going fun. It is also a time to beware of the tendency for estranged family members to delve into substance abuse in order to try to fit in or avoid confrontations. Later, as the Moon enters Aries, some folks might decide to let out their anguish, distress, and suppressed feelings. Don't let a perfectly good turkey dinner go to waste – keep lots of containers on hand for leftovers. Try to remain cool, calm, and collected. Celebrate with music, song, and art.

**Mercury trine Mars** (occurring Nov. 21 – 28) Mercury in Sagittarius is trine to Mars in Leo. This aspect is especially stimulating in a positive way when it comes to communications among family and friends. Thoughts, words and speech inspire activity, and the messages coming across often give us the incentive to get in on the action. Mercury trine Mars brings news and communications into a most favorable position when it comes to taking action. The trine aspect acts like a gift, and this is a superb time to communicate and to receive positive and uplifting information, which will inspire others to take affirmative action where needed. This is the only time Mercury and Mars will be trine this year.

**Venus square Neptune** (occurring Nov. 21 – 29) This may be a difficult time to be drawn to or to meditate on spiritual matters or activities. Art with a spiritual approach may appear more phony than ethereal. Feminine expression may be set back by antiquated beliefs. Love matters could be rocky due to a conflict of beliefs. Venus is in Scorpio, which intensifies the art of attraction, while Neptune is in Aquarius, formulating a new spiritual outlook for humankind. Venus influences beauty, attraction, and magnetism. Neptune is the higher spiritual vibration of the feminine spirit, the higher octave of Venus herself – the imperfect yet alluring mortal versus the perfect and irresistible goddess. When these two planets are in conflict, it is a time when women are being sent mixed messages about how to live up to a higher standard of the self. The influences of this aspect are not as harsh for those who understand that true attraction and beauty are found in the core of feminine, and that magnetic attraction goes beyond temporal beauty. This aspect last occurred June 25 – July 4, reaching its peak on July 1 with Venus in Taurus.

# November 27th Friday

| Moon in Aries | PST | EST |
|---|---|---|
| Moon opposite Saturn | 12:19 AM | 3:19 AM |
| Moon trine Sun | 5:30 AM | 8:30 AM |

*Mood Watch*: The waxing Aries Moon is often an active time when many folks are focused on whatever is new, fast, or thrilling. Sun in Sagittarius and Moon in Aries is a prime time for competitive sports. This would be a good time to physically work out all of the emotional aggressions which may have been brought on by the events of yesterday's long void-of-course Pisces Moon. Predictable or mundane situations may cause a great deal of restlessness or boredom. Confidence and a firm handshake bring opportunities, but if it's a job you're applying for, be sure to know who the boss is, and to show him or her that you are capable of control as well as compliance while following directions. No one will be impressed with a young upstart attitude, but they may be willing to settle for a go-getter.

# November 28ᵗʰ Saturday

| Moon in Aries | PST | EST |
|---|---|---|
| Moon trine Mars | 2:39 AM | 5:39 AM |
| Moon trine Mercury | 7:26 AM | 10:26 AM |
| Moon sextile Jupiter | 9:35 AM | 12:35 PM |
| Moon sextile Neptune goes v/c | 3:32 PM | 6:32 PM |
| Mercury sextile Neptune begins (see December 1) | | |

*Mood Watch*: Sun in Sagittarius and Moon in Aries is an active time. The Sun and Moon are both in fire signs. This brings creativity, enthusiasm, and courageousness. This is a good time to explore new avenues of thought and expression. Today's lunar aspects are positive and energetic. However, by late afternoon/early evening the waxing Aries Moon goes void-of-course, and this is a really bad time to point your nose where it isn't welcome and doesn't belong. The void-of-course Aries Moon brings impatience around delays and traffic. It also brings a tendency towards false starts and aggressive attitudes. This evening will be a good time to avoid butting heads and Saturday night brawls.

# November 29ᵗʰ Sunday

| Moon in Aries / Taurus | PST | EST |
|---|---|---|
| Moon enters Taurus | 2:33 AM | 5:33 AM |
| Mercury sextile Jupiter | 3:53 AM | 6:53 AM |
| Moon trine Pluto | 6:23 AM | 9:23 AM |

*Mood Watch*: The Moon enters Taurus this morning. Already we are looking ahead to December and the pending holiday season. Taurus Moon has a way of focusing our attention on finances, physical needs, and material concerns. This Moon brings an industrious vibration, a stubborn tenacity to bring what we need and want most. It also focuses our attention on the need for pleasure, comfort, and security. While Mercury is sextile to Jupiter (see below) we are likely to utilize today's lunar influence in constructive ways.

**Mercury sextile Jupiter** (occurring Nov. 26 – 30) Mercury in Sagittarius is sextile to Jupiter in Aquarius. Mercury influences news and talk, while Jupiter influences commerce, wealth, and prosperous advancement. This would be an excellent time to inquire about opportunities, to discuss potential work or career related advancements and to communicate visions and goals. This is also a good time to help people to improve their skills and apply them. Putting our minds to work on explorative, open-minded, and enterprising information, particularly while Mercury is in Sagittarius, is the sort of thing that gets noticed by employers and business partners. Opportunity is out there for both the employer and the employee. This is a good time to share information and promote your capabilities. Mercury sextile Jupiter brings joyful, philosophical, and mind expanding conversations. This aspect last occurred April 2 – 5, reaching its peak on April 4 with Mercury in Aries.

# November 30ᵗʰ Monday

| Moon in Taurus | PST | EST |
|---|---|---|
| Moon square Mars | 8:50 AM | 11:50 AM |
| Mercury square Uranus | 11:52 AM | 2:52 PM |
| Moon square Jupiter | 2:58 PM | 5:58 PM |
| Moon sextile Uranus | 6:02 PM | 9:02 PM |
| Moon square Neptune | 8:03 PM | 11:03 PM |
| Venus sextile Saturn begins (see December 4) | | |

*Mood Watch*: As for our moods, there's a lot of juggling going on today. First, Moon square Mars brings complex kinds of aggression. Later today, Moon square Jupiter brings a tendency for us to focus on our financial struggles, and we may seem less than generous, or find it difficult to get in touch with our sense of joy and prosperity. This evening, Moon sextile Uranus brings restlessness and a desire for freedom, or for unusual kinds of entertainment. Later, the last lunar aspect of the day brings complexity to our beliefs, and we may be easily confused by what we are feeling. The best solution: if possible, turn in early and get some rest.

**Mercury square Uranus** (occurring Nov. 26 – Dec. 2) Mercury in Sagittarius square Uranus in Pisces creates explosive mental states and causes some people to speak abrasively or to promote overly radical ideas. Tact and diplomacy are likely to go right out the door when religion is discussed. Communications and philosophical debates may come up against unusual or explosive viewpoints. Spiritual harmony is always best achieved when we exercise discretion. This really is a time to watch what you say: communications have the potential to shake matters up considerably. This aspect last occurred June 28 – July 3, reaching its exact peak on July 1, when Mercury was in Gemini.

# December 1ˢᵗ Tuesday

| FULL MOON in GEMINI | PST | EST |
|---|---|---|
| Moon opposite Venus goes v/c | 5:38 AM | 8:38 AM |
| Moon enters Gemini | 6:23 AM | 9:23 AM |
| Mercury sextile Neptune | 6:52 AM | 9:52 AM |
| Moon trine Saturn | 11:28 AM | 2:28 PM |
| Uranus goes direct | 12:28 PM | 3:28 PM |
| Venus enters Sagittarius | 2:03 PM | 5:03 PM |
| Moon opposite Sun | 11:29 PM | 2:29 AM |

*Mood Watch*: A new month begins and the Moon is full. For less than an hour, the day may start off somewhat lazily with the Moon going void-of-course in Taurus. As the Moon enters Gemini, a whirlwind of details begins to fill our brains. December is really here and this is one of the busiest months of the year. Let the Moon in Gemini trine with Saturn bring an afternoon of organization, clarity, and keenness of thought!

**Mercury sextile Neptune** (occurring Nov. 28 – Dec. 2) Mercury in Sagittarius sextile Neptune in Aquarius reassures us that communicating our philosophies and our beliefs also empowers our belief in humanity. This is an opportunistic time to cautiously attempt communication with regard to beliefs and spiritual matters. Mercury is in Sagittarius placing a philosophical emphasis of talk on

244

such Neptune related subjects as spiritual growth, guidance, and inspiration. Take this opportunity to transmute thoughts and beliefs into a workable understanding and to share it with others in a way that encourages them. Prayers, channeling, and spells are all very effective with Mercury sextile Neptune. This is the time to get the word out to Great Spirit, and to reinforce a sense of faith. This aspect last occurred April 5 – 8, reaching its peak on April 7.

**Uranus goes direct** (Uranus direct: Dec. 1, 2009 – July 5, 2010) Since July 1, Uranus, known for stirring up calamity, has been retrograde. Now the planet of chaos and rebellion moves steadily forward at the 22 degree mark of Pisces, awakening the spiritual needs of humanity, perhaps even inspiring breakthroughs in human rights, or promoting creativity in art and music. The work of radical and revolutionary forces resumes course as Uranus moves direct until early July, 2010. We all feel the need to break out of oppressing conditions of life. As Uranus moves forward, the volatile quality of its work demands the utmost intelligence and knowledge as each level of urgency is unveiled. Uranus is the ruler of Aquarius and teaches us to seek higher levels of intelligence through unusual, brilliant, and open minded measures. The next time the urge for unabashed rebellion makes you kick up your heels, remember to kindle the light of love for humankind's wisdom. This is, after all, the Age of Aquarius.

**Venus enters Sagittarius** (Venus in Sagittarius: Dec. 1 – 25) Now the planet of love and of the expression of affection is enhanced by the inspired character of Sagittarius. Venus in Sagittarius brings out a love of the arts, travel, philosophy, cultural exploration and sports achievements. With this comes a positive and optimistic spirit of camaraderie among people in general, and the effort to take affections beyond the usual bounds is certainly present. Philosophical theories justify love matters. Venus in Sagittarius will help to boost the love life and affections of our Sagittarius friends. This is your time, Sagittarius people, to reaffirm your visions of how to enhance the beauty and the love you are enjoying in your lives.

# December 2nd Wednesday

| Moon in Gemini | PST | EST | |
|---|---|---|---|
| Moon sextile Mars | 11:57 AM | 2:57 PM | |
| Moon trine Jupiter | 5:36 PM | 8:36 PM | |
| Moon square Uranus | 8:02 PM | 11:02 PM | |
| Moon trine Neptune | 10:02 PM | 1:02 AM | (December 3) |
| Mercury conjunct Pluto begins (see December 7) | | | |

*Mood Watch*: **Full Moon in Gemini** (Moon opposite Sun) often brings moods that may seem overwhelmed by mutable thoughts just when we are trying to make decisions. This Gemini Moon, in all of its glorious fullness, brings amazing talk, speeches, mind games, and intellectual pursuits. People may tend to babble sense-lessly, and very few are able to keep their minds on what they're doing, thinking, or feeling for very long. Ideally, this is a good time astrologically to pace oneself and relax the mind at various intervals. It may also be a time when our minds are relentlessly active and difficult to calm or ease. Full Moon in Gemini goes straight to charging our nervous systems, and we quickly discover that quieting

245

down or easing an overworked nervous system takes some extra time after it has been running at top speed. Take it easy on the caffeine.

# December 3rd Thursday

| Moon in Gemini / Cancer | PST | EST |
|---|---|---|
| Moon opposite Mercury goes v/c | 2:27 AM | 5:27 AM |
| Moon enters Cancer | 8:00 AM | 11:00 AM |
| Moon opposite Pluto | 11:45 AM | 2:45 PM |
| Moon square Saturn | 1:13 PM | 4:13 PM |

Mars-opposite-Neptune-non-exact (occurring from December 3 to 30 – see below)
Mercury square Saturn begins (see December 7)
Sun trine Mars begins (see December 10)

*Mood Watch*: The classic mental hangover of a post-full Gemini Moon is accentuated by this morning's void-of-course experience. We may find ourselves at a loss for words, or just plain careless with our thoughts. As the Moon enters Cancer our moods will become a great deal more responsive and sympathetic. On the other hand, there may also be a twinge of defensiveness, or a blithe lack of concern towards people who do not seem important. Moodiness can be thick on a post-full Cancer Moon. The lunar aspects are challenging today and it probably will be better if we try not to get too entangled by the way we feel. Genuine pampering is in order.

*Mars-opposite-Neptune-non-exact* (occurring Dec. 3 – 30) This aspect never reaches a peak due to the fact that Mars will go retrograde on December 20. Mars will go direct on March 9, 2010, and this aspect will begin occurring again in late May 2010. However, just as Mars finally begins to catch up to this Neptune opposition, the slow moving Neptune goes retrograde on May 30, 2010, and the aspect will dissipate again before reaching a peak. Just because these two planets don't reach a peak opposition does not mean we aren't experiencing its affects – perhaps just not as strongly. Individual integrity (Mars in Leo) is challenged by, or opposed to (opposite), humanity's belief in science (Neptune in Aquarius). Mars activates and stirs up action, while Neptune calms and dissolves all concern. When in opposition these two planets create an acute awareness of our spiritual beliefs and the manner in which those beliefs are acted upon and absorbed. For some, this aspect can create a spiritual breakthrough, while for others it may be that events are forging a strong spiritual awareness challenging personal beliefs. Sometimes we lash out at the world for draining so much of our energy. Perhaps this is a healthy sign that we need to re-structure our priorities, to take action towards finding a peaceful sanctuary where we can recharge our batteries. With Mars in Leo and Neptune in Aquarius, actions which relate to the self and the family are sometimes at odds with outside beliefs, or beliefs imposed by society. Establishing a more healthy attitude towards defending the self – and one's own beliefs – is the best remedy for the opposing outbursts that affect our spiritual wellbeing. This opposition last reached a full peak on June 21, 2008.

# December 4th Friday

| Moon in Cancer | PST | EST |
|---|---|---|
| Venus sextile Saturn | 3:44 AM | 6:44 AM |
| Moon trine Uranus goes v/c | 9:08 PM | 12:08 AM (December 5) |

*Mood Watch*: There's not a long list of lunar aspects crowding the celestial events today. This means that our waning Cancer Moon moods will be relatively smooth, generally unhindered by complexity, and the way we are feeling is not likely to be not be cluttered by misapprehension or high expectations. Nonetheless, the Cancer Moon does not change who we are, it only accentuates what we are feeling. For those who make it a habit to create complexities, there will probably be complications in their expressions of emotion. This is a good time to tap into your true feelings and to make adjustments with positive assurances and affirmations. Later tonight Moon trine Uranus occurs as the Moon goes void-of-course; this stirs up feelings, but usually in a good way.

**Venus sextile Saturn** (occurring Nov. 30 – Dec. 5) Venus is in Sagittarius sextile to Saturn in Libra. Venus in Sagittarius invites an attraction to traveling, adventurous love play, and uplifting social encounters. Venus sextile Saturn brings the opportunity for us to gain some control of our love relationships, and to better understand our boundaries and limitations. Saturn in Libra brings an even-tempered and civil-minded attempt to apply discipline in relationships. It is through this aspect that love relationships are given an opportunity for stronger levels of commitment and responsibility. This is the time to protect loved ones with guidance, and to teach them about discipline. Perfect timing brings pleasure. Venus sextile Saturn teaches us how to hold on to and maintain the things we love – those places, people, and things that matter to us. True love has a binding and lasting affect, and this aspect often shows us the ways in which love stands the test of time. This aspect last occurred August 15 – 21, reaching its peak on August 19, when Venus was in Cancer sextile to Saturn in Virgo.

# December 5th Saturday

| Moon in Cancer / Leo | PST | EST |
|---|---|---|
| Moon enters Leo | 9:07 AM | 12:07 PM |
| Mercury enters Capricorn | 9:24 AM | 12:24 PM |
| Moon sextile Saturn | 2:35 PM | 5:35 PM |
| Moon trine Venus | 5:43 PM | 8:43 PM |

*Mood Watch*: Throughout the night, the Moon has been void-of-course in Cancer. Waves of emotional responses lap against the morning beach-home of our thoughts. Moodiness is a classic symptom of this time. As the Moon enters Leo, there is a definite propensity to call up that ray of sunshine that brings hope, gaiety, and entertaining fun. People will be more inclined to seek amusement and leisurely activities. Families in search of something new and exciting will crowd the shopping malls on this first Saturday of December. The lunar aspects are positive today, and as a general rule, we can expect a cool, laid-back course of mood.

**Mercury enters Capricorn** (Mercury in Capricorn: Dec. 5, 2009 – Feb. 10, 2010) While Mercury travels through Capricorn, communications tend to be more serious and to the point, although not necessarily less complex. In negotiations, there is an emphasis on enterprise. While this versatile planet goes through Capricorn, our realms of communications have a determined and persistent quality of expression, like a demanding voice waiting to be heard and received with hospitality. This fits with the solar days of Capricorn, when the harsh realities of winter demand clarity of purpose in our communications. Mercury will remain in Capricorn for a longer than usual time, as it will go retrograde, December 26, 2009 – January 14, 2010. Mercury retrograde in Capricorn brings miscommunications over large scale contracts, issues of control and time restraints. Communication is one of the tools of survival, and this is an important time to use those skills wisely and sensibly.

# December 6th Sunday

| Moon in Leo | PST | EST | |
|---|---|---|---|
| Moon trine Sun | 9:29 AM | 12:29 PM | |
| Moon conjunct Mars | 3:51 PM | 6:51 PM | |
| Moon opposite Jupiter | 9:23 PM | 12:23 AM | (December 7) |

*Mood Watch*: The weekend continues to slip by with a comfortable, relaxing quality of mood while the Moon wanes in Leo. Today's lunar aspects are relatively promising as they bring an interest in personal hobbies, family endeavors, and leisurely activities. There will be a lot of activity in fact, as people are inclined to move about with an outgoing spirit. The Sun and Moon are in fire signs and this brings creativity, excitement, and an engaging spirit. Much later, as the Moon opposes Jupiter, some folks may toss and turn over the fact that they may have spent too much, or they may be sleepless over what it will take to afford the events of the pending holiday season. Restlessness over what we do and don't have is a sign that we may need to reevaluate our concepts of prosperity. Those who keep their goals simple and attainable are likely to feel the most prosperous.

# December 7th Monday

| Moon in Leo / Virgo | PST | EST |
|---|---|---|
| Moon opposite Neptune goes v/c | 12:58 AM | 3:58 AM |
| Mercury conjunct Pluto | 1:12 AM | 4:12 AM |
| Moon enters Virgo | 11:06 PM | 2:06 PM |
| Moon trine Pluto | 3:14 PM | 6:14 PM |
| Moon trine Mercury | 4:47 PM | 7:47 PM |
| Mercury square Saturn | 6:35 PM | 9:35 PM |

*Mood Watch*: Our Monday morning moods are driven by laziness, forgetfulness and, in some cases, sheer selfishness. Don't wield the sword of blame – it's just the waning void-of-course Leo Moon messing with our sensibilities. For awhile today, we can expect a fair bit of moping or lollygagging. As the Moon enters Virgo, a more cautious quality of moods leads us to be more discerning, courteous, and relatively tactful. Virgo Moon churns our curious juices and gets us in the mood to investigate, research, and examine the possibilities. Eventually, this will allow us to work more amicably through the challenging aspects of the day (see below).

**Mercury conjunct Pluto** (occurring Dec. 2 – 9) Mercury conjunct Pluto raises issues of power. The areas of our lives that have required challenge, struggle, sac-

248

rifice and transformation now bring us to a place where we can talk about them. With Mercury and Pluto newly in the sign of Capricorn, a very strong sense of duty is instilled in the delivery of messages. This is a time when people instinctively know their own fate. Mercury conjunct Pluto in Capricorn allows us to voice our hardships, and to contemplate and deliberate over the powerful occurrences that challenge and change our lives. There will be a great deal of intensity in our conversations at this time, especially with regard to the fate of the world and our ongoing efforts to end hardship and suffering.

**Mercury square Saturn** (occurring Dec. 3 – 10) Mercury in Capricorn square Saturn in Libra may be a difficult time to ask for favors, or to make requests of others in a way that they don't feel as if they're being used or taken advantage of. It may be a challenging time to communicate instructions or to inform someone of the end of something. It may also be challenging to sell someone on a product, or to successfully request a raise or promotion. Whatever the desired effect may be, it is wise to use caution when attempting communications during Mercury square Saturn. Saturn is newly in Libra (see Oct. 29), creating limitations and structural changes in matters of law, justice, marriage, and relationships. This aspect makes it difficult to put a message out there and be taken seriously, or sometimes, we are taken *too* seriously. Some people may become very tongue-tied and feel quite off track. Mercury square Saturn last occurred June 21 – 27, reaching its peak on June 26, when Mercury was in Gemini and Saturn was in Virgo.

# December 8th Tuesday
## LAST QUARTER MOON in VIRGO PST     EST

| | PST | EST |
|---|---|---|
| Moon square Venus | 12:53 AM | 3:53 AM |
| Moon square Sun | 4:13 PM | 7:13 PM |
| Sun square Uranus begins (see December 14) | | |

*"All we are saying, is give Peace a chance..."* - John Lennon

*Mood Watch*: The **Last Quarter Moon in Virgo** (Moon square Sun) calls for the release of doubt. These are the days of Sun in Sagittarius; applying the vision of how one wants to see their future-self is not an easy task, especially if poisonous and debilitating addictions are involved. However, the Sagittarian outlook often projects selfhood in an outward fashion in order to envision the demands of an expanding spirit. That same Sagittarian awareness is just as capable of traveling inward and perceiving the needs of the inner self. Let the doubts and fears of your life be flushed away at this time so that, through clarity, you may achieve the benefits of your visionary picture of health, wealth, and wellbeing.

# December 9th Wednesday

| Moon in Virgo / Libra | PST | EST | |
|---|---|---|---|
| Moon opposite Uranus goes v/c | 3:05 AM | 6:05 AM | |
| Moon enters Libra | 3:47 PM | 6:47 PM | |
| Moon square Pluto | 8:13 PM | 11:13 PM | |
| Moon conjunct Saturn | 10:07 PM | 1:07 AM | (December 10) |

*Mood Watch*: As the Moon wanes in Libra, our moods focus our attention on balancing the inconsistencies of relations with partners, loved ones, and friends. Libra

249

Moon emphasizes the need for teamwork and this will be a good time to delve into coordinating and collaborating with others. There are a number of adjustments being made right now, particularly later this evening as the Moon squares Pluto. Big shifts in energy always require the cooperation of others. This may also be a crucial time of decision, especially with regard to those decisions that affect the people who share our life and work. This is a good time to attempt to drop grudges and to make peace.

# December 10ᵗʰ Thursday

| **Moon in Libra** | PST | EST |
|---|---|---|
| Moon square Mercury | 2:46 AM | 5:46 AM |
| Moon sextile Venus | 10:29 AM | 1:29 PM |
| Sun trine Mars | 5:18 PM | 8:18 PM |
| Sun sextile Jupiter begins (see December 14) | | |

*Mood Watch*: At the earliest hour, Moon square Mercury has a mind-boggling affect on our moods. However, as the morning and afternoon progress, the congenial nature of the Libra Moon atmosphere is accentuated by the positive affects of Moon sextile Venus. Peaceful and hopeful feelings bring pleasantries and kindness among people. Where these traits don't exist, the Libra Moon brings a desire for us to strive for the best or to utilize the law to create protection and cordial civil duty. Overall, Libra Moon energy focuses on harmony.

**Sun trine Mars** (occurring Dec.3 – 14) This occurrence of Sun trine Mars particularly affects those Sagittarius people celebrating birthdays from December 3 – 14. There will be loads of energy to work with, and a strong need to activate the personality and accomplish goals. Creative work abounds. There are special gifts of triumph for those Sagittarius folks who activate their dreams and desires, allowing them to easily utilize existing energy. This is a time to exercise the will and the internal sense of primal might, to stir the personal agenda into a state of action. Heated matters will come to the surface in an advantageous manner. Through the act of making things happen, personal achievement will shine forth like a long needed blessing in the year to come for these birthday folks. Keep it active, Sagittarians.

# December 11ᵗʰ Friday

| **Moon in Libra / Scorpio** | PST | EST |
|---|---|---|
| Moon sextile Mars | 12:52 AM | 3:52 AM |
| Moon sextile Sun | 1:25 AM | 4:25 AM |
| Moon trine Jupiter | 7:01 AM | 10:01 AM |
| Moon trine Neptune goes v/c | 9:45 AM | 12:45 PM |
| Moon enters Scorpio | 8:32 PM | 11:32 PM |
| Sun sextile Neptune begins (see December 15) | | |

*Mood Watch*: Upbeat moods may kick off the day, but by late morning/afternoon, the waning Libra Moon goes void-of-course, and with this comes a long day and night of indecision and confusion. The void Libra Moon has a way of causing people to disagree. This makes it difficult to schedule, plan, deliberate, apply

250

patience, and to act civil. Much of the day will seem like a juggling act towards making adjustments. This is why it's wise to seize the day in the early a.m. hours, and to hold off on carrying out big plans in the later part of the day. Temper your expectations; this is a time when people's ability to collaborate may be taxed by the hazy clouds of the waning void-of-course Libra Moon. Later, as the Moon enters Scorpio, our moods will be inclined to react to the stresses and strains of the day. Secrets may come to the surface. Emotions are easily unleashed. It's a good time for therapeutic endeavors, and to try to get some rest.

# December 12th Saturday
### Chanukah begins (ends December 19)

| Moon in Scorpio | PST | EST |
|---|---|---|
| Moon sextile Pluto | 1:17 AM | 4:17 AM |
| Moon sextile Mercury | 3:22 PM | 6:22 PM |
| Venus trine Mars begins (see December 17) | | |

*Mood Watch*: There is beauty, sensation, and an electrical field of awareness at work. The events of the day may seem laced with strong doses of emotion. A waning Moon in Scorpio calls to us to let go of strong destructive tendencies and challenges us to cease hurting ourselves and others by transforming our lower impulses into higher aspirations. Under amicable circumstances, this is a good time to let go of the pain you've been concealing. Sexual activity is the tension reliever that many will be seeking. Weekend shopping crowds are thickening this time of year. If you're not up to the intensity, now is not the time to risk the potential for stress. On the other hand, the waning Scorpio Moon has a way of leading us directly to the pulse-point of activity. The lunar aspects are not so bad, and if it's excitement you're looking for, you won't have to go far.

# December 13th Sunday

| Moon in Scorpio | PST | EST |
|---|---|---|
| Moon square Mars | 8:24 AM | 11:24 PM |
| Moon trine Uranus | 2:44 PM | 5:44 PM |
| Moon square Jupiter | 3:07 PM | 6:07 PM |
| Moon square Neptune goes v/c | 5:17 PM | 8:17 PM |

*Mood Watch*: This morning/afternoon's Moon square Mars brings the potential for temperamental moods and harsh agitation may be evident. The waning Scorpio Moon has a way of leading us to the core of our feelings. Transformations bring profound feelings, but where simple and lighthearted expressions of joy and happiness are entertained, the profoundness can be illuminating. The moods conjured by Moon trine Uranus brings the desire for excitement and sensationalism. Later today, Moon square Jupiter bring less than generous, or less than bountiful, feelings. By evening, Moon square Neptune brings doubtfulness, uncertainty, and complexity to our faith, especially since the Moon goes void-of-course. The evening Moon is a good time to retire with (as P.G. Woedhouse's classic character, *Jeeves* would say) "an improving book." Many people may appear tired, exasperated, or just plain mysterious. No fear – it will pass.

# December 14ᵗʰ Monday

| Moon in Scorpio / Sagittarius | PST | EST |
|---|---|---|
| Moon enters Sagittarius | 4:25 AM | 9:25 AM |
| Sun square Uranus | 7:26 AM | 10:26 AM |
| Moon sextile Saturn | 11:46 PM | 2:46 PM |
| Sun sextile Jupiter | 4:16 PM | 7:16 PM |
| Venus square Uranus begins (see December 19) | | |

*Mood Watch*: In the wee small hours of the morning, our moods may seem suspicious, strange, or unreasonable. The Moon is in a detrimental place while it's in Scorpio, and it is equally challenged by its void-of-course state, which has been occurring since last evening. Soon enough, however, the morning Moon enters Sagittarius. At this time, the Moon is especially dark, as it works its way towards the new stage, set to take place on Wednesday morning. This is a time when deep philosophical insights tap at our conscience, and we can endeavor to create optimistic and uplifting visions, and to empower them with internal reflection.

**Sun square Uranus** (occurring Dec. 8 – 17) This occurrence of Sun square Uranus particularly affects Sagittarius people celebrating birthdays December 8 – 17. The square of Uranus (in Pisces) to these Sagittarius folks' natal Sun brings about challenging events and a strong dose of unrestrained chaos. This may be the year for you Sagittarius birthday folks to surrender to those aspects of life that are truly out of your control, and to concentrate more rationally on those facets of life over which you do have control. Sometimes the aftermath of Uranus's influence is an improvement, but with the square aspect at work, it is likely these people will feel personally challenged. It is important to understand that some types of personal challenges are best left alone, while others must be confronted directly without causing destructive damage, particularly to the self. On the other hand, birthday Sagittarius folks, if your life has no foundation, there is no point in holding onto the illusion of stability at this juncture of your sojourn. This aspect will pass, and it is vital not to give this rapid change too much resistance, lest you be bound to the reversals of trying to fight chaos with logic at a time when resistance is futile. Matters will settle down in due time; try to be detached from chaotic events as they occur, and the outcome will seem less costly. If you need it, project the picture of peace and it will be there for you at the other end. This aspect last occurred June 10 – 20, reaching its peak on June 17, when the Sun was in Gemini square Uranus is Pisces.

**Sun sextile Jupiter** (occurring Dec. 10 – 17) This aspect brings those Sagittarius people celebrating birthdays from December 10 – 17 into a favorable natal Sun position to Jupiter. It's a time of opportunity and expansion for these birthday folks if they act on their desires and work towards their goals. Skills learned throughout this year will support their overall plans for career advancement and fortune building. This aspect last occurred April 5 – 12, reaching its peak on April 10, bringing a similar affect to the birthday Aries people of that time.

252

# December 15ᵗʰ Tuesday

**Moon in Sagittarius**

| | PST | EST |
|---|---|---|
| Moon conjunct Venus | 2:17 PM | 7:17 PM |
| Sun sextile Neptune | 4:16 PM | 7:16 PM |
| Moon trine Mars | 6:04 PM | 9:04 PM |

*Mood Watch*: The Sagittarius Moon wanes darkly on the New Moon Eve. Introspection runs strongly in our moods. Today's positive, warm, and uplifting aspects will alleviate current pressures. This is a good time to contemplate and review important decisions about your life. This busy time of year often makes it difficult to stop and do such things. Nonetheless, the Sagittarius Moon opens pathways into the soul, especially when it wanes in the balsamic position. A simple meditation and positive affirmation may be all that's required to recharge your batteries and give you the confidence to move past the busy storms of late autumn.

**Sun sextile Neptune** (occurring Dec. 11 – 17) This occurrence of Sun sextile Neptune creates an opportunistic time for those Sagittarius people celebrating birthdays from December 11 – 17. These Sagittarius folks are experiencing an opportunity to awaken in the realm of spirituality and creativity. There is an awareness of the self that goes deep here, and these birthday people are likely to appear distracted and difficult to reach while this phenomenon of great depth is occurring. This will be your year, birthday folks, to explore personal opportunities of spiritual growth. It may be a time to get away from it all, and find a sanctuary in which to meditate and open up to some valuable answers to old questions. These folks are in a place that gives them an opportunity to better understand the work of their path, but this is probably only true if they act on their own intuitive sensibilities, without the influences of others. That shouldn't be too hard for the adventurous, open-minded, and outgoing Sagittarius natures among us. This will be your year (Sagittarius birthday people) to enhance and strengthen your intuition and primal instincts by tapping into them while they are easily available. This aspect last occurred April 11 – 17, reaching its exact aspect on April 15, when the Sun was in Aries.

# December 16ᵗʰ Wednesday

**NEW MOON in SAGITTARIUS**

| Moon in Sagittarius / Capricorn | PST | EST | |
|---|---|---|---|
| Moon square Uranus | 12:22 AM | 3:22 AM | |
| Moon sextile Jupiter | 1:33 AM | 4:33 AM | |
| Moon sextile Neptune | 3:05 AM | 6:05 AM | |
| Moon conjunct Sun goes v/c | 4:02 AM | 7:02 AM | |
| Moon enters Capricorn | 2:32 PM | 5:32 PM | |
| Moon conjunct Pluto | 8:00 PM | 11:00 PM | |
| Moon square Saturn | 10:24 PM | 1:24 AM | (December 17) |

*Mood Watch*: The **New Moon in Sagittarius** (Moon conjunct Sun) inspires us to look at life in a whole new way. A hopeful outlook is felt strongly as the Moon reaches the new mark this morning. New Moon in Sagittarius encourages us to start exercise programs, look into original philosophies, and to explore new territory in our lives. Sagittarius says, "I see," so vision and insight are the primary incentives to explore fresh ground. Today is a good day to optimistically look ahead and get in touch with an innovative vision for the coming month and year. Bear in mind that as soon as the Moon reaches the new mark, it goes void-of-course. A long day of spacey tendencies and inattention may cause our moods to be irritable at times, especially if we are trying to accomplish a lot at once. This evening's Moon in Capricorn will bring a bright picture of how to sensibly proceed through the final course of this busy week and this busy time of year.

# December 17th Thursday

| Moon in Capricorn | PST | EST |
|---|---|---|
| Venus  trine Mars | 4:39 AM | 7:39 AM |
| Moon  conjunct Mercury | 11:52 PM | 2:52 AM |
| Venus sextile Jupiter begins  (see December 20) | | |
| Venus sextile Neptune begins  (see December 20) | | |
| Sun conjunct Venus begins (peak date occurs on Jan. 10, 2010 / ends on Jan. 21, 2010 – for an explanation, see March 27) | | |

***Mood Watch***: Moon in Capricorn provides our moods with a steady persistence to meet important goals and make progress with our work. Let the progress of your work shine, and take joy in your accomplishments! Today's Capricorn Moon is preparing us for the pending season that awaits us – winter solstice, a busy time of year. In these final days of the Sun in Sagittarius, the Capricorn Moon gives us the unwavering determination needed to get through this time. For some, the excitement of the holiday season gives them the wherewithal to do the impossible. For others, the Capricorn Moon allows them to put off all those holiday distractions and get down to some integral effort to do some work. Either way, our busy moods are set on the idea of achievement, and it gives us what it takes to get things done.

**Venus trine Mars** (occurring Dec.12 – 19) Venus in Sagittarius is trine Mars in Leo. Adventurous, outgoing, and bold expressions of affection will bring very energetic and romantic interactions between loved ones. Venus trine Mars brings love in action. When Venus and Mars are well harmonized by this ideal aspect, there is a greater opportunity for peace and healing in relationships, and often gifts are exchanged. These are gifts which help people to understand how masculine and feminine expressions are harmonized. It starts with the effort to make things better, concentrating on the positive, not the negative, and continues with the persistence to bring out the best in your partner – no matter how stubborn at first (s)he may seem. This is the only time Venus trine Mars will occur this year.

# December 18th Friday

| Moon in Capricorn | PST | EST |
|---|---|---|
| Moon  sextile Uranus goes v/c | 12:08 PM | 3:08 PM |
| Sun conjunct Pluto begins  (see December 24) | | |
| Sun conjunct Venus begins (occurs Jan. 11, 2010, ends Jan. 23, 2010 – an affectionate time for Capricorns born between Dec. 18 – Jan. 23) | | |

*Mood Watch*: The Capricorn Moon youthfully waxes and many folks will be too busy to stop and check how they, or the folks around them, are feeling. In fact, we may find we are so preoccupied that we may not notice that, at times, we will be running around in circles. The Capricorn Moon goes void-of-course this afternoon, and although many people will remain determined, it is very likely that the busy rush of traffic and holiday hubbub will also slow down our sense of progress considerably. This evening would be a very good time to drop all the grudges that go along with not being able to achieve certain goals. By tomorrow, a new set of moods will put us on the right path. This is also no time to attempt to soul search with others – our moods will tend to be distant, lost in thought, and less than sympathetic towards the needs of others.

# December 19th Saturday

**Moon in Capricorn / Aquarius**

| | PST | EST |
|---|---|---|
| Moon enters Aquarius | 2:38 AM | 5:38 AM |
| Moon trine Saturn | 10:57 AM | 1:57 PM |
| Venus square Uranus | 5:52 PM | 8:52 PM |
| Sun square Saturn begins (see December 25) | | |

*Mood Watch*: The waxing Aquarius Moon sets the mood for our encounter with the hustle and bustle of humanity. Early in the day, Moon trine Saturn gives us the keen ability to apply precision and accuracy in all that we do. Aquarius Moon activities emphasize a focus on science, technology, social affairs and galas, and political events. The simple act of applying knowledge will lead us to some very educational experiences.

**Venus square Uranus** (occurring Dec. 14 – 22) Venus is in Sagittarius squaring to Uranus in Pisces. A love for travel may be stifled by chaotic changes. This aspect tends to put obstacles between love and freedom. Be careful not to become too personally affronted by explosive or radical love matters. This influence may be testing the power of love to withstand chaos. Be assured in self-love and empower affection with personal integrity and a strong loving vision. People are changing at a rapid rate and it is essential to let love take its course concerning issues of personal freedom. This aspect last occurred July 23 – 31, reaching its exact peak on July 28 with Venus in Gemini.

# December 20th Sunday

**Moon in Aquarius**

| | PST | EST | |
|---|---|---|---|
| Mars goes retrograde | 5:27 AM | 8:27 AM | |
| Moon opposite Mars | 6:43 PM | 9:43 PM | |
| Venus sextile Jupiter | 8:52 PM | 11:52 PM | |
| Venus sextile Neptune | 9:23 PM | 12:23 AM | (December 21) |
| Mercury sextile Uranus begins (peak date occurs on Feb. 5, 2010 / ends on Feb. 8, 2010 – for an explanation, see April 24) | | | |

*Mood Watch*: Sun in Sagittarius and waxing Moon in Aquarius generally bring insightful, brilliant, and inspired incentives and moods. That said, it must be noted that Moon opposite Mars tends to bring emotional storms, particularly while Mars is at a standstill and about to go retrograde (see below). We may be affronted by anger or heated emotions of some nature; we may also be especially charged up to do the impossible in a very short period of time. Despite the heat, the Aquarius Moon is a superb time to plan (or carry out) social endeavors and charitable events. This is also a good time to share and discuss strategies and theories.

**Mars goes retrograde** (Mars retrograde: Dec. 20, 2009 – March 9, 2010) Now the god of war, Mars, goes retrograde in Leo. Those who have overextended themselves may be due for a recreational healing period. Mars retrograde is also likely to stir up heated energy in the lives of Leo people as Mars is crossing over their natal Sun. Mars retrograde in Leo will undoubtedly cause difficulties and numerous energy shifts in the lives of Taurus and Scorpio people as Mars squares to their Sun signs for an extended period of time. Aquarius people are likely to feel overwhelmed with hot emotional energy – or even a fever – while Mars is retrograde in opposition to their natal Sun. As this energy moves backward instead of forward, it will take a little longer than a couple of months before all these folks are likely to get their activity modes and energy levels in smooth running order. While Mars is retrograde in Leo, this is really the time to learn to kick back intermittently and relax. Don't get impatient over projects that are slow to take off or allow hot emotions to get out of hand. For some people this may be a time of having to let go of emotional baggage that has caused them to be angry for too long. As Mars travels retrograde through Leo, the red planet's sometimes violent, forceful, or reactionary energy may be seen in a susceptibility to burn-out, defensiveness, and fear. Beware of the tendency to act on dangerous impulses, as Mars retrograde is not a good time to take risks – they may lead to disruptive and sometimes fateful accidents.

**Venus sextile Jupiter** (occurring Dec. 17 – 22) This aspect is currently reaching an exact peak for the fourth time this year. Venus is in Sagittarius, bringing a powerful sense of adventure and a joyful outreach towards the need to discover love's capabilities. Jupiter is in Aquarius, the place of humanitarian exploits and accomplishments. An attraction to adventure, travel, and the exploration of beauty and pleasure (Venus in Sagittarius), leads to unusual and intellectually stimulating opportunities in science, technology, social affairs, and charities (Jupiter in Aquarius). It is here that love and beauty are potentially found in the experience of going beyond the limits. This is an excellent time to shower loved ones with gifts and compliments. A lovers' getaway may be just the ticket to recapture some romance. This is the time to allow expansion to occur in love matters, and to take the next step towards enlivening and enhancing life. This aspect also occurred on February 16, March 11, and June 2, when Venus was in Aries sextile Jupiter in Aquarius.

**Venus sextile Neptune** (occurring Dec. 17 – 22) Venus in Sagittarius sextile Neptune in Aquarius brings inspirational and creative love to the art of spirituality. The sextile of Venus to Neptune brings the opportunity for us to find spiritual enhancement in the adventure of love, and to spread its healing power around for all to share. This serves as an excellent time to reach out spiritually to those we love as well as to our spirit guides. This aspect will last occurred May 28 – June 4, reaching its exact aspect on June 2.

# CAPRICORN

Key Phrase: " I USE "
Cardinal Earth Sign
Ruling Planet: Saturn
Symbol: The Goat
December 21st, 2009 through
January 19th, 2010

## December 21st Monday
**Winter Solstice**

| Moon in Aquarius / Pisces | PST | EST | |
|---|---|---|---|
| Jupiter conjunct Neptune | 12:50 AM | 3:50 AM | |
| Moon conjunct Neptune | 4:06 AM | 7:06 AM | |
| Moon conjunct Jupiter | 4:09 AM | 7:09 AM | |
| Moon sextile Venus goes v/c | 4:53 AM | 7:53 AM | |
| Sun enters Capricorn | 9:46 AM | 12:46 PM | |
| Moon enters Pisces | 3:41 PM | 6:41 PM | |
| Moon sextile Sun | 6:15 PM | 7:15 PM | |
| Moon sextile Pluto | 9:41 PM | 12:41 AM | (December 22) |

*Mood Watch*: Early this morning, the Moon is first conjunct with Neptune and then with Jupiter. This puts us in touch with today's conjunction of Jupiter and Neptune (see below). The waxing Aquarius Moon then goes void-of-course and remains void for a hefty portion of the day. We are now on the brink of winter season, and this can surely be felt with the Moon traversing in the winter signs of the zodiac. The void Aquarius Moon may connect us with a sense of how feeble or vulnerable we humans seem to be. Even though we have advanced technologically, we are often at the mercy of technological equipment, and we're sometimes stranded, at a loss, or blindsided without this equipment. Even with technology, we are sometimes frustrated by it as a result of its imperfections, or its inability to satiate specific needs. This is a time when many of us may feel the necessity to get back to the basics, to help and guide each other, and to deal with the great effort and stamina often required to get back on the right path. Later, as the Moon enters Pisces, we are reminded of the need for many folks to slip into fantasy, escape from troubles, and to enjoy a higher level of consciousness by consciously changing our environment. Through brave determination, we can finally reach a place of tranquility and enjoyment.

**Jupiter conjunct Neptune** (occurring Oct. 30, 2009 – Jan. 8, 2010) Jupiter conjunct Neptune in Aquarius brings limitless possibilities for spiritual advancement in humankind. Due to the retrograde patterns of Jupiter and Neptune this

257

year, this rare-occasion conjunction is reaching its peak for the third and final time this year. For a recap on the story of this fascinating conjunction between Jupiter and Neptune, *see May 27*, when it first occurred this year. This aspect also reached its peak on July 10.

**Sun enters Capricorn** (Sun in Capricorn: Dec. 21, 2008 – Jan. 19, 2009) Spark up the lights – it's **Winter Solstice**! Today the Sun King returns from the ashes of the longest night. This is the time of Saturn-ruled Capricorn. Sun in Capricorn is the time to step into success. Jack Frost is nipping at our heels, but the Sun King returns! The lengthening days of the Sun are finally here and a new season and cycle begins. The symbol of Capricorn is the mountain goat. The Capricorn goat consciousness is revealed to us through the high and lofty heights the goat commands. No mountain is too high for the true archetypal Capricorn, and the focus of this season is always placed on accomplishing the highest of goals and achievements. The working pace for the New Year is established here. Capricorn energy emphasizes corporate growth, the creation and maintenance of institutions, construction and development, and the use and control of industrial services and equipment. Many outstanding Capricorns are devoted to their careers and lifestyles with unyielding tenacity. Capricorn days of the Sun are splendid times to focus on goals, and to discipline one's nature to make daily tasks add up to something worth accomplishing. Although tedious and often predictable, the Capricorn nature makes sure the job is done – and done well.

# December 22nd Tuesday
**Moon in Pisces –** *No Exact Aspects*

*Mood Watch*: The waxing Pisces Moon is a fabulous time to get artistic, intuitive, romantic, poetic, imaginative, and to enjoy the brazen creativity of music and the arts. There are no exact aspects impeding on the purity of this spirit, and although this will not prevent us from experiencing the usual ups and downs, we are more likely to feel the acceptance of whatever comes along a great deal more easily than if there were a bunch of specific lunar aspect influences. The Christmas holiday, and all the holidays surrounding it, embodies this kind of mood-setting. Sooner or later, even those who are in denial are swept up by the illuminating lights and festive mood of the Christmas season. If there is ever a time to give in and go with the flow, the waxing Pisces Moon is that time. There is very little to stand in the way of this celebratory candor. This is an excellent time to tap into your creative resources and to create the festive mood of your desire.

# December 23rd Wednesday
| Moon in Pisces | PST | EST |
|---|---|---|
| Moon  sextile Mercury | 10:04 AM | 1:04 PM |
| Moon  conjunct Uranus | 1:42 PM | 4:42 PM |
| Venus conjunct Pluto begins  (see December 27) | | |

*Mood Watch*: The lunar aspects suggest an outgoing spirit. Our minds will be full and communicative this morning/afternoon with Moon sextile Mercury. Later in the day/early evening, Moon conjunct Uranus will have us feeling a little crazy.

258

Okay, *a lot* crazy. This is to be expected anyway, given the time of year. Fortunately, there is a certain degree of acceptance and nebulous approval of everything going on around us; this commonly occurs during the course of the waxing Pisces Moon. Sun in Capricorn and Moon in Pisces brings productivity and whimsical creativity. Everything seems to move at an alarming pace. Today, we can intuit our way through this industrial, yet abstract atmosphere. Bubbly, talkative moods lead to cheerful artistry.

# December 24ᵗʰ Thursday

**FIRST QUARTER MOON in ARIES / Christmas Eve**

| Moon in Pisces / Aries | PST | EST |
|---|---|---|
| Moon  square Venus goes v/c | 12:08 AM | 3:08 AM |
| Moon  enters Aries | 3:39 AM | 6:39 AM |
| Sun  conjunct Pluto | 9:31 AM | 12:31 PM |
| Moon  square Pluto | 9:34 AM | 12:34 PM |
| Moon  square Sun | 9:34 AM | 12:34 PM |
| Moon  opposite Saturn | 12:00 PM | 3:00 PM |
| Venus square Saturn begins  (see December 28) | | |

*Mood Watch*: This Christmas Eve brings the **First Quarter Moon in Aries** (Moon square Sun). Waxing Aries Moon energizes our moods, and inspires an upbeat, outgoing, and forward manner. Aries Moon is a superb time to get in tune with your own personal levels of energy, strength, and vitality. The First Quarter Moon is a good time to apply diligence and inspired ability to your work. Aries Moon brings on an expression of courageous vigor, as well as a sense of bold adventure. As a general rule, moods are marked by confidence and sometimes by cantankerous forcefulness and the drive to make a lasting impression. Santa Claus is coming. Do you believe? In the eighteenth century his name appeared in the American press as "St. A Clause," but we got to know the fully Americanized version of this northern dwelling Dutch-American elf by his name, "Saint Nick" in the classic 1823 poem, "The Night Before Christmas" by Clement Clarke Moore.

**Sun conjunct Pluto** (occurring Dec. 18 – 27) The Sun is conjunct with Pluto in the sign of Capricorn. Pluto, a.k.a. God of the Underworld, entered the Saturn ruled sign, Capricorn in January, 2008. Pluto represents transformation – in particular, those ways in which the generations of humankind affect change and make their mark. Pluto in Sagittarius (1995/96 – 2008) has been the eye opener of global awareness. This occurrence of Sun conjunct Pluto strongly affects late born Sagittarians and early born Capricorns – most specifically, those who are celebrating birthdays December 18 – 27. These Sagittarius/Capricorn birthday folks will experience challenges of mind-altering proportions. Sun conjunct Pluto affects the core of the personality and diminishes those parts of the self which are weak and no longer viable. Pluto's energy melds with the personality to bring out the strongest points of one's character, the very best that one can muster. Pluto removes all impurities by transforming the old self through unpredictable trials. Take this opportunity to make some personal breakthroughs, birthday folks, and find your power! Learn to harness your power willingly and responsibly while great transformation is occurring in your life. Give in but don't give up.

259

# December 25th Friday

## Christmas

| Moon in Aries | PST | EST | |
|---|---|---|---|
| Venus enters Capricorn | 10:17 AM | 1:17 PM | |
| Sun square Saturn | 3:57 PM | 6:57 PM | |
| Moon trine Mars | 5:00 PM | 8:00 PM | |
| Moon square Mercury | 9:14 PM | 12:14 AM | (December 26) |

*Mood Watch*: The waxing Aries Christmas Moon does not lend itself to an attitude of patience. Oh no, today there will be headfirst charging into gift unwrapping, festive events and playfulness. For some, however, rudeness will get them down – and perhaps gluttony, selfishness, and inconsiderate attitudes will hurt them, too. It's Christmas! Does this not bring out the kid in everyone? Let's face it – we're spoiled here in North America! We want *everything!* Nevertheless, it is always wise to show some appreciation and gratitude, especially on Christmas. Do your part, and have a good time. Remember always: Peace on Earth, Goodwill to Humankind. Meanwhile, perhaps you've noticed that uncertainty or confusion is beginning to set in? People are starting to stop mid-sentence, uncertain of how to proceed accurately with their thought form. That's not just the holiday fervor at work; that's the stationary condition of Mercury, about to begin its retrograde cycle for the fourth time this year (see tomorrow – Mercury retrograde).

**Venus enters Capricorn** (Venus in Capricorn: Dec. 25, 2009 – Jan. 18, 2010) Now Venus will be grounded in the stoic and serious focuses of Capricorn. Venus in Capricorn brings out an attraction for the staunch and ardent duty of accomplishing goals as well as a love of predictability. This type of expression creates stable ground for the development of relationships, and the general course of affections will be oriented towards making impressions, with a hard and ambitious drive towards providing well for loved ones. This is the time when the general populace is attracted to getting in shape. Venus in Capricorn will certainly bring out a more serious approach to love matters in general, especially while it is conjunct with Pluto (see Dec. 27). While being so serious, it may also be difficult to execute love matters smoothly since Venus is square to Saturn (see Dec. 28). It is important to have respect and maturity in matters of love if we are to be taken seriously by loved ones while Venus is in Capricorn.

**Sun square Saturn** (occurring Dec. 19 – 28) This occurrence of Sun in Capricorn (at the Sagittarius cusp of Capricorn) square Saturn in Libra especially affects Sagittarians and Capricorn who are celebrating birthdays December 19 – 28. These folks may experience personal challenges of impatience, loss of control, a poor sense of timing, or difficulty identifying with current obligations. The challenge is to overcome obstacles that intrude on one's discipline and accuracy. This may be a time of sacrifice, loss or compromise, and may also be a time of complexity and insecurity for these birthday folks. Saturn represents those things in life we are willing to work for and maintain. It also represents our sense of discipline and our application of effort and focus, and helps us learn about our limitations and where our strengths can be realized. This is a good time for Sagittarius and Capricorn birthday folks to conserve energies and take losses and difficulties in stride. Through the tests of this time, a stronger human being emerges to take on future tests with greater confidence and ability. Avoiding responsibilities or hard-ships now will only make life more difficult later. Back when Saturn was in Virgo, this aspect last occurred May 20 – June 8, reaching its peak on June 5, affecting the Gemini birthday people of that time. Now that Saturn is newly in Libra (since October 29), the Saturn square aspect will be affecting the natal sun signs of Cancer and Capricorn people until Saturn enters Scorpio in early October 2012.

# December 26ᵗʰ Saturday

**Boxing Day**

| Moon in Aries / Taurus | PST | EST | |
|---|---|---|---|
| Moon sextile Neptune | 2:10 AM | 5:10 AM | |
| Moon sextile Jupiter goes v/c | 3:43 AM | 6:43 AM | |
| Mercury goes retrograde | 6:39 AM | 9:39 AM | |
| Moon enters Taurus | 12:24 PM | 3:24 PM | |
| Moon trine Venus | 3:11 PM | 6:11 PM | |
| Moon trine Pluto | 6:07 PM | 9:07 PM | |
| Moon trine Sun | 10:37 PM | 1:37 AM | (December 27) |

*Mood Watch*: The post holiday world of travel will be downright frustrating today, especially during the morning. Early this morning, the Aries Moon goes void-of-course. People may seem impatient, headstrong, irritable, and overly aggressive at times. To make matters even more intolerable, Mercury goes retrograde (see below) and there may be a tendency for misinformation to botch up certain plans – or the lack of plans. It isn't until this afternoon that the Moon enters Taurus and by then we may be heavily preoccupied by the material world and the expenses of life. Taurus Moon puts us in touch with the need to find a good deal, a stable environment, and pleasurable and uplifting comforts. In the p.m. hours, the Moon will be trine with Venus, Pluto and, much later, the Sun. Despite everything, this succession of trine aspects brings a jovial and upbeat spirit. The Moon is exalted in Taurus and this is a good time to seek and find pleasure, wherever possible.

This is **Boxing Day**. Shopping on the day after Christmas is what Boxing Day represents to most of modern North America. Boxing Day is actually a British tra-dition. The custom represents this time after Christmas when extra gifts are boxed up and traditionally given to household employees and other service workers. Some relentless shoppers think of it as the time to box up those inappropriate gifts and take them back to the stores for exchanges. Other folks may use this time to share their extra gifts with friends and extended families.

**Mercury goes retrograde** (Mercury retrograde Dec. 26, 2009 – Jan. 14, 2010) Retrograde cycles of Mercury occur three times a year. Next year's three cycles begin early – in fact, one of them begins today. That makes this the *fourth* time this year that Mercury begins a retrograde cycle. Mercury will be retrograde in the sign of Capricorn for the next few weeks, until January 14, 2010. Mercury retrograde in the cardinal earth sign, Capricorn, is likely to bring a number of communication mishaps over building contracts, corporate mergers, and in matters with regard to authority and control – sound familiar? This is similar to the way we began this year with Mercury retrograde through Aquarius and Capricorn (Jan. 11 – Feb. 1).

261

Kicking off the New Year may seem confusing and tedious with Mercury retrograde in Capricorn, especially if it involves taking orders from a new boss. This is a good time to attempt communications more than once or twice, and to be persistent as well as patient. At first it may be difficult to sit through everyone's excuses and misinformation, but eventually there will be a logical explanation to Mercury related setbacks. For more information on Mercury retrograde, see the section in the introduction about *Mercury retrograde periods.*

# December 27ᵗʰ Sunday

## Moon in Taurus

| | PST | EST | |
|---|---|---|---|
| Moon square Mars | 10:48 PM | 1:48 AM | (December 28) |
| Venus conjunct Pluto | 10:49 PM | 1:49 AM | (December 28) |

*Mood Watch*: The Moon in Taurus is strongly waxing and it brings a firm desire for satisfaction, reassurance, and sensual pleasures. On a more mundane level, people will be pursuing material fulfillment, the security of money, and a stable environment to temper the holiday madness. This is a good time to relax and find comfort. People will tend to work at a kicked-back pace. Those who weren't satisfied with their gifts are likely to be out searching for the things they wanted but didn't receive this past Christmas. This is a time when the material world is commonly reassessed and put into some kind of workable order to suit personal needs.

**Venus conjunct Pluto** (occurring Dec. 23 – 30) This conjunction often places affections and love right where they are needed most: the areas of life that are deeply challenging and sometimes traumatic. It also intensifies love related efforts and, at times, our affections may seem overpowering or daunting in some way. Venus represents love and beauty, while Pluto (in Greek myth) represents the god of the underworld, who lured the goddess of love, Persephone, away from heaven with the rich scent of a narcissus flower. This single act of peculiar passion lead the youthful goddess into a fateful entanglement that would later force her to descend into the depths of Earth every autumn to join the underworld god until spring season. She represents the life of spring and summer, and when she is absent, planet Earth remains barren or dormant during autumn and winter. Venus (Persephone) conjunct Pluto (Hades) represents the union of beauty and strength. In the end, there is always a rich price to pay for the pursuit of passion, but true love and beauty are everlasting. This is a time when the intensity or hardship of love and attraction create richly striking images and perspectives of which we must eventually let go completely in the hope that love and beauty will transform our lives once again. Love and beauty are far richer experiences when they are met by the transformation demanded by Plutonian tests. Pluto brings loss through illness, death, and decay. Venus brings love that is renewed through all hardships, even loneliness. This is a time of deep confessions and secrets revealed. One of the powers of love is that we can always find it, even when we are alone, or in a barren or dormant state of being. Venus conjunct Pluto is occurring in Capricorn. This emphasizes the sobering awareness that is taking place with regard to the transformation process of love and attraction. This is a good time to find love's powers and unite them within.

# December 28ᵗʰ Monday

**Moon in Taurus / Gemini**

| | PST | EST | |
|---|---|---|---|
| Moon trine Mercury | 2:35 AM | 5:35 AM | |
| Moon sextile Uranus | 5:15 AM | 8:15 AM | |
| Moon square Neptune | 7:47 AM | 10:47 AM | |
| Moon square Jupiter goes v/c | 9:52 AM | 12:52 PM | |
| Moon enters Gemini | 5:13 PM | 8:13 PM | |
| Venus square Saturn | 10:54 PM | 1:54 AM | (December 29) |

*Mood Watch*: This Monday starts off comfortably with the waxing Taurus Moon. By late morning/mid-afternoon, the Moon goes void-of-course, and many people will be feeling the pangs of laziness or stubbornness, and they may feel generally overwhelmed by the massive material mayhem that was left behind after the Christmas holiday. This evening, the traffic may be somewhat trying. By the time the Moon enters Gemini, talkative moods are likely to occur. Now that Mercury is retrograde, there seems to be a lot of detail that needs to be sorted out. The strongly waxing Gemini Moon keeps us busily thinking about all kinds of things.

**Venus square Saturn** (occurring Dec. 24 – 31) This aspect creates obstacles and restrictions concerning the timely expression of love. Venus in Capricorn is square to Saturn in Libra. It may be difficult to engage in romance, particularly when restrictions play too strong a part in holding together relationships. It might seem that repeated security measures are always getting in the way of basic pleasures. Venus square Saturn sometimes creates blocks in the flow of care and love due to external responsibilities and restrictions that create separation. Sometimes people are distracted from properly providing care and concern where it is most needed due to the high demands of the world at large. While this aspect is occurring, it is wisest to work a little harder for the things that attract us, and at love related matters. This aspect last occurred July 15 – 24, and it reached its peak on July 21 with Venus in Gemini and Saturn in Virgo.

# December 29ᵗʰ Tuesday

**Moon in Gemini**

| | PST | EST |
|---|---|---|
| Moon trine Saturn | 12:42 AM | 3:42 AM |

*Mood Watch*: Versatility is the name of the game during this strongly waxing Gemini Moon. Overnight, the only aspect for today, Moon trine Saturn, puts us in a positive light and teaches us (probably through dreams at this late hour) how to pace ourselves and make some progress through the pending transition of the New Year. People usually tend to slow down in the final days of December, especially after the bulk of the holiday madness passes. Nevertheless, the Gemini Moon keeps our minds very busy. Today people will be making connections and correcting communication errors, especially while Mercury is newly retrograde (Dec. 26, 2009 – Jan. 14, 2010). Additionally, people will be prone to create misinformation – especially those among us who may be considered a great deal more pretentious – or naïve – by nature. In general, the Gemini Moon keeps us talkative and inquisitive as it waxes brightly towards fullness. It's a good time to enjoy the company of others, especially those folks who are interesting to be around and are full of entertaining information.

# December 30ᵗʰ Wednesday
*Full Moon Eve*

| Moon in Gemini / Cancer | PST | EST |
|---|---|---|
| Moon sextile Mars | 12:56 AM | 3:56 AM |
| Moon square Uranus | 7:29 AM | 10:29 AM |
| Moon trine Neptune | 9:54 AM | 12:54 PM |
| Moon trine Jupiter goes v/c | 12:28 PM | 3:28 PM |
| Moon enters Cancer | 6:44 PM | 9:44 PM |

*Mood Watch*: The Gemini Moon captures our imaginative and inquisitive thoughts throughout the day. The morning activities may seem chaotic or unusual while the Moon is square to Uranus. Later in the morning/afternoon, Moon trine Neptune tempers our moods with calmness, and there may seem to be a stronger need to seek tranquility. In the afternoon the heavily waxing Gemini Moon goes void-of-course; at this point, it will be wise to avoid getting caught up in conversations that have the potential to turn into heated arguments. People may tend to say things that they'll regret, especially while the Moon is so full and void in Gemini at the same time Mercury is retrograde. Gemini is ruled by Mercury, but when the odds of smooth communications are stacked against the nearly full Gemini Moon atmosphere, misinformation and deception are extremely common pitfalls. Later, as the Moon enters Cancer, deep feelings of compassion, desire, or perhaps – loneliness, may lead some people to seek some motherly advice. Many folks will feel that the need for care and nurturing is essential. We are now on the brink of a particularly unusual set of circumstances with the pending Full Moon (see tomorrow) and this is a good time to apply love and care in the places where they're needed most.

# December 31ˢᵗ Thursday
**FULL MOON in CANCER – Blue Moon – Partial Lunar Eclipse**

| Moon in Cancer | PST | EST |
|---|---|---|
| Moon opposite Pluto | 12:02 AM | 3:02 AM |
| Moon square Saturn | 1:58 AM | 4:58 AM |
| Moon opposite Venus | 6:34 AM | 9:34 AM |
| Moon opposite Sun | 11:12 AM | 2:12 PM |

*Mood Watch*: Today's Full Moon will be phenomenal. It is a Blue Moon, which is characterized by the rare event of being the second Full Moon that occurs within one calendar month – hence the term, "once in a Blue Moon." The term Blue Moon has taken on many meanings over the years and is often used incorrectly. Historical documents first showed the term used in the 1600s. The definition then was that when a *season* (the period between Solstices and Equinoxes, or Equinoxes and Solstices) had four full Moons, rather than the usual three, the fourth Full Moon was a "Blue Moon." That phenomenon is very rare. During the 1900s, two scientific articles misinterpreted the definition with the second article even misrepresenting the information in the first article. Then in 1980, in an attempt to explain this phenomenon, a popular radio show incorrectly cited the aforementioned articles, and got the idea even more wrong. This further distorted its meaning. So what exactly is a **"Blue Moon?"** After having the incorrect definitions repeated so often in the media, the commonly used definition today for a "Blue Moon" phenomenon is that when there are two Full Moons in a calendar month, the second Full Moon is a Blue Moon. This is a far cry from the original 17th century description. However, the term can also be referenced to describe a sad emotion, an event that rarely happens or, for some people, an event that never happens at all. Today also brings a Partial Lunar Ecliptic Moon, making this an especially rare occasion to have both of these infrequent events (Blue Moon and Lunar Eclipse) occur at the same time. To boot, it's the **Full Cancer Moon** (Moon opposite Sun) – Cancer being the sign the Moon rules and where it is naturally at home. Classically, emotions run especially high around this Moon; for more details on the Full Moon in Cancer, see January 10, when it last occurred.

**Partial Lunar Eclipse** – A lunar eclipse occurs when the Earth moves between the moon and the sun, blocking the light that reflects off the moon's surface back to Earth. Every year there are at least two lunar eclipses, this year there are four. Obviously, today brings the last of the four lunar eclipses. The other three lunar eclipses were penumbral lunar eclipses, which occurred on February 9, July 7, and August 5. Today's final eclipse is a partial lunar eclipse. Some view the shadowy affect on the moon as a dark time; this is mere superstition to some folks, while others may base this belief on their personal experiences. Needless to say, this is a good time to apply a great deal of caution during the festivities of the Ecliptic Blue Cancer Moon of New Year's Eve.

Cheers to All! Bright Blessings, And Happy New Year!

## Ephemeris 2009 Noon GMT
## Longitudes based on Greenwich Mean Time (GMT) at Noon

**JANUARY 2009**

| Date | ☉ | ☽ | ☿ | ♀ | ♂ | ♃ | ♄ | ♅ | ♆ | ♇ |
|---|---|---|---|---|---|---|---|---|---|---|
| 1 | 11♑13 | 05 55 | 00♒07 | 27♒48 | 03♑54 | 29♑03 | 21♍44 | 19♓15 | 22♒27 | 01♑16 |
| 2 | 12 14 | 18♓24 | 01 21 | 28 53 | 04 39 | 29 16 | 21 44 | 19 17 | 22 29 | 01 18 |
| 3 | 13 15 | 01♈10 | 02 30 | 29 58 | 05 24 | 29 30 | 21♍44R | 19 19 | 22 31 | 01 21 |
| 4 | 14 16 | 14 18 | 03 35 | 01♓03 | 06 09 | 29 44 | 21 44 | 19 20 | 22 33 | 01 23 |
| 5 | 15 17 | 27 50 | 04 34 | 02 08 | 06 54 | 29 58 | 21 43 | 19 22 | 22 35 | 01 25 |
| 6 | 16 18 | 11♉49 | 05 27 | 03 12 | 07 40 | 00♒12 | 21 42 | 19 24 | 22 37 | 01 27 |
| 7 | 17 20 | 26 13 | 06 13 | 04 16 | 08 25 | 00 26 | 21 42 | 19 26 | 22 39 | 01 29 |
| 8 | 18 21 | 11 00 | 06 50 | 05 20 | 09 11 | 00 40 | 21 41 | 19 28 | 22 41 | 01 31 |
| 9 | 19 22 | 26 04 | 07 19 | 06 23 | 09 57 | 00 54 | 21 40 | 19 30 | 22 43 | 01 33 |
| 10 | 20 23 | 11♋16 | 07 37 | 07 26 | 10 43 | 01 08 | 21 39 | 19 32 | 22 45 | 01 35 |
| 11 | 21 24 | 26 26 | 07 45 | 08 29 | 11 28 | 01 22 | 21 38 | 19 35 | 22 47 | 01 38 |
| 12 | 22 25 | 11♌25 | 07♒41R | 09 31 | 12 14 | 01 36 | 21 37 | 19 37 | 22 49 | 01 40 |
| 13 | 23 26 | 26 04 | 07 26 | 10 33 | 13 00 | 01 50 | 21 35 | 19 39 | 22 51 | 01 42 |
| 14 | 24 27 | 10♍19 | 06 59 | 11 35 | 13 45 | 02 04 | 21 34 | 19 41 | 22 53 | 01 44 |
| 15 | 25 28 | 24 07 | 06 20 | 12 36 | 14 31 | 02 19 | 21 33 | 19 43 | 22 55 | 01 46 |
| 16 | 26 30 | 07♎27 | 05 31 | 13 36 | 15 16 | 02 33 | 21 31 | 19 46 | 22 57 | 01 48 |
| 17 | 27 31 | 20 22 | 04 32 | 14 37 | 16 02 | 02 47 | 21 29 | 19 48 | 22 59 | 01 50 |
| 18 | 28 32 | 02 56 | 03 25 | 15 36 | 16 48 | 03 01 | 21 27 | 19 51 | 23 01 | 01 52 |
| 19 | 29 33 | 15 12 | 02 13 | 16 36 | 17 33 | 03 15 | 21 25 | 19 53 | 23 03 | 01 54 |
| 20 | 00♒34 | 27 16 | 00 56 | 17 35 | 18 19 | 03 29 | 21 23 | 19 55 | 23 05 | 01 56 |
| 21 | 01 35 | 09♐10 | 29♑39 | 18 33 | 19 05 | 03 44 | 21 21 | 19 58 | 23 07 | 01 58 |
| 22 | 02 36 | 21 00 | 28 22 | 19 31 | 19 52 | 03 58 | 21 19 | 20 01 | 23 10 | 02 00 |
| 23 | 03 37 | 02♑48 | 27 09 | 20 28 | 20 38 | 04 12 | 21 17 | 20 03 | 23 12 | 02 02 |
| 24 | 04 38 | 14 38 | 26 01 | 21 25 | 21 24 | 04 26 | 21 14 | 20 06 | 23 14 | 02 04 |
| 25 | 05 39 | 26 32 | 24 59 | 22 21 | 22 10 | 04 40 | 21 12 | 20 08 | 23 16 | 02 06 |
| 26 | 06 40 | 08♒33 | 24 06 | 23 17 | 22 57 | 04 55 | 21 09 | 20 11 | 23 18 | 02 08 |
| 27 | 07 41 | 20 41 | 23 20 | 24 12 | 23 43 | 05 09 | 21 06 | 20 14 | 23 21 | 02 09 |
| 28 | 08 42 | 02♓59 | 22 44 | 25 06 | 24 29 | 05 23 | 21 03 | 20 17 | 23 23 | 02 11 |
| 29 | 09 43 | 15 28 | 22 16 | 26 00 | 25 15 | 05 37 | 21 01 | 20 19 | 23 25 | 02 13 |
| 30 | 10 44 | 28 11 | 21 57 | 26 53 | 26 01 | 05 51 | 20 58 | 20 22 | 23 27 | 02 15 |
| 31 | 11 45 | 11♈07 | 21 47 | 27 45 | 26 47 | 06 06 | 20 54 | 20 25 | 23 29 | 02 17 |

**FEBRUARY 2009**

| Date | ☉ | ☽ | ☿ | ♀ | ♂ | ♃ | ♄ | ♅ | ♆ | ♇ |
|---|---|---|---|---|---|---|---|---|---|---|
| 1 | 12♒46 | 24♈20 | 21♑45D | 28♓37 | 27♑33 | 06♒20 | 20♍51 | 20♓28 | 23♒32 | 02♑19 |
| 2 | 13 47 | 07♉50 | 21 50 | 29 27 | 28 19 | 06 34 | 20 48 | 20 31 | 23 34 | 02 20 |
| 3 | 14 48 | 21 39 | 22 02 | 00♈17 | 29 05 | 06 48 | 20 45 | 20 34 | 23 36 | 02 22 |
| 4 | 15 49 | 05♊47 | 22 21 | 01 06 | 29 52 | 07 02 | 20 41 | 20 37 | 23 38 | 02 24 |
| 5 | 16 49 | 20 12 | 22 46 | 01 54 | 00♒38 | 07 16 | 20 38 | 20 40 | 23 41 | 02 25 |
| 6 | 17 50 | 04♋51 | 23 16 | 02 42 | 01 25 | 07 30 | 20 34 | 20 43 | 23 43 | 02 27 |
| 7 | 18 51 | 19 39 | 23 52 | 03 28 | 02 11 | 07 45 | 20 31 | 20 46 | 23 45 | 02 29 |
| 8 | 19 52 | 04♌30 | 24 32 | 04 13 | 02 58 | 07 59 | 20 27 | 20 49 | 23 48 | 02 30 |
| 9 | 20 52 | 19 16 | 25 16 | 04 58 | 03 45 | 08 13 | 20 23 | 20 52 | 23 50 | 02 32 |
| 10 | 21 53 | 03♍50 | 26 05 | 05 41 | 04 32 | 08 27 | 20 19 | 20 55 | 23 52 | 02 34 |
| 11 | 22 54 | 18 06 | 26 56 | 06 23 | 05 18 | 08 41 | 20 16 | 20 58 | 23 54 | 02 35 |
| 12 | 23 55 | 01♎58 | 27 52 | 07 04 | 06 05 | 08 55 | 20 12 | 21 01 | 23 57 | 02 37 |
| 13 | 24 55 | 15 26 | 28 50 | 07 44 | 06 51 | 09 09 | 20 08 | 21 04 | 23 59 | 02 38 |
| 14 | 25 56 | 28 29 | 29 51 | 08 22 | 07 38 | 09 23 | 20 03 | 21 07 | 24 01 | 02 40 |
| 15 | 26 56 | 11♏09 | 00♒54 | 08 59 | 08 24 | 09 36 | 19 59 | 21 11 | 24 04 | 02 41 |
| 16 | 27 57 | 23 29 | 02 00 | 09 35 | 09 11 | 09 50 | 19 55 | 21 14 | 24 06 | 02 43 |
| 17 | 28 58 | 05♐34 | 03 08 | 10 10 | 09 57 | 10 04 | 19 51 | 21 17 | 24 08 | 02 44 |
| 18 | 29 58 | 17 29 | 04 18 | 10 43 | 10 44 | 10 18 | 19 47 | 21 20 | 24 10 | 02 45 |
| 19 | 00♓59 | 29 18 | 05 30 | 11 15 | 11 30 | 10 32 | 19 42 | 21 23 | 24 13 | 02 47 |
| 20 | 01 59 | 11♑07 | 06 43 | 11 45 | 12 17 | 10 46 | 19 38 | 21 27 | 24 15 | 02 48 |
| 21 | 03 00 | 22 59 | 07 59 | 12 13 | 13 04 | 10 59 | 19 33 | 21 30 | 24 17 | 02 50 |

**FEBRUARY 2009 (Cont'd)**

| Date | ☉ | ☽ | ☿ | ♀ | ♂ | ♃ | ♄ | ♅ | ♆ | ♇ |
|---|---|---|---|---|---|---|---|---|---|---|
| 22 | 04♓00 | 04♒58 | 09♒16 | 12♈40 | 13♒51 | 11♒13 | 19♍29 | 21♓33 | 24♒19 | 02♑51 |
| 23 | 05 00 | 17 07 | 10 34 | 13 05 | 14 38 | 11 27 | 19 24 | 21 37 | 24 22 | 02 52 |
| 24 | 06 01 | 29 29 | 11 54 | 13 28 | 15 25 | 11 40 | 19 20 | 21 40 | 24 24 | 02 53 |
| 25 | 07 01 | 12♓05 | 13 16 | 13 49 | 16 12 | 11 54 | 19 15 | 21 43 | 24 26 | 02 54 |
| 26 | 08 02 | 24 55 | 14 39 | 14 09 | 16 59 | 12 07 | 19 11 | 21 47 | 24 28 | 02 56 |
| 27 | 09 02 | 07♈59 | 16 03 | 14 26 | 17 46 | 12 21 | 19 06 | 21 50 | 24 31 | 02 57 |
| 28 | 10 02 | 21 16 | 17 28 | 14 42 | 18 33 | 12 34 | 19 01 | 21 53 | 24 33 | 02 58 |

**MARCH 2009**

| Date | ☉ | ☽ | ☿ | ♀ | ♂ | ♃ | ♄ | ♅ | ♆ | ♇ |
|---|---|---|---|---|---|---|---|---|---|---|
| 1 | 11♓02 | 04♉46 | 18♒54 | 14♈55 | 19♒20 | 12♒48 | 18♍57 | 21♓57 | 24♒35 | 02♑59 |
| 2 | 12 03 | 18 28 | 20 22 | 15 06 | 20 06 | 13 01 | 18 52 | 22 00 | 24 37 | 03 00 |
| 3 | 13 03 | 02♊20 | 21 51 | 15 15 | 20 53 | 13 14 | 18 47 | 22 04 | 24 39 | 03 01 |
| 4 | 14 03 | 16 22 | 23 21 | 15 21 | 21 40 | 13 27 | 18 43 | 22 07 | 24 42 | 03 02 |
| 5 | 15 03 | 00♋31 | 24 52 | 15 26 | 22 27 | 13 41 | 18 38 | 22 10 | 24 44 | 03 03 |
| 6 | 16 03 | 14 48 | 26 25 | 15 27 | 23 14 | 13 54 | 18 33 | 22 14 | 24 46 | 03 04 |
| 7 | 17 03 | 29 09 | 27 58 | 15♈27R | 24 01 | 14 07 | 18 28 | 22 17 | 24 48 | 03 05 |
| 8 | 18 03 | 13♌32 | 29 33 | 15 24 | 24 48 | 14 20 | 18 24 | 22 21 | 24 50 | 03 06 |
| 9 | 19 03 | 27 53 | 01♓09 | 15 18 | 25 35 | 14 33 | 18 19 | 22 24 | 24 52 | 03 07 |
| 10 | 20 03 | 12♍05 | 02 45 | 15 10 | 26 22 | 14 46 | 18 14 | 22 28 | 24 54 | 03 07 |
| 11 | 21 03 | 26 06 | 04 24 | 14 59 | 27 09 | 14 59 | 18 09 | 22 31 | 24 57 | 03 08 |
| 12 | 22 03 | 09♎50 | 06 03 | 14 46 | 27 57 | 15 11 | 18 05 | 22 34 | 24 59 | 03 09 |
| 13 | 23 03 | 23 14 | 07 43 | 14 30 | 28 44 | 15 24 | 18 00 | 22 38 | 25 01 | 03 10 |
| 14 | 24 02 | 06♏17 | 09 25 | 14 12 | 29 31 | 15 37 | 17 55 | 22 41 | 25 03 | 03 10 |
| 15 | 25 02 | 18 58 | 11 07 | 13 51 | 00♓18 | 15 49 | 17 50 | 22 45 | 25 05 | 03 11 |
| 16 | 26 02 | 01♐21 | 12 51 | 13 28 | 01 04 | 16 02 | 17 46 | 22 48 | 25 07 | 03 12 |
| 17 | 27 02 | 13 28 | 14 36 | 13 03 | 01 51 | 16 14 | 17 41 | 22 52 | 25 09 | 03 12 |
| 18 | 28 01 | 25 24 | 16 23 | 12 36 | 02 38 | 16 27 | 17 36 | 22 55 | 25 11 | 03 13 |
| 19 | 29 01 | 07♑14 | 18 10 | 12 07 | 03 25 | 16 39 | 17 32 | 22 58 | 25 13 | 03 13 |
| 20 | 00♈01 | 19 03 | 19 59 | 11 36 | 04 11 | 16 51 | 17 27 | 23 02 | 25 15 | 03 14 |
| 21 | 01 00 | 00♒57 | 21 49 | 11 04 | 04 58 | 17 04 | 17 23 | 23 05 | 25 17 | 03 14 |
| 22 | 02 00 | 12 59 | 23 41 | 10 30 | 05 45 | 17 16 | 17 18 | 23 09 | 25 19 | 03 15 |
| 23 | 02 59 | 25 16 | 25 33 | 09 55 | 06 32 | 17 28 | 17 14 | 23 12 | 25 21 | 03 15 |
| 24 | 03 59 | 07♓49 | 27 27 | 09 19 | 07 20 | 17 40 | 17 09 | 23 15 | 25 23 | 03 16 |
| 25 | 04 58 | 20 40 | 29 22 | 08 42 | 08 07 | 17 51 | 17 05 | 23 19 | 25 24 | 03 16 |
| 26 | 05 58 | 03♈51 | 01♈19 | 08 05 | 08 54 | 18 03 | 17 00 | 23 22 | 25 26 | 03 16 |
| 27 | 06 57 | 17 20 | 03 16 | 07 27 | 09 41 | 18 15 | 16 56 | 23 26 | 25 28 | 03 17 |
| 28 | 07 57 | 01♉04 | 05 15 | 06 49 | 10 28 | 18 26 | 16 52 | 23 29 | 25 30 | 03 17 |
| 29 | 08 56 | 15 00 | 07 15 | 06 12 | 11 15 | 18 38 | 16 47 | 23 32 | 25 32 | 03 17 |
| 30 | 09 55 | 29 04 | 09 16 | 05 35 | 12 02 | 18 49 | 16 43 | 23 36 | 25 33 | 03 17 |
| 31 | 10 55 | 13♊12 | 11 17 | 04 58 | 12 49 | 19 01 | 16 39 | 23 39 | 25 35 | 03 17 |

**APRIL 2009**

| Date | ☉ | ☽ | ☿ | ♀ | ♂ | ♃ | ♄ | ♅ | ♆ | ♇ |
|---|---|---|---|---|---|---|---|---|---|---|
| 1 | 11♈54 | 27♊21 | 13♈20 | 04♈23 | 13♓35 | 19♒12 | 16♍35 | 23♓42 | 25♒37 | 03♑18 |
| 2 | 12 53 | 11♋29 | 15 23 | 03 48 | 14 22 | 19 23 | 16 31 | 23 46 | 25 39 | 03 18 |
| 3 | 13 52 | 25 35 | 17 27 | 03 15 | 15 09 | 19 34 | 16 27 | 23 49 | 25 40 | 03 18 |
| 4 | 14 51 | 09♌38 | 19 31 | 02 44 | 15 56 | 19 45 | 16 23 | 23 52 | 25 42 | 03♑18R |
| 5 | 15 50 | 23 36 | 21 36 | 02 14 | 16 42 | 19 56 | 16 19 | 23 55 | 25 44 | 03 18 |
| 6 | 16 49 | 07♍30 | 23 40 | 01 47 | 17 29 | 20 07 | 16 16 | 23 59 | 25 45 | 03 18 |
| 7 | 17 48 | 21 16 | 25 44 | 01 21 | 18 16 | 20 18 | 16 12 | 24 02 | 25 47 | 03 18 |
| 8 | 18 47 | 04♎52 | 27 47 | 00 57 | 19 03 | 20 28 | 16 08 | 24 05 | 25 48 | 03 17 |
| 9 | 19 46 | 18 16 | 29 49 | 00 36 | 19 50 | 20 39 | 16 05 | 24 08 | 25 50 | 03 17 |
| 10 | 20 45 | 01♏25 | 01♉49 | 00 17 | 20 38 | 20 49 | 16 01 | 24 11 | 25 51 | 03 17 |
| 11 | 21 44 | 14 18 | 03 48 | 00 00 | 21 24 | 20 59 | 15 58 | 24 14 | 25 53 | 03 17 |
| 12 | 22 43 | 26 53 | 05 45 | 29♓46 | 22 11 | 21 09 | 15 54 | 24 18 | 25 54 | 03 17 |

## APRIL 2009 (Cont'd)

| Date | ☉ | ☽ | ☿ | ♀ | ♂ | ♃ | ♄ | ♅ | ♆ | ♇ |
|------|------|------|------|------|------|------|------|------|------|------|
| 13 | 23♈42 | 09♐13 | 07♉39 | 29♓34 | 22♓58 | 21♒19 | 15♍51 | 24♓21 | 25♒56 | 03♑16 |
| 14 | 24 40 | 21 19 | 09 30 | 29 25 | 23 45 | 21 29 | 15 48 | 24 24 | 25 57 | 03 16 |
| 15 | 25 39 | 03♑14 | 11 19 | 29 18 | 24 31 | 21 39 | 15 45 | 24 27 | 25 59 | 03 16 |
| 16 | 26 38 | 15 04 | 13 04 | 29 14 | 25 17 | 21 49 | 15 42 | 24 30 | 26 00 | 03 16 |
| 17 | 27 36 | 26 53 | 14 45 | 29 12 | 26 04 | 21 58 | 15 39 | 24 33 | 26 01 | 03 15 |
| 18 | 28 35 | 08♒46 | 16 22 | 29♓12D | 26 50 | 22 08 | 15 36 | 24 36 | 26 03 | 03 15 |
| 19 | 29 34 | 20 50 | 17 55 | 29 15 | 27 37 | 22 17 | 15 33 | 24 39 | 26 04 | 03 14 |
| 20 | 00♉32 | 03♓09 | 19 24 | 29 20 | 28 23 | 22 26 | 15 31 | 24 42 | 26 05 | 03 14 |
| 21 | 01 31 | 15 48 | 20 49 | 29 28 | 29 10 | 22 36 | 15 28 | 24 45 | 26 06 | 03 13 |
| 22 | 02 29 | 28 49 | 22 08 | 29 37 | 29 56 | 22 45 | 15 26 | 24 48 | 26 07 | 03 13 |
| 23 | 03 28 | 12♈14 | 23 23 | 29 49 | 00♈43 | 22 53 | 15 23 | 24 50 | 26 09 | 03 12 |
| 24 | 04 26 | 26 03 | 24 33 | 00♈03 | 01 30 | 23 02 | 15 21 | 24 53 | 26 10 | 03 12 |
| 25 | 05 25 | 10♉11 | 25 38 | 00 19 | 02 16 | 23 11 | 15 19 | 24 56 | 26 11 | 03 11 |
| 26 | 06 23 | 24 33 | 26 38 | 00 36 | 03 03 | 23 19 | 15 17 | 24 59 | 26 12 | 03 10 |
| 27 | 07 22 | 09♊03 | 27 32 | 00 56 | 03 49 | 23 28 | 15 15 | 25 02 | 26 13 | 03 10 |
| 28 | 08 20 | 23 35 | 28 22 | 01 17 | 04 36 | 23 36 | 15 13 | 25 04 | 26 14 | 03 09 |
| 29 | 09♉18 | 08♋02 | 29 06 | 01 41 | 05 22 | 23 44 | 15 11 | 25 07 | 26 15 | 03 08 |
| 30 | 10 17 | 22 22 | 29 45 | 02 05 | 06 08 | 23 52 | 15 09 | 25 10 | 26 16 | 03 08 |

## MAY 2009

| Date | ☉ | ☽ | ☿ | ♀ | ♂ | ♃ | ♄ | ♅ | ♆ | ♇ |
|------|------|------|------|------|------|------|------|------|------|------|
| 1 | 11♉15 | 06♌30 | 00♊18 | 02♈32 | 06♈54 | 23♒59 | 15♍07 | 25♓12 | 26♒17 | 03♑07 |
| 2 | 12 13 | 20 27 | 00 46 | 03 00 | 07 40 | 24 07 | 15 06 | 25 15 | 26 18 | 03 06 |
| 3 | 13 11 | 04♍13 | 03 00 | 03 30 | 08 26 | 24 15 | 15 05 | 25 18 | 26 18 | 03 05 |
| 4 | 14 10 | 17 48 | 01 25 | 04 01 | 09 12 | 24 22 | 15 03 | 25 20 | 26 19 | 03 04 |
| 5 | 15 08 | 01♎11 | 01 37 | 04 33 | 09 58 | 24 29 | 15 02 | 25 23 | 26 20 | 03 03 |
| 6 | 16 06 | 14 24 | 01 43 | 05 07 | 10 44 | 24 36 | 15 01 | 25 25 | 26 21 | 03 02 |
| 7 | 17 04 | 27 25 | 01♊44R | 05 42 | 11 30 | 24 43 | 15 00 | 25 27 | 26 21 | 03 02 |
| 8 | 18 02 | 10♏14 | 01 40 | 06 18 | 12 16 | 24 50 | 14 59 | 25 30 | 26 22 | 03 01 |
| 9 | 19 00 | 22 50 | 01 31 | 06 56 | 13 03 | 24 57 | 14 58 | 25 32 | 26 23 | 03 00 |
| 10 | 19 58 | 05♐14 | 01 18 | 07 34 | 13 49 | 25 03 | 14 57 | 25 35 | 26 23 | 02 59 |
| 11 | 20 56 | 17 25 | 01 00 | 08 14 | 14 35 | 25 09 | 14 57 | 25 37 | 26 24 | 02 58 |
| 12 | 21 54 | 29 26 | 00 38 | 08 55 | 15 21 | 25 15 | 14 56 | 25 39 | 26 25 | 02 57 |
| 13 | 22 52 | 11♑18 | 00 13 | 09 37 | 16 06 | 25 21 | 14 56 | 25 41 | 26 25 | 02 55 |
| 14 | 23 49 | 23 07 | 29♉45 | 10 20 | 16 52 | 25 27 | 14 55 | 25 44 | 26 26 | 02 54 |
| 15 | 24 47 | 04♒55 | 29 14 | 11 04 | 17 38 | 25 33 | 14 55 | 25 46 | 26 26 | 02 53 |
| 16 | 25 45 | 16 48 | 28 42 | 11 49 | 18 23 | 25 38 | 14 55 | 25 48 | 26 27 | 02 52 |
| 17 | 26 43 | 28 51 | 28 08 | 12 34 | 19 08 | 25 44 | 14 55 | 25 50 | 26 27 | 02 51 |
| 18 | 27 41 | 11♓09 | 27 33 | 13 21 | 19 54 | 25 49 | 14 55 | 25 52 | 26 27 | 02 50 |
| 19 | 28 39 | 23 48 | 26 58 | 14 08 | 20 39 | 25 54 | 14♍55D | 25 54 | 26 28 | 02 49 |
| 20 | 29 36 | 06♈51 | 26 23 | 14 56 | 21 24 | 25 59 | 14 56 | 25 56 | 26 28 | 02 47 |
| 21 | 00♊34 | 20 21 | 25 50 | 15 45 | 22 10 | 26 03 | 14 56 | 25 58 | 26 28 | 02 46 |
| 22 | 01 32 | 04♉19 | 25 18 | 16 35 | 22 55 | 26 08 | 14 57 | 26 00 | 26 28 | 02 45 |
| 23 | 02 29 | 18 40 | 24 48 | 17 25 | 23 41 | 26 12 | 14 57 | 26 01 | 26 29 | 02 44 |
| 24 | 03 27 | 03♊21 | 24 21 | 18 16 | 24 27 | 26 16 | 14 58 | 26 03 | 26 29 | 02 42 |
| 25 | 04 25 | 18 13 | 23 57 | 19 07 | 25 12 | 26 20 | 14 59 | 26 05 | 26 29 | 02 41 |
| 26 | 05 22 | 03♋08 | 23 36 | 19 59 | 25 58 | 26 24 | 15 00 | 26 07 | 26 29 | 02 40 |
| 27 | 06♊20 | 17 57 | 23 19 | 20 52 | 26 43 | 26 28 | 15 01 | 26 08 | 26 29 | 02 38 |
| 28 | 07 18 | 02♌35 | 23 06 | 21 45 | 27 28 | 26 31 | 15 02 | 26 10 | 26 29 | 02 37 |
| 29 | 08 15 | 16 56 | 22 57 | 22 39 | 28 13 | 26 35 | 15 03 | 26 11 | 26 29 | 02 36 |
| 30 | 09 13 | 00♍59 | 22 52 | 23 33 | 28 58 | 26 38 | 15 05 | 26 13 | 26 29 | 02 34 |
| 31 | 10 10 | 14 44 | 22♉52D | 24 28 | 29 42 | 26 41 | 15 06 | 26 14 | 26 29 | 02 33 |

## JUNE 2009

| Date | ☉ | ☽ | ☿ | ♀ | ♂ | ♃ | ♄ | ♅ | ♆ | ♇ |
|------|------|------|------|------|------|------|------|------|------|------|
| 1 | 11♊08 | 28♍11 | 22♉56 | 25♈24 | 00♉27 | 26♒43 | 15♍08 | 26♓16 | 26♒29 | 02♑32 |
| 2 | 12 05 | 11♎22 | 23 05 | 26 19 | 01 12 | 26 46 | 15 09 | 26 17 | 26♒29R | 02 30 |
| 3 | 13 03 | 24 18 | 23 18 | 27 16 | 01 56 | 26 48 | 15 11 | 26 19 | 26 29 | 02 29 |

## JUNE 2009 (Cont'd)

| Date | ☉ | ☽ | ☿ | ♀ | ♂ | ♃ | ♄ | ♅ | ♆ | ♇ |
|---|---|---|---|---|---|---|---|---|---|---|
| 4 | 14♊00 | 07♏00 | 23♉36 | 28♈12 | 02♉41 | 26♒50 | 15♍13 | 26♓20 | 26♒29 | 02♑27 |
| 5 | 14 58 | 19 31 | 23 58 | 29 10 | 03 26 | 26 52 | 15 15 | 26 21 | 26 28 | 02 26 |
| 6 | 15 55 | 01♐51 | 24 24 | 00♉07 | 04 10 | 26 54 | 15 17 | 26 22 | 26 28 | 02 24 |
| 7 | 16 52 | 14 00 | 24 55 | 01 05 | 04 55 | 26 56 | 15 19 | 26 24 | 26 28 | 02 23 |
| 8 | 17 50 | 26 02 | 25 30 | 02 04 | 05 40 | 26 57 | 15 21 | 26 25 | 26 27 | 02 21 |
| 9 | 18 47 | 07♑56 | 26 09 | 03 02 | 06 25 | 26 58 | 15 23 | 26 26 | 26 27 | 02 20 |
| 10 | 19 45 | 19 45 | 26 52 | 04 01 | 07 09 | 26 59 | 15 26 | 26 27 | 26 27 | 02 18 |
| 11 | 20 42 | 01♒32 | 27 39 | 05 01 | 07 54 | 27 00 | 15 28 | 26 28 | 26 26 | 02 17 |
| 12 | 21 39 | 13 21 | 28 30 | 06 01 | 08 38 | 27 01 | 15 31 | 26 29 | 26 26 | 02 15 |
| 13 | 22 37 | 25 14 | 29 24 | 07 01 | 09 22 | 27 01 | 15 34 | 26 30 | 26 25 | 02 14 |
| 14 | 23 34 | 07♓17 | 00♊23 | 08 01 | 10 06 | 27 01 | 15 37 | 26 30 | 26 25 | 02 12 |
| 15 | 24 31 | 19 35 | 01 25 | 09 02 | 10 50 | 27♒01R | 15 39 | 26 31 | 26 24 | 02 11 |
| 16 | 25 28 | 02♈12 | 02 30 | 10 03 | 11 34 | 27 01 | 15 42 | 26 32 | 26 24 | 02 09 |
| 17 | 26 26 | 15 13 | 03 39 | 11 05 | 12 18 | 27 01 | 15 45 | 26 33 | 26 23 | 02 08 |
| 18 | 27 23 | 28 40 | 04 52 | 12 06 | 13 01 | 27 01 | 15 49 | 26 33 | 26 23 | 02 06 |
| 19 | 28 20 | 12♉35 | 06 08 | 13 08 | 13 45 | 27 00 | 15 52 | 26 34 | 26 22 | 02 05 |
| 20 | 29 18 | 26 57 | 07 27 | 14 10 | 14 29 | 26 59 | 15 55 | 26 34 | 26 21 | 02 03 |
| 21 | 00♋15 | 11♊42 | 08 49 | 15 13 | 15 13 | 26 58 | 15 59 | 26 35 | 26 21 | 02 02 |
| 22 | 01 12 | 26 44 | 10 15 | 16 15 | 15 57 | 26 57 | 16 02 | 26 35 | 26 20 | 02 00 |
| 23 | 02 09 | 11♋52 | 11 44 | 17 18 | 16 41 | 26 55 | 16 06 | 26 36 | 26 19 | 01 58 |
| 24 | 03 07 | 26 58 | 13 17 | 18 22 | 17 24 | 26 53 | 16 09 | 26 36 | 26 18 | 01 57 |
| 25 | 04 04 | 11♌54 | 14 52 | 19 25 | 18 08 | 26 51 | 16 13 | 26 36 | 26 18 | 01 55 |
| 26 | 05 01 | 26 32 | 16 31 | 20 29 | 18 51 | 26 49 | 16 17 | 26 37 | 26 17 | 01 54 |
| 27 | 05 58 | 10♍48 | 18 13 | 21 32 | 19 35 | 26 47 | 16 21 | 26 37 | 26 16 | 01 52 |
| 28 | 06 56 | 24 40 | 19 57 | 22 36 | 20 18 | 26 45 | 16 25 | 26 37 | 26 15 | 01 51 |
| 29 | 07 53 | 08♎09 | 21 45 | 23 41 | 21 01 | 26 42 | 16 29 | 26 37 | 26 14 | 01 49 |
| 30 | 08 50 | 21 16 | 23 36 | 24 45 | 21 43 | 26 39 | 16 33 | 26 37 | 26 13 | 01 48 |

## JULY 2009

| Date | ☉ | ☽ | ☿ | ♀ | ♂ | ♃ | ♄ | ♅ | ♆ | ♇ |
|---|---|---|---|---|---|---|---|---|---|---|
| 1 | 09♋47 | 04♏04 | 25♊29 | 25♉50 | 22♉26 | 26♒36 | 16♍38 | 26♓37 | 26♒12 | 01♑46 |
| 2 | 10 44 | 16 36 | 27 25 | 26 54 | 23 09 | 26 33 | 16 42 | 26 37 | 26 11 | 01 45 |
| 3 | 11 42 | 28 54 | 29 24 | 27 59 | 23 52 | 26 30 | 16 46 | 26 37 | 26 10 | 01 43 |
| 4 | 12 39 | 11♐01 | 01♋25 | 29 05 | 24 34 | 26 26 | 16 51 | 26 37R | 26 09 | 01 42 |
| 5 | 13 36 | 23 00 | 03 28 | 00♊10 | 25 17 | 26 23 | 16 56 | 26 37 | 26 08 | 01 40 |
| 6 | 14 33 | 04♑53 | 05 32 | 01 16 | 26 00 | 26 19 | 17 00 | 26 37 | 26 07 | 01 39 |
| 7 | 15 30 | 16 42 | 07 38 | 02 21 | 26 43 | 26 15 | 17 05 | 26 36 | 26 06 | 01 37 |
| 8 | 16 28 | 28 30 | 09 46 | 03 27 | 27 26 | 26 11 | 17 10 | 26 36 | 26 05 | 01 36 |
| 9 | 17 25 | 10♒18 | 11 54 | 04 33 | 28 08 | 26 06 | 17 15 | 26 36 | 26 03 | 01 34 |
| 10 | 18 22 | 22 10 | 14 03 | 05 39 | 28 51 | 26 02 | 17 20 | 26 35 | 26 02 | 01 33 |
| 11 | 19 19 | 04♓09 | 16 13 | 06 46 | 29 33 | 25 57 | 17 25 | 26 35 | 26 01 | 01 31 |
| 12 | 20 16 | 16 16 | 18 22 | 07 52 | 00♊16 | 25 52 | 17 30 | 26 34 | 26 00 | 01 30 |
| 13 | 21 14 | 28 37 | 20 32 | 08 59 | 00 58 | 25 47 | 17 35 | 26 34 | 25 58 | 01 28 |
| 14 | 22 11 | 11♈15 | 22 41 | 10 06 | 01 40 | 25 42 | 17 40 | 26 33 | 25 57 | 01 27 |
| 15 | 23 08 | 24 13 | 24 49 | 11 13 | 02 22 | 25 37 | 17 45 | 26 33 | 25 56 | 01 26 |
| 16 | 24 05 | 07♉34 | 26 56 | 12 20 | 03 03 | 25 31 | 17 51 | 26 32 | 25 55 | 01 24 |
| 17 | 25 03 | 21 21 | 29 02 | 13 27 | 03 45 | 25 25 | 17 56 | 26 31 | 25 53 | 01 23 |
| 18 | 26 00 | 05♊34 | 01♌08 | 14 34 | 04 27 | 25 20 | 18 02 | 26 30 | 25 52 | 01 21 |
| 19 | 26 57 | 20 10 | 03 11 | 15 42 | 05 08 | 25 14 | 18 07 | 26 29 | 25 51 | 01 20 |
| 20 | 27 54 | 05♋06 | 05 14 | 16 50 | 05 50 | 25 08 | 18 13 | 26 29 | 25 49 | 01 19 |
| 21 | 28 52 | 20 13 | 07 15 | 17 57 | 06 32 | 25 02 | 18 18 | 26 28 | 25 48 | 01 17 |
| 22 | 29 49 | 05♌24 | 09 14 | 19 05 | 07 14 | 24 55 | 18 24 | 26 27 | 25 46 | 01 16 |
| 23 | 00♌46 | 20 28 | 11 11 | 20 13 | 07 55 | 24 49 | 18 30 | 26 26 | 25 45 | 01 15 |
| 24 | 01 44 | 05♍17 | 13 07 | 21 21 | 08 37 | 24 42 | 18 36 | 26 25 | 25 43 | 01 13 |
| 25 | 02 41 | 19 45 | 15 02 | 22 30 | 09 18 | 24 36 | 18 42 | 26 24 | 25 42 | 01 12 |
| 26 | 03 38 | 03♎48 | 16 54 | 23 38 | 10 00 | 24 29 | 18 48 | 26 22 | 25 41 | 01 11 |
| 27 | 04 36 | 17 24 | 18 45 | 24 47 | 10 41 | 24 22 | 18 54 | 26 21 | 25 39 | 01 10 |

**JULY 2009 (Cont'd)**

| Date | ☉ | ☽ | ☿ | ♀ | ♂ | ♃ | ♄ | ♅ | ♆ | ♇ |
|---|---|---|---|---|---|---|---|---|---|---|
| 28 | 05♌33 | 00♏35 | 20♌34 | 25♊55 | 11♊22 | 24♒15 | 19♍00 | 26♓20 | 25♒38 | 01♑08 |
| 29 | 06 30 | 13 22 | 22 21 | 27 04 | 12 02 | 24 08 | 19 06 | 26 19 | 25 36 | 01 07 |
| 30 | 07 28 | 25 49 | 24 07 | 28 13 | 12 43 | 24 01 | 19 12 | 26 17 | 25 34 | 01 06 |
| 31 | 08 25 | 08♐01 | 25 51 | 29 21 | 13 23 | 23 54 | 19 18 | 26 16 | 25 33 | 01 05 |

**AUGUST 2009**

| Date | ☉ | ☽ | ☿ | ♀ | ♂ | ♃ | ♄ | ♅ | ♆ | ♇ |
|---|---|---|---|---|---|---|---|---|---|---|
| 1 | 09♌23 | 20♐02 | 27♌34 | 00♋31 | 14♊04 | 23♒46 | 19♍25 | 26♓15 | 25♒31 | 01♑04 |
| 2 | 10 20 | 01♑54 | 29 14 | 01 40 | 14 44 | 23 39 | 19 31 | 26 13 | 25 30 | 01 03 |
| 3 | 11 17 | 13 43 | 00♍53 | 02 49 | 15 25 | 23 31 | 19 37 | 26 12 | 25 28 | 01 02 |
| 4 | 12 15 | 25 31 | 02 31 | 03 58 | 16 05 | 23 24 | 19 44 | 26 10 | 25 27 | 01 01 |
| 5 | 13 12 | 07♒20 | 04 06 | 05 08 | 16 46 | 23 16 | 19 50 | 26 09 | 25 25 | 01 00 |
| 6 | 14 10 | 19 13 | 05 40 | 06 17 | 17 26 | 23 09 | 19 57 | 26 07 | 25 24 | 00 58 |
| 7 | 15 07 | 01♓13 | 07 13 | 07 27 | 18 06 | 23 01 | 20 03 | 26 06 | 25 22 | 00 57 |
| 8 | 16 05 | 13 21 | 08 43 | 08 37 | 18 47 | 22 53 | 20 10 | 26 04 | 25 20 | 00 56 |
| 9 | 17 02 | 25 39 | 10 13 | 09 46 | 19 27 | 22 46 | 20 16 | 26 02 | 25 19 | 00 56 |
| 10 | 18 00 | 08♈10 | 11 40 | 10 56 | 20 07 | 22 38 | 20 23 | 26 01 | 25 17 | 00 55 |
| 11 | 18 57 | 20 54 | 13 06 | 12 06 | 20 47 | 22 30 | 20 30 | 25 59 | 25 15 | 00 54 |
| 12 | 19 55 | 03♉55 | 14 29 | 13 16 | 21 26 | 22 22 | 20 37 | 25 57 | 25 14 | 00 53 |
| 13 | 20 52 | 17 15 | 15 52 | 14 27 | 22 05 | 22 14 | 20 43 | 25 55 | 25 12 | 00 52 |
| 14 | 21 50 | 00♊54 | 17 12 | 15 37 | 22 45 | 22 06 | 20 50 | 25 53 | 25 11 | 00 51 |
| 15 | 22 48 | 14 55 | 18 31 | 16 47 | 23 24 | 21 59 | 20 57 | 25 52 | 25 09 | 00 50 |
| 16 | 23 45 | 29 16 | 19 47 | 17 58 | 24 03 | 21 51 | 21 04 | 25 50 | 25 07 | 00 50 |
| 17 | 24 43 | 13♋55 | 21 02 | 19 09 | 24 42 | 21 43 | 21 11 | 25 48 | 25 06 | 00 49 |
| 18 | 25 41 | 28 47 | 22 15 | 20 19 | 25 21 | 21 35 | 21 18 | 25 46 | 25 04 | 00 48 |
| 19 | 26 39 | 13♌47 | 23 26 | 21 30 | 26 00 | 21 27 | 21 25 | 25 44 | 25 02 | 00 47 |
| 20 | 27 36 | 28 45 | 24 34 | 22 41 | 26 39 | 21 20 | 21 32 | 25 42 | 25 01 | 00 47 |
| 21 | 28 34 | 13♍34 | 25 40 | 23 52 | 27 18 | 21 12 | 21 39 | 25 40 | 24 59 | 00 46 |
| 22 | 29 32 | 28 06 | 26 44 | 25 03 | 27 56 | 21 04 | 21 46 | 25 38 | 24 57 | 00 45 |
| 23 | 00♍30 | 12♎14 | 27 46 | 26 14 | 28 35 | 20 56 | 21 53 | 25 36 | 24 56 | 00 45 |
| 24 | 01 28 | 25 56 | 28 45 | 27 25 | 29 14 | 20 49 | 22 00 | 25 34 | 24 54 | 00 44 |
| 25 | 02 26 | 09♏12 | 29 41 | 28 36 | 29 52 | 20 41 | 22 07 | 25 31 | 24 53 | 00 44 |
| 26 | 03 23 | 22 02 | 00♎35 | 29 48 | 00♋30 | 20 34 | 22 15 | 25 29 | 24 51 | 00 43 |
| 27 | 04 21 | 04♐30 | 01 25 | 00♌59 | 01 08 | 20 26 | 22 22 | 25 27 | 24 49 | 00 43 |
| 28 | 05 19 | 16 41 | 02 12 | 02 11 | 01 46 | 20 19 | 22 29 | 25 25 | 24 48 | 00 42 |
| 29 | 06 17 | 28 39 | 02 56 | 03 22 | 02 24 | 20 12 | 22 36 | 25 23 | 24 46 | 00 42 |
| 30 | 07 15 | 10♑29 | 03 36 | 04 34 | 03 01 | 20 04 | 22 44 | 25 20 | 24 45 | 00 41 |
| 31 | 08 13 | 22 17 | 04 12 | 05 46 | 03 39 | 19 57 | 22 51 | 25 18 | 24 43 | 00 41 |

**SEPTEMBER 2009**

| Date | ☉ | ☽ | ☿ | ♀ | ♂ | ♃ | | ♅ | ♆ | ♇ |
|---|---|---|---|---|---|---|---|---|---|---|
| 1 | 09♍11 | 04♒05 | 04♎44 | 06♌58 | 04♋16 | 19♒50 | 22♍58 | 25♓16 | 24♒41 | 00♑41 |
| 2 | 10 09 | 15 59 | 05 11 | 08 09 | 04 53 | 19 43 | 23 06 | 25 14 | 24 40 | 00 40 |
| 3 | 11 07 | 28 00 | 05 34 | 09 21 | 05 31 | 19 37 | 23 13 | 25 11 | 24 38 | 00 40 |
| 4 | 12 06 | 10♓11 | 05 52 | 10 33 | 06 08 | 19 30 | 23 20 | 25 09 | 24 37 | 00 40 |
| 5 | 13 04 | 22 34 | 06 05 | 11 45 | 06 45 | 19 23 | 23 28 | 25 07 | 24 35 | 00 40 |
| 6 | 14 02 | 05♈09 | 06 12 | 12 58 | 07 23 | 19 17 | 23 35 | 25 04 | 24 34 | 00 40 |
| 7 | 15 00 | 17 56 | 06♎13R | 14 10 | 08 00 | 19 10 | 23 42 | 25 02 | 24 32 | 00 39 |
| 8 | 15 58 | 00♉56 | 06 08 | 15 22 | 08 36 | 19 04 | 23 50 | 25 00 | 24 31 | 00 39 |
| 9 | 16 57 | 14 09 | 05 56 | 16 35 | 09 13 | 18 58 | 23 57 | 24 57 | 24 29 | 00 39 |
| 10 | 17 55 | 27 35 | 05 39 | 17 47 | 09 49 | 18 52 | 24 05 | 24 55 | 24 28 | 00 39 |
| 11 | 18 53 | 11♊14 | 05 14 | 19 00 | 10 26 | 18 46 | 24 12 | 24 52 | 24 26 | 00♑39D |
| 12 | 19 52 | 25 08 | 04 43 | 20 12 | 11 02 | 18 41 | 24 20 | 24 50 | 24 25 | 00 39 |
| 13 | 20 50 | 09♋15 | 04 05 | 21 25 | 11 37 | 18 35 | 24 27 | 24 48 | 24 23 | 00 39 |
| 14 | 21 48 | 23 35 | 03 22 | 22 38 | 12 13 | 18 30 | 24 35 | 24 45 | 24 22 | 00 39 |
| 15 | 22 47 | 08♌05 | 02 32 | 23♌51 | 12 48 | 18 24 | 24 42 | 24 43 | 24 21 | 00 39 |
| 16 | 23 45 | 22♌43 | 01 38 | 25♌03 | 13 24 | 18 19 | 24 49 | 24 41 | 24 19 | 00 39 |
| 17 | 24 44 | 07♍22 | 00 39 | 26♌16 | 13 59 | 18 14 | 24 57 | 24 38 | 24 18 | 00 40 |